Family Ties & AGING

To my family, in order of appearance . . .
My parents, I. Lilla Arnet and Andrew J. Connidis . . .
My siblings, Kristine, Michael, Justin, Angela, Stephanie,
and Melina, and their families . . .
My husband, Craig Boydell, and his family, and . . .
My children, Michael, Patrick, and their families, and . . .
Kai and Nora,
With thanks and love.

Family Ties & AGING

INGRID ARNET CONNIDIS

Sage Publications
International Educational and Professional Publisher
Thousand Oaks ▪ London ▪ New Delhi

For information:

Sage Publications, Inc.
2455 Teller Road
Thousand Oaks, California 91320
E-mail: order@sagepub.com

Sage Publications Ltd.
6 Bonhill Street
London EC2A 4PU
United Kingdom

Sage Publications India Pvt. Ltd.
M-32 Market
Greater Kailash I
New Delhi 110 048 India

Printed in the United States of America

Library of Congress Cataloging-in-Publication Data

Connidis, Ingrid Arnet, 1951-
    Family ties and aging / by Ingrid Arnet Connidis.
        p.   cm.
    Includes bibliographical references and index.
    ISBN 0-7619-1957-0 (pbk.: alk. paper)
    1. Aged—United States—Family relationships. 2. Aged—Canada—Family relationships. I. Title.
    HQ1064.U5 C61135 2001
    305.26'0971—dc21   2001000089

03   04   05   06   07   7   6   5   4   3   2

Acquiring Editor: Jim Brace-Thompson
Editorial Assistant: Karen Ehrmann
Production Editor: Diana E. Axelsen
Editorial Assistant: Kathryn Journey
Typesetter/Designer: Tina Hill
Indexer: Mary Mortensen
Cover Designer: Ravi Balasuriya

Contents

PART I
Introduction and Overview

PART II
Intimate Ties

PART III
Intergenerational Relations

PART IV
Sibling Relationships

PART V
Research and Policy Issues and Directions

Preface

When I read a book, I like to know something about the author, including how to pronounce his or her name if there is some doubt. "Ingrid" does not pose a problem but, over the years, I have heard many variations on "Connidis." To paraphrase some lyrics from the Gershwin brothers' song, "Let's Call the Whole Thing Off," "I say Con-NEE-dis."

Originally, my plan was to write a book about siblings in middle and later life (and that may happen yet). But as I put together another sociology course on family ties and aging, I was struck—again—by the absence of a recent book that provided an integrated and thorough representation of what we know about this broad topic. Yet the field has flourished over the 15 years since I prepared a Canadian book about older persons and their families. So I wrote this book about family relationships in middle and later life in an attempt to fill this gap. The purpose of *Family Ties and Aging* is to weave the vast range of information we now have about the many facets of family relationships and aging into a critical, comprehensive, and integrated whole. The intended audience is all of those interested in the topic but particularly those who are learning more about family ties and aging as part of their education, research, or policy planning. Chapter 1 provides a more detailed overview of the book's approach and content.

Throughout the book, I have included groups and relationships that typically receive short shrift in commentaries about family life, to the extent that current research allows. Although ties to a spouse and to children and grandchildren are central family connections for many older persons, these are not the only relationships that matter to them. Indeed, these ties are not even a part of the family networks of significant numbers of older Americans and Canadians. What is the experience of those who are not married? Or those who do not have children? Whose intimate ties are not formalized by marriage? What do we know about sibling relationships in middle and older age? What kinds of family ties are forged by gay and lesbian persons over the life course? These questions beg to be answered if we are to have a comprehensive understanding of family life among older adults.

Family ties can be studied in multiple ways, as they are in this book. How prevalent is a given relationship? What is the nature of the tie? Does a particular relationship serve as an important source of support? What are its qualitative dimensions? In the following pages, these questions are discussed as I consider the ties of older persons to a partner (spouse or live-in, gay or straight), children, grandchildren, and siblings. Along the way, I explore the unique family situations of those who are childless, single, divorced, and widowed and the implications of transitions such as divorce for other family relationships. In the final chapter, I discuss research and policy issues.

One of the nice developments in scholarly writing over the past few years has been the open recognition of the influence an author's experience has on the perspective taken to a given subject. Although one may presume that a book such as this one has limited latitude for individual expression and bias, there is still room enough for authors to take quite different approaches—in the topics they choose to include, in the interpretation they give to mixed findings, and in the way they extend current knowledge to commentary about future directions and social action. So I offer some words about myself to allow you to judge how my experience might slant my views of family ties in middle and later life.

When this book is published, I will be 50 years old. Although I am somewhat surprised by how resilient my views about aging and family relationships have been, there is no doubt that increasing age has shifted my standpoint. I am the oldest of seven children, five girls and two boys, as we still think of ourselves, even though it is some time since we could accurately be described as girls or boys. My parents are in their 70s, still thriving with their exuberance for life, their mental dexterity, and their physical ability. So they instill a sense of optimism about aging. I am married and am mother to four children, two of whom are technically stepchildren but whom I think of simply as my children, if one can think of children simply. My children span two generations, my two oldest sons, Michael and Patrick, in their 30s by the time this is in print; my son, Kai, in early adolescence (14), and my daughter, Nora, 11 going on 15 or 5, depending on the mood and occasion. I am mother-in-law to two very special women, Nina and Nikki, and grandmother (Mormor) to a delightful little boy, Jackson. I have had a daughter die, little Karl, an experience that stands as an enduring reminder of how valuable close family ties can be.

By many standards, my family life, although hardly flawless, is an embarrassment of riches. Perhaps this makes me unduly positive about the possibilities of family ties. But if so, it is not because my family life is a traditional one. The combined experiences of my extended family include single life, straight and gay partnerships, marriage, divorce, remarriage, parenthood, childlessness, step ties, grandparenthood, great-grandparenthood, responding to special needs, dual-career couples, stay-at-home mothers, the loss of family members, and the addition of new ones. One benefit of a large family is the opportunity to have one's horizons and empathy expanded by close-at-hand experiences that are far more diverse than most of us can squeeze into our own lifetimes.

Professionally, I am a sociologist, and this leads me to focus more on the social than the psychological aspects of family ties and aging. When I trained as a sociologist, I took one course in the family that I didn't like very much. I felt surrounded by students hoping for important tips on how to find a husband and, indeed, the course focused heavily on courtship and marriage. Fortunately, things have changed. I didn't take a course on aging—there weren't any. Instead, my efforts as a graduate student concentrated on deviance and criminology, not the standard beginning to a career in aging or family. But, I think, it was a useful one, sensitizing me early to the atypical and how much it teaches us about both the typical and atypical, raising fundamental questions about how we come to see some situations, actions, lifestyles, and people as ideal and others not, and how we define possibilities for various social groups on this basis. We have a lengthy list of expectations about family life, of "dos and don'ts," based on gender, class, race, sexual orientation, and age. A fundamental challenge to exploring family ties and aging is to peel away these expectations and expose them as social creations, opening the door to many possible and equally acceptable ways for families to be created and recreated.

I hope that you read this book with questions in mind. May the book provide good answers to many of them. And may your unanswered questions be the ones that lead us to new directions in our understanding of family ties and aging.

Acknowledgments

When I first approached Sage about the possibility of writing a book on family ties and aging, I was delighted to be directed to Bert Adams and David Klein, coeditors of the Sage series, **Understanding Families.** I first met with Bert Adams in 1998 at the American Sociological Association meetings in San Francisco, and that marked the beginning of this book. My sincere thanks to Bert for a warm reception and initial encouragement. It was a treat to meet a man who garners deep respect for his long-standing and continuing scholarly contributions and for the very personable individual he is. Bert Adams's other commitments kept him busy, and Dave Klein served as a consulting editor for this book. Many many thanks, Dave, for quick and helpful feedback, delivered directly, often with wonderful comic relief and always reflecting a startling breadth of knowledge. You have been a valued touchstone throughout the process, and working together has been a pleasure.

My thanks to two Jims at Sage. First, to Jim Nageotte for agreeing to publish the book and getting the process started. And second, to Jim Brace-Thompson, for seeing it through with a very professional, friendly, and supportive style. Thanks also to Karen Ehrmann and Diana Axelsen for steering the book through production, Marilyn Powers Scott for able and pleasant copyediting, Ravi Balasuriya for patient consultation about the book's cover, and Tina Hill for typesetting and design.

To my colleagues in Canada, a special thank you: to Barry McPherson who, as Editor, encouraged me (and others) to write a book monograph for the Butterworths (Canada) series on Individual and Population Aging years ago, cementing a transition in my research focus—and for occasional lapses back to his former editorial role in useful suggestions made for this book. To Lori Davies and Julie McMullin, friends and colleagues at Western, for listening to me think out loud or describe yet another interesting article I'd just read, for asking regularly how things were going, for celebrating various stages of completion, and for support when it was needed most: Thank you. To Anne Martin-Matthews and Carolyn Rosenthal for their ongoing interest and for serving periodically as sounding boards. And to Anne, Carolyn, Barry, and Victor Marshall—a most impressive and supportive quartet, thank you.

To colleagues in the United States who reviewed the book manuscript, Toni Antonucci, Rosemary Blieszner, Victor Cicirelli, and Sarah Matthews, many thanks for taking the time to provide helpful commentary, prompting responses that I believe have improved the book. And thanks for your generosity—in the care you took and the praise you gave. I hope that you like the changes I have made.

To students in my Sociology 476 (and sometimes 565) course, thank you for providing the point of view most central to this book's objective, with helpful observations of strengths and weaknesses. To Jarrett Petroski, thank you for tracking down references and helping to keep them in order. To Angela Conti, thank you for compiling data. And to Cheryl McNeill, thank you for your skill and patience at the computer, pulling together the final submission under pressure, with grace and calm.

Thank you to those from whom I have learned in my various research projects and whose words make ideas come alive. For financial support of those studies, thanks to the Social Sciences and Humanities Research Council of Canada and to the Ontario Mental Health Foundation. And thank you to the many researchers whose work served as pieces of the puzzle I was putting together.

For a complete and satisfying diversion from the rest of my life and for their warm camaraderie, many thanks to Fred Harrison and the Tuesday night Art Group. Thanks also to Judy Everett for ongoing interest in the book and for lending a hand by entertaining my children and dog.

And to my family—all of you. Thank you for inspiring my interest in family relationships by virtue of being the dynamic people you are and for the richness you add to my life. To Michael and Patrick, thank you for always asking and for being steady forces in my life. To Craig, Kai, and Nora, thank you for being there for me, day to day, even when I have not been there for you because I was busy writing. We have traveled far together while this book was in progress. Thank you.

PART I

Introduction and Overview

1

Older Persons in a Family Context

My family has always been an essential part of my life, but the older you get, the more you feel . . . how much you need each other. As long as you are together, it is like a tree growing. . . . The longer the tree is there, the stronger the branches become and the more you are knit into one. So, the more you are together, the more you realize how important it is to be together and stay together.

—66-year-old married father of two

Perhaps no topic strikes as personal a chord as family relationships. All of us have had the direct experience of being family members and, whatever the nature of that experience, it is likely to have been profound. For some, family life may represent the idyllic safe haven from a heartless world; for others, early family experiences may set the stage for a lifetime of surviving harsh circumstances at the hands of loved ones. For most, family life falls somewhere in between these two extremes. In this book, we explore the family lives and families of older persons, bearing in mind that they have a history that goes back to childhood. Family ties in later life are the culmination of a lifetime of decisions made, roads taken and not taken, and changing times and social worlds.

Because older persons' family ties involve individuals from several generations, our exploration necessarily takes us beyond the particular experiences and situations of older persons only, to considering how factors in the lives of younger persons affect family relationships in older age. As a convention, older persons are considered to be aged 60 to 65 years or older, reflecting common practices of entitlement, such as pension and security benefits. We need not be quite that precise here, recognizing that family processes may follow different trajectories depending on such facts as age at first marriage or birth of first child. For convenience, we shall assume that we are generally speaking of people aged 60 or more when we talk about older persons, realizing that there are substantial variations within this age group.

Families and Family Ties

Who do you think of as your family? Who considers you part of their family? Are there any older persons in your family? If so, who is in their family? When we think of families, we tend to concentrate on the nuclear family, that is, parents and their children living together in one home. Depending on our stage of life, this may refer to the family of orientation, comprising parents and siblings, or the family of procreation, consisting of spouse and children. Over time, the nuclear family model has become less applicable as more families break the traditional pattern through cohabitation, divorce, single parenthood, and remarriage, for example. This model also downplays the significance of the single (never married) and the childless in family networks and minimizes the family relationships of those past the child-rearing stage—the middle-aged and elderly. As well, emphasis on the nuclear unit leads to the treatment of other arrangements as abnormal or less desirable (Ganong, Coleman, and Mapes, 1990; Nydegger, 1983). However, diverse familial arrangements reflect fundamental forms of diversity in society. Moreover, the nonnuclear family households that are common in later life are usually the outcome of typical life course transitions by family members, such as leaving home in young adulthood.

Because the life experiences of any age group are so closely tied to the family, examining the family ties of older individuals can lead to a better understanding of later life. In this book, the focus is on familial relationships in older age rather than later-life families. This emphasis avoids some of the pitfalls of attempts to define a later-life family. For example, childless couples are often excluded in definitions that focus on the age and stage of children to define the family of later life (Brubaker, 1990). Alleviating this problem by selecting a chronological age as the time when such couples become later-life families still excludes the never married. Yet both the childless and single are active participants in family life as children, nieces, nephews, siblings, aunts, uncles, and cousins. Therefore, they are an important part of the family network and do experience "family" life. Our focus on family ties and aging emphasizes the fact that nearly all older persons are family members and that the process of aging is associated with transitions in family relationships.

Definitions of family have both substantive and practical implications. At the substantive level is the general issue of recognizing diversity. This means going beyond both the nuclear family and beyond the household to include nonresident kin as well as those who consider themselves to be family by virtue of the obligations that they feel and the support that they extend and receive (Scanzoni and Marsiglio, 1993). Practical implications may be most acutely felt when the state adopts definitions of family that either include or exclude particular individuals as family. Such applications can result in having someone rely on an unreliable family member for support by virtue of qualifying as the "closest" tie (legally or biologically) or having someone miss the opportunity for support from someone who is not defined as family but would have acted as family (e.g., a gay partner; Bould, 1993). Those with few "real" family members often consider their closest friends family, a tie termed *fictive kin* by some (MacRae, 1992). One essential fact about the family is that it does not take one fixed form (Cheal, 1993).

Most relationships in older age are continuations of those begun earlier in life, and their nature is shaped by past patterns. Poor relationships will probably not become good ones simply because one reaches old age, whereas good ones are likely to remain that way. Thus, there is continuity in the relationships of later life, given both the probability that their character is unlikely to change dramatically and the fact that most family ties began earlier in life. However, change also occurs. Some long-term relationships are lost, primarily through death, whereas others are gained, most notably through birth (grandchildren, great-grandchildren) and remarriage. Change in the nature of past relationships may also occur in response to other changes associated with aging. Widowhood may lead to a reorganization of family ties and more time spent with other family members. Retirement may alter the marital relationship, and health declines may lead to shifts in helping patterns and dependency. Change in the lives of other family members may also have profound effects. A child's divorce, for example, may alter dramatically the relationship between a grandmother and her grandchildren. Thus, family life in older age is dynamic and involves both continuity and change.

The Place of Older People in
Families of the Past and Present

Myths About the Past

Several myths about family life persist despite numerous studies over the years that do not support them (Hareven, 1991, 1996; Nett, 1993; Shanas, 1979). One predominant myth is that the elderly are neglected or abandoned by their families, especially their children. This Golden Age myth assumes a better past for older people, based on several assumptions: that three-generation households predominated in times gone by, that three-generation households signify better family relationships, and that the respect accorded older persons in the past can be equated with affection (Nydegger, 1983; Shanas, 1979).

Contrary to popular belief, the typical 19th-century family household throughout the Western world, including the United States, Canada, and Europe, was nuclear, with one generation of parents and their children (Darroch and Ornstein, 1984; Hareven, 1996; Nett, 1993). In the past, much higher mortality rates and lower life expectancy across the life course made the likelihood of multiple generations living together a rarity. As young countries founded in their current form by immigrants, both the United States and Canada were even less likely to have multiple generations nearby. Thus, only recently have multigenerational households in large numbers become a possibility.

The emphasis on debunking the myth of the multigenerational family risks understating the fact that the coresidence of older parents with one of their children was more common in earlier times (Ruggles, 1996). Again, however, one must go beyond the fact of coresidence to understanding the context in which it occurred. Many have argued that a major reason for the shift toward living alone in old age has been the improved financial situation of older persons. However, research using U.S. census data (Ruggles, 1996) indicates that, in the late 19th and early 20th centuries, coresidence was more likely among those with higher incomes, leading to the conclusion that "rising incomes cannot explain the decline of coresidence" (Ruggles, 1996:255). This association is consistent with two patterns of earlier times: older parents' control of land and property and the common placement of impoverished older persons in poor houses, the only institutional alternative available to those families who could not afford to support an older parent. Rising incomes over time have had the greatest impact on the poor elderly who now qualify for state-funded pensions and support. As well, then as now, coresidence of older parents and their children typically followed a lengthy period of independent living in nuclear households by both generations, rather than the continuation of three-generation households as a dominant family form (Hareven, 1996).

Research from several countries demonstrates that when three generations did coreside, it was either a function of inheritance laws and the control by older parents of property or because one parent had died, leaving the other alone. For example, in 1871, three-generation Canadian households were usually formed as a consequence of a widowed parent moving in with a child and his or her family. When a child lived with older parents, it was more often sons than daughters who did so, "as one would expect in a society where control of property was largely vested in the male line" (Darroch and Ornstein, 1984: 164). In New England, among parents whose children were born from 1920 to 1929, the typical pattern was close proximity to at least one child, with coresidence an outcome of a parent's widowhood and only after attempts were made to assist the widowed parent's independent living (Hareven and Adams, 1996). In this case, the youngest daughter was most likely to care for an older parent. Thus, three-generation households reflected either the power of older parents through control over land or the dependence of parents on their children following the loss of a spouse (Hareven, 1996).

Did the more common custom of taking an older parent into the home signal closer ties between an older parent and his or her (but usually her) children? At the turn of the century, publicly funded assistance for older people was either nonexistent or extremely limited, making three-generation households in many ways a forced choice for those elderly who could no longer function alone. In both Norway and Sweden, as examples, declines in informal care and increases in formal support have been attributed in substantial measure to the availability of state-supported alternatives, not the demise of the family (Daatland, 1990; Tedebrand, 1996). Similarly, solitary living among older persons is related to income; overall increases in income among older persons account for more of them living alone, and among older persons, greater income increases the chances of living on one's own (Kinsella, 1995).

Comparisons of two cohorts of children in the United States (Hareven and Adams, 1996) do suggest that the simple availability of formal support is not enough to ensure its use; one must also be accustomed to receiving state support in a variety of forms. Children for whom the welfare state was a new concept were more likely to find placing their parent(s) in a nursing home problematic, whereas their younger siblings, more familiar with the idea, considered it a reasonable alternative to coresidence. This suggests that it is the experience of change rather than of caring options per se that made the use of formal support difficult for those parents and children going through the transition in caring alternatives. Even for this cohort of children, however, coresidence occurred "only in cases of dire need, when aging parents experienced chronic illness, handicap, or dementia, and needed help with their daily activities" (Hareven and Adams, 1996:278). Although living with children in old age might, therefore, have been more probable, it did not necessarily reflect a happier or more desirable situation. Indeed,

> All the children . . . who had taken care of aging parents in their own homes expressed a strong desire never to have to depend on their own children in their own old age. They considered living with their children the greatest obstacle to maintaining their independence. (Hareven and Adams, 1996:283)

We discuss this issue further in Chapter 8.

Although the elderly in times gone by appear to have received greater respect from younger family members and the community at large, such respect was based on economic power rather than either age itself or being more loved than the elderly of today (Nydegger, 1983). Indeed, in those instances where accumulated power among the elderly occurs, the consequence is typically intergenerational conflict and competition, not improved familial relations. The debate over intergenerational equity (see Chapter 14) in which the old are portrayed as getting too much from the government at the expense of the young is a current example of the price the old pay when they improve their economic situation. Attempts to find evidence of a "Golden Isle"—a place in the world where the old are revered—have also led to the general conclusion that age alone is very rarely a basis for preferred status in any culture (Nydegger, 1983). Moreover, studies of hunting tribes, such as the Inuit and other North American aboriginal groups, provide support for the predominance of nuclear families throughout most of human history (Gough, 1971). Thus, the present household structure typified by the nuclear family is not a new phenomenon.

Realities of the Present

Of course, discounting the assumptions that comprise the myth of a Golden Age does not establish that families of today provide better rela-

Photo 1.1. Increased longevity means that more older people are living to see their great-grandchildren.

tionships or support for older adults. Nonetheless, the family has clearly not deserted its older members and continues to provide extensive support (Brubaker, 1990; Finch and Mason, 1993; Johnson, 1995; Wellman, 1990, 1992). The network of contact and exchange among nuclear households has resulted in the characterization of today's family as *modified extended* (Shanas, 1979). Family ties beyond the nuclear family household operate on a principle of revocable detachment wherein "dormant emotional ties can be mobilized when they are needed or desired" (George, 1980:79). Thus, although the extended family does not typically live together, multiple generations are available to one another when needed, as Photo 1.1 reflects. The history of immigration and greater life expectancy means that there are now more families than ever with multiple generations in the United States and Canada.

   Living longer also means lengthening the amount of time spent in particular familial relationships (Farkas and Hogan, 1995; Kinsella, 1995). Marriage and other intimate ties, relationships between parents and their children, between grandparents and grandchildren, and between siblings all have the potential to last longer. Thus, for example, parents can expect to know their children into their middle age, and increasing numbers of grandparents are living to see their grandchildren reach adulthood and become parents. This, combined with less restrictive definitions of what constitutes family membership, makes family relations more complex and could actually widen the net of family carers, despite times of lower fertility. Even if grandchildren do not directly assist their grandparents, providing other types of familial support may enhance their parent(s)' ability to do so. Last, speedier methods of communication (telephone, E-mail) and travel (car, air) enhance the opportunity for contact among family members. In sum, the near-universal provision of family care and support for older members in different cultures and historical periods indicates greater continuity than change in the responsibility family members assume for their elders.

The potential for conflict in families may be greater today, not because there is less love shared or because older family members are neglected, but rather because the demands and expectations are greater. Laslett (1978:478) argues that the family has increased in importance "as a source of personal identity and satisfaction in life." However, these demands on the family often exceed the family's ability to meet them, thus creating a potential source of guilt and conflict. Contrary to popular belief, then, the importance of the family has in some ways been heightened, not diminished. But this creates additional strains within the family. Regarding marriage, for example, Gillis (1996:151) argues that the increased expectations of marriage in which "the perfect couple now must be everything to one another—good providers, super sexual partners, best friends, stimulating companions" combine with longer life expectancies to make sustaining romance over the course of a marriage very difficult.

Conflict can be expected in other family ties, too. For example, the fact that parents and children share adulthood may increase the likelihood of counter opinions as older children behave more like peers than like younger children. At the same time, the greater likelihood of sharing more of life's transitions may enhance empathy between the generations. The heightened emotional significance of the family and its isolation as an appropriate forum for expressing strong feelings increase "the likelihood that emotionally charged interactions—both positive and negative—will occur" (Laslett, 1978:487). This underlines the importance of exploring the *qualitative* aspects of older people's familial relationships—closeness, solidarity, and loyalty. It also stresses the need to consider the negative aspects of family life that may occur because of structural strains in the kinship system and in society. The coexistence of both positive and negative sentiments and the competing demands of familial relationships may be the basis for ambivalent inter- and intragenerational ties (Luescher and Pillemer, 1998; see Chapter 7).

Assessing Family Ties

Despite the fairly long-standing rejection of a Golden Age for families, the current hold of the family values debate illustrates just how attractive a myth this is. One can only speak meaningfully of the family's decline by assuming that there were better times. There is no question that both the ideals of family life and family life itself have *changed* over time (Gillis, 1996; Snell, 1996), but the monolithic treatment of "the family" as an institution in decline makes several questionable assumptions. First is the assumption that change signals decline. After dispelling the myth of idyllic family relations in the past, Snell (1996:4) concludes that "for both women and men in the past, old age was often a difficult time." But, he emphasizes, "this is not to argue that the nature of aging and of being old has not changed." Change is often discomfiting, leading us to favor old ways of doing things. This tendency must not serve as the basis for concluding that change has been for the worse. Instead, we must first identify the real ways in which family life has changed and then examine the consequences of any observed changes for *various family members*. As Atchley (Atchley and Lawton,1997:187) observes more generally about age-related deficits, "negative changes do not necessarily have negative consequences."

The tendency to focus on the negative consequences of change is part of a larger phenomenon of looking at family life in relative terms. Thus, for example, when proposing that individuals should be considered active agents in their own destiny, Scanzoni and Marsiglio (1993:109) promote the view of family members as "persons struggling to create *better* lives for themselves and their families (italics added)." Although the general argument is sound, why better lives? Better than what? Most of us are not necessarily striving to shape our lives, including our ties with family members, in such relative terms. Instead, we might more accurately be said to be striving to create lives that we consider desirable, acceptable, satisfactory, good, or fulfilling. Moving away from implicit comparative treatments of family life will help us avoid some of the ideological pitfalls of many writings on family ties, including those on older persons.

A second problematic assumption embedded in much research on the family is the view that all members of a family share uniform experiences of family membership. Thus, the impact of change is assessed in relation to "the family" rather than from the point of view of different family members. For example, rising divorce rates are often equated with familial decline. But does divorce necessarily have the same impact on all family members (husbands, wives, children, parents, grandparents, grandchildren)? The apparent success of marriage in earlier days, measured in terms of duration, often came at the expense of both the happiness and welfare of particular family members. Women were often financially dependent on their spouses and could not leave their marriages, either legally or practically, even in the face of harsh circumstances, such as being the victims of abusive partners. Did children in such marriages necessarily benefit from the lasting union of their parents? Addressing such issues requires considering the impact of both continuity and change from the vantage point of different family members. In the context of aging and family ties, this means considering the points of view of the older person and other family members. Thus, for example, the issue of support will be considered from the perspective of the giver and of the receiver, emphasizing the fact that older persons serve as both, operating within a system of family relationships.

Views of the place of older persons in families have followed ironic twists and turns that correspond to general concerns regarding family life in North America. During the 1970s and early 1980s, there was serious concern in the aging field about the predominantly negative view of old age, including the portrayal of older family members as a drain on family resources. Embedded in this concern was an empathetic stance toward meeting the needs of older persons, both within families and through social policy. This negative stereotype gave way to an equally inaccurate positive stereotype that focused on the virtues of old age, placing heavy emphasis on independence and the possibility of remaining youthful. Despite the good intentions of such a portrayal, including the view that a more positive view would be the basis for greater inclusion of the older population, we find ourselves in a new century dealing with debates on intergenerational equity. In these debates, older persons are characterized by some as "greedy geezers," taking far more than their share of the public purse at the expense of younger generations, particularly children (see Chapter 14). We have in a sense come full circle, returning to a negative view of older persons as a serious drain on resources. But this view can only be sustained by ignoring family dynamics and the significant contributions made by older persons to the younger generations of their families over a life time (Stone, Rosenthal, and Connidis, 1998). Thus, a focus on family ties helps redress major inaccuracies in the broader public debate concerning an aging population and its implications for public policy.

Theoretical Orientation

As research areas, family life and aging share long-standing public and policy interest. Although this has aided research in these areas, it has perhaps hindered theoretical development, as funders of research sought information (data) to inform policy decisions or to create a foundation of knowledge. Discussions of theory in the two areas suggest that the area of the family has enjoyed more theoretical development than the area of aging (Cohler and Altergott, 1995). Conversely, aging research has generated data that fill important gaps in the family literature, particularly concerning family ties that fall outside the nuclear household (Cohler and Altergott, 1995).Thus, there are benefits to be gained from bringing the two areas together, building on their respective strengths. The point of view taken when one's interest is in older persons and their family relationships brings into question traditional approaches to family life. Being an outsider to a field has the advantage of freeing the observer from the weight of history within a particular specialty; in a sense, one can think theoretically, unfettered by old approaches to the subject (Mann, Grimes, Kemp, and Jenkins, 1997). Thus, researchers in the aging field can bring fresh insight to theoretical thinking about the family, and vice versa.

A current debate concerning family sociology is whether theoretical approaches have become more diverse and critical (Cheal, 1991) or whether they continue to be grounded in the functionalist perspective and its focus on stability and the maintenance of the status quo (Mann et al., 1997). Reflecting the general dominance of functionalist thought in sociology, the areas of both the family and aging have their functionalist equivalents. In the area of the family, the Parsonian view assumes that the nuclear family has evolved as the ideal family form for modern society and that this form is most evident in middle-class families. Thus, the assumed middle-class family is held up as the ideal, against which other family forms are to be measured and found wanting (dysfunctional). In the area of aging, the disengagement perspective assumes that it is functional for both the individual (allowing older persons to shore up limited reserves) and society (enhancing its smooth functioning) for older persons to disengage (primarily in the form of retirement but in other spheres as well) from the usual activities of adulthood (Cumming and Henry, 1961).

In both fields, these functionalist approaches have been severely criticized on a number of points. Primary among them is their bias in favor of middle-class life, the importance of maintaining the status quo while ignoring the conflicting interests of different groups within society, the view of the individual as someone who follows norms rather than being an active agent in setting his or her course, and the failure to link societal or macro-level phenomena to individual or micro-level experience (for example, the impact of a gendered society on family relations). Although one may debate the extent to which any specialty has totally rid itself of assumptions embedded in the functionalist paradigm, researchers of aging and of the family have engaged in a parallel critique of the perspective and moved toward a more critical and interactionist approach to studying how social life works. This trend mitigates against specifying ideal types and encourages observing the lived reality of family life. Combining the two areas of family and aging by examining the family ties of older persons also moves us in this direction.

This book does not aim to provide exhaustive coverage of theoretical developments about the family or about aging. However, I do make five underlying theoretical assumptions, and these frame how available information on family ties in later life is presented. First, the family ties of later life are best understood in the context of a life course perspective. This means that an older person's familial relationships are in substantial measure an outcome of decisions, actions, and circumstances in younger years. Thus, older persons' relationships represent both continuity and change. This also means that when striving to understand such issues as reciprocity in family relationships, one should take a long-term view of the exchanges that have occurred rather than focusing on one point in time (usually the present).

Second, understanding the family ties of older persons requires examining relationships, not only families, as entities in their own right. This has several implications. Family ties are not captured fully in a structural arrangement referred to as "the family." Most older persons do not live with most of their family members. Furthermore, a relationship has at least two points of view, not just the point of view of the older person, and these points of view may conflict with one another. Thus, one must strive for balance in understanding the nature of the relationship between an older person and other family members by considering both vantage points. Also, no party in a relationship only gives or only receives, although the contributions of the two at a given point in time may be imbalanced. When considering family ties in later life, we must not assume that an older person is necessarily the dependent party in a relationship. Instead, we must examine what both older *and* younger persons give and receive in their familial relationships. Last, dyadic relationships (relationships involving two people) are embedded in the broader context of a family network or system that is influenced in turn by a society's structural arrangements. Thus, for example, our society's tendency to organize family life on the basis of gender provides a fundamental parameter for family relationships. Such parameters can be one basis for conflicting interests among family members and must be negotiated by the players involved.

Third, family membership should be defined broadly and not restricted to a traditional notion of what constitutes family. Although in practice this is often made difficult by limited information on particular familial arrangements, it must nevertheless remain the goal. One can distinguish between formal and social families (Scanzoni and Marsiglio, 1993) to capture the difference here. Formal families are defined by such criteria as having a blood (biological parents and children) or legal (marriage, adoption) tie. This excludes many who develop social families that either cannot be formalized (e.g., unions between same-sex partners) or are not considered "real" family (e.g., friends who act as family in the eyes of the involved parties). Defining families broadly means a more inclusive treatment of family membership. In the typical family textbook, family life follows a trajectory starting with childhood, moving into early and middle adulthood, and, in some books, ending with old age. Along the way, certain groups tend to be dropped from the discussion. For instance, once the topic of marriage comes up, the never married tend to disappear, and once the discussion of family formation arises, the childless are eliminated from discussion. Yet those who remain single or do not have children, by choice or circumstance, remain family members. They may have active ties with parents, siblings, aunts or uncles, nieces or nephews, grandparents, and so on. Looking at families broadly and in terms of relationships rather than as fixed groups enhances the likelihood of inclusiveness in the examination of family life.

Fourth, the arrangements of social life, what is commonly termed *social structure,* both encourage and constrain individual action, but they do not completely determine what individuals do. The fact that individuals in very similar circumstances can and do act in very different ways attests to the importance of individual agency, that is, the ability to act on one's own behalf. At the same time, our position within the social structure will influence how much this is possible. A key challenge to appreciating how family relationships actually work is to understand their connection to the bigger social picture. Although none of us mindlessly follows a prescribed set of norms, none of us completely creates family life just as we would choose to have it. Instead, we work within the pressures exerted by social structure to negotiate as best we can what we consider to be a desirable family life. Key bases of social organization include gender, class, race and ethnicity, age, and sexual orientation (Bury, 1995; Ginn and Arber, 1995; McMullin, 1995). Our negotiations of family life will be influenced by our place in current structural arrangements, and the families of which we are a part will reflect the diversity that these structural arrangements create (Calasanti, 1996; Calasanti and Zajicek, 1993). To the extent that these change, we can expect that the nature of negotiating family ties will also change.

Fifth, the negotiation of family relationships takes place in the context of social structural arrangements that are imbued with cultural views of an ideal family. Thus, the meaning of family at both the cultural and individual level is an important facet of understanding how ties are both negotiated and evaluated by family members and by others (see Marshall, Matthews, and Rosenthal, 1993). The ideals of family life may not be realized in practice, but they are typically the benchmark by which family life is judged (Gillis, 1996).

Dimensions of Family Ties and the Plan of the Book

Four dimensions of familial relationships in older age are discussed when we examine intimate ties, intergenerational relationships, and sibling ties in this book. First, the availability of kin is addressed in the next chapter through the presentation of data on the marital status and the number of children, grandchildren, and siblings of older persons. Second, the extent of contact and interaction with available kin is discussed at the beginning of each chapter. Third, the ties between older family members and various kin are examined as potential avenues for providing, receiving, and exchanging support. However, contact with and exchange of services among kin do not address the quality of kin relations. Thus, the fourth dimension of family ties is the quality of familial relationships in later life.

The focus of this book is the United States and Canada. Although the culture, the structure, and the dynamics of family life of the two countries differ in important ways, in some areas, such as the relationships between adult children and their older parents, similar patterns are evident. Although the emphasis here is on research conducted in the United States and, to a lesser extent, in Canada, work from other countries is also included, providing some comparative context.

Throughout the book, I will refer to published as well as unpublished work from three of my studies. In the earliest study, 1981, interviews averaging 1 hour and 45 minutes took place in the homes of a stratified random sample of 400 residents aged 65 and over (see Connidis, 1989a; Connidis and Davies, 1990; Connidis and Rempel, 1983). The second more qualitative study involves a convenience sample of 60 sibling dyads or 120 respondents ranging in age from 25 to 89 (see Connidis, 1992). Thirty of the sibling pairs both lived in London, Ontario, whereas the other 30 pairs included one sibling who lived in town and another who lived elsewhere. Between 1988 and 1990, siblings were interviewed separately in their home or by phone. Over half of the interview followed an open-conversation format and was tape-recorded. In the third study, a multistage quota sample of 678 persons aged 55 and over was interviewed in their homes for an average of 70 minutes, in 1990 and 1991 (see Connidis and McMullin, 1993). The sample overrepresents men, the single (never married), divorced, and childless to ensure large enough numbers of these groups for statistical analysis. Additional quotes are taken from a study on multigenerational families in progress as I write.

All of these studies include quite detailed information about both the participant and all of his or her children, siblings, and parents. This means that the impact of both respondent and family characteristics, as well as dyad and network characteristics, can be studied. Personal observations from participants in these studies are provided from time to time to make the somewhat lifeless findings of research take on human dimensions. As you read each chapter, I encourage you to consider how your experiences and those of persons to whom you are close compare with the general conclusions drawn from research.

Thinking Ahead

There is now a fairly long-standing North American tradition of addressing the needs of families and of older persons through government policy. As researchers and experts in the area of family ties and aging, there is a responsibility to consider the implications of what we know for social policy. The final chapter of the book focuses on policy implications. As you read each chapter, consider the extent to which intervention by the state can improve conditions for older persons and their families. To aid in this consideration, be aware of the biases that are embedded in our current social arrangements and in your own way of thinking about individual versus social responsibility. To what extent do you think individuals and their immediate families should assume responsibility for their own welfare? And to what extent do you believe there is a social responsibility to ensure a reasonable quality of life for all citizens, including the old? This distinction between individual and social responsibility was made by C. Wright Mills (1959) some time ago, when he distinguished between approaching problems from a private troubles versus public issues perspective. When we take a private troubles approach, we assume that individuals and those close to them should take care of themselves; when we take a public issues approach, we assume that there is some social responsibility for both creating and solving the challenges that citizens face. As we shall see, for many of the issues concerning family ties and aging, there are elements of both individual and social responsibility. The challenge is to find a balance between the two that recognizes the power of and limits to both individual and social action in creating a social world that benefits all citizens.

2

The Availability of
Family Ties in Later Life

Although having a particular family tie does not guarantee an active relationship with that relative, not having one certainly precludes it. Therefore, as a starting point, it is useful to consider the availability of various kin in later life as one parameter of family life. As well, combining a knowledge of trends with a knowledge of the nature of different kin relationships, such as children, helps us to anticipate changes in family form and function in the future. However, existing familial arrangements are a product of their time, so we cannot simply apply trend data to our current way of doing things and assume that we have seen a complete picture of what lies ahead. Thus, consider the information in this chapter as one parameter of family ties in later life, knowing that changes in the availability of specific kin ties are likely to be met by adaptations in the way that other relationships are negotiated. In later chapters, the nature of specific family ties in terms of their intensity (type and amount of contact), supportiveness (the degree and direction of support exchange between older persons and particular family members), and quality is examined.

We begin by looking at trends in marital status, fertility, and the availability of siblings and grandchildren. We then examine the living arrangements of several age cohorts. These demographic and social trends set some boundaries to family life; they do not portend a particular destiny for any age cohort (see Connidis, 1999a; Friedland and Summer, 1999). However, these trends are an essential element of the social context in which family members negotiate. The number of grandchildren and siblings we have are not under our direct control, whereas fertility and living arrangements more often involve choice. However, fertility will affect the likelihood of having grandchildren, and living arrangements can be seen in part as a function of the availability of particular family members (marital status and fertility). Our focus is on marital partners, children, siblings, and grandchildren. However, most older persons also have nieces, nephews, and cousins, and substantial numbers of those in their 60s have parents, aunts, and uncles as well.

The Availability of a Marital Partner

Marital status establishes a parameter of family life with both short-term and long-term consequences for social networks and social support. Table 2.1 shows the very similar distribution of marital status for 10-year age groups in the United States (1995) and Canada (1996). Whereas the majority of all individuals aged 25 to 74 years are married, this continues to be true for men for all age groups but for women only up to the age group of 65 to 74 years. Among those aged 65 to 74, 80% of men are married, whereas 55% of women are. By the ages of 75 to 84 years, three fourths of men are still married, whereas not quite one third of women have a spouse. Among the oldest age group (85 and over), one half of men have spouses but only about 1 in 10 women do so.

These differences in the likelihood of being married are due primarily to differences in widowhood rates. At the ages of 65 to 74, not quite 1 in 10 men are widowed, compared with one third of women. This difference grows with age; for those aged 75-84, not quite 1 in 5 men are widowed, compared with 3 in 5 women, and by the ages of 85 years and over, 2 in 5 men are widowed, compared with 4 in 5 women. These gender differences in the proportion of persons who are married and widowed apply to all races and reflect the longer life expectancy of women than men and the cultural tradition of an age difference between partners in which men are older than women.

In the United States, however, there are substantial differences by race in marital status distribution (see Table 2.2). Overall, White persons are the most likely to be married and least likely to be widowed, followed by Hispanics, and then by Blacks, who are the least likely to be married and most likely to be widowed of the three groups. Thus, for example, among men aged 75 to 84 years, the percentage married is 76 for Whites, 62 for Hispanics, and 55 for Blacks. Corresponding figures for women in this age group are 33% of Whites, 26% of Hispanics, and 20% of Blacks. The distribution of widowed

TABLE 2.1 Percentage Distribution of Current Marital Status by Gender and Age: United States, 1995; Canada, 1996

	Single				Married				Divorced				Widowed			
	Men		Women		Men		Women		Men		Women		Men		Women	
Age	U.S.	Canada	U.S	Canada	U.S.	Canada	U.S.	Canada	U.S.	Canada	U.S.	Canada	U.S.	Canada	U.S.	Canada
25-34	38	39	26	27	53	58	62	66	8	4	12	7	0	0	0	1
35-44	17	16	10	11	72	75	70	75	10	10	19	13	0	0	1	1
45-54	8	8	6	7	77	80	72	75	14	11	19	15	1	1	4	3
55-64	5	6	4	5	81	82	67	71	12	10	16	12	3	3	13	12
65-74	4	6	4	6	80	79	54	55	7	7	9	8	8	8	33	32
75-84	4	6	4	8	74	71	32	30	4	5	5	4	18	18	59	58
85+	5	7	5	10	51	51	11	10	3	4	2	2	41	39	81	79

SOURCE: Data from U.S. Bureau of the Census (1996) and Statistics Canada (1996a).

TABLE 2.2 Percentage Distribution of Current Marital Status By Gender, Age, and Race: United States, 1995

Race and Age	Single Men	Single Women	Married Men	Married Women	Divorced Men	Divorced Women	Widowed Men	Widowed Women
White								
25-34	35	22	56	66	9	12	0	0
35-44	15	8	71	74	13	17	0	1
45-54	7	5	79	74	14	17	1	3
55-64	4	4	82	70	11	15	3	11
65-74	4	4	81	56	7	8	8	32
75-84	3	4	76	33	4	5	17	58
85+	4	5	52	12	4	2	41	81
Black								
25-34	53	46	38	39	9	15	0	0
35-44	28	24	51	47	21	27	1	2
45-54	16	13	62	51	20	29	2	8
55-64	12	8	65	47	17	23	6	21
65-74	5	7	65	37	14	17	16	40
75-84	10	5	55	20	7	7	28	66
85+	11	5	52	7	0	3	38	84
Hispanic								
25-34	37	24	55	65	8	11	0	1
35-44	18	11	69	66	13	21	0	2
45-54	8	8	77	68	14	20	1	5
55-64	5	6	79	62	13	19	3	14
65-74	2	8	70	45	14	17	14	30
75-84	5	6	62	26	11	7	22	61
85+	5	3	50	16	5	3	41	78

SOURCE: U.S. Bureau of the Census (1996).

men aged 75 to 84 is 17% of Whites, 22% of Hispanics, and 28% of Blacks and, of widowed women, 58% of Whites, 63% of Hispanics, and 70% of Blacks. These differences clearly set the stage for racial variations in living arrangements and support networks in older age.

For both the United States and Canada, the percentage of currently divorced individuals hits the double digits for those under the age of 65 and is in the single digits for those aged 65 and over, with a slightly higher percentage of currently divorced persons in the United States than in Canada. The fact that the percentage divorced is higher for all age groups under the age of 65 than for those over 65 indicates that more older individuals in future cohorts will be divorced. Again, there are some differences by race. For Blacks and Hispanics, the percentage of persons aged 65 to 74 who are divorced is slightly higher than the percentage of those aged 25 to 34 who are divorced. For all races and ages, men are consistently less likely than women to be divorced, due largely to men's higher rates of remarriage.

The single constitute a relatively small proportion of older persons. Of those aged 65 to 74, 4% of Americans and 6% of Canadians never married. For those aged 85 and over, 5% of Americans and 7% (men) to 10% (women) of Canadians are single. This slight trend downward within the older population reflects the high marriage rates of the parents of the baby boom cohort. Being single is more common among Black men and women than either their White or Hispanic counterparts. The high percentage of single persons under the age of 35 represents in part later age at first marriage but may also indicate an increase in the proportion of single adults in the future. However, although not married, some of these single individuals are cohabiting, and some are gay or lesbian. Greater acceptance of alternative lifestyles may mean more awareness and recognition of cohabiting and same-sex partnerships.

Data on marital status by gender over time among those aged 65 or over (Table 2.3) show that the distribution has remained quite stable since 1971-1972. In the United States, approximately 4% of older women and men are single, 77% of men and 42% of women are married, 14% of men and 47% of women are widowed, and 6% of men and 7% of women are divorced as of 1995. A slight decline in the percentage of seniors who are single has occurred over this 25-year period.

Since the early 1970s in the United States, there has been a steady increase in the percentage of women who are married, with a corresponding decline in widowhood. Similar but less dramatic trends are evident among men. This shift reflects longer life expectancy for both men and women and the more recent "catch-up" in male life expectancy. Although women still live longer than men, the difference in life expectancy is shrinking, leading to an increase in shared survivorship (Kinsella, 1995). These trends are less evident in Canada.

TABLE 2.3 Percentage Distribution of Marital Status for Population Aged 65+, by Gender: United States, 1972–1995; Canada 1971–1996

Marital Status and Gender	1972 U.S.	1971 Canada	1981 U.S.	1981 Canada	1991 U.S.	1991 Canada	1995 U.S.	1996 Canada
Never Married								
Men	5	11	4	9	4	7	4	7
Women	7	11	6	10	5	8	4	7
Married								
Men	75	72	78	76	77	74	77	73
Women	35	39	37	40	41	40	42	41
Divorced								
Men	3	1	4	2	6	5	6	7
Women	4	1	4	2	6	5	7	6
Widowed								
Men	18	17	16	14	15	13	14	14
Women	56	49	54	49	48	47	47	47

SOURCE: U.S. Bureau of the Census, *Current Population Reports* (Population Characteristics, Marital Status and Living Arrangements, March 1972, P-20 No. 242, Table 1; March 1981, P-20 No.372, Table 1; March 1991 P-20 No. 461, Table 1; March 1995, P-20 No. 491, Table 1) and Statistics Canada, *Census of Canada,* Canada Yearbook, 1975. Table 4.15, p. 167, Statistics Canada Catalogue 92-901, *Census of Canada, 1981.* Vol. 1, Table 4, Statistics Canada Catalogue 93-312, Census Canada, The Nation.

Although the numbers remain small, the most dramatic rate of change is in the percentage of divorced individuals aged 65 and over, which has roughly doubled in the United States since 1970 (Table 2.3). The number of persons who reach old age divorced will continue to increase. As well, the number of couples who actually divorce after age 65 has increased, a trend that is likely to continue (Uhlenberg and Myers, 1981). These trends indicate growing acceptance of divorce as an option to a poor marriage among all age groups. The greater economic security of women due to employment and to changes in social policy that ensure a divorced woman's receipt of a share of her former husband's pension benefits may also facilitate divorce in older age.

There are variations in these trends among White, Black, and Hispanic Americans (see Table 2.4). The percentage who are single has gone down for

TABLE 2.4 Percentage Distribution of Marital Status for Population Aged 65+,
by Gender and Race: United States, 1972–1995

Marital Status, Race, and Gender	1972	1981	1991	1995
Never Married				
White Men	5	4	4	4
White Women	7	6	5	4
Black Men	4	5	5	7
Black Women	3	5	5	6
Hispanic Men	6	5	3	3
Hispanic Women	3	8	5	8
Married				
White Men	77	79	78	78
White Women	36	37	42	44
Black Men	65	68	63	64
Black Women	30	29	31	29
Hispanic Men	63	71	78	70
Hispanic Women	30	38	42	39
Divorced				
White Men	2	4	5	6
White Women	3	4	6	6
Black Men	7	11	16	12
Black Women	8	10	13	13
Hispanic Men	7	10	8	13
Hispanic Women	8	6	11	14
Widowed				
White Men	17	15	14	13
White Women	55	54	48	47
Black Men	29	23	23	22
Black Women	65	60	55	56
Hispanic Men	29	19	14	18
Hispanic Women	65	50	45	44

SOURCE: U.S. Bureau of the Census, Current Population Reports, Population Characteristics, Marital Status and Living Arrangements March 1972, P-20 No. 242, Table 1; March 1981, P-20 No.372, Table 1; March 1991 P-20 No. 461, Table 1; March 1995, P-20 No. 491, Table 1.

Whites and for Hispanic men. In contrast, it has gone up for Black women (6% in 1995) and men (7%) and for Hispanic women (8%). Despite declines in the percentage who are widowed, an increase in the percentage who are married has not occurred for Black women or for Hispanic women since 1981 (see Ries and Stone, 1992). Black men have actually experienced a decline in the percentage aged 65 and over who are married and who are widowed. Although the rate of change in divorce has been slower for Blacks and Hispanics, the actual percentages of these groups who are divorced are higher. For example, whereas 6% of White women are divorced, 13% of Black women and 14% of Hispanic women are.

The data discussed here focus on current marital status, so figures of those who have ever been divorced would be higher. For example, in 1990, 1 in 5 Canadian women aged 50 to 59 had divorced at least once (Gee, 1995). Indications are that divorce rates are rising steadily in both Canada and the United States, with higher rates in the United States than Canada (Ries and Stone, 1992). Thus, divorce has affected more older persons than is indicated by the numbers of currently divorced individuals.

Summarizing, the majority of men in older age have a spouse and the majority of women do not. This creates a very different perspective on later-life intimate relationships for men and women. Clearly, the qualitative dimensions of marriage are of relevance to a greater proportion of older men than women. In turn, the issue of life alone following widowhood affects a majority of older women but only a minority of older men. When combined with the single and the divorced, the percentages and numbers of unattached older men and women are substantial, and the unique nature of their family ties requires separate attention. The steady increase in divorce rates affects all ages, both directly, in terms of the elevated frequency of divorce at all stages of the life course, and indirectly, in terms of the repercussions of divorce in one generation for other generations.

The Availability of Children

Although one can generally equate singlehood with childlessness in the older population, this is not true of the younger population. Thus, singlehood can no longer stand as a proxy for childlessness, although the tabulation of births for ever-married women only in Canada until 1991 appeared to make this assumption. Birth rates have declined over the past several decades in the United States and Canada. However, focusing on birth rates can provide a distorted picture of family life. Instead, the data presented here focus on family size and show number of children by age group (see Table 2.5).

Data on births (see Table 2.5) show that 79% or more of American women up to the age of 80 in 1990 had at least one child. Similarly, among ever-married Canadian women in 1991, 85% or more did so (note that Canadian data are for ever-married women only, whereas U.S. data are for all women). As well, although overall birth rates have gone down over time, so too have the percentages of women who are childless or who had only one child. For example, among American women aged 45 to 64 in 1990, the number of women who are childless is down to 11% compared with 21% of those aged 75 to 79 years. Declining birth rates are predominantly a function of the lower proportion of the youngest women who have five or more children, offset somewhat by an increase in the proportion who have two or three children (Connidis, 1999b). Although rates of childlessness are likely to be higher among younger cohorts of women than among mothers of the baby boom (children born from 1947 to 1967 in the United States and slightly later in Canada), they are unlikely to exceed those of women now aged 80 and over.

In some cases, childlessness and small family size are due to the death of children. Speaking of her deceased daughter, a London, Ontario, widow of 92 notes the unexpected nature of such loss: "It never occurred to me that I would end my days without her. We were very, very close and we had so much to do with the family." However, even taking this possibility into account, the vast majority of older Americans and Canadians (80%; Gee, 1995) have at least one living child.

There are clear parallels between the older segments of the current cohort of elderly persons (those marrying and bearing children in the Depression and post-Depression years) and those presently in their childbearing years. Compared to other time periods, both groups share low fertility, a similarity that is frequently overlooked in discussions about the future elderly. The parents of the baby boom represent the more novel case in having a *larger* pool of children from whom to receive support. Thus, with respect to family size, the experience of many of today's older persons may be of particular relevance to those who are now of childbearing age, although the factors affecting childbearing decisions may be quite different.

TABLE 2.5 Percentage Distribution of Number of Children Ever Born To Women Aged 45+ By Age Group: United States, 1990; Canada, 1991

No. of Children	45-54		55-64		65-69		70-74		75-79		80-84		85+	
	U.S.	Canada	U.S.	Canada	U.S.	Canada	U.S.	Canada	U.S.	Canada	U.S.	Canada	U.S.	Canada
0	11	7	11	9	14	10	17	12	21	15	23	21	24	15
1	11	10	11	8	13	10	15	12	17	14	19	19	18	19
2	28	37	22	22	24	20	25	24	24	24	23	21	21	19
3	23	25	22	23	20	20	18	18	16	15	14	16	14	17
4	13	12	15	15	12	15	11	14	9	12	8	8	9	10
5+	13	8	19	24	17	25	14	20	13	20	13	16	14	20

SOURCE: U.S. Bureau of the Census, 1990. *United States Census* Public Use Microdata Sample (1% Sample). Data are for all women. Statistics Canada, 1991. *Census of Canada.* Data are for ever-married women.

The Availability of Grandchildren

Of Americans aged 35 and over, 80% report being members of three-generation families, and 16% are in families of four generations (Szinovacz, 1998). Among all Americans and Canadians aged 65 and over, 80% have at least one grandchild (see Table 2.6). The numbers are even higher if one focuses on those who have children. Among older Canadian parents, 80% of those aged 55 to 64 and over 90% of those aged 65 or more also have grandchildren. Similarly, among older Americans, 95% of those whose youngest child is at least 40 years old are grandparents (Szinovacz, 1998). Looked at from the vantage point of younger men and women aged 19 to 26 years, from 73% (Black) to 78% (White and Hispanic) have at least one living grandparent, and at least 1 in 5 have three living grandparents (Szinovacz, 1998). Thus, for a majority, ties to a grandparent extend into adulthood, and old age includes grandchildren.

The Availability of Siblings

Changes in patterns of fertility also affect the availability of siblings. With declining fertility, the number of siblings decreases. However, when the parents of the baby boom and the baby boomers are compared, low fertility in the family of procreation has been preceded by higher fertility in the family of orientation, and high fertility in the family of procreation has been preceded by lower fertility in the family of orientation. Therefore, on average, those having small families themselves (those who are among the older elderly and the baby boom) tend to come from larger families and have more siblings available. Those who come from smaller families (the parents of the baby boom) tend to have larger families themselves. Declining fertility leads to a decline in the number of children and siblings for the same age cohort only when successive generations have similarly low levels of fertility.

In both Canada and the United States, the vast majority of all age groups have siblings. As the data in Table 2.7 show, over 90% of Americans and Canadians of all ages have had siblings. Most continue to have surviving siblings into old age. In Canada, three quarters of older persons aged 80 and over have at least one living sibling, and over half have more (Connidis, 1999a). A variety of surveys in the United States also indicate the availability of siblings to most older persons (Cicirelli, 1995). In sum, the majority of older persons

TABLE 2.6 Percentage Distribution of Those With Grandchildren by Age Group: United States, 1994; Canada, 1995

Percentage With Self-Defined Grandchildren	United States							Canada	
	Male				Female				
	Total	Black	White	Hispanic	Black	White	Hispanic	All Persons	Parents Only
55-64	78	86	74	95	86	82	69	70	80
65-74	—	—	—	—	—	—	—	80	93
75-84	—	—	—	—	—	—	—	79	91
85+	—	—	—	—	—	—	—	77	96
65+	81	85	84	90	79	79	91	—	—

SOURCE: U.S. data are from Wave 2 (1994) of the National Survey of Families and Households (Sweet, Bumpass, and Call, as reported in Szinovacz, 1998, p. 43). Statistics Canada 1995, *Canadian General Social Survey, 1995.*

TABLE 2.7   Percentage Distribution of Number of Siblings by Age Group:
United States, 1996; Canada, 1995

Age Group	Number of Siblings					
	0	*1*	*2*	*3*	*4*	*5+*
25-34						
United States	5	20	18	20	14	23
Canada	9	22	24	16	9	19
35-44						
United States	4	14	21	18	12	30
Canada	6	14	20	17	13	30
45-54						
United States	5	17	21	18	12	28
Canada	9	15	16	15	11	35
55-64						
United States	6	17	19	15	11	33
Canada	9	13	13	13	11	41
65-74						
United States	8	13	15	13	14	38
Canada	7	11	13	11	9	48
75-84						
United States	6	12	16	15	14	39
Canada	7	11	12	14	9	47
85+						
United States	—	17	15	8	8	52
Canada	5	10	12	11	10	52

SOURCE: Davis and Smith, 1996; Statistics Canada, 1996.

have both inter- and intragenerational family members. In subsequent chapters, we shall explore the nature of these various family ties in later life.

Living Arrangements in Later Life

The living arrangements of older persons are indicative of both their continued involvement in family settings and a trend toward living alone in the absence of a spouse (Davis, Moritz, Neuhaus, and Barclay, 1996; Kinsella, 1995). Only a relatively small proportion (5% in the United States; Burr, 1990; Lugaila, 1992; for Canada, estimates range from 5% to 8.5%) of all those aged 65 and over currently live in institutional settings. Institutionalization is more likely among women than men, those with fewer children, the nonmarried, Whites, and older seniors (Angel, Angel, and Himes, 1992; Belgrave and Bradsher, 1994; Belgrave, Wykle, and Choi, 1993; Carrière and Pelletier, 1995). The lower institutionalization rates of Blacks when compared with Whites are offset somewhat by their greater reliance on paid home care and informal care but are also due to simply going without care (Wallace, Levy-Storms, Kington, and Andersen, 1998). The presence of at least one daughter or sibling minimizes the chances of being placed in a nursing home (Freedman, 1996), providing a link between the availability of ties and their impact on social life in older age.

The living arrangements of older Americans and Canadians are shown in Table 2.8. The majority of people aged 65 and over live with a family member, predominantly a spouse (Kinsella, 1995). Living with family is more common in the United States than in Canada but is the norm among older persons in both countries. However, there are substantial differences between men and women, with men much more likely to be in this situation than women. Thus, whereas about 80% of American and Canadian men lived with family members in 1991, this was true of only 56% of American and 49% of Canadian women. These gender differences reflect primarily the higher widowhood rates among women due to the custom of husbands being older than their wives, the greater life expectancy of women, and the higher remarriage rates of men.

A general trend in the Western world since 1960 is the growing proportion of elderly people, particularly women, who live alone (Kinsella, 1995; Wolf, 1990). Among older persons in the United States in 1995, more than twice as many women (43%) as men (19%) lived alone (see Table 2.8), again, in substantial measure because women are more likely to be widowed (Kinsella, 1995). The fact that widowed women are more likely to live on their own if they did so for at least 3 months prior to the age of 60 (Bess, 1999) suggests that solo living will continue to increase among women because living alone at earlier stages of the life course is increasingly common. On the other hand, the mothers of the baby boom may represent a temporary drop in living alone, given the association between number of children and coresidence with a child (Wolf, 1995).

TABLE 2.8 Percentage Distribution of the Population Aged 65+, by Type of Living Arrangement and Gender: United States, 1972–1995; Canada, 1961–1991

| | *Family* | | | *Nonfamily* | | | |
| | *Primary* | | *Secondary* | *Primary Individual Living Alone* | | *Living With Others*[b] | *Collective Dwelling*[a] |
	U.S	Canada	Canada	U.S.	Canada	Canada	Canada
1972 U.S., 1971 Canada							
All Men	84	67	3	16	11	16	4
All Women	60	41	2	40	24	28	5
1981 U.S. and Canada	Families			Householder			
All Men	85	72	—	15	13	8	5
All Women	57	42	—	43	32	15	8
1991 U.S. and Canada	Families			Householder			
All Men	83	78	2	17	15	4	—
All Women	57	49	6	43	38	6	—
1995 U.S., 1996 Canada	Families			Householder			
All Men	81	81	—	19	16	3	—
All Women	57	52	—	43	38	10	—

SOURCE: Saluter, 1992, 1996; Statistics Canada, 1973, 1982, 1992, 1996; U.S. Bureau of the Census, 1972, 1981.
NOTE: Living Arrangement: Census Families are groups of two or more persons residing together and related by blood, marriage, or adoption. Primary Families include the head of a household. Primary Individuals are household heads with no relatives in the household; they are included as "householder" from 1981 on.
a. Primarily institutional settings; excluded in 1991.
b. Includes lodgers and noncensus family members (e.g., adult siblings).

The living arrangements of Black, White, and Hispanic Americans vary somewhat (see Table 2.9). Among men, there are differences by race and ethnicity in the proportion who live with family members; in 1995, 72% of older Black men did so, compared with about 80% of White and Hispanic men. Among women, Hispanic Americans are more likely to live with family

TABLE 2.9 Percentage Distribution of the Population Aged 65+, by Type of Living Arrangement, Gender, and Race: United States, 1972–1995

1972	Family, Primary	Nonfamily, Primary Individual Living Alone
White Men	84	15
White Women	59	41
Black Men	76	24
Black Women	66	34
Hispanic Men	78	22
Hispanic Women	65	35
1981	*Families*	*Householder*
All Men	85	15
All Women	57	43
White Men	86	14
White Women	57	43
Black Men	72	28
Black Women	61	39
Hispanic Men	82	18
Hispanic Women	75	25
1991	*Families*	*Householder*
All Men	83	17
All Women	57	43
White Men	82	17
White Women	56	44
Black Men	74	26
Black Women	60	40
Hispanic Men	86	14
Hispanic Women	70	30
1995	*Families*	*Householder*
All Men	81	19
All Women	57	43
White Men	82	18
White Women	57	43
Black Men	75	25
Black Women	58	42
Hispanic Men	82	18
Hispanic Women	65	35

SOURCE: U.S. Bureau of the Census, 1972, 1981, 1991, 1995.

members then are White or African Americans. The aggregate data presented here mask additional differences. For example, when living with family is divided into the three categories of living with a spouse only, living with a spouse and other kin, and living with other kin only, White persons aged 60 and over are far more likely to be living with a spouse only, whereas Asian, Black, Hispanic, and Native American persons are far more likely to be living with other kin only (Himes, Hogan, and Eggebeen, 1996).

When adult children and their older parents do live together, the usual assumption is that the parents are living with their children and that, if there is an issue of dependency, it is the older generation who depends on the younger one (Coward and Cutler, 1991). However, coresidence may also represent the dependence, sometimes temporary, of adult children. Some children may never have left home, often due to long-term disability; others may have returned home following unemployment or divorce. Census data are generally an unreliable way of determining whether parents are living with children or children are living with parents, although some have used the status of household head to determine which party is dependent (Coward and Cutler, 1991). Canadian data on three-generation households show that activity limitations are spread across generations. The first *and* second generations *each* account for just over one third of the activity limitations reported for such households, and the remaining 25% applies to the youngest generation (Che-Alford and Hamm, 1999). Thus, in the case of three-generation households, at least, coresidence provides support for family members with disabilities of all generations, not just the old. Family size affects who lives with whom; nonmarried women with more children are more likely to have someone living with them than to be living with someone (Mutchler, 1990). The increased return of children to the empty nest is examined in Chapter 8.

To address more broadly the extent to which the elderly are supported or neglected by their families, it is necessary to examine reasons for living alone. There is no doubt that older people prefer to maintain their independence, including independent living, for as long as possible (Mack, Salmoni, Viverais-Dressler, Porter, and Garg, 1997). In Western culture, older persons also prefer receiving help from formal service agencies rather than from their children, especially if the need for care is lengthy or personal (Daatland, 1990; Wielink, Huijsman, and McDonnell, 1997). In the eyes of older persons, the desire for independence seems to be maintained more effectively by receiving services from the community rather than from children. Factors other than preference are influential in living arrangement outcomes. These include economic resources (are they sufficient to sustain independent living?), health (is one healthy enough to live on one's own?), and the availability of kin, particularly children and a spouse (Zsembik, 1996). Economic security, health, and family ties are differentially distributed across the older population, which helps explain why some groups are more likely than others to live alone.

We have noted already the impact of marital status on living arrangements and the greater probability of women living alone that results from their greater likelihood of being widowed. Variations in fertility rates among the older population also help account for differences in both stated preferences and actual living arrangements. For example, the greater likelihood of older Latinos and Latinas to prefer to reside with children is typically explained as the outcome of a shared cultural tradition of honoring filial obligation through coresidence (Zsembik, 1996). However, studies that consider diversity *within* this group show that preferences for and actual coresidence of parents with children vary. For example, the apparently greater desire among Latinos of Cuban origin than of Mexican Americans to live alone is due to having fewer children with whom to coreside. When number of children is held constant, older Cubans hold a significantly stronger preference for living with children than do Mexican Americans (Zsembik, 1996), and Cuban fathers are actually more likely to do so (Zsembik, 1993). Further differences are found among older Mexican Americans based on place of birth, with those who were born outside the United States more likely than the native born to live with their children and to prefer doing so (Angel, Angel, McClellan, and Markides, 1996). These results provide an important caveat to attend to diversity within groups that are often assumed to be homogeneous.

Data from several countries indicate that the odds of living alone decrease as the numbers of children and siblings increase (Mutchler, 1990; Wolf, 1990). The desire for independence is more readily realized by today's elderly, even widowed homemakers, who, as a group, enjoy greater financial security than past generations (Gratton and Haber, 1993; Kinsella, 1995). In the United States, the increase in living apart from children that began in the mid-20th century was an outcome of "neither neglect nor desertion but the implementation of the welfare state" (Gratton and Haber, 1993:191). Indeed, during the early 1900s, "when women could, they delayed becoming dependents in the homes of the young; they preferred to maintain 'intimacy at a distance'" (Gratton and Haber, 1993:192). The preference for independence is realized by older women today through solitary living in their own homes. The significance of economic resources is reflected in the fact that women with higher incomes are more likely to live alone (Wolf, 1990). One probable consequence of more women of all ages being in the labor force is a further increase in the rate of living alone.

Even after variations among White, Black, Hispanic, and Asian older persons in the distribution by age, gender, and marital status are taken into account, the impact of race and ethnicity on living arrangements persists (Himes, Hogan, and Eggebeen, 1996). Based on 1990 U.S. census data, standardized figures show that extended family living is more typical among older Blacks, Hispanics, and Asians than among Whites, reflecting important cultural differences based on ethnicity and race. Overall, older White, Black, and Native Americans are more likely to live alone than are Hispanics and Asians. However, the greater income and fewer children of white women are two reasons that older, *nonmarried,* white women are more likely than their Black counterparts to live alone (Mutchler, 1990).

Generally, extreme limits in the ability to function independently and being in poor health make living alone less likely (among Canadian widows, Bess, 1999; Waite and Hughes, 1999; Wolf, 1990). But comparisons of White and Black unmarried women show that net worth and health affect the living arrangements of White women only, indicating that race has independent effects on the living arrangements of older unmarried women that may reflect cultural differences (Mutchler, 1990; re: health, see also Angel et al., 1992; Belgrave and Bradsher, 1994). Taking into account the impact of various resources, Black women are more likely to head a multiperson household in older age. In turn, White women are more likely to both live alone and to be nonhead members of multiperson households (see also Peek, Henretta, Coward, Duncan, & Dougherty, 1997).

Similar trends are evident in the probability of living in an institution. The chances of doing so are lower among older Blacks and Hispanics than among Whites (Angel et al., 1992; Belgrave and Bradsher, 1994; Belgrave et al., 1993), and there are differences in some of the predictors of doing so among Black versus White unmarried older persons (Burr, 1990). For example, being widowed rather than single or divorced decreases institutional rates for White but not Black older persons. Although both Black and White unmarried women share an increased chance of living in an institution if they have fewer children, the impact is far greater for White women. These outcomes highlight the contrasting contexts and dynamics of family life among Black and White women over a lifetime and go beyond the impact of differential resources alone. At the same time, however, the significance of serious economic disadvantage and racism must not be minimized, including their role in fostering supportive kinship networks among African Americans (Belgrave et al., 1993).

Cultural differences in coresidence are also evident in Canadian patterns of three-generation households. Although a fairly small proportion (3%) of all households fit this pattern, there has been a 39% increase in three-generation families from 1986 to 1996 (Che-Alford and Hamm, 1999). In 1996, nearly half of all such households were headed by immigrants and, among those who arrived between 1986 and 1996, Asians composed 75% of three-generation household heads. American older persons of European origin also vary in their living arrangements. Regardless of how many past generations have resided in the United States, older persons of Southern, Central, and Eastern European ancestry are more likely than those of Northwestern European ancestry to live with relatives (Clarke and Neidert, 1992). In sum, ethnicity and race are important short-term and long-term factors in the living arrangements of older persons.

Last, a broader issue of living arrangements is migration. Patterns of migration among the elderly have significant implications for their welfare and for public policy. Older persons may concentrate in particular localities for three major reasons: accumulation, where older residents are left behind in communities that younger residents leave in order to find more prosperous locations; recomposition, when older persons migrate to an area that younger persons are leaving; and congregation, in which case older migrants outnumber younger migrants but persons of all ages are moving in (Morrison, 1990). Typically, congregation involves relatively well-off older persons seeking to improve their situation by moving to a desirable location, such as Arizona. In contrast, accumulation usually occurs in economically disadvantaged communities, for example, the Mississippi delta, leaving older persons with fewer resources to fend for themselves. The poorer economy of these regions also limits the ability to offer locally supported community support to older residents. The accumulation that results from aging in place while younger persons migrate, a trend evident in both the United States and Canada, requires mechanisms for the redistribution of wealth by higher levels of government (Moore and Rosenberg, 1997).

Summary and Conclusion to Part I

In Chapter 1, you saw that older family members of the past did not enjoy a particularly advantaged position in our society. Today, older people are more able to maintain chosen independence due to improved social security measures. Understanding family life in old age requires going beyond definitions of family as the traditional nuclear household and recognizing the families of single and childless older persons as siblings, children, aunts and uncles. Family relationships are negotiated in the context of a given family and of the larger society. Family members may have quite different views of how their families work. As particular family ties are examined, it is important to consider whether the challenges of family life and of aging should be considered private troubles or public issues.

In Chapter 2, some broad parameters of family life were established by looking at trends in the availability of various family members in later life. The data presented in that chapter documented that most older persons have children, grandchildren, and siblings. Nonetheless, there are significant variations in the availability of family ties, depending on gender, age, race, and ethnicity. For example, most old men have a spouse, whereas most old women do not. These factors are highlighted in subsequent chapters about the central family ties of older people. Each chapter begins with a discussion of contact with the family member in question before examining support exchanges and qualitative dimensions of the relationship. Let us begin by exploring intimate ties in later life.

PART II

Intimate Ties

3

Intimate Ties in Later Life

> The term *pure relationship* . . . refers to a situation where a social relation is entered into for its own sake, for what can be derived by each person from a sustained association with another; and which is continued only in so far as it is thought by both parties to deliver enough satisfactions for each individual to stay within it. Love used to be tied to sexuality, for most of the sexually "normal" population, through marriage; but now the two are connected more and more via the pure relationship.
>
> —*Giddens (1992:58)*

Struggling to find a term that captures those unique intimate relationships that differ from friendship and from those family ties that are created by others (e.g., parents and siblings) indicates the need to create new terms that incorporate the shifting boundaries of chosen bonds. Although many relationships may well be intimate in terms of emotional attachment, this chapter deals specifically with relationships that include sexual intimacy or are formalized by marriage. Traditionally, this chapter could have been titled "marriage in later life," or something like it, and been accepted as covering the intimate relationships of older persons. Now, such a focus is too exclusive. Although it is still the case that marriage represents the intimate relationship of their lives for most older persons, this is not true of all older persons and will be less common in the future. Yet typically excluded are those whose heterosexual intimate relationship parallels marriage but has not been formalized, cohabiting same-sex partners (whose relationships cannot currently be formalized legally by marriage), and the ongoing intimate ties of both heterosexual and homosexual older persons that do not involve living together.

To date, there has been little attention paid to either long-term same-sex partnerships or intimate heterosexual ties outside of marriage, as is reflected in this chapter where much of the discussion pertains to marital ties. However, we must begin with an awareness of these serious gaps in research and with an appreciation for the broader context of intimate ties. For example, as we know from Chapter 2, the majority of older women are not married. To discuss only marital ties excludes other intimate relationships that some of these women may have. As well, discussions of single persons tend to assume that there are no intimate relations occurring when, in fact, some of these persons may be gay or lesbian and some, whether gay or straight, may have ongoing intimate ties. Our failure to ask about this side of life in older age makes it unlikely that we will discover much about it. But it is intimacy, not marriage per se, that is important to well-being and health (Traupmann and Hatfield, 1981). Therefore, we need to better understand the intimate relationships of older married *and* unmarried individuals.

Do sexual relations have to be present in order for a tie to be considered intimate? Not necessarily. A relationship may qualify as intimate based either on *assumptions* of sexual intimacy as a hallmark of institutionalized relationships, such as marriage, or on the *presence* of sexual intimacy in the case of noninstitutionalized relationships. In our society, sexual interdependence is typically a restricted exchange; that is, the exchange is confined to two persons (a dyad), and a third party is not considered a legitimate alternative to either player (Scanzoni and Marsiglio, 1993). Even outside marriage, serial relationships are socially sanctioned to a far greater degree than are multiple partners, reflecting the restricted exchange associated with sexual relationships. When other intrinsic exchanges are added to sexual interdependence, the resulting relationship has been described as erotic friendship and as a sexually bonded primary relationship (Scanzoni and Marsiglio, 1993). We might as readily use Giddens's term, pure relationship, to describe such ties.

Intimate ties as discussed here include pure relationships as well as those ties formalized by marriage. In some ways, to qualify as intimate ties, pure relationships have a greater burden of proof (the presence of sexual relations) than do marriages (where sexual relations may or may not occur). At the same time, however, the institution of marriage carries with it a heavy burden of obligation to provide mutual support. At the very least, intimate ties as discussed here parallel Huyck's (1995:181) view of "marital-like partnerships" as presuming "potential sexual sharing." Although other familial ties as well as friendship may offer emotional intimacy, they are characteristically different from these intimate ties and cannot serve as full substitutes for them.

The Significance of Marital Status

Marital status is a central variable in structuring social life and is related to living arrangements, loneliness, suicide, psychological well-being, and health. As noted in Chapter 2, higher widowhood rates among women make living alone more likely among women than men. However, when unmarried men and women aged 60 and over are compared, they are equally likely to live alone (Burch and Matthews, 1988). Thus, being married ensures a companion, whereas absence of a spouse means living alone for the majority of older men and women. The type of housing in which one lives is, however, far more dependent on marital status among women, who tend to rent rather than own their home once widowed, whereas most widowed men retain ownership (Connidis and Rempel, 1983). Although the single elderly have a smaller network of immediate family because they have always been spouseless and, with very few exceptions, childless, they more often live with someone else than do their previously married peers (Stull and Scarisbrick-Hauser, 1989). Among the never married who do live alone, solo living is more often a long-established lifestyle than is the case for the widowed.

Marital status is also related to health, both psychological and physiological. Life satisfaction and well-being tend to be lower for the widowed, divorced, and separated and higher for the never married and married (Cotten, 1999). The lower morale of the widowed compared to the single indicates the greater negative impact of desolation (feeling forsaken and lonely) than isolation (being on one's own); Gubrium, 1974). However, special occasions, such as weddings, provide opportunities for those who have lost a partner to be part of their larger family networks, as illustrated in Photo 3.1. The moderate position of the single is echoed in a 17-nation study of marital status and happiness that finds that both married and cohabiting individuals are significantly happier than single persons who, in turn, are happier than the separated, divorced, and widowed (Stack and Eshleman, 1998). Simply having a partner has benefits, but being married enhances happiness far more than does cohabiting

Photo 3.1. Special occasions, such as weddings, bring family members together, including those who are widowed.

(Stack and Eshleman, 1998). Loneliness is also greater among the unmarried who have had previous relationships than among those who have not (Peters and Liefbroer, 1997), indicating the greater impact of losing a partner than simply not having one. A dramatic indicator of the link between marital status and psychological well-being is the higher suicide rates among the unmarried than married (Lauer, Lauer, and Kerr, 1995). For all ages, marriage lowers the risk of suicide to a greater extent among men, in part because women more effectively maintain a pool of affiliative ties comprising family and peers (Cumming and Lazer, 1981).

Black married women are less satisfied with their marriages than White women, and Black men and women report less harmonious marriages than do White Americans (Broman, 1993). The less rewarding marriages of African Americans are due in part to their lower levels of spousal support and financial satisfaction. Nonetheless, although African American older women show more depressive symptoms than White women, being married means better well-being for both White and Black women (Cochran, Brown, and Mc-Gregor, 1999). As is true of heterosexuals, a committed monogamous relationship increases life satisfaction among gay and lesbian older persons. Gay men with such intimate ties are less lonely and depressed and more happy than those who are unattached (Brown, Sarosy, Cook, and Quarto, 1997). Loneliness among heterosexuals is also offset by having a partner but more so for men than for women (Peters and Liefbroer, 1997).

Overall, regardless of age, married persons are the most healthy, followed by single, widowed, divorced, and separated persons (Verbrugge, 1979). This pattern holds for morbidity and mortality. Cohabitation tends to mimic the positive effects of marriage on health. However, important variations appear if age and living arrangement are considered. Counter to most research, data from the U.S. Longitudinal Study of Aging find that single (never-married) women are healthier than married women (Goldman, Korenman, and Weinstein, 1995). British research (Murphy, Glaser, and Grundy, 1997) suggests why this might be. Among those up to 70 years old in Great Britain, long-term illness is least likely among those in their first marriage, followed by the remarried, the widowed and divorced, and then the single. However, single persons aged 75 and over who live in the community have the *lowest* rates of long-term illness. Why this reversal? Being single makes it much more likely that poor health will result in moving into an institution, a consequence of the smaller family network available to single persons. Thus, it is important to recognize that community-based samples of older adults include particularly healthy single persons who are able to live independently.

The relationship of marriage to health is not only a function of the selection process in which the healthy are more likely to marry, whereas the unhealthy remain single or fail to remain married (Verbrugge, 1979). Marriage also has protective effects over the life course (Murphy et al., 1997). Being married is actually conducive to better health because a partner encourages behavior that contributes to health and provides support when ill (Schone and Weinick, 1998; Umberson, 1992a). Living with someone else and having greater economic security, for women particularly, are additional reasons that marriage enhances health (Hahn, 1993; Waite, 1995; Zick and Smith, 1991). Marriage reduces the need to rely on formal services, a common measure of illness or health decline, and is the basis for a broader range of informal support, especially among older men (Connidis and McMullin, 1994). The better health of the never married than the previously married suggests again that desolation is more stressful than simply being unmarried.

Clearly, marital status is a critical variable in shaping social life. The preceding discussion illustrates the necessity to distinguish among various forms

of being unmarried (widowed, divorced, separated, and single) and the different impact that marital status has on men versus women. Just as important is
the need to consider marital history and variations in marital quality. Most research focuses on current marital status, but this masks differences among
older persons of the same status. For example, work in the Netherlands (Peters
and Liefbroer, 1997) shows that the more relationship breakups one has experienced, the lonelier one feels, regardless of current marital status. Time does
tend to heal and loneliness abates as the time lapse grows since a breakup.
Variations in marital quality also make a difference. Although being in a relationship generally enhances well-being, being in an unhappy one does not, in
which case being alone is a better alternative (Ross, 1995).

Before exploring in greater detail the variations among older persons
based on their marital status and partnership history, we first consider an
aspect of later life that is, to date, profoundly affected by marital status:
sexuality.

Sexuality and Aging

Sexuality . . . is now a means of forging connections with others on the basis of
intimacy, no longer grounded in an immutable kinship order sustained across
the generations.

—*Giddens (1992:175)*

Although much of the research on sexuality and aging focuses more on the
mechanics of sex than feelings about it, it does clarify some misconceptions
about aging and sexual activity. "Ageism" is now a familiar concept. One long-
standing example of agist attitudes is the view of older persons as asexual
adults who are not and should not be interested in sex. Fortunately, this view
has softened among all age groups, and today, older persons are more open to
discussing and engaging in sexual activity (Hooyman and Kiyak, 1999). The
incredible media attention paid to impotence and sex-enhancing drugs, such
as Viagra, has brought the issue of aging and sex into the open, even though relatively few men actually use the drug (American Association of Retired Persons, 1999a).

Two shortcomings of the limited research on sexuality in old age have
distorted our understanding of this topic (Hooyman and Kiyak, 1999). First,

attention is focused on the frequency of heterosexual intercourse to assess the significance of sex to older persons' lives. This approach excludes discussion about the quality and meaning of sex and excludes gay and lesbian sexual relations altogether. Among heterosexuals, declines in intercourse alone need not signal a decline in either the interest older persons have in sexual relations or in the importance of sex to their intimate relationships. Sexuality is a far broader concept than sexual intercourse, and touching, caressing, holding hands, and kissing are important forms of sexual expression in older age (Neugebauer-Visano, 1995).

Second, most research on sexual activity is cross-sectional so that the activity of one age group is compared with the activity of other age groups. Such a comparison shows that older persons engage in sexual intercourse less often than other groups but cannot tell us about changes in sexual activity over time. Research that does address sexual activity over the life course finds that our practices as younger adults are carried into old age; those who are active in younger years remain that way in old age, given the opportunity (Hooyman and Kiyak, 1999). As well, older people who are more sexually active are more satisfied with their sex lives (Matthias, Lubben, Atchison, and Schweitzer, 1997), and their view of themselves and their competence is bolstered by sexual activity (Marsiglio and Donnelly, 1991). Thus, sexuality remains a significant component of intimate relationships in later life.

Recent research on sexuality and aging reported by AARP (1999a), in an article titled "Great Sex: What's Age Got to Do With It?," has updated our understanding of later-life sex and identified important issues on this topic among heterosexuals. The AARP study is based on mail surveys completed by 1,384 adults aged 45 and older in 1999. Two thirds of the men and almost 60% of the women believe that a good sexual relationship is an important contributor to their quality of life. Among men and women with sexual partners, 60% of those aged 45 to 59 have sexual intercourse once a week or more; one quarter of those aged 75 and over do so. More than 75% of this group have sex once a month or more.

Specifying that we are talking about people with partners is an important qualifier, as information on this group alone masks several gaps among older persons. There is a *partner gap* that is related to age and gender. As we know from Chapter 2, men are far more likely than women to have partners, particularly spouses. Because being married is overwhelmingly the most significant predictor of sexual activity among heterosexual women (Matthias et al., 1997), differences in marital status are important to our understanding of gender variations in sexual activity. Indeed, among those who are married, there are not gender differences in sexual activity (Marsiglio and Donnelly, 1991).

Sexual invisibility is an experience often reported by older women, who have mixed views about it. Those who would like to be noticed find this a drawback of aging. One group that is especially prone to experiencing invisibility is lesbian women (Auger, 1995). The combination of being old, women, and lesbian makes them a particularly marginal group, of limited interest to mainstream culture and research. Many remain "in the closet," fearful of coming out to others, including children and grandchildren. But for some, older age provides some license to explore their sexuality:

> When [my daughter] told me that she was gay I thought about it quite a lot. I have also loved women, liked them better than men. Now, I just wish that there was someone I could meet so that I could have a lesbian relationship. I have given it a lot of thought and I am ready for that thrill. No one cares about little old ladies of 70 anyway, so I should be able to get away with it until I die. (Woman in her 70s; Auger, 1995:109)

For some women, such as well-known feminist Gloria Steinem, the invisibility of old age is a welcome relief from a lifetime of attention. At 65, in an interview with Claudia Dreifus, she observed,

> The sexual response of men you're not attracted to can be awful. . . . [Invisibility] is a complaint many older people have, but it's not a problem for me. While most women have had too little visibility in their lives, I've had an overdose of it. (AARP, 1999b)

Such mixed responses are also evident in letters to advice columnists from women whose partners are taking Viagra. Although many are delighted that their spouses can engage in desired sexual activity once again, some feel cheated of the relief from sexual obligations that impotence provided.

The AARP (1999a) study also reports *gender and age gaps* in views on sexual activity. Sexual activity is considered a more important dimension of life quality by men than by women, and its significance declines somewhat with age. However, these differences are likely to reflect the acceptance of limited opportunity (the absence of a partner or health limitations) and a focus on other sources of satisfaction in later life rather than innate differences between men and women or a feature of aging itself.

Last, a *generation gap* regarding appropriate sexual activity makes it probable that future cohorts of older persons will more freely engage in sexual relations outside of marriage. As well, the acceptance by young and middle-aged adults of sexual activity that extends beyond intercourse (AARP, 1999a; Giddens, 1992) will make declines in male performance (e.g., erectile dysfunction) less central to satisfactory sex for future older persons. In addition, aging itself may improve sexual satisfaction, as some evidence suggests that men and women become more similar in their sexual preferences as they age (AARP, 1999a; 1999c), once the transition through midlife menopause and viropause (the male parallel to menopause, also called *andropause*) is complete. Other conditions also converge to potentially enhance sexual satisfaction after 50: more free time, no fear of pregnancy, no children at home, and enjoying sex beyond "the Act" (AARP, 1999c).

What about sexual activity among older persons who are not married? The available information is sketchy. Unfortunately, the nature of regular partners is not specified in the AARP study, so we do not know how many of these regular partnerships are marriages or other arrangements. Among those who do not have regular sexual partners, fewer than 1% of women and 6% of men aged 60 and over have intercourse once a week or more (AARP, 1999c). These numbers, although very low, are not surprising, as they probably capture casual sexual liaisons with changing partners, an activity one would not expect to be common for most adults.

Earlier work reports that older married men are two and a half times more likely than unmarried men (31%) to be sexually active (Matthias et al., 1997). The ratio is much greater for women: Married women are 11 times more likely than unmarried women (5%) to engage in sexual activity. More recent findings from a study of persons aged 70 and over (Matthias et al., 1997) show a much smaller margin of difference between married (47%) and unmarried (31%) men in the likelihood of having had sexual relations in the past month. Meanwhile, married women (43%) are still much more likely than their unmarried counterparts (3%) to have done so. Thus, marriage is currently much more critical to sexual activity among older women than among older men.

Unlike heterosexual ties, gay and lesbian sexual relationships are not associated with reproduction at any age (Giddens, 1992). Thus, as barriers to sexual activity outside marriage are broken down, gay and lesbian relationships could prove instructive about the nature of sex in later life for everyone.

The extent of sexual activity among older gays and lesbians is unclear, largely due to the reliance on unrepresentative samples. Generally, gays and lesbians engage in more episodic sex (gay men more so) and have more serial monogamous relationships than straight persons do (Giddens, 1992). As is true among heterosexuals, the level of sexual activity declines with age. In a small sample of gay men ($n = 87$; Pope and Schulz, 1990), more than four fifths of men aged 50 and over reported that they continue to engage in sexual activity, with two fifths of those aged 60 and over stating that they had sex once per week. Gay couples have sex more often than do lesbian partners, but sexual activity is the norm for both, with its frequency declining over time (Schwartz and Rutter, 1998). With increasing age, the number of partners with whom gay men are active declines, with the majority restricting their activity to one person (Berger, 1996).

In sum, aging brings with it a decline in sexual activity, but for those with partners, a history of an active sex life is carried into older age. Sexual activity remains important to older persons of all sexual orientations, but access to a partner can prove difficult, especially for women. Studies of sexuality and aging must pay more attention to alternative ways of sexual expression, the fundamental significance of intimate bodily contact, and the meaning of sexual intimacy to older persons. Such broader conceptions of sexuality highlight the benefits of intimate ties, the challenges of not having a partner, and the failure of formal responses to care to accommodate this important dimension of later life. Even those married couples who have private rooms in institutional settings find that expressing their sexuality is constrained. An 88-year-old husband observes, "we just get started, and it takes longer to start these days, when they come in here. It is so embarrassing. We don't feel we are able to have a normal life or a complete marriage any longer" (Neugebauer-Misano, 1995: 25). In the next chapter, we examine long-term intimate partnerships, primarily marriage, in later life.

4

Intimate Partnerships

Interdependence in
Long-Term Intimate Partnerships

A close relationship has been defined as one of high interdependence that is "reflected in intense activity and interaction" (Kelley, 1981:279). Interdependence varies because four of its properties vary among couples. These properties are (a) the degree of interdependence, (b) the balance of dependence between spouses (equal versus unequal), (c) commonality versus conflict of interests, and (d) dependence on individual versus joint action (Kelley, 1981). In considering life events that are characteristic of older age, a central issue is their impact on these dimensions of the marital or intimate relationship. For example, some changes may increase interdependence, thus contributing to a closer relationship, whereas others may disrupt prior patterns of interdependence and threaten the earlier closeness between partners.

As a rule, aging is associated with greater interdependence in the marital relationship. Most married persons aged 50 and over maintain considerable reciprocity in support exchanges with their spouse (Depner and Ingersoll-Dayton, 1985), indicating ongoing interdependence. In part because there is a decreased pool of social contacts and leisure activities in older age, the companionship and communication provided by a partner take on heightened importance as sources of satisfaction. A shortage of shared interests is the greatest threat to gratifying interaction between spouses.

Interdependence in the marital tie is shaped by culture and by circumstance. For example, Japanese couples are much more likely to emphasize complementarity in their mutual dependence on one another's gender-based roles than are White Americans, who focus more on equity in later-life marriage (Ingersoll-Dayton, Campbell, Kurokawa, and Saito, 1996). African American couples are also highly interdependent, but in their case, both partners develop parallel skills so that they can substitute for one another when needed, an innovative response to the more frequent necessity to have both partners in the labor force.

Couples, gay or straight, in which partners value independence are less satisfied with their relationships than are those who value interdependence (Julien, Chartrand, and Begin, 1999; Kurdek, 1992). This suggests that changes associated with aging may actually enhance intimate ties. We will later consider the impact of two major transitions associated with older age, retirement and health decline, on intimate relationships, particularly marriage. These transitions may increase the need for interdependence between partners and contribute to a decreased emphasis on gender in structuring household responsibilities among heterosexual couples.

We now turn to a closer examination of marriage in later life, the marital status most common among today's older persons for most of their lives. Because this currently means a focus on heterosexual couples, long-term gay and lesbian relationships are discussed in the following section.

Marriage in Later Life

There is an intrinsic and inescapable conflict in marriage. Human beings want incompatible things. . . . They want excitement and adventure. They also want safety and security. These desiderata are difficult to combine in one relationship. Without a commitment, one has freedom but not security; with a commitment, one has security but little freedom.

—*Bernard (1972:89)*

Among the married, satisfaction with their romantic relationship increases with age (Broman, 1993), and those who are more satisfied and happy with their marriage enjoy better mental health and well-being (Quirouette and Gold, 1995). Persistent marital strain has more detrimental effects on mental health than does divorce, and ongoing conflict between spouses concerning daily roles may lead to depression (Keith and Schafer, 1985). A poor marriage may also threaten physical health. For example, coronary heart disease is more common among those who are dissatisfied with their marriage (Traupmann and Hatfield, 1981). These findings underscore the need to attend to the qualitative dimension of marriage as well as the impact of marital status.

Marital Satisfaction Over the Life Course

Although marital satisfaction generally has positive effects on well-being (Lauer et al., 1995), the effect is greater for men than for women. One reason for this difference is that women, particularly older women whose marriages are more traditional, are more emotionally responsive to their partner (Quirouette and Gold, 1995). Another is that both husbands and wives agree that when marriages or phases of them are inequitable, it is the men who gain and the women who lose (Peterson, 1995). Exploring trends in marital satisfaction over the life course suggests additional reasons for differences between older men and women and identifies sources of change over time in this pattern.

Traditionally, research on changes in a couple's marital satisfaction over time has focused on the impact of the family life cycle, typically employing the eight stages of family life, or variations on them, initially proposed by Duvall (1967). This model uses age of the oldest child to determine the stages of the family cycle, beginning with the married couple without children and ending with aging families (retirement to death of both spouses). Couples who are childless following 7 years of marriage are often excluded, and only individuals or couples whose marriages remain intact tend to be included. This makes generalizations to all married couples problematic. As well, the extensive reliance on a cross-sectional design (comparing the marital satisfaction of different age groups at one point in time) means that observed differences may occur because the younger age groups include unhappy couples who eventually divorce, whereas the later stages include only those couples whose marriages have survived. Also, those who have been married for a long time may be more likely to report being satisfied with their marriages to justify having stayed married for so long.

Based on such work, the conventional wisdom for years was that marriages follow a curvilinear pattern in which marital satisfaction starts out relatively high, decreases for a time until children are launched, and then increases in the later stages, after children have left home (Lupri and Frideres, 1981; Rhyne, 1981; Vaillant and Vaillant, 1993). At all ages, men are significantly more satisfied than women. Children appear to be central to the assessment of a marriage among parents, and more childless spouses than parents describe their marriage as "very happy" (Lupri and Frideres, 1981). However, although marital happiness is enhanced by childlessness throughout the family cycle, the curvilinear pattern between family cycle and marital satisfaction appears to hold for couples with and without children.

The factors deemed important to a good marriage vary with time. Midlife couples place greater emphasis on the role performance of their spouse than either newlyweds or older couples when evaluating their marriages (Thurnher, 1976). Unlike middle-aged couples, preretiree couples are also concerned with personal attributes, emotional ties, and companionship when evaluating their marriage. The transition to the postparental stage involves shifts in priorities for both genders (Rhyne, 1981). Among men, the three most important aspects of marriage during the launching phase are friendship, sexual gratification, and help at home. After the children have left home, friendship remains most important and is followed very closely by the love and interest shown by their spouse. Among women, interest, friendship, and love are the three most essential components of marital quality in the launching phase. Once children are launched, love becomes most important, followed by sexual gratification, friendship, and interest. The heightened interest in sex among older women may be because declines in sexual activity, in the view of both men and women, are usually due to the husband rather than the wife (Ade-Ridder, 1990).

Are the observed improvements in marital satisfaction over the life course real? Age-related changes in the criteria of assessment may help account for apparent gains in marital satisfaction in later life. As an 80-year-old woman in one of my studies observed, one becomes "a little easier with people, a little less critical perhaps, as you get older. You can see your own faults and perhaps you are a little more tolerant with other people's faults." Indeed, when retrospective accounts of marriage are compared with prospective accounts, patterns of marital satisfaction are quite different (Vaillant and Vaillant, 1993). In the first case, when long-term marital partners reflect on their marriages, they observe the standard curvilinear pattern with a dip in satisfaction during the child-rearing or midlife years of marriage. However, when the same individuals report on the current state of their marriage at different points in time, marital satisfaction is remarkably stable over the middle and later years. Prospective accounts are favored as "truer" accounts of what "really" happened. However, one might also argue that it is only with the advantage of hindsight that one can actually judge the relative merits of a marriage over time.

Another recent study (Glenn, 1998) suggests that observations of change in marital satisfaction are actually a function of cohort effects, that is, differences among cohorts in marital stability and quality rather than differences over time in the course of all marriages. Rather than following a curvilinear pattern, marital success, gauged in terms of staying together and of assessing an intact marriage as very happy, tends to experience quite a dramatic downturn in the first two decades and a slower downturn thereafter. There is no evidence of an upturn in marital quality in the later years of long-term marriages. Thus, the apparent improvement in marriages over time is a function of relying on cross-sectional designs that fail to take into account divorce and its increase over succeeding cohorts. Consequently,

> Persons in the earlier durations of their marriages should not expect them to mature into a golden stage in the normal course of events. A mid-term upturn in marital quality seems unlikely . . . unless spouses are diligent in maintaining their relationship and put forth special efforts to make improvement occur. (Glenn, 1998:576)

On balance, older couples appear to be more satisfied with their marriages than their younger counterparts. Whether this is a function of looking at marriage through rose-colored glasses in later life, of selectivity with only the better marriages lasting a long time, of stage in the family life cycle, or of an "old-fashioned" commitment to marriage that is waning, the fact remains that today's older men and women in long-term marriages tend to enjoy relatively high levels of marital satisfaction (Lauer et al., 1995). The fact that the vast majority of couples whose children refill the empty nest are very satisfied with their marriages suggests that long-term marriages develop their own resiliency, making couples able to handle unexpected trajectories in the life plans of other family members (Mitchell and Gee, 1996). We will now take a further look at the unique features of long-term unions.

The Nature of Long-Term Unions

Do long-term marriages have qualities that are different from their shorter-term counterparts? The decline in companionate and passionate love over time (Traupmann and Hatfield, 1981) suggests that the nature of love changes in marriages that endure to old age. Older couples tend to be more reliant on one another for companionship and support (Zube, 1982). Partners in long-term marriages have assessed the following factors as central to the success of their relationship: having an intimate tie with someone they like and whose company they enjoy, being committed to one's partner and to marriage as an institution, sharing humor, and holding similar views on a range of topics (Lauer et al., 1995). Although commitment to marriage seems like a self-evident precursor of a successful union, this commitment is shared by unhappy couples; it is commitment to the partner that differentiates happy from unhappy marriages (Lauer et al., 1995).

A unique feature of marriage and similar intimate ties is its sexual component. As Ade-Ridder (1990:65) concludes, "other relationships can impart feelings of closeness and intimacy, but the emotional closeness experienced in a marriage of self-defined high quality is different because it is sexual, whether intercourse is a part of the expression or not." The same probably applies to other intimate, sexual partnerships that are not formally sanctioned by marriage.

Sexual intimacy continues to be important in long-term marriages, and among sexually active couples, greater sexual interest and activity are related to happier marriages (Ade-Ridder, 1990). Older persons typically describe their sexual partners (usually a spouse) as their best friend and as kind and gentle, reflecting qualitative dimensions of the sexually active relationship (AARP, 1999a). It is somewhat surprising, however, that the cessation of sexual activity, usually due to the husband's inability to perform, is not related to lower marital quality (Ade-Ridder, 1990). This suggests that when factors outside the couple's control make sexual activity impossible, alternative ways of providing intimacy and happiness to one another are found. Indeed, having a good relationship is important to more older people (9 out of 10) than is a good sexual relationship (67% of men and 57% of women; AARP, 1999a).

For some couples, the passage of time actually improves sexual relations. A 68-year-old man says,

> My wife and I have been married for 40 years and I have never looked back. She's the light of my life, and as sexy as ever . . . our sex life is better now than when we first got married. (Neugebauer-Visano, 1995:21)

One reason for this is suggested by a 70-year-old wife's observation: "I find it easier to talk about my [sexual] needs in my old age." Similarly, a husband, aged 69, says, "After a while you feel comfortable enough to ask your partner to do things that you only dream about doing, without being shy about it" (Neugebauer-Visano, 1995:21). The importance of building trust and comfort over time raises the question of causal order. Although it may be that sexual activity enhances marriage, the reverse may also apply, namely, that the quality of a relationship is important to a good sex life, particularly in older age (AARP, 1999a).

Older men report greater marital satisfaction than older women and greater satisfaction of the need for love and communication in their marriage. Are there features of the social networks of men and women that might account for their differing priorities in marriage and the greater satisfaction derived from marriage by men when compared to women?

Women do have a more extensive network of intimate relationships than men. They are more involved than men in maintaining family contacts and make a greater emotional investment in family and friend relationships. Although men and women have similar numbers of primary relatives, men restrict confidant status primarily to their wives, whereas women consider all primary relatives as confidants (Depner and Ingersoll-Dayton, 1985; see also Connidis and Davies, 1990, 1992). There is greater closeness between female kin (e.g., mother-daughter and sister-sister) than between female-male and male-male combinations (see Chapters 7 and 11). Women also have closer ties to friends and more friends whom they consider confidants. As a consequence, men more often than women rely on their spouses as sole confidant. Women's broader array of potential confidants provides a basis for comparison that may sometimes favor another relative or friend over a spouse, leading women to judge their marriages more harshly than men do (Depner and Ingersoll-Dayton, 1985). With fewer alternatives, men may place a higher value on the spousal relationship.

The two most commonly listed trouble spots in longer marriages are having different values and philosophies of life and lack of mutual interests (Sporakowski and Hughston, 1978). These dimensions of marriage tend to be relatively enduring, indicating an incompatibility between spouses that is unlikely to surface for the first time in older age. Older couples may not necessarily have fewer disagreements but rather better mechanisms for dealing with conflict. There appears to be very little struggle for dominance between spouses in long-term marriages, which would serve to minimize conflict for older couples. If a marriage can last into old age, it would appear that there are many benefits to be enjoyed. Therefore, it is important to highlight the continuity of the marital relationship, for it is rare that an unhappy marriage becomes a happy one in old age. Among those with marriages characterized by unhappiness and conflict, barring divorce, the prognosis is further deterioration in the marital relationship as they enter old age.

We now turn to consider long-term gay and lesbian relationships. We will then explore how two key transitions, retirement and declining health, affect long-term unions. Reflecting the available research, the focus of the latter discussion is marriage.

Gay and Lesbian Partnerships

In August 1999, *Maclean's Magazine* (Canada's equivalent to *Time* or *Newsweek*) ran a cover story titled, "Sex and Marriage: Can passion survive kids, careers and the vagaries of aging?" (August 9). In a subsequent issue (August 23, 1999:4), a reader wrote from New York City,

> You may not realize how cool it was to feature a gay couple among the pairs profiled in your "Sex and Marriage" cover story. Even better, the two men received no special treatment; they were integrated matter-of-factly into the piece. As a reader, I value that kind of fairness.

The extent to which gay and lesbian relationships are "integrated matter-of-factly" into discussions of intimate ties is a measure not only of fairness but also of our progress toward truly respecting and accepting diversity. At the moment, the tendency to ignore same-sex partnerships makes it necessary to give these relationships special attention both because there is less known about them and because we must emphasize the importance of including them. Photo 4.1 gives a glimpse of the richness of extended family ties for some same-sex partners.

A reluctance to grant legitimacy to gay and lesbian partnerships and a tendency to focus on homosexual identity and the coming-out process have resulted in very little research on same-sex *relationships,* particularly those in later life (O'Brien and Goldberg, 2000). Recent attempts to legalize same-sex partnerships create a picture of gay and lesbian partners attempting to "catch up" with their heterosexual counterparts. Yet as Giddens (1992:15) argues, "Gay women and men have preceded most heterosexuals in developing relationships. . . . For they had to 'get along' without traditionally established

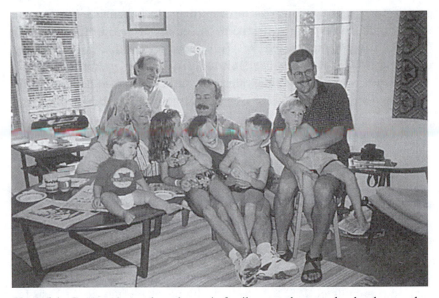

Photo 4.1. Gay couples are key players in family networks as uncles, brothers, and sons.

frameworks of marriage, in conditions of relative equality between partners." Thus, we should avoid assuming that heterosexual unions are the ideal to which homosexual partnerships should aspire and assume, instead, that understanding more about gay and lesbian relationships can extend our understanding of how to create intimate relationships.

The general invisibility of the old in our society is heightened for those who are old and gay or lesbian (Grossman, 1997; Lee, 1989). In the discussion that follows, the reader must remember that research to date has relied heavily on small and unrepresentative samples of gay and lesbian persons. This is especially true of older persons who faced far greater stigma due to their sexual orientation than is true of those in younger cohorts. One consequence of this difference is variation among cohorts in the likelihood of having public, same-sex relationships. In contrast to younger and middle-aged adults, one study finds that those older gays and lesbians who conceal their sexual orientation at work and are not very involved with the gay community are *more* satisfied with life (Adelman, 1991). Thus, for some older persons at least, concealment of a homosexual orientation appears to have been an effective strategy for managing stigma. But this contributes to their invisibility. The fact that younger cohorts tend to adjust better to a gay or lesbian identity when they disclose their orientation and are visibly involved in the gay community reflects an important generational shift due to social change (Adelman, 1991). More recent work indicates that improving attitudes toward homosexuality have also increased openness about being gay among older men (Brown et al., 1997).

Some argue that dealing with the stigma of homosexuality leaves older gay persons better equipped for dealing with the challenges of aging (Friend, 1996). Such a conclusion may reflect biased samples of relatively affluent and active gay and lesbian persons (Ehrenberg, 1997). For many older persons, occupying two stigmatized statuses—being gay or lesbian and being old— may make older age *more* of a challenge (Grossman, 1997). Age-related declines in health and a consequent need for social services may force the issue of disclosure for older gay and lesbian individuals, leading either to coming out more publicly in older age or to isolating themselves from needed support (see Fullmer, 1995). As well, health problems may be the basis for public questioning of a long-term partner's right to serve as a care provider or guardian. This creates unique challenges to same-sex relationships that are not part of the challenge posed by poor health among heterosexual, particularly married, couples.

There are other variations among gay and older persons that must be considered. Coming out tends to be more difficult for members of ethnic minorities (Manalansan, 1996) and, among gay men at least, for members of the working class (Chapple, Kippax, and Smith, 1998). Such differences are likely to influence both the probability of forming long-term same-sex ties and the success of such partnerships when they are formed because the concealment of a homosexual identity from family members and negative reactions from family produce strained relationships (Peplau, Venergas, and Campbell, 1996). Ethnicity and class are shared with other members of one's family but, typically, being gay or lesbian is not (Fullmer, 1995), heightening the potential for isolation not only from mainstream society but also from family.

The issue of disclosure is unique to gay and lesbian couples and is one reason that new typologies of long-term relationships other than those of heterosexual marriage are needed (Cruikshank, 1991). On balance, although the vast majority of gays and lesbians favor a couple relationship, and most would marry if legally able to do so (Lever, 1994, 1995, cited in Schwartz and Rutter, 1998), fewer are actually in such a partnership. Nonetheless, serial monogamy is typical, and 40% to 60% of gay men and 45% to 80% of lesbians are part of a live-in couple relationship at any one time (O'Brien and Goldberg, 2000). These numbers are mirrored in the living arrangements of gay men and women aged 50 or more; over a third of gay men and 60% of lesbians in one study live with someone else, most often a partner (58%) or friend (16%; Quam and Whitford, 1992). Another study finds that 60% of older gay men live with someone, most often a lover (Berger, 1996). Although these numbers are substantially lower than the proportion of heterosexuals who are married, they are impressive given that the institutionalized support of marriage is missing. They also suggest that aging may bring an increased desire to maintain a long-term monogamous partnership:

> F and I have been together 18 years now . . . we don't want or need to be with anyone else. When you get older you need more stability in your life. I've had my flings—I know what it is like to love other women, but I want to be settled down and get on with what's left of our lives together, so that when either one of us is gone the other will have wonderful memories to look back on. (58-year-old lesbian; Auger, 1995:111)

Similarly, a gay man of 65 says,

> I've been with Ryan for 10 years and I've never been happier. . . . We were made for each other. I only wish we had met sooner. It would have saved me some heartache. . . . Love improves with age and I think our sex life has improved too. (Neugebauer-Visano, 1995:24)

What type of attachments do gay and lesbian older persons form, and how do they compare with heterosexual partnerships? Three family forms are the most common among older lesbians and gays: long-term committed relationships; social networks that include friends, significant others, and those biological family members who exchange help; and family-of-origin roles that reflect their special social position (Fullmer, 1995). Heterosexual couples appear to be more committed to monogamy in both principle and practice than is true of same-sex partners, especially gay couples, the majority of whom engage in extrarelationship sex (Schwartz and Rutter, 1998). Nonetheless, same-sex and opposite-sex couples use the same criteria for assessing the quality of their relationships, have comparable perceptions of the quality of and satisfaction with their relationships (Julien et al., 1999; Kurdek, 1998), fall in love in parallel ways, and experience similar levels of intimacy (Julien et al., 1999) and relationship dynamics (Kurdek, 1994).

Although both gay and lesbian couples report more autonomy than opposite-sex couples (Kurdek, 1998), gay couples tend to maintain greater independence from each other, whereas lesbian couples are more inclined to merge their identities and to equate sex and love (Fullmer, 1995). The gendered nature of sexual relations is also evident in heterosexual marriages, with men far more likely than women to have affairs (Schwartz and Rutter, 1998). Homosexual unions tend to be more egalitarian. The majority of gay and lesbian couples are both in the labor force and thus enjoy relative economic independence (Peplau et al., 1996). This may help explain the fact that gay and lesbian partners do not engage in a gendered division of labor based on "masculine" and "feminine" tasks. Instead, their relationships have been compared with "best friendships" because the partners share a similar status and power position (Peplau et al., 1996). This lays the foundation for both members of the relationship to secure greater financial security in older age and to make a smoother transition following retirement than is true of heterosexual couples.

The potential significance of long-term intimate relationships may be greater among older gay men and lesbians than among heterosexuals because, on balance, their family networks tend to be smaller. In some cases, homosexuality may be the basis for estrangement from one's family of orientation (parents and siblings) as well as a partner's family, and only a small minority of same-sex couples have children. Those who have passed as heterosexuals by marrying and having children, a phenomenon more likely among today's older gays and lesbians than among their younger counterparts, are exceptional in this regard. In the more usual context of gay and lesbian networks, a long-term intimate tie and a family-like network of primarily gay friends, sometimes referred to as fictive kin or chosen families, are central to attaining effective social support (Brown et al., 1997; Fullmer, 1995).

Long-term relationships between gay and lesbian partners offer support, acceptance, a shared history, and memories, and their quality does not differ from that of heterosexual bonds (Fullmer, 1995; see also Berger, 1996). Also, like straight couples, life satisfaction is higher among same-sex couples who are happy and communicate well (Lee, 1990). However, the potential isolation of the same-sex partnership from other family ties may heighten its intensity and may present unique challenges to sustaining a good, long-term relationship. The fact that the support offered to straight couples by family members, especially parents and in-laws, enhances the marital success of longer-term marriages (Bryant and Conger, 1999) underscores the challenge to gay and lesbian partnerships that lack such support. AIDS is also likely to increase the value placed on long-term exclusive relationships among middle-aged gay men, partly as a way of reducing the risk of infection but more important, because the experience of AIDS has highlighted the significance of such ties: "In a crisis, only friends and family count" (Berger and Kelly, 1996).

Research on younger same-sex couples is suggestive about future differences in the experiences of older same-sex partners. Same-sex younger couples have more friends and more overlap in their social relationships than do opposite-sex couples, but they have similar numbers of kin in their social networks (Julien et al., 1999). However, conjugal adjustment is better among gay couples who depend less on their separate and joint friends, among lesbian couples who have fewer separate friends and depend less on their respective kin, and among straight couples who include their families of origin equally. These findings suggest an improved response to same-sex partnerships by family members, the risk to such partnerships of relying too heavily on friends, and the uniqueness of each type of relationship.

There is much research to be done on long-term gay and lesbian partnerships. Existing evidence suggests notable parallels in the factors that contribute to the success of gay, lesbian, and straight relationships. Learning more about gay and lesbian couples will inform us not only about their situation but also about fundamental features of forging intimate ties across the life course.

The Impact of Life Transitions on Intimate Ties

Two major age-related transitions in later life have an impact on intimate partnerships: retirement and declining health. To date, most related work has focused on married couples, especially research on the effects of retirement. The HIV/AIDS epidemic has encouraged research on caregiving among gay couples, but the literature on how life transitions affect same-sex relationships remains sparse.

Retirement

Although retirement is usually treated as an individual decision, plans to retire are heavily influenced by one's spouse, particularly among men

(Henkens, 1999; Smith and Moen, 1998). Thus, married couples have already contemplated retirement and its consequences, as a couple. Although most married men retire by age 65, unmarried men retire at younger ages. Conversely, married women both plan to (Morgan, 1992) and do retire earlier than unmarried women. This is partly a matter of economics (married men and unmarried women need their incomes more than their same-sex counterparts) and partly due to the desire of married women to retire at the same time as their generally older husbands. As well, those couples who have happy marriages and enjoy spending time together may retire earlier than less-happily-married couples.

What is the impact of retirement on a couple's relationship? The effect of retirement on the gendered division of labor and, in turn, on marital quality has several facets: equity in the actual division of labor (who is doing how much of what), perceptions of its fairness, and the attitudes held toward the traditional division of labor based on gender. Retirement of one or both partners has the potential to change the division of household labor between partners. Some argue that aging itself leads to less gender differentiation and more similarity in definitions of masculinity and femininity (Brubaker, 1985). Among men, aging is associated with greater sensitivity, familial affiliation, passivity, and introspection and, among women, with increased aggression, dominance, and assertiveness (Zube, 1982). Is the potential for gender role flexibility that these gender-associated changes suggest realized in retirement?

Despite the dramatic rise of women's labor force participation throughout Canada and the United States, the division of labor in the home is slow to change. In practice, women of all ages take on more of the responsibilities of housekeeping, kinship, and child care, whether or not they work outside the home. Most studies find that both genders tend to remain involved primarily in gender-linked tasks over the course of long-term marriages (Ward, 1993). Thus, for example, women are more engaged in traditionally "feminine" tasks, such as cooking, laundry, and housekeeping, whereas men focus more on "masculine" tasks, such as taking out the garbage, household repairs, and cutting the lawn. The most typical change in household duties is an increase among men in the number of masculine tasks they perform in older age (Askham, 1995). However, retired men do perform more feminine tasks than do employed men (Brubaker 1985; Dorfman, 1992; Vinick and Ekerdt, 1992). The employment status and history of wives makes a difference to the household labor of husbands. Retired men whose wives are in the labor force as well as those whose wives have a longer work history do more housework than their counterparts (Szinovacz, 2000). When their wives retires, these men curtail their household efforts.

At younger ages, the presence of children in the household increases the imbalance in the gendered division of labor by adding disproportionately to the woman's share of household tasks, whether or not women are in the labor force. By contrast, with children no longer living at home, older spouses carry a more balanced share of *all* responsibilities in running the household, even when they follow a traditional division of labor. In this sense, aging and retirement can be said to contribute to more egalitarian ties even though little real change occurs in sharing the household responsibilities that remain.

A considerable portion of the literature on retirement adjustment concerns changes in the activities of the male retiree and assumes that wives are full-time homemakers. Information on couples with a retired husband and a working wife or with both spouses retired from the labor force is quite recent. The patterns established prior to retirement are critical determinants of the effect retirement has on marriage. Couples who continue to share recreational interests begun earlier in their marriages tend to deepen their relationship (Henkens, 1999). But if over the course of a marriage, spouses spend little time together and develop few mutual interests, more time together following retirement may present a greater challenge to their marriage. Because working-class couples are more likely to have divergent interests (Kelley, 1981), they may have more difficulty in adjusting to the husband's retirement.

Retirement demands more of spouses than a simple increase in the amount of time spent together. In the absence of coworkers and a job, the bolstering of self-esteem and the maintenance of a positive self-image occur primarily within the marital dyad, particularly for men (Ade-Ridder and Brubaker, 1983). Without a positive sense of self-worth, spouses of either gender are inclined to act as either so-called doormats or aggressors intolerant of any discordant views (Medley, 1977). This creates considerable potential for friction in postretirement marriages if changed needs are not met by the spouses (usually the wife). Housewives are more likely to report disadvantages of their spouse's retirement than are their retired husbands (Keating and Cole, 1980). The most frequently mentioned disadvantages among women concern changes within the spousal relationship, such as shrinking personal freedom, too much time together, and too many demands on their time. The increased dependence of retired men on their wives for companionship, a sense of usefulness, and self-affirmation may instill a level of interdependence between spouses that either enhances their relationship or creates an imbalance that threatens it. Yet the fact that marriage in the retirement years tends to be as good or better than in earlier stages suggests that the net effect of the retired male's increased dependence is a more equitable balance in dependency between husband and wife.

The rise in dual-career couples has heightened interest in the concept of equity in marital relationships at various stages in the life course. Whereas some conclude that equity in the areas of food preparation, housekeeping, being the provider, and companionship contributes to marital satisfaction among long-term spouses (Keith, Schafer, and Wacker, 1995), others find that equity only makes a difference in perceptions of marital quality through its effect on perceived spousal support. Among women in their 50s to 70s, especially those who are employed, unequal sharing of household labor leads to dissatisfaction with spousal support, which leads, in turn, to lower assessments of marital quality (Pina and Bengtson, 1995; see also Suitor, 1991). Equity also contributes to the marital satisfaction of younger working couples married for an average of 15 years, but, in this case, its effect is filtered through gender (Wilkie, Ferree, and Ratcliff, 1998). Men, more inclined to see economic support of the family as their domain, experience a greater improvement in marital satisfaction than do women when there is greater equity in breadwinning; women, generally held to be more responsible for domestic labor, enjoy greater enhancement of their satisfaction with marriage when there is greater equity in household labor.

Perceptions of fairness rather than equity itself may be key to a marriage's success. Among older couples, perceived fairness of household labor, but not the number of hours engaged in housework itself, enhances marital happiness among women (Szinovacz, 1996; Ward, 1993). This apparent contradiction suggests the importance of the views one holds about the nature of marriage and gender. Examining the impact of different retirement configurations among later-life couples is instructive here. Possible configurations include employed husband and retired wife, retired husband and employed wife, both retired, employed husband and housewife, and retired husband and housewife. Although couples in which the husband is retired and the wife employed appear to have lower marital satisfaction, this is only true among couples who hold traditional views of gender roles (Szinovacz, 1996). In turn, traditional couples are highly satisfied with their marriages when the wife is retired and the husband is still in the labor force. At the same time, when employed wives first join their husbands in retirement, marital quality declines; the reverse is not true. This may be a function of wives feeling pressured to retire by their (usually older) husbands.

The impact of traditional views of gender and work is also evident in the varying effects of occupational prestige. Among employed women, the prestige of a wife's job has a negative effect on marital satisfaction, whereas the prestige of a husband's job and increasing age have a positive effect (Cassidy, 1985). In contrast, neither the prestige of the husband's nor the wife's past employment has a carryover effect on marital quality following retirement. Thus, in cases where the high prestige of a wife's occupation creates tension in a marriage, her retirement is particularly likely to enhance marital quality. On the other hand, couples reliant in part on the satisfaction derived from the prestige of the husband's job may find retirement has a detrimental impact on their relationship.

As we look ahead to future cohorts of older persons, the implications of the dramatic shifts in labor force participation among women, and consequent shifts in expectations of and actual division of labor in the household, must be examined. More power for women in the larger social world is likely to enhance the ability of future wives to negotiate effectively with their husbands (Scanzoni and Marsiglio, 1993). At the same time, the variable effects of retirement on marital quality suggest that retirement can pose challenges to the later-life marriage.

Central to discussing the impact of retirement on marriage is the issue of health. Although it is rare that retirement leads to poor health, one reason for retiring is declining health (Atchley and Miller, 1983). A change in health status of either spouse may have the most profound effect of all on the nature of marriage in later life.

The Impact of Declining Health

Reflecting the available literature, the focus here is on the marital dyad, although a number of our observations are likely to apply to all long-term intimate relationships. The health of one's spouse is related to both marital and life satisfaction. Among older married persons, good health enhances happiness (Crompton and Kemeny, 1999). Among married men only, so too does the good health of one's spouse. Men in poor health derive considerable benefit from having a healthy wife in terms of being happier and experiencing less mental distress. Conversely, the happiness and distress levels of women in poor health are not offset by their partner's good health. This may be because the life satisfaction of women is directly related to the life satisfaction of the husband and only indirectly related to his health (Atchley and Miller, 1983). Thus, among men, poor functional health of a spouse lowers life satisfaction, whereas, among women, a spouse's poor health depresses life satisfaction only if it does so for her spouse. Does this reflect differences between men and women in the response to becoming either a sick dependent or caregiver?

The illness of one partner may be the basis for a couple's symbiotic inter-dependence (Depner and Ingersoll-Dayton, 1985). Kelley (1981) proposes that severe illness and disability create imbalanced dependence between part-ners that leads, in turn, to rifts between them based on their conflicting inter-ests. The ill partner has negative feelings about the illness, the need for help, and perhaps most important, the compliance expected in return for care. At the same time, the helper feels the responsibility to provide care, the need for acknowledgment of the sacrifices being made, and difficulty in finding time to meet his or her own needs. Although the helping spouse may derive satisfac-tion from behaving altruistically and performing roles previously assumed by the ill spouse, difficulties in mastering new skills may arise and create frustra-tion. Similarly, the care recipient experiences ambivalent feelings as the help provided by a spouse is both a positive reflection on the marital relationship and an ongoing reminder of the need for help. As Rose and Bruce (1995:119) observe, "for the cared for, the inability to do things which they had done in the past, either for the couple or for themselves, was a matter of continuing regret and for some of them, rage." Both partners experience the altered nature of their relationship deeply and meet its challenges in part through using "a rhet-oric of coping" (e.g., "in sickness and in health," "you have to laugh"; Rose and Bruce, 1995:124), and a restrained expression of loss.

Given the greater likelihood that men will be married in later life, the experience of caring for a spouse is, consequently, much more likely for women. Demographics alone ensure that more older women than men will both care for an ill spouse and rely on someone other than a spouse to care for them, should help be needed. Thus, one must not deduce that women are turning to daughters and others for care simply because they have been ne-glected by their husbands. That said, the expectation to fill the caregiver role is greater for women than for men (Allen, Goldscheider, and Ciambrone, 1999; Thompson, 1993), and married women are more likely than married men to serve as primary carer to their spouse. In two quite different situations, one in which a spouse is in the advanced stages of cancer and another in which a partner is limited in the ability to carry out usual daily activities, husbands more often than wives name their spouses as either their primary caregiver (Allen et al., 1999) or as a helper (Barrett and Lynch, 1999). Furthermore, for both husbands and wives, greater emotional closeness makes naming a spouse as the primary source of care more likely (Allen et al., 1999). These findings highlight two crucial dimensions of support in intimate relationships: the gendered nature of caring and the importance to instrumental exchanges of a relationship's qualitative dimensions.

Caring Among Same-Sex Couples

Caregiving among same-sex couples has received sparse research attention. Sadly, the key impetus for conducting such research has been the spread of HIV and AIDS, particularly among gay men. A striking difference between gay versus married couples involved in caring is their much younger age. Examinations of older gay couples tend to include those who are 50 years or more rather than the conventional cutoff of 60 or 65 years. Caregiving in the context of HIV/AIDS is also unique because of the stigma associated with the illness and the marginal status of same-sex relationships (Ory, Zablotsky, and Crystal, 1998). Furthermore, a gay person caring for a partner with HIV or AIDS is likely to share with his partner associated risk factors and either the illness itself or survival guilt for not being ill (Brennan and Moore, 1994). These factors combine to create a challenging caregiving context for gay men with HIV/AIDS. However, like their straight peers, gay persons are most likely to receive care from a partner (Brennan and Moore, 1994). However, as is also true of married couples, others are engaged in providing care to gay persons with HIV/AIDS, but because of their younger age, sexual orientation, and usual childless status, parents are the family members most likely to be key caregivers (Mullan, 1998).

Gay partnerships that involve caregiving fundamentally transform the gendered nature of caring that predominates among heterosexual couples (Mullan, 1998). Men caring for partners with HIV/AIDS face particular challenges due to their relatively young age and isolation from family. Indeed, gay caregivers are more likely to seek support from friends in the gay community than from family and to rank support received from gay peers as most helpful and support from family members as least helpful (Mullan, 1998). However, the stigma of HIV/AIDS leads some couples to keep the diagnosis secret, limiting their ability to reach out to others for help (Brennan and Moore, 1994).

This is particularly true among gay members of minority populations, where the stigma of homosexuality, and consequently, AIDS, is especially high (Brown and Sankar, 1998). Among African Americans, the greater influence of religious institutions that have publicly denounced homosexuality reinforces the stigma of AIDS and further undermines the support received from family members (Brown and Sankar, 1998). For some gay persons, however, the illness serves as a catalyst for contact among previously estranged family members, challenging caregivers to negotiate a changed relationship with their partners' families (Brennan and Moore, 1994). Because gay partnerships tend to rest more heavily on egalitarianism and relative independence, the imbalance created by illness can be more disruptive than is true in marriage.

Gender and Interdependence in the Caregiving Relationship

Gender-based distinctions between heterosexual partners tend to extend into advanced old age (Wilson, 1995). However, when a partner becomes ill, such distinctions and a couple's interdependence may be altered dramatically. Examinations of shifting dependence usually focus on the increased dependency of the person receiving care. However, providing care can also create dependency, as the caregiver withdraws from other activities to meet a partner's needs. Similarly, the dependency brought on by ill health is usually assumed to decrease the relative power of the ill partner. Again, however, the partner providing care may also lose power in the relationship by becoming increasingly subject to the needs of the ill spouse. In other words, being the ill person does not always mean being the most dependent partner in an intimate relationship, nor does being the care provider guarantee having the most power. Indeed, other factors such as gender may be more important in determining power balances. For example, women who look after their spouses often feel unable to have visitors in their home for fear of upsetting their husbands (Rose and Bruce, 1995). Generally, men have more influence in the negotiation of the caregiving-receiving relationship, regardless of their position.

The nature of marriage prior to the onset of illness is critical to the development of a good caregiving relationship. Close partnerships lay a foundation for successful caring, whereas a poor marriage increases the risk that illness will result in negative physical and psychological consequences for both spouses (Allen et al., 1999). As well, older couples in shorter-term marriages find the adjustment to one partner's dependency more difficult (Rose and Bruce, 1995), in part because they have had less time to accumulate a history of problem-solving strategies. Length of marriage heightens mutual positive sentiments between spouses where one partner is caring for the other (Chappell and Kuehne, 1998). In turn, such shared sentiments enhance well-being for both partners.

Advanced old age (aged 75 and over) is associated with far less concern about domestic power as both men and women focus more on day-to-day survival (Wilson, 1995). The growing dependency due to the illness or disability of one or both partners is met with an "over-riding desire for independence" that "erodes previously gender-determined allocations of tasks, even before the demands of extreme dependency leave little choice other than to do what needs doing or to accept separation and institutionalization" (Rose and Bruce, 1995:120). This suggests that the illness of one of the partners may lead older couples toward the interdependent ideal of marriage with its emphasis on care, commitment, mutual nurturing and encouragement, and the acknowledgement by both partners of their need for each other (Thompson, 1993). The failing health of one partner does heighten closeness among long-term couples, especially when the wife is ill, because this situation fosters more nurturing by the husband (Ingersoll-Dayton, Campbell, Kurokawa, and Saito, 1996).

Generally, caregiving spouses are less healthy than spouses who are not engaged in caring for a partner (Wallsten, 2000). Nonetheless, the majority of spouses express positive sentiments about their marital relationship (Chappell and Kuehne, 1998). But women who care for their husbands are much more likely to express negative sentiments about their partners than are husbands who care for their wives (Chappell and Kuehne, 1998; Wallsten, 2000). Furthermore, women experience greater burden and health strain than do men when providing care to their spouse (Miller, 1990). Comparisons of husbands and wives who care for spouses with husbands and wives who do not, show that the greater psychological costs of caring experienced by wives are a function of caregiving itself and not an artifact of general gender differences (Rose-Rego, Strauss, and Smyth, 1998). What might account for such variations?

The psychological toll of caregiving is reduced by having a larger helping network (Smerglia and Deimling, 1997). Among the married, women are more likely than men to be the sole care provider to their spouses and to provide both more hours and more types of help to them (Allen, 1994; Stoller and Cutler, 1992). When cared for by spouses, women more often face unmet needs in the area of household maintenance than do men, but needs for personal care appear to be equally well met by spouses (Allen, 1994). Among very ill women, the deficit in help with household tasks is made up for by other helpers, but this is not true among married women who are less ill. Furthermore, when unable to function independently, married women are more likely than married men to receive simultaneous support from a child, sibling, friend, or formal service provider (Barrett and Lynch, 1999). Thus, the larger social networks negotiated by women are helpful in terms of additional support when a married woman is herself ill, but they do not translate into additional assistance in caring for an ill spouse. Conversely, married men receive more help from others in providing assistance to their spouses. This is consistent with a gendered view of helping in which women are assumed to be more adept at providing care on their own.

Another factor that may account for gender variations in the burden of spousal caregiving is the contrast in their histories of caring for others (Fitting, Rabins, Lucas, and Eastham, 1986). For women, particularly mothers, caregiving is the resumption of an activity recently (or never) relinquished, whereas for men, it is often newly acquired, following many years of labor force participation. An extreme example from my research is a mother of nine who raised two grandchildren, provided concurrent care for her mother and father-in-law until they died, and was then faced with caring for her husband as he died of cancer. Another widowed mother with five sons tells her story:

> After [my sons] grew up, I had my ill husband to look after for 7 years. . . . I couldn't get out. I was always there. . . . The only chance that I had of getting out was when the boys (sons) would come to look after him. . . . I guess the easiest time that I had was after he died.

Dementia: A Unique Caregiving Relationship

Much of the current research on caring for an ill spouse focuses on dementia, a health problem that presents special challenges to the family. Those who look after a spouse with dementia, including Alzheimer's disease, are especially prone to experience threats to their own mental and physical health because they invest more time in caregiving than those helping someone with other health problems (Hooker, Monahan, Bowman, Frazier, and Shifren, 1998; Ory, Hoffman, Yee, Tennstedt, and Schulz, 1999). Spouses and children are most likely to describe caring for a demented elder as difficult when the severity of the dementia, not the level of physical burden, is high. Among husbands caring for wives, the extent of memory and behavioral problems directly increases strain (Kramer, 1997). Yet the fact that both wives and husbands increase their tolerance for dealing with these problems over time (Johnson, 1985; Kramer, 1997) indicates their adaptability to a stressful situation. Caring for a spouse with dementia presents universal challenges that may transcend other differences. For example, in an African American's personal profile of caring for her husband, "race and culture do not play a major role in her story or care methods. Rather, her story emphasizes the basic human trials of coping with a debilitating disease." (Miller, 1998:511 reviewing Shanks, 1996).

Whether African American or White, men and women caring for a demented partner give the same types of care to their spouse, even though caregiving is often considered "women's work" (Miller and Kaufman, 1996). Women and Whites are more inclined than their male and Black counterparts to view caregiving as gendered (Miller and Kaufman, 1996). The more egalitarian views of African Americans suggest that age-related transitions, in this case, a spouse's illness, are more likely to be the grounds for increased interdependence between Black than White couples, regardless of which spouse is ill. Those who hold gendered views of caregiving emphasize women's greater capacity for compassion, caring, emotional strength, household work, and child care. In turn, men are considered better at repairs, financial acumen, and tasks requiring physical strength, notably lifting an ill spouse.

The view of caregiving as women's work and women's stronger belief that looking after a demented spouse is emotional work (Miller and Kaufman, 1996) help account for gender differences in the distress created by this unique caring situation. These factors are also the basis for what has been termed the "pet rabbit relationship" adopted when a husband cares for his wife (Rose and Bruce, 1995). This evocatively captures the argument that men experience greater pride in successfully caring for their spouses, in substantial measure because they emerge as "Mr. Wonderful" for fulfilling a role that is usually the purview of women. Conversely, precisely because caring is considered normal and natural for women, caring for a husband is not as effective a diversion from grieving his partial loss to dementia. The potential for violence is a unique feature of dementia and other illnesses (e.g., strokes) that impair cognitive functioning. This leaves women much more likely than men to be frightened by actual or possible violent outbursts because of their relative inability to defend themselves, heightening the extent to which caregiving controls their lives (Rose and Bruce, 1995).

Last, in the case of dementia, it is difficult to speak meaningfully of the impact of illness on the quality of marriage because the situation resembles having lost a spouse. This feeling makes adjustment to the caregiving role particularly hard. Because the spouse is alive, mourning seems inappropriate, but severe impairment limits the spouse's ability to satisfy the needs of the caregiver, including companionship. Describing older couples in their study, Rose and Bruce (1995:118-19) emphasized the significance of emotional work in this adaptation: "Emotional labour on one's own feelings was a large part of the invisible work carried out by carer and cared for as they struggled to survive disabilities and illnesses that were laying siege to their quality of life."

Summary

In sum, the interdependence that characterizes many older marriages provides a foundation for adapting to the need for care when one spouse becomes ill. The transition to the roles of care provider and care recipient heightens the interdependence of older spouses, contributing to a sense of closeness. At the same time, both partners must make considerable adaptations, and unique forms of conflict, though typically minimal, sometimes emerge in response to the illness of a spouse. Such conflict is often based on the fear of being abandoned through death (Johnson, 1985). The spouse of an older person who suffers major mental impairment due to dementia or stroke faces a particularly challenging situation—he or she confronts the loss of the spouse while having to care for him or her, often for many years. Even in this situation, however, caregiving should not be treated solely in negative terms; for many, "spouse caregiving may provide a complex challenge, giving a sense of competence and satisfaction that may compensate for the losses experienced" (Wells and Kendig, 1997:672).

Our examination of spousal caregiving indicates the significance of gender to understanding support in later life. The models of support that have dominated research on caregiving in later life (see Chapter 8) emphasize assumed features of particular relationships and fail to consider how gender structures family ties so that they are characteristically different for women and men (Allen et al., 1999). Even in old age, when health losses by one or both partners require greater interdependence and gender differences appear to diminish, family life continues to be organized around gender, and the "his and hers" marriage described by Jessie Bernard (1972) 30 years ago remains evident.

Although caring for a spouse may heighten interdependence in the marriage, it often leads to isolation of the couple (Johnson, 1985a). The comments of a 67-year-old childless woman from one of my studies exemplify how her husband's illness has cut them both off from the outside world:

> My husband is very possessive since he nearly died. I have got to be here. He had been very sick . . . and I have been very afraid since then. He nearly died. I have the feeling that he is very afraid. He doesn't like to be alone. So I try to understand, but it does not make me feel good. Like, if I say that I am going to go to the shopping mall, he says, "Oh no." I am not free.

Should illness be followed by death, extreme interdependence can prove debilitating to the surviving spouse, as commitment to the caregiving role may have deprived the surviving spouse of ongoing contact with others. Once again, the gendered nature of social relations is critical as it creates variations in the impact of one's own and one's partner's health on contact with others. Regardless of their own health status and that of their spouse, older married women maintain high contact with other social network members. Conversely, the health of married men is irrelevant to the amount of contact they have with others, provided that their wife is healthy (Crompton and Kemeny, 1999). However healthy they may be, married men suffer a notable drop in social contact if their spouses are ill. This situation reflects the greater emphasis on network development and maintenance among women than men, a difference with important implications following the loss of a spouse (see Chapter 6).

In marked contrast to those who spend most of their adult years married are those who remain single for their lifetime. We turn now to consider their experience.

5

Being Single in Later Life

The term *single* refers to the never married, in contrast to the *unmarried* who are widowed, divorced, or separated. Unfortunately, much research does not make such a distinction and, instead, includes single, divorced, separated, and widowed persons in one category or isolates widowed persons as a separate category. However, single persons are unique, in part because they usually have neither children nor spousal kin in their family network, unlike those who are widowed or divorced.

Images of being single have changed over time. The large number of baby boomers born from the mid-1940s to mid-1960s initially combined with the availability of birth control and the women's movement to increase sexual activity among single persons (Schwartz and Rutter, 1998). For the first time, the opportunity for sex outside of marriage was considered acceptable for both men and women, although still more so for men, lending an attractive aura to singlehood. However, as the front-runners of the baby boom reached adulthood, the women experienced a demographic squeeze, there being more of them than of slightly older men of desirable age for marrying. This situation was the basis for extensive media attention in the 1980s. For example, in June 1986, *Newsweek*'s cover story was titled "Too Late for Prince Charming?" and reported that well-educated women of 35 had only a 5% change of marrying. This news was described as "traumatic" and as confirming the widely held view that good-looking women with high-paying jobs could not have husbands too. The actual impact of the demographic squeeze was both over-stated and dramatized. In fact, the appeal of marriage to women was waning somewhat while men were finding it more difficult to find jobs, a major imped-iment to marrying (Siegel, 1995). Nonetheless, the flurry generated by this report and others like it demonstrated how highly valued the state of marriage remained.

And remains. By 1991, the situation reversed, and the number of eligible American men outnumbered single women (Faludi, 1991), a result of the smaller cohort following the baby boom. This left the men at the end of the baby boom to compete for mates from a smaller pool of women roughly 2 years younger than themselves. At the beginning of a new century, this trend is the one featured in the headlines. "The Man Glut," cried one newspaper (McLaren, 2000)—"Two Boys for Every Girl. Remember when they said a single woman was as likely to be attacked by terrorists as find a hus-band? Well, now the demographic tables have turned." The article contin-ues, "Some observers say this turnabout has profound social implications. It may make men stubbornly marriage-minded and competitive, while young women, by contrast, are free to take their own sweet time starting families" (p. R1). In a dozen years or so the tables will have turned again. And the focus will probably still be on the odds of marrying rather than exploring single life. However, recent media treatment of being single has had a more positive spin in both Canada (*Maclean's Magazine*, May 8, 2000, p. 37: "I Am Single—More Canadians than ever before are choosing to live alone—and lik-ing it.") and the United States (*Time,* August 28, 2000, p. 37: "Flying Solo—More women are deciding that marriage is not inevitable, that they can lead a fulfilling life as a single.").

A vacuum in knowledge surrounds the area of single life and the role of single persons in families. This is especially true of older single individuals. As well, little is known about variations among single individuals, especially the ways in which race, ethnicity, and class shape single life (Barrett, 1999). Possibly, some of the trepidation about never marrying is a fear of the un-known. Examining the experiences of older persons informs us about their present circumstances and how they have negotiated their family lives as sin-gle persons, providing us with a glimpse into the future for younger persons who do not marry. In this section, we will examine trends in singlehood, the transition and pathways to being permanently single, the objective situation of single persons (e.g., the nature of their social networks), and the subjective experience of being single.

Trends in Singlehood

Among those aged 65 and over, the percentage who are single has remained fairly stable since 1981, at about 5% (see Chapter 2). However, although rates of singlehood among the elderly have remained fairly constant, because the proportion of the population that is old has increased significantly, so too have the absolute numbers of single elders. The substantially higher proportion of single persons aged 35 to 44 (17% of men, 10% of women) and 25 to 34 (38% of men, 26% of women) in 1995 suggests that the likelihood of remaining single will increase among younger cohorts. This is particularly true for Black Americans, among whom the proportion who remain single is higher than among White and Hispanic Americans for all age groups. Indeed, among those aged 45 to 54 years, the proportion of Blacks who are single is 16% for men and 13% for women. This difference between Black and White Americans is likely to continue as rates of singlehood are rising more quickly among Blacks than Whites (Waite, 1995). The higher probability of being single among African Americans may result in less stigma attached to being single and less of a difference between those who do and do not get married (Barrett, 1999).

The trends that underlie increased rates of singlehood among younger age groups reflect the interplay of social change and demographic shifts. In all age groups, educated women are a readily identifiable group with elevated rates of singlehood (Barrett, 1999; Doudna and McBride, 1981). The greater economic independence of women and a decline in the stigma associated with being single, in general, and being a single parent, in particular, are likely to sustain increased rates of singlehood, especially among women (Duncan, 1986; Siegel, 1995).

Whereas older single women are more educated than their married counterparts, single men tend to be less well off financially than married men. Does this represent a selection effect, or is there something about marriage that enhances income among men? Research on marital status transitions shows that men with higher earnings are more likely to marry and, once married, are more likely to stay that way (Nakosteen and Zimmer, 1997). The increasing challenge of finding secure, well-paying jobs among the younger baby boomers and the subsequent cohort, sometimes referred to as "Generation X," may account for some of the increase in remaining single.

Some argue that when demographic shifts lead to a sex ratio favoring women, as was the case for those born at the end of the baby boom, the probability of major social change, such as the women's movement, escalates (Doudna and McBride, 1981). As unmarried, educated women sought to find a place for themselves outside the traditional family unit, attempts to change socially structured barriers to their progress occurred, in areas such as the labor force. In turn, a sex ratio of more marriageable-age men than women tends to encourage conservatism as men engage in more traditional courting rituals (e.g., an evening out dining rather than drinking), as their focus on getting married is heightened (McLaren, 2000:R6).

Other factors associated with staying single among men include an unhappy childhood and lower occupational prestige (Duncan, 1986). Among older women, commitments to family, particularly parents (O'Brien, 1991), and the pursuit of higher education and a career were key reasons for staying single. Reflections on the motherhood of well-educated, single (mostly never-married) mothers with an average age of 41 years are suggestive about additional reasons for singlehood (Siegel, 1995). On balance, single mothers have a less positive view of men than do married mothers. They often hold a very idealistic view of marriage, but their experience of disappointing ties with their father or their parents' poor marriage has led them to believe that the ideal is unattainable. As well, single mothers express a stronger preference to be in control and a desire to avoid compromises assumed to be inevitable in marriage. On balance, the primary difference between single and married mothers concerns their views of relationships with men rather than of motherhood.

The Transition to Singlehood

Being single may be voluntary or involuntary and may be a temporary or stable (permanent) state (Stein, 1981). Combining these two dimensions creates four categories of single persons. Singlehood that is voluntary and temporary includes those who are postponing marriage but are not opposed to the idea of marriage. Voluntarily stable singles are those who choose to be single and oppose the idea of marriage. Also included in this group are those whose religious commitments include celibacy. Those who view being single as involuntary but temporary have actively sought a partner but have yet to find one. Involuntarily stable single persons wanted to marry but have not found a mate and have accepted being single as their probable life state. Older singles are likely to be stable singles, but when does this change in identity occur?

To date, little is known about the transition from temporary to stable singlehood because, typically, staying single is not treated as a life transition (Davies, 2000). This is in part because, unlike childlessness (especially for women), there is not a clear line of demarcation between a time when changing one's status is possible and a time when it is not. Unlike marrying, divorcing, or being widowed, there is neither a ceremony nor another party involved. However, in our culture, most adults expect to marry, and when this does not happen, a transition from defining oneself as someone who will marry to someone who is permanently single occurs. When they are about 30, an age by which many have married, women who are still single start to consider their status in relation to their expectation to marry (Gordon, 1994). For some women, in part because of the association of singlehood with childlessness, the initial redefinition of oneself as single may be experienced as a crisis, but eventually, most women appear to experience this transition positively (Peterson, 1982). Some suggest that men do not go through an equivalent transition and, instead, experience singlehood fairly uniformly over the life course (Waehler, 1996). In her qualitative study of middle-class, childless, single persons aged 40 to 57, Davies (2000) reports that most of the men and women do experience a transition to singlehood, holding the view that they do not anticipate getting married but remain open to the possibility of an intimate relationship. At this point in their lives, "they are comfortable with their singlehood, aware of its advantages, and focused on enjoying those advantages" (Davies, 2000:10).

What signals the transition to singlehood? A birthday is often a key event, although the particular age that marks singlehood varies considerably (Davies, 2000). Middle-aged women also view buying a house as a marker of considering oneself permanently single:

> I always thought you got married, you bought a house. Well, I bought a house and I'm not married. . . . I've laid down roots. . . . You're sort of saying, "Okay, this is it." And it makes you feel more settled. (Davies, 2000:12)

The dissolution of a serious relationship or engagement, instigated either by the respondent or his or her former partner, also precedes defining oneself as single.

Circumstances of a given time and family may lead some individuals to drift into, rather than choose, singlehood. For example, obligations to their family of orientation (parents and siblings) took precedence over personal aspirations related to education, work, and marriage among single women of advanced age and various class backgrounds (Allen and Pickett, 1987; O'Brien, 1991). In the words of one woman,

> My parents were my whole life. . . . [My mother] was quite bad [ill] when I was in high school, and that probably contributed some to the fact that I didn't go on. . . . They were basically years when I was just sort of stuck with my mother, and I didn't have too many young friends. (Allen and Pickett, 1987: 523)

Hitting marriageable age in the 1920s and 1930s, a time when the heavy emphasis placed on the familial obligations of women was reinforced by the Depression for some, fundamentally shaped the prospects of marriage for women of this cohort. For some, it was delayed; for others it was postponed forever. Such circumstances are key to understanding why "[n]one of the women claimed to have made a conscious decision not to marry. Nor did marriage appear to have been an important goal in any of their lives" (O'Brien, 1991:309). Thus, although singlehood was not chosen, it was not actively resisted either, a reflection of the strongly entrenched familistic ideology of the time (Allen, 1989; Allen and Pickett, 1987). Like all women of their day, these single women were honoring their family responsibilities. Consequently, they paralleled their married counterparts as involved family members; they simply engaged in an alternative family career (Allen, 1989; Allen and Pickett, 1987).

When singlehood is the outcome of such circumstances, should it be viewed as voluntary or involuntary? Middle-aged respondents often view their singlehood as a result of a lifetime of choices and decisions, even when there was never a deliberate choice to be single (Davies, 2000). Similarly, older women who assigned priority to caring for their parents did not necessarily choose to stay single. The dichotomy between voluntary and involuntary singlehood is limiting in assuming that only those who choose to stay single act with agency in their lives. No doubt, some single individuals may have been captives of circumstances, but for others, singlehood is an indirect consequence of other choices. Thus, the dimension of voluntary versus involuntary singlehood is probably best conceived of as two continua rather than a dichotomy, reflecting varying degrees of both circumstance and choice in staying single.

The Objective Situation
of Older Single Persons

Among today's older population, being single typically means being childless. Thus, childlessness can be considered one objective consequence of remaining single, given the very strong proscription against having children outside of marriage. Although older single women in one study did not express regret about being single, some were sorry not to have had children (O'Brien, 1991). This association between being single and being childless is weakening, however. Birth rates have risen dramatically among younger, never-married American women so that, by 1990, about 1 in 4 single women aged 18 to 44 years had at least one child (Siegel, 1995). These figures vary greatly by race; half of the Black American women in this age group are mothers, compared with 15% of White American women. However, the birth rates are rising most dramatically among single, college-educated women and women in professions or management (Siegel, 1995). Thus, the family structure of single persons, especially women, is undergoing a striking transformation. This change will in turn affect the kinds of ties that single persons negotiate with other family members. As we examine the social networks of today's older single persons, consider how this change is likely to affect intergenerational relationships as well as the future family and friendship ties of single persons.

For single women, not marrying means working. This puts older single women of today in a unique situation when compared with their married peers. In their day, getting married meant leaving the workforce. Thus, work was both a cause and outcome of singlehood; for some, the desire to have a career meant not marrying; for others, not marrying meant finding work (O'Brien, 1991). Labor force participation has paid off in old age when single women enjoy far more stable and secure financial circumstances than do widowed, divorced, and separated women because of their longer and continuous work careers (McDonald, 1997). Historically, older single women have had both more education and higher incomes than single men (Buunk and van Driel, 1989). But these differences between single men and women have diminished over time (Davies, 1995; Seccombe and Ishii-Kuntz, 1994).

The single are often assumed to be, by definition, isolated and have been typed by some as lifelong isolates (Gubrium, 1975), in part because their overall contact with others is lower than is true for the married and widowed. One must consider different forms of social involvement to better appreciate the impact of being single on social networks. Older single persons do appear to be less socially involved than both their married and previously married peers, as indicated by overall levels of informal interaction (Barrett, 1999). Furthermore, contact with relatives, friends, and neighbors declines with age among single persons but increases among the ever married (Barrett, 1999). Similarly, among singles ranging in age from 35 to 64 years, single persons spend less time with their relatives than their married peers (Seccombe and Ishii-Kuntz, 1994). As well, older (Barrett, 1999) and middle-aged (Marks, 1996) singles are less likely to report having a confidant than are ever-married seniors.

However, there are important differences in social involvement within the single population. Regarding gender, single women maintain relatively large social networks of siblings and their families, friends, and neighbors; see family and friends more often; and receive far more familial support than do single men (Barrett, 1999; Longino and Lipman, 1981; Mugford and Kendig, 1986). Among middle-aged singles, a similar pattern emerges, with single women in far greater contact with relatives from whom they receive more emotional support than do single men (Seccombe and Ishii-Kuntz, 1994). Race also makes a difference, with non-Whites interacting less often than Whites with relatives, friends, and neighbors (Barrett, 1999). Last, among older single persons, higher education levels enhance levels of interaction and socioemotional support (Barrett, 1999).

Of course, most older single persons have neither a spouse nor children. What about their ties with other family members? Older single women continue very strong attachments with surviving family members and describe their childhood relationships with parents and brothers and sisters very positively (O'Brien, 1991). The single tend to maintain especially close ties with siblings, nieces, and nephews when compared with either married people with children or childless, widowed individuals (Rubinstein, Alexander, Goodman, and Luborsky, 1991). A lifetime of less competition from other relationships (no spouse) permits single individuals to maintain sibling relationships more effectively than those who marry. When questioned about feeling lonely, older single persons are most likely to mention that they would like more contact with siblings, parents, and friends (Gubrium, 1975).

Among older single persons, friends generally take on greater significance than they do in the lives of the married, widowed, and divorced. Greater investment in friends is evident in forming more friendships (Keith, 1986; Longino and Lipman, 1981) and in maintaining greater contact with them (Seccombe and Ishii-Kuntz, 1994; Stull and Scarisbrick-Hauser, 1989). Not only is the amount of contact with friends greater among single persons, so too is the propensity to consider friends as confidants and part of one's inner circle (Rubinstein, 1987; Strain and Chappell, 1982). Given that friendship is a crucial source of intimacy among younger single persons as well (Stein, 1981), the place of friends in the social network of older single persons represents continuity in their lives. However, older single women generally favor basing their friendships on "voluntary mutuality" rather than dependency and thus do not tend to view friends as potential caregivers in old age (Rubinstein et al., 1991). Nonetheless, friendships often take the place of family and provide enduring, trusting, and supportive ties in later life. However, there are important gender differences here, with older single men more likely to receive help from friends, whereas older single women are more likely to be helped by family members, including children (Barrett and Lynch, 1999). Both older single men and women are more likely than married persons to rely on paid help for assistance with daily activities, a difference that may reflect a long-term pattern among the single of relying on such help as a way of maintaining independence (Connidis and McMullin, 1994).

Older singles have a higher rate of coresidency than the divorced and widowed, with over one third living with someone else (Stull and Scarisbrick-Hauser, 1989). This is largely because living with someone who is unrelated or with siblings, cousins, aunts, or uncles is more common among the single. For many single elders who live alone, solitary living is a transition that occurred in midlife to later life, following the death of a parent, sibling, or other person with whom they lived (Rubinstein, 1987; Rubinstein et al., 1991). A 68-year-old woman in one of my studies did not worry about her future until her mother died 6 years prior to retirement:

> I lived with my mother till . . . [s]he died when she was 91. It was lovely living together. When she was with me, I didn't think much about retirement because I was thinking about her. But after she died, I started thinking about it. I was anxious about where I would live and if I'd have enough money.

Thus, it cannot be assumed that living alone in older age is a familiar and well-established tradition for all single persons.

In sum, older single persons experience greater continuity in their lives than is true of other unmarried groups. Single persons are less likely to experience a change in residence in older age, having typically made such a transition in midlife. Instead, a sizeable portion of single persons reach old age with an established pattern of living, either alone or with others. As well, most single persons are not isolates and maintain quite active ties with relatives and, particularly, friends. On balance, they are likely to be at less risk than their previously married peers of being institutionalized in old age (Stull and Scarisbrick-Hauser, 1989).

The Subjective Experience of Being Single

One would think that choosing to be single would create a happier state than involuntary singlehood, but as yet, there is no research on the subject. Perhaps, by the time one has been single for 60 years or more, the reason for being single matters little. However, those who see singlehood as desirable are less lonely in old age (Dykstra, 1995), indicating the significance of one's view of being single on subjective feelings. Some single seniors, especially men, may consider marrying in the later years when the obligations and obstacles of earlier times no longer preclude marriage (Rubinstein, 1987). Such a change in attitude among older men is matched by potential opportunity given the imbalanced sex ratio favoring women in old age.

Some assert that an advantage of being single in old age is that one avoids the desolation of a spouse's death (Gubrium, 1975). This view minimizes the attachment single persons have to their closest friends or relatives and the impact on their lives of losing these individuals. A qualitative study concludes that, for older single men, "loss, with disruptive consequences, does occur in late life or loss occurs earlier in life and some of its effects may linger" (Rubinstein, 1987:111). Although the necessity to forge "uncharted territory" may make single persons more adaptable than their ever-married peers (Stein, 1981), the depth of their attachments and the extent of their loss when significant persons in their lives die or move away are substantial. Rather than assume that single persons are somehow impervious to desolation because they have no spouse to lose, one might ask instead if not having a spouse or children detracts from their lives. Studies on the well-being of older singles help address this query.

Although the single are more satisfied that any other group with their material situation in later life (Stull and Scarisbrick-Hauser, 1989), overall, the never married are less satisfied than their married peers (Barrett, 1999). However, single women are more satisfied than are single men. Yet single women report more hassles in their networks than do single men, possibly reflecting the greater likelihood that, as single women, there are high expectations about the help they will offer other family members, especially parents and siblings (Barrett, 1999). As well, among single women, psychological well-being is related to age; older single women are better off than younger single women and than older single men (Davies, 1995). There are racial differences as well, with single White persons more satisfied than single non-White persons, even though non-Whites report fewer hassles from network members by virtue of being single (Barrett, 1999). Parallel observations apply to middle-aged persons; single women in their early 50s do not differ from married women in distress levels, but single men experience greater distress than their married peers (Marks, 1996). On the other hand, single men and women do not fare as well as their married counterparts in terms of self-acceptance, environmental mastery, positive relations with others, a sense of purpose in life, and personal autonomy and growth. These differences at middle age may reflect cohort differences. Alternatively, they may mark a transitional phase to permanent singlehood and later become the more positive views reported by older single persons, particularly women.

Like most situations, being single is seen to have advantages and disadvantages. Among women ranging in age from 35 to 69, being alone, being in control, being free to engage in chosen activities and pursuits, and freedom are assets of being single (Gordon, 1994). Costs of singlehood include the need to ensure social contact, loneliness, the expense of single living, feeling peripheral in a couple-oriented society, and the stigma of being single. The combination of viewing being alone as an advantage and loneliness as a disadvantage of being single suggests that being single creates the risk of emotional but not social isolation (see Weiss, 1973), an interpretation supported by the active social ties with family and friends noted earlier.

When reflecting on their lives, older single women (aged 80 and over) express no regret about having met familial obligations to parents and siblings or about remaining single, but some regret not having children (Allen, 1989; O'Brien, 1991). When asked directly whether they felt any regret about never marrying, a small majority of single men and women said they did (Rubinstein, 1987). At the same time, only a minority believed that life after 65 is more difficult for those who never marry (Rubinstein, 1987). The greater loneliness of single than married persons (Dykstra, 1995; Rubinstein, 1987) underscores one of the losses of never marrying. In turn, however, the greater loneliness of formerly married compared to single persons (Dykstra, 1995; Rubinstein, 1987) illustrates the adaptation to single life made by most single individuals by the time they reach older age. As well, loneliness is offset by friendship support (Dykstra, 1995), a reward for the greater involvement of single persons in friendship ties. The relative adaptability of single individuals may be due in part to the stability created through a lifetime of work. When compared with older widows, single retirees "felt better about themselves . . . , friendlier toward others . . . , and more in control of their own lives" (Norris, 1980:142).

Dating and Cohabiting in Later Life

Being single does not necessarily mean the absence of intimate ties. Unfortunately, however, little is known about dating and cohabiting among older single persons, partly due to our tendency to make traditional assumptions about intimacy in older age; one is either married or celibate. As well, when these topics are explored, the activities of the previously married tend to receive more attention than those of the ever single. Thus, dating and cohabitation tend not to be viewed as the ongoing arrangements of single persons but rather as the follow-up to marital dissolution. This orientation also limits examinations of same-sex relationships that cannot be legally sanctioned. Because most studies on dating and cohabiting concern younger people, their findings are generally irrelevant to the experience of older persons. This means that we need more information about the extent to which these phenomena occur, more attempts at understanding why they occur, and more research on their unique features in later life.

Gender has a huge impact on the likelihood of either dating or cohabiting. Men are far more likely to report both activities, and the key reason for the difference is the relative availability of suitable partners. The combination of women's longer lives and men's involvement with younger women leaves fewer opportunities for heterosexual coupling among older women. In the case of dating, almost a third of previously married unattached men aged 55 and over report having dated someone at least once in the past month, compared with only 7% of women (Bulcroft, R. A., and Bulcroft K. A., 1991). For both men and women, the likelihood of dating declines with age, from highs of 44% for men and 18% for women aged 55 to 59 to lows of 13% for men and 2% for women aged 75 and over. Among women and men who do date once a month or more, almost half describe themselves as being involved in steady dating. Yet only a small percentage of dating older persons think it likely that they will marry (16% of men and 5% of women) or live with an intimate partner (15% of men and 5% of women).

These findings support qualitative research that suggests different reasons for dating among older persons (Bulcroft and O'Conner, 1986). Whereas younger persons tend to date as part of a mate selection process, older persons date in the hope "of establishing a long-lasting, gratifying, and intimate personal relationship that will serve as a sexual outlet and a hedge against loneliness" (Bulcroft, K. A., and Bulcroft, R. A., 1991:248). Companionship and sexual activity typify steady dating relationships in older age, distinguishing them from friendships and supplanting the search for traditional marriage (Bulcroft and O'Conner, 1986). The timeless experience of meeting and falling in love are evident in the comments of a 75-year-old man:

> We met five years ago at a singles' dance. I saw her across the room. I thought she was the most perfect creature, extremely lovely to look at. I could tell that she found me attractive as well. When our eyes met, we both knew it was destiny. (Neugebauer-Visano, 1995:22)

The ongoing significance of sexual attraction also shines through in a 72-year-old woman's observations: "My love and I are very attracted to each other. Oh definitely, he is very handsome and distinguished looking. He does it to me" (Neugebauer-Visano, 1995:22).

A study of heterosexual cohabitation in the United States (Chevan, 1996) shows a steady increase in the number of cohabiting older couples. In 1990, Among Americans aged 60 or more, there were 407,000 persons living with someone of the opposite sex. Although this represents only 2.4% of that age group, the rise since 1960 is dramatic, particularly in light of the proscription against cohabitation among older persons. In 1990, 11% of those aged 40 to 59 were living with someone, indicating that the number of cohabiting older persons will continue to go up. Again, men are more likely (6% of those 60 and over) than women (1%) to cohabit. Cohabitation is also more likely among the very poor, the young-old, those who have divorced or separated (a number that we know is also growing), and residents of the Sunbelt states, where a seniors subculture free of outside (family) influence is more likely to have emerged than anywhere else in the United States (Chevan,1996).

Although a relatively small percentage of older persons either date regularly or cohabit, these numbers are likely to change along with changing views of sexuality, increases in the numbers remaining single and divorcing, and the greater propensity to cohabit among younger cohorts. When compared with younger persons, older men and women are much less likely to date to find someone to live with or marry. Similarly, marriage is less likely to follow cohabitation in older age (Chevan, 1996). These differences suggest the *greater* significance of both dating and cohabitation in old age as sources of intimacy in their own right, rather than as stepping stones to another form of relationship or another stage of life, such as childbearing.

Summary

In sum, older single people, particularly women, appear to negotiate involved familial and friendship ties and successful work careers over the course of their lives, offsetting the lost potential advantages of marrying. They define single life as "normal" and derive satisfaction from sources other than family life. But they also remain active family members, extending their responsibilities for and attachments to their family of origin into adulthood. As well, they actively negotiate ties to friends over the life course, with some friends serving family-like roles in their lives. Nonetheless, although most single persons do not feel lonely, they are more likely to do so than are their married counterparts. They also receive less emotional, social, and instrumental support from family than do the married, primarily because they do not have a spouse or children, in most cases.

On balance, research to date indicates the need for a reconceptualization of single life that does not implicitly accept marriage as the exclusive intimate relationship of adult life. It is also important to emphasize the place of single persons in family networks and the crucial support that they provide to various family members. We need to know more about the romantic attachments of single persons in older age, an area that we are more likely to explore as acceptance of sexuality in later life grows.

6

Transitions in Marital Status

Widowhood, Divorce, and Remarriage

Today's older persons are far more likely to experience widowhood than divorce. As well, although many are widowed once older, some lose a spouse earlier in life. Thus, widowhood in old age is a transition for some and a status already acquired earlier in life for others. Because divorce usually occurs at younger ages, the experience of divorce in later life most often concerns the long-term consequences of an event that took place some time before. Reflecting the greater numbers to whom it applies, this chapter begins by considering widowhood. We then explore the experience of being divorced in later life. Some older persons follow widowhood or divorce with remarriage, the final topic of this chapter.

Widowhood

Widowhood is a different way of life. My husband was frail for several years and needed a lot of attention and care. I had to give up so many things that I was doing before and lost so much contact with so many of my friends. After his death it was difficult for me to pick up the pieces. . . . I was 80 when my husband died. . . . I had a friend who lost her husband when she was young and she had a tiny boy. I remember so well her saying to me, "After my husband died I made up my mind that I was not going to sit around and mope all the time because if I did, I would lose all my friends." You know, I never forgot that. That's what I thought when my husband died. I wasn't going to sit around and mope all the time. It wasn't going to do him any good and it certainly wasn't going to do me any good.

—*Widow, aged 92*

As was the case for this widow, caregiving often precedes widowhood in later life for both men and women (Wells and Kendig, 1997). Although the percentage of widowed men and women has decreased, women remain much more likely than men to be widowed (see Chapter 2). Consequently, widowhood is often considered a women's issue, and "the knowledge we have of 'widowhood' and 'widowed elderly persons' is gendered. What we know of widowhood in later life is of *women's* experiences of widowhood in later life" (Martin-Matthews, 1999: 41). When possible, we will examine the gendered nature of widowhood evident in the unique experiences of men *and* women who have made this transition. The overview presented here begins with the initial stage, bereavement, which lasts for roughly 2 to 4 years (Martin Matthews, 1991). Then, we examine the longer-term objective and subjective outcomes of widowhood.

Bereavement

In the initial stages of widowhood, individuals undergo a period of grieving and mourning characterized, initially, by profound psychological disorganization (Martin Matthews, 1991). The popularity of a timetable of "stages of grief" masks the fact that grieving is variable, both in terms of how long it lasts and how severely it is experienced. Grief and mourning can be viewed as a process that includes shock, intense pain, grief work, and, once ready to rebuild one's life as a widow(er), reality testing (Heinemann and Evans, 1990). Several dimensions of grief have been identified (Lopata, 1996). At first, emotions dominate and include a sense of shock, loss, regret, guilt, loneliness, anxiety, and sometimes, anger at the lost spouse. These strong sentiments can coexist with quite positive feelings of joy, happiness, and relief. Managing the emotional pain of loss follows, and involves feeling numb, willful self-control to stifle strong emotions, faith, distracting oneself through activity or passivity, and sharing feelings with others. A third phase of grief includes the dead spouse as he or she is incorporated into the surviving partner's life through images of heaven, hallucinations, memories, rituals, and conversation. Daily functioning may then change as the widow or widower is less committed to work and social encounters and, possibly, suffers declines in health. Eventually, relationships with other persons are altered, becoming either more close or distant. With varying degrees of success, the bereaved makes the initial adjustment to life without a partner.

The comments of an 84-year-old widow in one of my studies exemplify several dimensions of grief as she moved on with her life:

> My husband was suffering so much that I eventually got the idea that it wasn't fair to want him to go on doing that. Nevertheless, for about a year, I was absolutely numb. Everywhere I turned, I ran into things that I missed. However, I have a strong nature. I made up my mind that I couldn't do that, that it wasn't fair to my daughter and it wasn't fair to myself. The last words that my husband said to me were, "Now don't sit down and brood. Make all you can out of the rest of your life." And I have done so. There isn't a day in my life that I don't think about him. But it has developed now into just happy thoughts of the times that we had.

Widowhood is a more dramatic transition than caregiving, but the caring experience has implications for the transition to widowhood (Wells and Kendig, 1997). On one hand, those who cared for their spouse are less depressed once widowed than are those who were not caregivers. On the other hand, widowed persons who were caregivers have more sleeping problems, use tranquilizers more often, and report higher levels of strain than those who were not. An ongoing consequence of caregiving prior to widowhood is a heightened view of life as meaningless. Thus, even the "quasi-widowhood" experienced by those whose spouse is institutionalized (Ross, Rosenthal, and Dawson, 1997) does not necessarily leave older persons better prepared for widowhood.

These findings reflect the mixed results concerning whether adjusting to sudden death or death following a long illness is more difficult. Other things being equal, anticipating widowhood through the illness of a spouse tends to make adapting to losing one's partner easier (Martin Matthews, 1991). That said, a partner's death, either suddenly or after a prolonged illness, presents a tough challenge, and adjusting to widowhood depends on several circumstances, including age and class (Lopata, 1996). Generally, losing a spouse in later life—an age when it is expected —softens the loss, regardless of whether the loss is sudden (Arbuckle and de Vries, 1995; Lopata, 1996). However, this advantage is offset in extreme old age, when adjusting to a partner's death is made more difficult by having a smaller support network and poorer health (Martin Matthews, 1991). Class also helps define the widowhood experience. Widowhood is more clearly and positively defined in working-class than in middle-class and upper-class cultures, thus easing the process of bereavement for working-class women (Walker, MacBride, and Vachon, 1977). The family-based social network typical of the working class is also helpful in the initial stages of bereavement.

Lesbian and gay individuals tend to face somewhat different circumstances on the death of a long-term partner. Although the bereavement process itself is similar (Shernoff, 1998), the extent of social support may not be. Because homosexual unions are generally not recognized as marriage, sympathetic allowances in the work place and among acquaintances are likely to be fewer. Family members, particularly those of the deceased partner, may not be supportive, sometimes to the point of intervening in funeral and subsequent arrangements or discounting the relationship entirely (Fullmer, 1995; Peplau et al., 1996). Estrangement from other potential sources of support, such as religious institutions, may heighten the sense of loss that follows a partner's passing (Fullmer, 1995). Death due to AIDS adds additional stresses to losing a partner because of the stigma associated with the illness, the fact that death often occurs at younger ages, and, in some cases, survivor guilt (Peplau et al., 1996; Shernoff, 1998). As well, the loss of an intimate partner often occurs in the context of multiple losses due to AIDS within a closely knit community (Mullan, 1998).

Discussions of adjustment to widowhood suggest a process of recovery akin to that following illness. Yet the focus of many widows on surviving and prevailing as they take charge of their lives and become more independent suggests that adapting to widowhood represents a transformation rather than a recovery (Martin-Matthews, 1999). An 83-year-old woman, widowed for 14 years, observes, "I became more independent, a lot more my own person. You have to, to be on your own without your husband's help. . . . It makes you a stronger person" (Martin Matthews, 1991:28). For some widows and widowers, the passage of time heightens rather than diminishes grief (Lopata, 1996) and leads to personal changes judged to be negative (Martin Matthews, 1991). However, both widows and widowers feel more competent than do long-term married individuals, prompting the suggestion that "the experience of surviving one of life's most stressful events and maintaining independence . . . following the loss has enhanced these widows and widowers' knowledge of their own capabilities and increased their sense of self-confidence" (Arbuckle and de Vries, 1995:644). As well, in more extreme cases, widowhood brings relief from a painful marriage, an outcome that should be less likely in the future, as younger couples turn to divorce more readily than did today's older persons (Martin-Matthews, 1999). What are the longer-term consequences of widowhood?

The Impact of Widowhood on Objective Conditions

The reliance of women on their husband's earnings is reflected in the relative impoverishment of the current cohort of older women following widowhood (Heinemann and Evans, 1990; Martin-Matthews, 1999), an experience that men do not share if their wives dies. Employment and marriage, the two key sources of income among women, are both in extremely short supply (Lopata, 1996). Therefore, the financial hardship of widowhood is intractable without the support of family and the state. Indeed, a government pension is the key source of income for 70% of *retired* Canadian widows, compared with only 18% for whom a pension is the primary income source (McDonald, 1997). Retired widows who fall below the low-income cut-off are older, have less education and lower occupational prestige, are less likely to have planned for retirement, and are more likely to have retired to care for a family member than are retired widows who are above the low-income cut-off (McDonald, 1997). Similarly, in the United States, unmarried women rely more heavily on Social Security as an income source than either unmarried men or married couples (National Economic Council, 1998). Thus, to date, employment does not guarantee economic security among retired widows, largely because the meshing of work histories and family careers has resulted in intermittent employment in jobs with no or paltry pension benefits.

One outcome of widowhood for some is residential mobility. Although widows and widowers remain in their residence for an average of 15 years, the probability of moving peaks during the first year of widowhood (Chevan, 1995). Good health and higher incomes decrease the probability of moving once widowed. Among widows, home ownership is associated with having a larger number of close friends in the neighborhood, largely due to greater length of residency (Bess, 1999). In the longer run, being widowed alters living arrangements by increasing the chances of being placed in a nursing home or similar long-term care institution (Lopata, 1996; Wolinsky and Johnson, 1992).

Just as socially constructed gender relations limit the financial security of widows, they have a parallel effect on the social networks of widowers (Blieszner, 1993). On balance, women generally and widows in particular have a more extensive network of support from family and friends than do their male peers (Antonucci, 1990; Barrett and Lynch, 1999; Bengtson, Rosenthal, and Burton, 1990; Wister and Strain, 1986). Widowed men are less likely than married men and than women of all marital statuses to feel needed and appreciated and to have someone to accompany them when engaging in activities outside the home (Connidis and McMullin, 1994). Thus, unless they remarry, widowers tend to have social networks that are less diverse and involved than is true of widows (Barrett and Lynch, 1999).

The loss of a wife's homemaking and interpersonal skills requires a major adjustment of most widowed men. Although the traditional skills of a wife tend to be socially undervalued, they are fundamental to daily life (Thompson and Walker, 1989). Thus, acquiring the ability to prepare meals and keep dishes, clothes, and home clean—or finding someone else to do these tasks— is essential following a wife's death. However, older widowed men more readily acquire skills such as cooking than older widows acquire such traditionally male tasks as driving a car or house and yard upkeep (Kendig,1986; O'Bryant, 1991).

Children, especially daughters, are the central individuals in the family network of widowed men and women, and contact with them is higher among the widowed than the married (Barrett and Lynch, 1999; Martin Matthews, 1991; see Chapters 7 and 8). This relationship represents considerable familial stability for widowed parents, particularly in the initial stages of bereavement when contact with children is very helpful. The fact that widowed men and women are more likely than their married counterparts to confide in at least one child (Connidis and Davies, 1992) suggests that both the quality and the extent of interaction with children increase following widowhood. However, if support comes only from children, the benefits of filial support are diminished (Martin Matthews, 1999).

Widowhood also may elicit more involved ties with siblings, especially between widows and their sisters (Martin Matthews, 1991; see Chapters 12 and 13). Among those who note a change in their relationships with siblings following widowhood, most observe greater emotional closeness, improved ties, and more frequent and supportive contact (Connidis, 1992). When compared with the married, widowed men and women are more likely to receive help from siblings (Barrett and Lynch, 1999). The benefits of sibling contact are evident among rural widows for whom sibling contact staves off loneliness (Dugan and Kivett, 1994). Among childless widows, siblings compose a larger portion of the confidant network than is true of childless wives (Connidis and Davies, 1990). However, although siblings are important socioemotional ties for many widows, they tend not to provide instrumental help (Connidis, 1994b).

In American society, family tends to take precedence over friends, particularly among the working class (Lopata, 1996). Yet although some couple-based friendships may fade, friends emerge as important network members in widowhood (Lopata, 1996; Martin Matthews, 1991). Both widowers and widows are more likely than the married to consider a friend both a confidant and a companion, and friends occupy a larger portion of these networks among widowed persons (Connidis and Davies, 1990; 1992). However, widows tend to have more friends, many of whom became friends following widowhood, and are more likely to confide in them (Connidis and Davies, 1992; Martin Matthews, 1991). The reduction of loneliness and worry among widowed women and the generally positive effect of having friends and neighbors (Lee, Willetts, and Seccombe, 1998) underlines the benefits derived from maintaining and establishing personal relationships and the shortcomings of relying solely on family. The relative scarcity of fellow widowers leaves men more isolated than women and may partially explain their higher remarriage rates.

The greater reliance of working-class persons on a homogeneous network focused on relatives puts the working-class widow at greater risk of isolation if her children do not live nearby (Walker et al., 1977). A family-based network can also be counterproductive when the widow is ready to establish a new way of life with new activities and people. The more dispersed networks and higher education of middle-class widows put them at a relative advantage for making this transition (Lopata, 1996). Yet widowhood is more disruptive among the more highly educated women of the middle and upper classes because their relationships with their husbands were typically more interdependent.

In sum, the gendered experience of widowhood mirrors the gendered relations of our society. Women experience greater economic hardship and men greater isolation on the loss of a spouse. The impact of losing a spouse on objective conditions extends to the ability to live life independently as a widow. For example, the older widows who are best able to self-sufficiently perform "male" and "female" tasks, are those who spent the most years in the labor force (O'Bryant, 1991). Changing social structural arrangements in the areas of family and work are likely to make the experience of widowhood in later life easier in the future. However, the fact that women tend to work in jobs that do not include pension benefits and their greater tendency to work part time and intermittently make this an optimistic scenario (McDonald, 1997). As well, the cumulative negative effects of earlier divorce and prior widowhood on the financial security of married and widowed persons does not bode well for upcoming cohorts of women, given that women spend more years than men unmarried and "out from under the protective economic umbrella of marriage" (Holden and Kuo, 1996:389). The greater involvement of today's younger fathers in the lives of their children may have long-term benefits for their social networks in old age. Again, this has been a very gradual shift, and the extent of its impact remains to be seen.

The Subjective Impact of Widowhood

For men and women, widowhood creates a sense of loneliness because other family members cannot provide the unique companionship of a spouse. The following comments of a 65-year-old widow from one of my studies illustrate the intimacy of the spousal relationship.

> When Ted used to go on the night runs he used to come in at 2, 3, 4, o'clock in the morning. . . . Until he came home I knew that there was something missing in the house and he used to feel the same with me. . . . He used to play the most devilish tricks on me. . . . I used to come home and it wouldn't be any later than 11:30 but, you see, he would be on the early morning run. . . . I would come in the back door. I would have hung my night clothes in the bathroom and I would close the door very quietly and creep into the bathroom and close the door. . . . I would get dressed, changed, and wash my face and . . . creep along the passage. I can even see myself drop down on my hands and knees to go past him, as he would be laying on the edge of the bed, and go all the way around. . . . Now I would put my feet in the bed and he would have some damn thing down in the bottom—maybe one of the kid's toys or something cold, or he had fixed the bed so I can't push my feet down. . . . He has waited until I have got in and I would think to myself, "Oh, I haven't disturbed him" and he would turn around and say, "WELL!" I would go up in the air. . . . Those are the things that make us sit back and think, the things to look on you see.

As our earlier discussion of marital status and its effects showed, widowed persons have lower levels of psychological well-being than the married (Arbuckle and de Vries, 1995; see Chapter 3). One of the longer-lasting consequences of widowhood is elevated levels of loneliness (Dugan and Kivett, 1994), which can take many forms. Widows, for example, may miss their particular partner or be generally lonely for someone with whom to live, do things, or share intimacies (Lopata, 1996). All forms of loneliness may be offset by meeting someone new, but for women, the opportunity for solving loneliness through new male companions is limited.

On balance, men appear to experience greater psychological suffering than women when their spouses die (Lopata, 1996; Martin Matthews, 1991). Both men and women tend to underestimate their chances of being left alone as a result of widowhood (Holden and Kuo, 1996), but women are more inclined to expect widowhood and to imagine how they would handle it, a process referred to as anticipatory socialization, which aids adjustment (Martin Matthews, 1991). Men typically spend a shorter time than women in the widowed state, and psychological well-being does improve with time (Lee et al., 1998). Yet even when length of widowhood is considered, widowed men remain significantly more depressed than widowed women. But this may be because the much higher rates of remarriage among men are selective, leaving a pool of widowers who are particularly depressed (Lee et al., 1998).

Gender differences in objective conditions (see the preceding section) are directly related to variations in life satisfaction (Stevens, 1995). When compared with widows, widowers enjoy less financial stress, more education, fewer somatic symptoms, and more frequently have new intimate relationships, all factors that enhance life satisfaction. In contrast, widows have more financial stress, less education, more somatic symptoms, and tend not to have new partners, all of which depress life satisfaction. Their one relative advantage is more regular contact with friends. Yet when all of these factors are taken into account, widows are still more satisfied than widowers (Stevens, 1995). Women's virtuosity in nurturing a range of relationships (see Dykstra, 1990) clearly has benefits when meeting the challenges of widowhood. The importance of the gendered context of widowhood is also brought home by the fact that widows who live in retirement communities are more satisfied with life when the ratio of married to widowed persons is low (Hong and Duff, 1994). This may help explain the higher satisfaction of widows than widowers. In the broader community of older persons, widows' interactions with other women are mostly with widowed women; widowers' encounters with other men keep them in the social world of the married.

In sum, the lower psychological well-being of the widowed is not solely a direct consequence of widowhood per se. Instead, the association of widowhood with poorer health, poorer socioeconomic circumstances, and reduced social activity probably contributes to the poorer subjective state of widowed individuals. This link between negative objective states and the subjective feelings of the widowed means that there is the potential for social policy to intervene in an area typically considered a personal problem, that is, low morale. Dealing with some of the detrimental effects of widowhood through social policy can thus improve both objective and subjective conditions (see Chapter 14). More generally, many of the observations made here reflect socially constructed gender relations regarding work and family. Social change in these relations are fundamental to ameliorating the problems faced by both widows and widowers.

Divorce

Divorce is a radical departure in a person's life. It leads us to wonder why we marry in the first place, why marriages go wrong, and what it takes in these times to make a marriage endure. Divorce raises issues such as monogamy, morality, feminism, sexuality, misogyny, loyalty and betrayal, love, self-respect, and self-delusion. It asks us question the way we see ourselves as children, siblings, and parents and the way others perceive us—be it as failures, pariahs, threats, comrades, or role models.

—*Kaganoff and Spano (1995:xiii-xiv)*

As the figures in Chapter 2 showed, a relatively small proportion of today's older persons—about 6%—is divorced. Although divorce rates have gone up for all age groups over time, they have gone up more dramatically for younger than for older age groups (Uhlenberg, Cooney, and Boyd, 1990). The risk of divorce is greatest in the first few years of marriage, and younger persons account for the majority of all divorces (Hiedemann, Suhomlinova, and O'Rand, 1998). However, those who divorce in middle age are less likely than those who divorce at younger ages to remarry, resulting in growing numbers of individuals who will reach old age unattached due to divorce (Wu and Penning, 1997).

Substantially more older persons have been divorced at some point in their lives than are currently divorced. In 1990, 1 in 5 Canadian women aged 50 to 59 years had divorced at least once (Gee, 1995). In the United States, estimates are that about 1 out of 8 women aged 40 in 1983 can expect to have their *first* marriage end in divorce by the time they reach old age (Uhlenberg et al., 1990). Black women are more likely than women of other races to experience divorce in midlife (Hiedemann et al., 1998).

Currently, 44% of *all* American marriages and 1 in 3 Canadian marriages are predicted to end in divorce (Ambert, 1998). However, this general figure masks important cohort differences in the likelihood of divorcing, and there is a hint of a trend downward among those married in the 1980s and 1990s (Cherlin, 1992). Most notably, in relation to the general upward trend, the parents of the baby boom have unusually low *lifetime* divorce rates (about 25%), whereas their children are expected to have unusually high rates (Cherlin, 1992). Nonetheless, there is an increase in the numbers of persons who are entering and will enter old age with a marital history that includes one or more divorces (Counts, 1992). Thus, the long-term consequences of long-ago events and relationships are central to the study of being divorced in later life.

Dissolution of Same-Sex Relationships

Although technically one cannot speak of divorce among same-sex couples, one can speak of relationship dissolution. There are fewer barriers to dissolving a relationship among same-sex couples; there are generally neither legal nor religious supports for marriage nor impediments to breaking up and, socially, families are less likely to support a same-sex than an opposite-sex union (Kurdek, 1998). Despite this, the likelihood of breaking up over an 18-month period among longer-term couples (10 years or more) is very similar for straight, gay, and lesbian couples (Peplau et al., 1996). In shorter-term relationships (under 2 years), dissolution rates are lower for married couples but similar for cohabiting couples, regardless of sexual orientation. Unfortunately, the long-term effects of dissolving same-sex partnerships have received scant attention. One might expect, however, some parallels to the impact of divorce. In this chapter, we focus on the subjective and objective consequences of divorce and relationship dissolution for older persons. In Chapter 11, we consider the impact on intergenerational relations of both a parent's and an adult child's divorce.

The Transition From Marriage to Divorce:
The Subjective Impact

Including the separated in discussions of divorce, especially concerning older persons, is essential to accurately assessing the extent of marital breakup and the process of adjustment that follows. Although separated persons may not divorce, all divorced persons were once separated, and separation marks the beginning of the emotional and physical break with a partner. As well, among older individuals there may be fewer incentives to actually divorce (e.g., no other marriage prospects), even when the separation is considered a permanent rather than a temporary arrangement.

The first year of separation is marked by feelings of ambivalence that combine a sense of longing with a feeling of relief, regardless of which spouse triggered the separation (Cherlin, 1992). However, for the person who did not initiate the separation, the unexpectedness and the short time for anticipating the separation make the initial adjustment more difficult (Kitson, Babri, Roach, and Placidi, 1989). For most separated persons, the heightened anxiety, periodic depression, and personal disorganization typical of this period are followed by several years of reorganization during which a new identity and life style are negotiated (Cherlin, 1992).

Most older divorced men and women went through this transition earlier in their lives. For older women, the transition to divorce often meant making another key transition from being a homemaker to being a paid worker. On balance, women appear to experience greater psychological distress than men following divorce and feel more lonely, angry, sleepless, guilty, and anxious (Sev'er, 1992). Some of this variation may simply reflect gendered responses in how and when distress manifests itself. Men tend to react later and, sometimes, more severely in the form of higher rates of suicide, accidents, and psychiatric care.

Although both men and women aged 50 and over tend to see their lives after divorce as either the same as or better than life during the year before separation, women are more likely than men to note improvement in their social life and overall happiness and in being a parent (Hammond and Muller, 1992). Two to three years after a divorce, men are more likely than women to have friendly feelings toward and to feel preoccupied by their ex-spouse and to have lower well-being (Masheter, 1991). Race also has an impact, with Blacks adjusting better and feeling less stigmatized by divorce than Whites 4 years after separation (Kitson et al., 1989). Divorce has a cumulative effect so that those who have divorced two or more times have higher depression scores than those who have divorced once (Kurdek, 1991).

Generally, both the reasons for separation (desire for independence, differences in interests and in attitudes about sex, partner problems, including affairs) and its consequences (feelings of loneliness, anger, guilt, and confusion coupled with relief, happiness, and independence) are similar for same-sex and opposite-sex partners (Peplau et al., 1996). The following words of a 62-year-old woman about her lesbian partner could as readily have been spoken by a woman about her husband:

> When D said she wanted out of the relationship, to be with a younger woman, I was really devastated. I knew that things hadn't been going all that well for a while, but I really thought that after 22 years we would stay together forever. . . . I can't imagine who would want me now or where the hell I would ever meet anyone in this place. (Auger, 1995:110-111)

However, there are two key differences between the dissolution of same-sex versus straight relationships. First, same-sex couples experience the complexity of being gay or lesbian in a heterosexist society as a reason for breaking up (Peplau et al., 1996), a factor that is irrelevant to heterosexual couples. Second, gay and lesbian couples may be more likely than straight couples to renegotiate their relationships with expartners as friendships, possibly in part because they share a smaller and more closely knit community. An older gay respondent observed, "My sister has gone through three husbands and I have gone through three lovers. The difference is that I have remained good friends with all of my ex-lovers" (Berger, 1996:155).

The Objective Situation of Older Divorced Persons

One longstanding consequence of divorce is a decline in financial resources (Holden and Kuo, 1996). Although both men and women feel a sense of relative deprivation (Keith, 1985), the financial impact of divorce is far greater for women (Sev'er, 1992). Two key factors account for this difference: the greater likelihood that men are in the labor force and in better-paying jobs at the time of divorce and the higher probability that women have custody of children following divorce. These differences were particularly true for today's older women when they divorced. For men, divorcing later rather than earlier in life has greater economic consequences because they can no longer make significant financial gains in the work world to compensate for the expenses of dissolving a marriage (Keith, 1985). For both men and women, the financial setback of divorce carries over into the preretirement years, even following remarriage (Holden and Kuo, 1996). This helps account for the fact that divorced women in their 50s are more likely to work and to expect to retire later than their widowed and married peers (Morgan, 1992).

Reduced financial circumstances following divorce, particularly among women, heighten the challenge of living alone by restricting the potential for supporting a healthy, independent life style. Not surprisingly, recently divorced women are less likely than widowed women to live alone, and they have the lowest home ownership rates of all women (Uhlenberg et al., 1990). Clearly,

> Even though divorces that occur in later life are still relatively uncommon, there should be serious concern for the socioeconomic well-being of divorced women who will arrive at old age in the future, after having lived many years in the divorced state. (Uhlenberg et al., 1990: S10).

This concern extends to men as well, who also enjoy the protective effects of marriage and bear financial costs of marital separation (Holden and Kuo, 1996). Nonetheless, persistent poverty is most likely among female-headed households and particularly among Black female-headed households (Cherlin, 1992). The life course experience of poverty leaves divorced Black women in an especially weak economic position in old age.

In the period immediately following separation, both younger (under 50) and older (50 and over) men and, more so, women rely on multiple sources of emotional support, particularly parents, siblings, friends, and children (Hammond and Muller, 1992). Among parents divorced after at least 19 years of marriage, mothers rank their children as their most supportive tie during the early stages of divorce, whereas fathers rank their friends and parents above their children (Wright and Maxwell, 1991). Ongoing, supportive ties with former in-laws following divorce are unusual despite widespread normative support for them (Finch and Mason, 1990). Generally, older persons rely less than younger men and women on others for emotional support following separation.

Divorce erodes the support network, especially ties with married friends, more than widowhood, in part because the role of kin and friends is ambiguous, and the normative expectations for self and others are less clear and uniform (Brubaker, 1990; Martin Matthews, 1991). Nonetheless, the likelihood of receiving help from friends is greater among the divorced than the married (Barrett and Lynch, 1999). Although the social networks of divorced older women remain sizable, they are also homogeneous and are characterized by a tendency to rely on one close friend to satisfy most needs for emotional support (Gibson and Mugford, 1986). Older divorced men have the smallest social networks of all (Mugford and Kendig, 1986), reflecting a customary lack of involvement with their young children following a divorce earlier in life. Traditionally, research has focused on the effect of divorce on the lives of women and children. Yet although women are improving their economic independence, some argue that "in old age, as family relationships based on marriage and parenthood grow in importance, it is males who are at risk" (Goldscheider, 1990:531). Currently, divorced men receive considerably less support from their grown-up children than do divorced women (Barrett and Lynch, 1999). This relative social isolation of divorced men could be lowered if men became more directly involved in family ties, particularly with children. For both men and women, it will be some time before the gradual move toward a more common experience in the labor force (McDonald, 1997) and at home has dramatic effects on support networks among older divorced persons.

In sum, the stress of divorce manifests itself in different ways for men and women. The greater initial personal trauma experienced by women motivates them to make greater changes in their lives, which, in the longer run, appear to leave them better adapted and more content in later life. However, one dilemma of comparing long-term divorced men and women rests on the fact that remarriage rates are higher among men. Thus, there is a greater selection effect among men than women, potentially distorting the results of comparisons between men and women beyond the initial stages of separation.

Remarriage

Discussing rates of remarriage, like those of divorce, must be done with caution because the data are so often misinterpreted. A better understanding of family ties and aging is aided by knowing how many older persons are remarried following divorce or widowhood rather than married for the first time. This requires data that focus on the likelihood of remarriage among those who have been married before, not rates of remarriage as a proportion of all marriages. As well, knowing the probability that one will remarry should divorce or widowhood occur in later life is pertinent to understanding intimate ties in later life. Increases in cohabitation, especially at younger ages, require that we consider this arrangement as well as remarriage to capture the extent of longer-term intimate commitments in older age.

Since the 1970s, remarriage rates following divorce and widowhood have declined (Cherlin, 1992; Goldscheider, 1990; Lee et al., 1998; Uhlenberg et al., 1990). However, this decline is offset considerably by an increase in the likelihood of cohabiting following divorce, an arrangement that is often but not necessarily followed by marriage (Cherlin, 1992). Among couples with one previously married partner, remarried couples are more likely than cohabiting couples to be White and to have higher incomes (Wineberg and McCarthy, 1998). Rates of remarriage are markedly higher for men than women. Following widowhood, men are about 5 times more likely than women to remarry (Lee et al., 1998), partly because more unattached women than men result from women living longer and marrying older men.

Generally, remarriage is more common following divorce than widowhood, largely because divorce usually occurs at a younger age than widowhood. For example, among divorced Canadians born between 1920 and 1930, about two fifths of the women and three quarters of the men had remarried by the time they were 55 to 65 years old. Among their widowed counterparts, just over one quarter of the women and two fifths of the men had remarried (Burch, 1990). In the United States, the likelihood of women remarrying following divorce tends to be higher than in Canada—about two thirds of American women do so—whereas the proportion of all men who remarry is parallel at about three fourths (Cherlin, 1992). However, Black Americans are substantially less likely to remarry (about one third of Black women and one half of Black men remarry within 10 years of divorce; Cherlin, 1992). Overall, fewer than 1 in 10 Canadian men (8.5%) and women (8.4%) had ever remarried by the age of 65 (Burch, 1990).

For both men and women, increasing age decreases the likelihood of remarrying following either divorce or widowhood (Uhlenberg et al.,1990; Wu, 1995), making rates of remarriage in old age comparatively low. There are a number of reasons for this, including objective limitations (scarcity of older men, poorer health, reduced mobility, poorer finances), the absence of incentives common to younger ages (being pregnant, wanting children, proving adulthood, conformity to life cycle timing), a short future (making it harder to justify the necessary changes brought about by marriage on the basis of long-term advantages), and the social pressure to protect one's estate (Talbott,

1998; Treas and VanHilst, 1976). Among divorced women but not divorced men, socioeconomic status affects the chances of remarriage. High socioeconomic status discourages remarriage among women aged 25 at the time of divorce but increases the probability of marrying among those divorced at age 45 (Sweeney, 1997). This suggests that women who remain divorced as they enter old age are particularly prone to face financial difficulty.

Although the pool of potential mates is larger for older men, pool size alone does not account for remaining on one's own; there are men and women who simply choose not to remarry (Burch, 1990). Among men and women in advanced old age who had formed new relationships, women did not want to marry, whereas widowed men typically did (Wilson, 1995). One's past experience with marriage influences attitudes about remarrying. Among widows aged 61 to 85, those whose previous marriages had been particularly good or bad were least interested in remarrying, whereas those whose marriages were generally positive but with flaws were most open to considering remarriage (Talbott, 1998). Many older widows, most of whom had very traditional marriages, were reluctant to give up their independence, to return to taking care of a man, and to risk losing another partner (Heinemann and Evans, 1990). For example, a 66-year-old widow in one of my studies says she would not remarry because

> I am enjoying my freedom too much now. I brought up my children, and I looked after my husband to the best of my ability. I cared for my parents until they died, and it was a joy and I liked it, but I am enjoying the freedom now of not having to account to anybody for what I do.

An 81-year-old widow is even more direct:

> I wouldn't get married again for all the tea in China. . . . Oh no. . . . I am set in my ways, and I wouldn't want a young fellow running around all the time, and I wouldn't want an old man with one foot in the grave either. Then stop and think that you would have to wash for them, you would have to iron, you would have to have meals to suit them. Now, if I feel like eating, I eat, and if I feel like going out, I go out.

There are also those who do miss the companionship of a man and assume that any woman who claims that she is not interested in remarrying must be lying

(Talbott, 1998). This is, however, still the minority view among today's older women.

Among those who do remarry, marriage occurs far more quickly after widowhood in later life than at earlier ages (Lopata, 1996). Although discussions of family network change in older age often focus on losses, remarriage is a potential basis for enhancing one's kin network. Over time, remarriage can form the foundation for close family ties (see Chapter 11), as in the case of a 71-year-old man in my community study:

> I hear a lot of people around my age being lonely. Well, I don't know what it is to be lonely really. I have two sons and their families and my daughter. I have eight grandchildren. . . . We also have five great-grandchildren. I was married twice. I was married very young and then that marriage broke up, and my present wife and I have been married 31 years. Mary is the present wife's daughter and the other two are my first wife's sons. We see the boys frequently, and I am very happy that they are fond of my present wife, so we get along very well. . . . We are a very close family.

Once married, older remarried couples tend to enjoy positive support from their children, who are happy because their parent is happy (McKain, 1972; Vinick, 1978). This is fortunate, because marital success is enhanced by positive feedback from family and friends, and its absence can create considerable apprehension about the marriage's prospects for success. One outcome of remarriage is that more time is spent at home and less with friends and children. Hence, remarriage in later life has the potential for enhancing relations with children, who may now feel less burden, responsibility, or guilt, knowing that their parent is cared for by a spouse. On the other hand, the assumed threat to an inheritance or the fear that a mother will have to look after another partner may motivate some children to object to a mother's remarriage, a potent deterrent to making this decision (Lopata, 1996).

Generally, higher divorce rates for remarriages than marriages are due to elevated rates in the first few years of marriage, after which the rates for the two groups are parallel (Cherlin, 1992). The reasons one chooses to remarry can have a bearing on marital success. Older individuals most often remarry for companionship, a motive that includes the desire "to be useful to someone and to feel that another person's happiness was dependent on yours" (McKain, 1972:65). The next most frequent basis for remarrying among women is deep emotional attachment to and admiration for the personal qualities of the husband, whereas among men, it is the desire to be cared for (Vinick, 1978). Marital success is also more likely among those whose first marriage was successful, who have adjusted well to changes associated with aging, who are better off financially, and who begin their marriage in a new home rather than one previously shared with a former spouse (McKain, 1972). One reason for the greater stability of later-life remarriages is the long time that most remarried older persons have known their new spouse.

In sum, a relatively small percentage of today's older individuals either marry in later life or enter old age remarried. However, among those who are widowed or divorced, particularly at younger ages, a majority of men and a substantial minority of women eventually remarry, and most of them are happy with their marriages. There is still much that is unknown about remarriage in later life and its impact on other family relationships. The increase in divorce has changed the dynamic of remarriage because now more remarriages follow divorce rather than widowhood. In Chapter 11, the impact of divorce and remarriage of either older parents or their adult children on relationships between parents and their children and between grandparents and grandchildren is explored.

Summary and Conclusion to Part II

Intimate relationships are important across the life course. The need and desire for intimacy, including sexual relations, continue into old age, but venues and methods for its expression may change. A more inclusive view of intimate relationships encourages us to consider the intimate ties of older people outside as well as within marriage. Long-term couples, whether married or cohabiting, whether gay or straight, tend to derive considerable satisfaction from their relationships. Interdependence between partners is heightened in later years as a consequence of being together more of the time, sharing household tasks (primarily along traditional lines in the case of married couples), and the declining health of one or both partners. Such symbiosis permits older couples to live independently.

Providing care to an ill spouse for a long time can lead to isolation of both partners. This may leave a newly widowed person poorly prepared for dealing with life alone. Nonetheless, most older persons make the transition to widowhood successfully. Although widowhood is more common among women, it has repercussions for both men and women. Men are less likely to experience some of the objective losses, such as income, that are a consequence of widow-hood for many women. However, subjective losses seem to be greater for men, in large part because of their more exclusive reliance on a spouse for intimacy and sharing confidences. Women tend to turn to other family ties following widowhood, whereas men are more inclined to turn to another mate.

Although a relatively small proportion of older individuals have ever divorced, the numbers are increasing. The stigma associated with divorce can make initial adjustment problematic, especially among today's older persons, given the stronger commitment to marriage of this age cohort. However, women in particular tend to discover advantages to being alone, including increased self-worth and newly gained independence. As in the case of wid-owhood, following divorce, women more typically seek and receive support from family and friends, whereas men find support through remarriage. Di-vorced older men appear to be more isolated than other men and than women of all marital status groups.

Remarriage among today's older persons is generally successful. Several factors contribute to this success, including the support of other family mem-bers, especially children. Remarriage rates among all age groups have experi-enced a decline over the past two decades, in substantial measure because cohabitation has become more common. The ongoing advantage in life expec-tancy for women helps ensure that rates of remarriage and cohabitation will continue to be lower among older women than men.

Recent research indicates the continuing significance of sexual intimacy in old age. We need to learn more about the intimate ties of those who are un-attached—the single, divorced, and widowed—especially given that sexual relations are no longer seen as the exclusive domain of marriage. Contrary to common conceptions, older single persons, particularly women, are not iso-lated. Although their social networks are smaller, this is due to having fewer kin. Single individuals tend to cultivate lifelong friendships that complement their smaller family networks. They also develop closer attachments to some of their own kin, especially siblings and their families (see Chapter 9 on child-less older persons and Chapters 12 and 13 on siblings). Nonetheless, the single rely more on formal support services than the married and the widowed with children. As is true of the widowed and divorced, single women are more sat-isfied than single men. The consistency of these differences indicates the propensity of men to depend on a spouse whereas women develop broader familial networks. These proclivities by gender are also evident in intergen-erational ties, the subject of the next five chapters.

PART III

Intergenerational Relations

7

Exploring Intergenerational Relations

The two most central intergenerational relationships for most older persons are those with their adult children and with their grandchildren, as reflected in Photo 7.1. For both ties, amount of contact and of support exchange are major issues. However, the qualitative dimensions of these relationships are also central to appreciating the bonds of older persons with their children and grandchildren. Much has been written about adult children caring for their older parents. To better reflect the reality of parent-child ties during most if not all of a parent's old age, the discussion of caregiving is balanced with other facets of the parent-child relationship, including the extensive support that older parents give to their adult children (Chapter 8). As well, I take a comparative approach to exploring the significance of children in older age by considering the situation of childless older persons (Chapter 9). Last, the ties between grandparents and grandchildren are not independent of those between older parents and their adult children. The mediating role of the middle generation is therefore critical to grandparent-grandchild ties (Chapter 10). Two issues of growing significance to these relationships—changing gender relations and higher divorce rates—are considered throughout this section (see Chapter 11 for divorce). Related policy concerns are addressed later, in the book's final chapter.

Increased longevity means that we will spend more of our lifetime in many family relationships, including intergenerational ties between parents and children and between grandparents and grandchildren. Declining birth rates, however, have led to the "verticalization" of family structure. This means that the number of family members in each generation except the

Photo 7.1. Intergenerational ties between parents and children and between grandparents and grandchildren last longer due to greater life expectancy.

oldest (due to longevity) has decreased, whereas the number of generations has increased (Martin-Matthews, 2000a; McPherson, 1998). For a time, families of four and more generations were expected to become common, but this possibility has been offset by older ages at first marriage and at birth of the first child among younger cohorts. This creates an age-gapped structure wherein the number of years between generations increases. The fact that more individuals will share more of their adult lives with parents, children, and grandchildren requires a dynamic view of these ties. Parent-child and grandparent-grandchild ties must be negotiated and renegotiated to meet transitions and changing circumstances across the life course.

Some argue that the greater diversity and expansion of families through divorce, cohabitation, and remarriage are the basis for a new family structure, which they term a *latent kin matrix* (Riley and Riley, 1996). This matrix is defined as "a latent web of continually shifting linkages that provides the potential for activating and intensifying close kin relationships as they are needed" (Riley and Riley, 1996: 287). Reminiscent of the modified extended family model (see Chapter 1), the latent matrix places much greater emphasis on the voluntary relationships between former in-laws and stepfamily members. The authors speculate that this new family type will make the parent-child tie less focal by providing "a wide choice of kinship bonds" that will "transcend" age-based conflicts (Riley and Riley, 1996:290). Implicit in this argument are two important assertions: that the adult child-parent relationship is losing its significance in the overall network of family ties, and that the net effect of divorce, cohabitation, and remarriage is the enhancement of kin networks. Let us consider these points in light of current evidence about the relationships between generations and about the impact of life transitions, including divorce and remarriage, on these relationships.

Perspectives on Intergenerational Relations

Two approaches have dominated the study of intergenerational relations, especially those between parents and children. One focuses on solidarity and the other on problems (Luescher and Pillemer, 1998; Marshall, Cook, and Marshall, 1993). More recently, the concept of ambivalence has been applied to intergenerational ties as a way of establishing the coexistence of solidarity and conflict in these relationships (Connidis and McMullin, 2000; Luescher and Pillemer, 1998). These perspectives are briefly reviewed as a backdrop to our discussion of parent-child and grandparent-grandchild relations.

The intergenerational-solidarity perspective focuses on the extent of solidarity or strength of intergenerational bonds between parents and children (Bengtson and Schrader, 1982). Solidarity has six analytic dimensions: (a) associational (type and frequency of interaction and activities), (b) structural (factors such as geographic distance that influence the extent of interaction), (c) functional (exchange of assistance and support, especially instrumental help), (d) affectional (sentiments and feelings), (e) consensual (agreement between generations on opinions and values), and (f) normative (the extent to which family members share expectations of family life; Silverstein and Bengtson, 1997). Originally, all dimensions of solidarity were posited to contribute to overall intergenerational solidarity, but empirical tests of this perspective raised doubt about whether these various forms of solidarity are actually part of one analytic construct (Atkinson, Rivett, & Campbell, 1986).

The concept of solidarity and studies using this concept have encouraged theoretical thinking and have indicated the multidimensional nature of intergenerational relations. However, an ongoing concern about the solidarity perspective is its tendency to minimize family diversity and to treat problematic or conflictual features of intergenerational relationships as simply the absence of solidarity (Connidis and McMullin, 2000; Marshall et al.,1993). One consequence is that conclusions drawn from analyses applying this approach are somewhat proscriptive, with either implicit or explicit recommendations on how families can better reach the ideal of solidarity.

More recent applications of the solidarity perspective have tried to incorporate notions of paradox and conflict in family ties. Indeed, one of the ultimate paradoxes of intergenerational relations is the fact that solidarity and conflict coexist (Bengtson et al., 1996; Silverstein and Bengtson, 1997). Explorations of conflict have been primarily at the level of interpersonal relations—asking parents and children about their differences, disagreements, and disappointments with each other (Clarke, Preston, Raksin, and Bengtson, 1999). This attempt to incorporate conflict within the normative assumptions of solidarity places limits on examining conflict itself as a root to understanding intergenerational relationships (see Connidis and McMullin, 2000). Most likely to be ignored is the conflict that is embedded in social structure, such as the organization of family and work based on gender.

Another approach to intergenerational relations emphasizes problems and conflicts in families and is evident in much of the caregiving literature and in terms such as "caregiver burden." This approach focuses on the problems created for children and, sometimes, parents by caring for older parents (Marshall et al., 1993). Although some have termed this a conflict perspective (Luescher and Pillemer, 1998), in fact, most of this work does not deal directly with conflict beyond the level of interpersonal relations. In Chapter 8, conceptual approaches that focus on caregiving are presented. Earlier formulations would fall within the problems perspective because, like the solidarity approach, the examination of how structural conditions create conflict in families is not central, and particular relationships (e.g., spouses, parent-child, siblings) are assumed to have consistent features across families. Other formulations of caregiving take a more dynamic approach in their emphasis on the negotiation of relationships.

Recently, the concept of ambivalence was explored as a way to address the coexistence of solidarity and conflict, rather than emphasizing one or the other as the overriding feature of intergenerational relationships (Luescher and Pillemer, 1998). Intergenerational ambivalence refers to contradictions in parent-child ties, and these contradictions apply at both the psychological (primarily subjective) and sociological (institutional resources and requirements) levels. Because intergenerational ties are ambivalent, they must be negotiated in an ongoing process of family relations. Therefore, the study of intergenerational relations must address how social structural forces and individual interests create the contradictions and conflicts that family members must work out in their encounters with one another (Connidis and McMullin, 2000). This approach to understanding family relations is particularly compatible with feminist, critical, and symbolic interactionist theory.

In sum, intergenerational relationships are not static or uniform. Instead, they evolve as family members respond to both constancy and change over the life course, interacting in a social world of conflicting or contradictory interests and structural arrangements. Emphasizing the ambivalent nature of family ties encourages us to consider both sides of the solidarity-conflict coin. As well, we must consider how the dramatic shifts in family structure brought about by divorce, cohabitation, and remarriage affect the bond between parents and their children and between grandparents and grandchildren.

Intergenerational Ties of Older Gay and Lesbian Persons

Before we turn to parent-child relations, a word about the intergenerational ties of older gay and lesbian individuals. First, referring to "gay families" is no more appropriate than referring to "straight families," given that identity as gay or straight is an individual, not a familial characteristic (see Stacey, 1998). Rather, one might speak more accurately of the families of gay or straight individuals. To date, there is little exploration of intergenerational ties involving gay or lesbian parents, partly because of a reluctance to acknowledge the families of gay and lesbian individuals and partly because the impediments to family formation have meant that relatively few gay and lesbian persons have children. It has been estimated that there are 1 to 5 million lesbian mothers and 1 to 3 million gay fathers in the United States (Patterson, 1996). In turn, 6 to 14 million children are estimated to have gay or lesbian parents.

The need for generativity has been proposed as one explanation for the frequent age disparity between men involved in gay relationships, a difference that is not observed among older lesbians who more commonly have children (Ehrenberg, 1997). However, there are several routes to parenthood for gay and lesbian individuals, paralleling those of heterosexuals (O'Brien and

Goldberg, 2000). Lesbian mothers and gay fathers may have children from former marriages, a possibility that is more likely among older gays and lesbians given their greater tendency to pass as straight by marrying. Older gay and lesbian parents who have not come out may fear being rejected by their adult children or grandchildren should they do so (Quam and Whitford, 1992). Most divorced and separated gay fathers, like their heterosexual counterparts, do not have custody of their children (O'Brien and Goldberg, 2000). Lesbian mothers are less likely than straight mothers to maintain child custody (Patterson, 1996), reflecting a tendency to stigmatize lesbian mothers (Causey and Duran-Aydintug, 1997).

Gay and lesbian couples differ from straight couples because there is never more than one partner who is biologically linked to their child (O'Brien and Goldberg, 2000). However, like some heterosexual couples, gay and lesbian persons may elect to become parents through stepparenting, adoption, or by means other than standard heterosexual reproduction. Thus far, the research that has delved into the ties of gay or lesbian parents with their children has focused, understandably, on policy issues (see Chapter 14) and on younger children. The consequence is a dearth of research about the ties of adult children to their gay fathers or lesbian mothers and about grandparent-grandchild ties involving gay or lesbian grandparents.

Older Parents
and Their Adult Children

I can sit and listen to my children talking and feel pride in them because I see the way that they have grown inside. I see the characters that they have developed and things like this. It makes me feel good inside. And I think to myself, I was a part of all that, you know. They have been instrumental in building up my character, too, because many many things happened to them, as they do to all families.

—*66-year-old mother of five*

Much of the research on the parent-child relationship focuses on its potential for support, examining the extent to which children and parents engage in supportive exchanges with one another. Although often framed as an exchange, the emphasis has been on children as help providers and parents as care recipi-

ents, with a corresponding interest in caregiver burden, the sandwich generation, and women in the middle. However, help flowing from parent to child is
an ongoing component of parent-child relationships in old age (Stone et al.,
1998), making the focus on support *exchange* essential.

More recently, the continuing interest in support has been complemented
by a concern with the impact of children, including the support that they provide, on the quality of their parents' lives. This research includes an assessment of the impact of simply having children, and of specific aspects of
parent-child relations, on the well-being of older parents. As well, the parent-
child relationship is examined by some as it evolves over time and in response
to life transitions. Given that most persons spend most of their old age relatively independent, the nature of parent-child ties outside the context of caregiving is examined first. This is followed in Chapter 8 by an exploration of
support exchanges between parents and children. Throughout, bear in mind
that, like all relationships, this one has at least two vantage points, that of the
older parent and that of the older child, which often differ from each other
(Aquilino, 1994). Thus, when considering research results, pay attention to
the source of information about parent-child ties. Is it a parent's or a child's
perspective?

Contact With Children

As we saw in Chapter 2, the majority of older persons (about 80% of those
aged 65 or more) are parents. Declining mortality rates over the past century
offset the negative impact of smaller family size on the odds of having children
survive to old age. For example, Uhlenberg (1996) estimated that in the year
2000, nearly 90% of mothers aged 80 had a surviving son, whereas close to
90% of mothers aged 90 had a surviving daughter. How does this general availability of children translate into accessibility and contact?

Most older parents have at least one child living close by, reflecting the
preference of parents and children not to live far from one another. Among parents who do not live with a child, about three quarters reside within a 35-
minute drive of their nearest child, and half have a second child within this
radius (Lin and Rogerson, 1995; see also Hoyert, 1991; Morrison, 1990). One
quarter have a child less than 1 mile away. Factors associated with greater
proximity to the nearest child are family size (the more children a parent *and*
a child has, the closer the nearest child lives), health of the parent (healthier

parents are more geographically distant), age of parent (parents over 80 live nearer by), age of child (increasing age increases geographic distance from parent[s]), parent(s)' socioeconomic status (SES; higher SES means greater geographic distance), and parent(s)' marital status (married parents live nearer to the most proximate child than do divorced or separated parents; the most proximate combination is widowed mothers and their daughters; Lin and Rogerson, 1995). Remarried parents are more geographically distant from their adult children than are parents who remain married to each other (Lawton, Silverstein, and Bengtson, 1994).

The fact that the very old (80 and over) live nearer to their children reflects the growing expectation with age that older parents will move closer to adult children if they need support (Silverstein and Angelleli, 1998). Such moves have been described as reunions, with similar ambivalent feelings of both wanting to be there and fearing what it will be like (Moss and Moss, 1992). Both parent and child must renegotiate their relationship, setting boundaries and attempting to create a good balance between autonomy and dependency so that they may enjoy their renewed proximity.

Most parents see their children on a regular basis, with as many as 80% of older parents reporting weekly contact with at least one of their children (Chappell, 1992). Generally, greater distance limits personal contact, but proximity has no impact on the quality of parent-child ties (Rossi and Rossi, 1990; Waite and Harrison, 1992). Distant children are more likely to be in contact with their parents through infrequent overnight visits, telephone conversations, and letter writing (DeWit, Wister, and Burch, 1988). Nonetheless, rates of telephone contact are higher between parents and children who live closer by and who see each other most often (Cicirelli, 1983; Frankel and DeWit, 1988). Thus, greater geographic distance does not increase the amount of phone contact but does make the telephone a more crucial form of contact.

Generally, the social networks of the working class are composed to a greater extent of family members, including children, siblings and their families, aunts, uncles, and cousins (Nett, 1993). Thus, working-class older parents see their children more often than do their middle-class peers, a tendency that is compounded by their greater geographic proximity (Greenwell and Bengtson, 1994). Having established the general availability of children in terms of both proximity and contact, we now explore the nature of the relationship between older parents and their children.

The Nature of Parent-Child Ties in Later Life

> You never cease being a parent, you know. Now my daughter is married, she has a home of her own and a husband to take care of her and a family to look after, but when she is out on the road in the winter time and the roads are icy, I worry about her just as much as I did when she was a child coming home, you see. . . . We have become friends. . . . But she is also my daughter.
>
> *—76-year-old widow*

What are parent-child ties like once parents are older and their children adults? Getting together in person is often arranged by older parents, who take the view that their failure to oversee such contact would mean seeing less of their children (Eisenhandler, 1992). Typically, this situation is seen as reasonable, given that their children have less time and flexibility in their daily lives. Older men often act as family head, whereas older women play the roles of kinkeeper and comforter (Rosenthal, 1985, 1987). The kinkeeper serves to keep family members in touch with each other; the comforter provides emotional support and advice. Thus, older parents serve a cohesive function in the family, drawing members of different generations together as part of an extended family network.

There are several common themes regarding the nature of parenting in older age, despite the diversity of family types at this stage of life. Among middle-aged parents of children 21 to 44 years of age, the two most common hopes and dreams for children are their happiness and educational success (Ryff, Lee, Essex, and Schmutte, 1994). These are followed by career success, having a happy family, personal fulfillment, and being a good and healthy person. These priorities on behalf of children are shared by mothers and fathers and indicate a parental focus on the successful launching and independence of their adult children.

The value placed on independence carries on into old age, when parents in their 70s value their children's maturity and have a corresponding concern for having their own independence respected by their children (Eisenhandler, 1992). Older parents tend to consider parenting a role that is behind them and are most likely to view their tie to children positively if they are in good health, active in their own interests, and independent. Although appreciating that they may continue to be important in their children's lives, on balance, being a parent is not considered central to one's identity in old age for mothers or fathers, as it was earlier in their lives. The more "hands-off" approach to parenting in later life is evident in the comments of one older mother:

> My responsibility is to be there should the children need me . . . you know, just to be in the background. To be sort of an anchor. That is all. Not to be *in* their lives, you know, just to be on the peripheral edges. (Goodman and Rubinstein, 1996:307)

These tendencies are magnified in very old age, when parents in their late 80s and beyond no longer try to exert influence over their children and continue to value as much independence as they can maintain (Johnson and Barer, 1997). Their older children, in turn, have fewer competing commitments, leading to more relaxed support from child to parent.

Affectional ties between parents and children drop when children are adolescents, peak when they are in their 20s, and then drop slightly before leveling off during their 30s to levels similar to those when children were 10 years old (Rossi and Rossi, 1990). From the vantage point of older parents, children are key confidants, dominating the confiding networks of mothers and fathers when children are geographically proximate (Connidis and Davies, 1990). Although more distant children still comprise a substantial portion of their parents' confiding networks, friends become the modal confidants among parents whose children live more than an hour away. Although the majority of parents consider at least one child to be a confidant, previously married parents are more likely than married parents to do so (Connidis and Davies, 1992). Confiding between parent and child is typically reciprocal, with both parties seeking and giving advice and reassurance (Wenger and Jerome, 1999). These findings suggest close bonds between parents and children in later life, reflecting the growing egalitarianism of this tie with time. On the other hand, children do not typically serve as companions to older parents when they are engaged in activities outside the home (Connidis and Davies, 1990, 1992).

Gender plays an important part in shaping the bonds between parents and children. Generally, adult children feel closer to their mothers than to their fathers. In one study, nearly 75% of children reported feeling "very close" to their mothers, whereas 60% felt this close to their fathers (Silverstein and Bengtson, 1997). In turn, assessments of perceived distance between generations find that, when compared with fathers, mothers perceive stronger ties to their children (Lynott and Roberts, 1997). On balance, mothers report closer ties to both sons and daughters than do fathers, daughters report closer ties to both fathers and mothers than do sons, and daughters and mothers are closer to one another than any other parent-child combination (Rossi and Rossi, 1990).

Although the greater closeness between mothers and daughters is clearly and consistently found in a range of studies, the substance of this closeness is less clear. The unique attachment between mothers and daughters may be an outcome of gendered familial relationships in which women are expected to be close to one another, an extension of the traditional view of mothers as martyrs and daughters as dutiful (O'Connor, 1990). Yet older mothers and adult daughters tend to enjoy an enduring tie built on communication, shared closeness, and minimal conflict (Blieszner, Usita, and Mancini, 1996). Mothers and daughters who are not close to one another tend never to have been so.

As parents, older persons have two abiding concerns: leaving a fair will and resolving problematic relationships, either between themselves and a child or between their children (Eisenhandler, 1992). Indeed, parents consider having children "get along" a hallmark of good parenting. If children fail to do so, parents sometimes believe it is because their children perceive treatment by parents to be inequitable (Eisenhandler, 1992; see also Bedford, 1992). Based on their own descriptions of parenthood in later life, older mothers and fathers have been described as "emeritus parents" engaged in paradoxically "closely distant" or "distantly close" relationships with their children (Eisenhandler, 1992). This view is reflected in the comments of a 67-year-old woman in one of my studies:

> You would think that children are enough fulfillment, but actually they are not, because they are little people on their own, and they are going to grow up and they are gone. And they have their own little circle, their own little world, and you are not really part of it. You love them and they love you, but that is another unit, you know.

Although these observations describe common experiences of being parents in later life, intergenerational ties vary across families. Adult children's assessments of affinity (emotional closeness and similarity of opinions), opportunity structure (geographic proximity and contact), and functional exchange (the giving or receipt of instrumental support) with their parents are the basis for formulating five types of relationships between parents and adult children

TABLE 7.1 Intergenerational Types and Their Features

Intergenerational Type	Level of Affinity (High, Low)	Level of Opportunity Structure (High, Low)	Level of Functional Exchange (High, Low)	Percentage of Mothers Fitting Type	Percentage of Fathers Fitting Type
Tight-knit	High	High	High	31	20
Sociable	High	High	Low	28	23
Obligatory	Low	High	High	16	16
Intimate but distant	High	Low	Low	19	14
Detached	Low	Low	Low	07	27

SOURCE: Adapted from Silverstein and Bengtson (1997).

(Silverstein and Bengtson, 1997). These intergenerational types and some of their features are shown in Table 7.1.

Tight-knit intergenerational ties are characterized by high levels of affinity (emotional closeness and shared views), opportunity for contact, and instrumental exchange. Sociable parent-child ties share high levels of emotional and physical closeness and contact but do not involve much instrumental exchange. The difference between these two family types could simply be differing needs for support, a factor that was not included in the Silverstein and Bengtson (1997) study. Obligatory relations involve high levels of opportunity and support exchange but are lower on affinity. Conversely, intimate but distant intergenerational ties are strong emotionally but low on physical contact and functional exchange. Last, detached relationships are cases where parents and children are not engaged on any dimension. As can be seen in Table 7.1, the most common intergenerational types, overall, are tight-knit and sociable. However, when types of ties are examined separately for mothers and fathers, there are two striking differences between them. Ties with mothers are more likely than those with fathers to be tight-knit (31% vs. 20%), whereas ties with fathers are more likely than those with mothers to be detached (17% vs. 7%).

These family types provide an example of the diversity of intergenerational relationships. However, they do not capture the meaning or experience of being either a parent or child in any of these situations. Is it any better or worse to be in one type than another? Some of the predictors of intergenerational types suggest that each may have advantages for particular circumstances or at particular times in the relationship between parent and child. For example, with increasing age, children are generally more likely to have relationships with their parents that are sociable or detached rather than tight-knit (Silverstein and Bengtson, 1997). Although we tend to think of tight-knit ties as preferable, moving from a tight-knit to sociable or detached tie may allow for greater independence and reduced responsibility for each generation. Indeed, from the older person's point of view, intense involvement with children often has undesirable catalysts, such as their own changed needs, crisis in the life of a child, or the eruption of unresolved conflict (Eisenhandler, 1992).

Qualitative research on the attachments between older mothers aged 64 to 83 and their only child yields three types of ties between mother and child (Goodman and Rubinstein, 1996). Attached and dependent mothers are sorry to have had only one child, and this regret makes it difficult to separate themselves from their child, either physically or emotionally. These mothers continue to focus on their child to the virtual neglect of other family members and interests. The second type, "she's okay, I'm okay" mothers, are independent and do not consider themselves entitled to their child's concern. But they give mixed messages about the quality of the current relationship with their child. Last, detached and depressed mothers focus largely on themselves rather than their child, tending to hold a very negative view of the mothering experience as "a ball and chain affair" (Goodman and Rubinstein, 1996). Like many samples in qualitative research, this study is biased as it only includes women who have one child but wanted to have more. Thus, their current view of being mothers in later life may reflect this disappointment rather than the type of relationships that the mothers of one child (and their child) can expect. Although having only one child may have been a matter of default for today's older women, younger women may choose this alternative. Nonetheless, the profiles of these three types of mother-child relationships reveal an advantage of qualitative data: an evocative and revealing picture of how these ties are experienced.

As is true of all relationships, conflicts occur between parents and their grown-up children. Yet we know relatively little of this parent-child dynamic outside the caregiving situation or the extremes of elder abuse. Recent work on intergenerational ties examines sources of conflict between parents and children from both vantage points (Clarke et al., 1999). Comments regarding "things on which you have differed, disagreed, or been disappointed about" from parents (average age of 62) and children (average age 39) yield considerable similarity in their views (Clarke et al., 1999:262). Two thirds of both parents and children observe differences, disagreements, or disappointments with each other. The sources of these differences are: communication and interaction (25% of parents, 34% of children), habits and lifestyle choices (38% of parents, 30% of children), child-rearing practices (14% of parents, 16% of children), work orientation (10% of parents, 4% of children), and politics and religion (9% of parents, 15% of children).

Although each of these issues could and sometimes does serve as a tension point in parent-child ties, it is not clear that disagreements and differences necessarily translate into open conflict. For example, the key concerns raised about communication are its absence, method, and level of honesty. Some comments suggest a longing for more contact rather than an acceptance of limited communication. For example, one mother does not feel included by her child: "They are so into their own family . . . that I feel very left out at times" (Clarke et al., 1999:265). As well, differences in view do not always refer directly to the parent-child tie, as in the case of children who comment on how their parents communicate with each other. Similarly, disagreements about habits and lifestyles often reflect an ongoing concern with a parent or child's welfare or acceptance, rather than with intergenerational conflict. For example, a father worries about his daughter's failure to save for a rainy day, a daughter wishes her mother would support her choice to cohabit and not have children, and a son notes that his parents "have the money to do whatever they want, but yet they deprive themselves of things they can well afford" (Clarke et al., 1999:266). Nonetheless, observing parent-child differences corrects an unduly rosy view of this intergenerational tie once parents are in old age.

As is true of all close ties, those between parents and children typically involve tensions and ambivalence that may lead to conflict or be successfully negotiated. This has consequences for ties between parents and children throughout life. Positive relationships characterized by emotional support (feeling cared for, loved, and listened to) mean less psychological distress for parents and children; more negative relationships (critical and demanding) heighten distress (Umberson, 1992b). Unfortunately, the negative side of the parent-child relationship has a more powerful effect than the positive on levels of distress for both parties. Clearly, understanding the reality of parent-child ties and their impact requires moving beyond the idealized emphasis on harmony to analyzing their power dynamics (Pyke, 1999). The shifting needs and situations of parents and children over the life course can have a dramatic impact on the relative power of parent and child. We consider this issue in the next chapter.

8

Support Exchanges Between Older Parents and Their Children

Life Transitions and Parent-Child Ties

How do ties between parents and their children evolve over time? Children leaving the parental home, changes in a child's or parent's marital and parental status, and the declining health of a parent are typical age-related experiences that occur in the midlife and later life of parents. The lengthening of parent-child ties means that both generations will experience numerous life transitions that are likely to have an impact on their relationship with one another. For example, from the child's perspective, getting married improves a daughter's relationship with her parents, whereas having children improves mother-son ties but diminishes the father-daughter tie (Kaufman and Uhlenberg, 1998). Two key transitions with major consequences for parent-child ties are the divorce of either generation (see Chapter 11) and shifts in support exchanges as parents age. We turn now to a theoretical foundation for examining support exchanges in later life.

Perspectives on Support Exchanges
Between Adult Children and Older Parents

Obligation, duty and responsibility . . . are commitments developed by real people not abstract principles associated with particular relationships.

—*Finch (1989:181)*

There are two types of support, usually distinguished as formal versus informal. *Formal support* refers to the help provided by agencies, services, professionals, and workers whose job it is to supply particular forms of assistance.
Informal support refers to various forms of help, ranging from emotional support to hands-on nursing care, that persons receive from people they know, primarily family, friends, and neighbors. The vast majority of support provided
to older persons comes from family members, particularly women.

Four models of social support have dominated discussions and examinations of the help provided to older persons by family members. The
hierarchical-compensatory model (Cantor, 1979) assumes that older persons
have a hierarchy of favored relationships from whom all forms of support are
sought. A spouse and children are at the top of the list, but if these are not available, substitutes can be found from lower on the list. These substitutes compensate for the preferred but unavailable ties. The assumption is that those
without a spouse or children or both are missing a fundamental source of all
kinds of help. The *task-specificity* model (Litwak, 1985) focuses on tasks
rather than particular relationships and posits that certain forms of aid are best
provided by ties with complementary features. Thus, for example, help that
requires proximity is best provided by a neighbor. This suggests the importance of diversity in social networks.

Two other models offer a more varied and dynamic conception of informal support networks. The *functional-specificity of relationships* model
(Simons, 1984) is more flexible in taking the view that a particular relationship, for example, that with a sister, can be negotiated in different ways. For
some, a sister may be a very important source of support, whereas for others
she is not. Thus, in a particular person's life, a relationship may serve one or
many functions, and particular functions are not tied to specific relationships.
Again, diversity is an important dimension of social networks but not because
given relationships specialize in the same task for all persons. Last, the *convoy*

model of support (Antonucci and Akiyama, 1995) offers a dynamic view of social support. A convoy is a supportive network of persons to whom an individual is connected by the giving or receiving of support. As we move through life, the convoy changes as the nature of social exchanges shifts or as members join or leave the convoy. Thus, different ties may be significant, not only for different groups of individuals but also for the same individual at different points in the life course.

The hierarchical-compensatory and task-specificity models have fairly fixed notions of support networks, minimizing variability in the ways that ties to family, friends, and other individuals can be negotiated over time and by different individuals. In these models, emphasizing normative assumptions about particular familial bonds also fails to incorporate gender as an organizing feature of social life (Allen, Goldscheider, and Ciambone, 1999). The conventional view of family embedded in the hierarchical-compensatory model favors the traditional nuclear family (spouse and children) as the primary relationships in the lives of all adults. By definition, this excludes those without spouses or children and views their networks as inadequate (Connidis, 1994b). For these reasons, the functional-specificity and convoy models are superior perspectives for understanding the negotiation of informal support in later life.

One of the best ways to understand social support within families is to combine the influence of culture, social structure, family history, and individual preferences as central when discussing how obligations to family members represent negotiated commitments (Finch, 1989). These factors are embedded in the concept of legitimate excuses, which refers to socially accepted reasons for avoiding obligations to help in particular situations (Finch, 1989). For example, a married father in the labor force could argue effectively that his prior claims as father, husband, and worker excuse him from the responsibility of caring for his mother, especially given that his sister is a married homemaker and thus more available to help. The gendered nature of social life in general and of family life in particular means that such an excuse would carry the additional weight of different gender claims in the assumed responsibility to care.

Older parents give and receive assistance, but the imbalanced focus on help provided by children creates the impression that all older people need help and downplays their role as helpers in old age. Support between parent and child is more correctly viewed as an exchange relationship (Dowd, 1980), which includes assumptions of reciprocity (Gouldner, 1967). The degree of reciprocity or balance in a relationship affects its perceived quality. For example, emotional functioning is better among older persons whose exchanges are characterized by reciprocity (Black, 1985). More generally, reciprocal relationships enhance satisfaction with life for adults of all ages, although receiving either more or less than one's share in an exchange undermines well-being (Antonucci, Fuhrer, and Jackson, 1990).

Reciprocity is at the root of filial responsibility, reflected in the view that a primary reason children should look after their parents is because their parents looked after them when they were young (Dwyer, Lee, and Jankowski, 1994). Older parents in my study of 400 community-dwelling persons aged 65 or more enjoy considerable reciprocity in exchanges with their children. Almost two thirds both give and receive support in a variety of areas, just over one fifth give some assistance but receive none, and 15% receive some assistance but give none. These parents also judge their exchanges with children as fair: 95% of them believe that their children give them about the right amount of help, and 92% believe that they in turn give their children the right amount of help.

Nonetheless, there are limits in the extent to which the relationship between parent and child can ever be truly balanced. "Children have an irredeemable obligation toward parents. Nothing they do can ever make up for the initial parental gift" of life and nurturing (Berman, 1987:25). In turn, older parents experience irreplaceable loss. Although they may engage in new activities and make new friends in old age, they are unable to replace people and times that went before (Berman, 1987). Both parents and children may thus feel unable to offer as much to each other as they feel they owe (children) or would like to give (parents), creating an essential tension in parent-child relationships. The irredeemable obligation of children and the irreplaceable losses of parents cannot be resolved in daily interaction and provide an ongoing basis for ambivalence in intergenerational ties.

In sum, support between parents and their adult children flows in two directions. Although there are limits to which either party may feel that the intergenerational bond is a balanced one, reciprocity is preferred by both parents and children. Although our culture expects children to honor their responsibilities toward their parents, this is only one factor in the negotiation of support between parents and children. Structured social relations based on gender, class, ethnicity, and race, for example, all play a role in how intergenerational ties are negotiated. The history of relationships within a family also helps determine who will assume what obligation to support a family member. The negotiation process is rarely restricted to two parties. Instead, negotiating support for any family member, including a parent or adult child, involves a dynamic interplay of the interests and concerns of all those who could be implicated in providing that support. Even those who appear to be uninvolved are likely to have negotiated that position through claims to acceptable competing and overriding responsibilities as legitimate excuses for not offering support. These general issues are now applied to the respective roles of children and of parents as providers of support to one another.

Child Support to Older Parents

> When she was small, our daughter depended on us for decisions, for help from us in so many ways. Now, I find that the roles are somewhat reversed. She is much younger [than we], and she is out in the world more, and I think we tend to lean on her a little. We try not to, but there are times when I feel that we do. She is just like the Rock of Gibraltar.
>
> —*Married mother, 77 years old*

Despite laments about the decline of the family, estimates are that over 80% of the support received by older persons is provided by family members (Merrill, 1997). The most likely providers of this support are spouses and, in the absence of a spouse, children. Over a third of older persons who require daily help receive it from a child (Aldous, 1994). Children provide a broad range of help to their older parents, from emotional support to extensive, long-term, hands-on nursing care. Indeed, the range of support included in discussions of caregiving is simply too broad. Much of what is termed *support* and even *care* might be viewed more accurately as the usual stuff of close relationships, a difference captured in the distinction between "caring for" and "caring about" a family member (Martin-Matthews, 2000a). For example, is "emotional support" a form of caregiving, or is it an ongoing feature of a family tie?

Some of the terminology used to describe informal support to older parents is also problematic. Terms such as "eldercare" have seeped into the gerontological literature, but they tend, implicitly, to reduce older persons to a position paralleling that of infants (Martin-Matthews, 1996). Yet even the older family member who needs care is in a very different situation from that of a dependent child. The variability in definition of support is matched by variability in the samples used to study caregiving. Some studies are based on samples of all children in a family, but most focus on child caregivers only. Some samples include children who are in and out of the labor force, whereas others include labor force participants only. Some address a range of living situations, whereas others study coresident parents and their caregiving children. Last, there is also a considerable range in the amount of support that older parents actually require, which some studies take into account and others do not. Awareness of these differences is necessary to understanding apparently contradictory results in the research literature.

Several flaws in caregiving research further undermine our understanding of the real situation. First, most studies are cross-sectional, examining caregiving at one point in time. This snapshot view fails to capture the dynamics of the caregiving process, including the ebb and flow of involvement by different family members over time. This problem is heightened by a second weakness, the focus on a "primary caregiver," the person identified as being most responsible for looking after an older person. Again, this misses the negotiation of support through which some children may take turns offering more or less help according to the shifting needs of parents and their variable ability to offer support. Some children may find themselves more implicated in caregiving than others. The variety of pathways to care, discussed shortly, illustrates this dynamic.

Third, a gender bias in research favoring the kinds of support more traditionally offered by women heightens their apparent dominance as caregivers and effectively minimizes the support provided by sons (Dwyer and Coward, 1991; Stoller, 1990). When coupled with the assumption that more "feminine" forms of support are better for parents (Matthews and Heidorn, 1998), the efforts of sons and of less traditional daughters are treated implicitly as inferior and suspect. Consider these caveats as we explore the help that children give to their parents.

Pathways to Caring

The possibility that a child will provide care to an older parent is heightened if the parent is a mother, is not married, has fewer children, and is in greater need of help (Dwyer and Coward, 1991; Ikkink, van Tilberg, and

Knipscheer, 1999). The extensiveness of help given to an older mother by her children is a function of her need and of emotional closeness between them (Bengtson, Giarrusso, Silverstein, and Wang, 2000). Among daughters, not being married makes caregiving more likely, but having children and being employed make no difference (Himes, Jordan, and Farkas, 1996). Sons who act as primary caregivers are likely to be only children, to have no sister, or to have a sister living far away from the parent (Martin Matthews and Campbell, 1995). Among men, class also makes a difference in the likelihood of caring for parents, with working-class men more likely to do so (Martin Matthews and Campbell, 1995).

Race also affects caregiving dynamics, with African American caregivers more likely to be children, whereas among Whites, a spouse predominates (Connell and Gibson, 1997; Stommel, Given, and Given, 1998). This may help account for the fact that White primary caregivers more often provide care on their own, whereas Black primary caregivers receive more support from others (Stommel et al., 1998). Yet although the conventional wisdom is that older African Americans get more help from their families, this is largely an outcome of receiving more primary support from coresident children and grandchildren rather than general differences in all forms of support from all family members (Peek, Coward, and Peek, 2000). When all sources of informal support are considered (relatives and unpaid nonrelatives), Black elders actually receive less assistance than their White counterparts (Norgard and Rodgers, 1997). From the vantage point of older persons, Black elders are less likely to be institutionalized despite being in poorer health and receiving less care from relatives (Belgrave and Bradsher, 1994). However, as reported by caregivers, African Americans tend to provide more hours of support and to be caring for older persons who have more health limitations (Bowman et al., 1998). When health and wealth are taken into account, Black and White adult children are more inclined to help their parents financially and Hispanic children less so (Wong, Capoferro, and Soldo, 1999). On balance, Black adult children are most willing to sacrifice meeting their own needs to provide financial aid to their parents.

The apparent strength of family ties among non-White groups may create a false impression of needs being met. Research on Mexican American elders shows that, despite extensive family involvement, older persons' needs for instrumental aid are not being met adequately (Dietz, 1995). Similarly, although the informal networks of older Blacks are more likely to include someone other than a spouse, child, or child-in-law, they are no larger than those of older Whites (Burton et al., 1995). Thus, assumptions about the availability of family to older non-White persons must not detract from the necessity to improve accessibility to other forms of support.

We have focused thus far on the characteristics of the individuals who give and receive care as determinants of caregiving, but characteristics of families are also important. Families that manage conflict positively, engage in compromise, and work hard at conflict resolution tend to give far more help to an older member with Alzheimer's (Lieberman and Fisher, 1999). Somewhat counterintuitive is the fact that families in which decision-making authority is granted to one family member, with input from others, give more aid to elders than do more democratic families. However, families who have a high level of agreement between spouses and their children regarding the behavior of a coresident older person experience less stress and depression and greater satisfaction and mastery as a result of caregiving (Pruchno, Burant, and Peters, 1997a). Understanding these kinds of family dynamics is essential to understanding how the caring work of families gets done.

What motivates children to support their parents? A sense of filial responsibility has been noted as a prime reason for helping parents. There is a widely held view that children should help their parents, although not unconditionally (Finch and Mason, 1991). Children who subscribe most strongly to this view also give their parents more help (Ikkink et al., 1999), although a stronger sense of obligation appears to have a greater impact on the amount of help given by sons than by daughters (Silverstein, Parott, and Bengtson, 1995). Among those caring for older family members, filial responsibility means securing a safe and comfortable environment that respects autonomy; being sensitive to the older person's feelings and need for affection and reminiscence; and including the older person in daily activities, outings, and visits (Piercy, 1998). Generally, non-White caregivers have a stronger commitment to filial support than do Whites (Connell and Gibson, 1997).

Children's support of older parents is also considered indicative of close affectional bonds between them. In fact, children who feel close or extremely close to their parent do express greater concern about their parent's future health (Marshall et al., 1983). As well, parent-child ties characterized by affection earlier in life (Parrott and Bengtson, 1999) currently involve more exchanges of support (Silverstein et al., 1995), but for sons, this is a result of greater contact with their parents (Silverstein et al., 1995). Nonetheless, filial responsibility can override the impact of distant or conflictual ties. For example, previous conflict between children and their parents does not stop current support exchanges (Parrott and Bengtson, 1999). However, among daughters, obligation dominates affection as a motive for assistance with activities of daily living but not for more general forms of social support (Merrill, 1997). As well, exchanges that are motivated by obligation are uneven, with children giving far more than they get in return (Parrott and Bengtson, 1999).

Qualitative research about children caring for parents reveals several pathways to caring (Merrill, 1997). Some children were selected as the caregiver "de facto," meaning that no one else was available or perceived to be adequate to the task. Others became primary helpers following family meetings, usually held in response to a major change in circumstances. The typical outcome of such gatherings is for one child to emerge as the caregiver after others offer legitimate excuses (Finch, 1989; see Chapter 8) to justify their "inability" to serve as caregiver. However, some siblings decide to share caregiving equally (see Chapter 13). A third scenario, most common among working-class families, is for caregivers to be chosen by their parents, who express their preference on the assumption that the elected child is willing and able (Merrill, 1997). Other children report that the caregiving situation "just happened," evolving over time as situations shifted and the need for support intensified. The most uncommon pathway to caring is for a child to independently volunteer for the role, a decision generally considered a choice rather than a forced circumstance. Gender ideology pervades the road to caregiving and is reflected in the preference of fathers and mothers to have daughters provide care and the greater probability that sons perceive caregiving as a forced choice, whereas daughters are more likely to volunteer.

Gender and Caring for Parents

One response to population aging has been a heightened concern about the "sandwiched generation," women "caught in the middle" of caring for both their older parents (more often a mother) and their young children. Yet although the potential for this phenomenon has increased greatly because more parents are living into old age, the experience of caring for dependent parents and children simultaneously is not typical (Martin-Matthews and Rosenthal, 1993). Indeed, recent commentary on the sandwiched generation of women suggests that this is another instance of overselling demography (Martin-Matthews, 2000b; Rosenthal, 2000). For example, in Canada, although about a third of women in their late 40s are in the structural position of having an older parent, dependent children, and a job, the highest percentage of any age group (women aged 50 to 59) who were actually combining work and children with helping a parent once a month or more was only 7% (Rosenthal, Martin-Matthews, and Matthews, 1996; for similar U.S. results, see Spitze and Logan, 1990; Uhlenberg, 1993).

Although women trying to meet these competing responsibilities have a formidable task at hand, there is no purpose served in overstating the prevalence of this reality. Indeed, alarming claims that large numbers of stressed-out employees need support for caregiving may scare off work-based initiatives to support workers among the most well-meaning of employers (Martin-Matthews, 2000b). As well, there are both rewards and costs to caring for parents, and engaging in multiple roles itself does not appear to add to the stress of caring (Penning, 1998). The observation that parental caregiving at any one point in time is rare, particularly in combination with labor force participation and dependent children, must be tempered by two facts. First, among older women with a surviving parent, one third of those aged 60 to 75 provides parental care (Himes, 1994). Second, among women who have a living parent, 50% of those aged 45 to 49 will probably become a caregiver to that parent at some point in the future.

When parents are well, sons and daughters are equally active in supporting them (Ikkink et al., 1999). However, the worry about women in the sandwiched generation stems from the fact that they tend to dominate as caregivers. Gender differences in caring for parents provide an excellent example of the difference between attitude and action. Men and women do not differ in their expression of filial obligation, in their stated emphasis on equality and fairness in sharing responsibility (Finch and Mason, 1991), or in their reported ability to provide support to parents following hospitalization (Wolfson, Handfield-Jones, Glass, McClaran, and Keyserlingk, 1993). Yet under a broad range of circumstances, daughters are more likely than sons to care for parents and to provide a wider range of help (Dwyer and Coward, 1991; Dwyer and Seccombe, 1991). Even the possibility of a parental preference to receive care from a child of the same gender does not erase this difference. Although sons are more inclined to help fathers than mothers and daughters are more likely to help mothers than fathers, daughters are still more likely than sons to help both mothers and fathers (Lee, Dwyer, and Coward, 1993). As well, examinations of support provided to both self-sufficient and dependent mothers by daughters indicate that caregiving is the extension of long-established patterns of helping between generations of women (Walker and Pratt, 1991).

The lower level of help provided by sons is compensated for considerably by the far greater involvement of daughters-in-law than sons-in-law in hands-on assistance. Even when sons are primary caregivers, direct personal care often shifts to the son's wife (Merrill, 1997). Indeed, daughters and daughters-in-law are as likely to see themselves as primary caregivers and to report providing the same types of help; the difference is that daughters spend more time doing so (Merrill, 1993). They also experience differences in the support received from their husbands for their caregiving efforts; sons-in-law view their wife's help to her parents as too high a priority; sons view their wife's help to their own parents as critical (Suitor and Pillemer, 1994). These patterns are not duplicated among children and children-in-law who are all labor force participants. In this case, daughters provide more social and home-based support than sons, but daughters and sons provide similar levels of health care, and sons- and daughters-in-law provide parallel levels of help to their parents-in-law (Ingersoll-Dayton, Starrels, and Dowler, 1996). Most critical to the amount of help given to parents and parents-in-law is how much support they need. Gender of the parent is also influential, with mothers both giving and receiving more support than fathers (Ingersoll-Dayton, Starrels, and Dowler, 1996).

Sons Who Care

The gender bias of research suggests that parents who must "make do" with sons as caregivers are at risk of receiving inferior aid. Yet when sons take on primary caregiving responsibilities, their commitment is as stable as that of daughters, and the patterns of involvement become quite similar for sons and daughters (Martin Matthews and Campbell, 1995; Stoller, 1990). However, sons in families with no daughters negotiate directly with parents rather than with siblings and work hard to foster their parents' independence, an approach that may be preferable to the more traditional hands-on style of daughters (Matthews and Heidorn, 1998). As well, although women may be more involved than men with caring for parents, qualitative research on sons who care for their parents shows that sons provide a broad range of help, including personal care, as needed (Harris, 1998).

Like daughters, sons vary in the support that they give, in part based on circumstances such as their parent's health and marital status. Sons looking after a parent with dementia take four key approaches to caring (Harris, 1998). The dutiful son has an intense sense of duty toward his parents, which motivates him to help. The son who goes the extra mile usually has his parent(s) living with him, and his efforts mimic those of a spouse. The strategic planner is emotionally involved in the management strategies he uses to ensure that care is provided, by himself and others. Last, the son who shares the care works with a parent or siblings (or both) as equal team players. These caregiving sons receive emotional support from their wives but do not expect them to care for their parents. Filial responsibility is met in a nurturing and loving manner, in varying ways. More exploration of how caring for parents is carried out is likely to suggest stronger parallels across gender and greater within-gender differences than is assumed in the current conventional wisdom about gender and caregiving to parents.

Labor Force Participation and Caring

Because women are so prominent as providers of parental support, their increased involvement in the labor force prompts concerns about how these competing demands can be met. Women's paid work changes the way in which caring is carried out but not the likelihood of caring. Geographic location overrides work commitments in decisions about which child will care for an older parent (Stern, 1996). If a child is selected as the key caregiver, then decisions regarding adjustments at work are made.

Typically, labor force participants manage parent care by identifying needs and ensuring that some of them are met by others, including paid-for services. Thus, on balance, those who receive care from employed women receive as much of it but not necessarily directly from their daughter (Doty, Jackson, and Crown, 1998). Employed women and housewives provide similar levels of help with shopping, transportation, household maintenance, emotional support, and service management (Brody, Kleban, Johnsen, Hoffman, and Schoonover,1987; Brody and Schoonover, 1986), but traditional hands-on care is most usual among housewives. The picture is more complicated when one considers the relationship between hours at work and hours of care received by a parent. Among those who work up to 18 hours per week, hours of care increases with hours of work (Doty et al., 1998). However, after that point, increasing hours at work decreases both the number of hours of care a woman provides and the total number of hours of care received by a parent. We do not know whether this leaves the parents of daughters who are employed full-time in need of care or whether these women and their cohelpers provide care more efficiently.

Among caregivers, men are more likely than women to be engaged in the multiple roles of spouse, parent, worker, and son (Penning, 1998). Canadian research shows that, among the employed, men are as likely as women to aid their parents, except for personal care, which is much more likely among women (Martin-Matthews and Campbell, 1995). In the United States, there is striking similarity in the types of help given by employed sons and daughters, particularly helping with personal and health care and care management (Neal, Ingersoll-Dayton, and Starrels, 1997). But daughters provide more help overall, are more often primary carers, and give more socioemotional and household support.

The gendered nature of family and work life typically leads women to adjust work commitments to a greater extent than do men to help their parents. Women who work outside the home continue to support their old parents (Robison, Moen, and Dempster-McClain, 1995), largely by forfeiting leisure time and sleep, giving up opportunities for job advancement, using vacation and sick days for parent care, reducing work hours, enlisting the help of other family members, and cutting back on housework and nonessential dimensions of family life (Guberman and Maheu, 1999; Ikkink et al., 1999; Martin Matthews and Rosenthal, 1993). Despite the juggling act that combining work and caregiving requires, employment is often a positive counterpoint to caring for a parent (Martin-Matthews and Keefe, 1995; Murphy, Schofield, et al., 1997; Scharlach, 1994). One daughter observes, "Work is a break. I can finally use my brain. I am so busy, it takes my mind off everything here [at home]. I wouldn't want to give it up" (Merrill, 1997:82). In spite of the positive spin-offs of combining work and care for some, the psychological distress of employed midlife women caring for parents could be alleviated if the conflict between work and family were reduced (Marks, 1998).

Because the jobs held by working-class women are not as well paying as the careers typical of middle-class and upper-class women, women with lower-status jobs more often leave them in the face of demands for parent care than women with higher education and higher-status jobs (Brody et al., 1987). In one study of caregivers (Mutschler, 1994), 80% of whom are women, those in clerical and blue-collar jobs are most likely to leave work to care. Among workers who stay in the labor force, those in blue-collar jobs are most likely to reduce the number of hours they work as an initial strategy for assuming caring responsibilities. Rearranging schedules is the most common tactic for combining work and care, but managers, professionals, and clerks are almost twice as likely to use this approach. The alternative for those in sales, service, and blue-collar jobs is to take time off without pay. Longitudinal research suggests that work-related adjustments are prompted as soon as the need for care arises. However, these adaptations are often temporary as women discover ways to balance work and caregiving or the parent's need for care declines (Franklin, Ames, and King, 1994). As well, the stress associated with caregiving tends to decline over time (Martin-Matthews, 1999), indicating adaptation to caregiving responsibilities.

Consequences of Caring

Power Shifts

When older parents are healthy, exchanges with children typically involve reciprocity (Ikkink et al., 1999). The growing need for support imposed by health problems or disability often reduces the power of parents in exchanges with their children. Following a health crisis, for example, control over health care decisions is often in the hands of the child and health professional (Fischer, 1985). The comparatively powerless parent is sometimes left with only two resources, invoking the guilty feelings of their children or complying with their children's wishes. The irredeemable obligation felt by children can make guilt an effective weapon in parental attempts to regain power, although resorting to feelings of guilt is unlikely to contribute to good relations. However, children are often motivated to help by feelings of guilt that parents are quite unaware of evoking (Pyke, 1999). One consequence is that children report more demands for and greater burden from providing care than do their parents.

Children are also very aware of how much they have received from their parents and often view caregiving as their attempt to repay their parents for the many sacrifices they made for them. Such delayed reciprocity is evident in the fact that parents who gave more support to their children when they were younger receive more support from them in later life (Ikkink et al., 1999). One son observed,

> I was pleased that I was able in some small way . . . to pay her back. I think if she had died of a heart attack, I would never have had the chance to say to myself in some small way I had repaid her for what she did. Not that she ever made me feel like I had to, but I did. (Harris, 1998:347-348)

Children typically feel unable to truly reciprocate the lifetime of support received from their parents, as a daughter's comments illustrate: "I could never give her all of what she has given me, not in a million years" (Sheehan and Donorfio, 1999:171).

Compliance is a common response used by a dependent parent who seeks to appease and please his or her child (Dowd, 1980). Parents vary in their willingness to defer to their children, based on whether they are members of families that are individualist or collectivist in their stance toward familial support (Pyke, 1999; Pyke and Bengtson, 1996). In individualist families, both generations believe strongly in self-reliance and have very low expectations for, and provision of support to, older members. Collectivist families are the opposite; close family ties are valued, and high levels of support are expected and offered. But greater support has its price. The parents in collectivist families have less intergenerational power and exhibit greater deference to their children than is true of parents in individualist families (Pyke, 1999). Parents in individualist families resist receiving support from their children for as long as possible in an effort to maintain autonomy. However, in both family types, if help is provided and parents fail to repay support with compliance, children are resentful and respond by setting limits on the amount of support they are willing to provide. Thus, to maintain reciprocity in the caregiving situation, parents must trade power for support or support for power.

Subjective Impact on Children

Results are mixed about the impact on well-being of looking after an older parent, in part because measures of caregiving and well-being, as well as sample characteristics, vary greatly. A national sample of married adult children shows no difference in levels of well-being, marital quality, financial resources, and satisfaction with leisure time between those who assume simultaneous obligations to their parents or parents-in-law and children that require "a lot or quite a bit of time and energy," and those who do not (Loomis and Booth, 1995). The fact that those with happier marriages are more likely to take on this responsibility means that these findings may simply reflect the unique situation not just of married persons but of married persons with strong relationships. Other research indicates that the well-being of children who have emotional support (Sheehan and Donorfio, 1999) or have partners (Murphy, Schofield, et al., 1997) is not adversely affected by caring for their parents, whereas those without a partner are more likely to resent caregiving (Murphy, Schofield, et al., 1997). A parent's declining health and the provision of some types of support contribute to deteriorating relations with parents and less happiness among children, according to some studies (Kaufman and Uhlenberg, 1998; Strawbridge, Wallhagen, Shema, and Kaplan, 1997).

The strain of caring for an older parent is primarily emotional, although the resulting restrictions placed on time and freedom are also problematic. Yet most research on caregiver burden is quantitative. These studies view caregiving as a series of tasks, emphasize the "costs of caring," and neglect the emotion work of caring (MacRae, 1998; Sheehan and Donorfio, 1999). This orientation removes the caregiving experience from the emotional context of deep family bonds. Although we tend to think of emotions as rather spontaneous and free ranging, "emotions themselves are subject to normative guidelines" (Finch, 1989: 207), which some have termed "feeling rules" (Hochschild, 1983). Failure to manage the mix of emotions that may accompany caring—anger, frustration, sadness, love, guilt, resentment, fear—according to these feeling rules, is itself stressful for caregivers (MacRae, 1998). Emotional reciprocity may also break down when an older parent's illness interferes with the usual ability to follow feeling rules. Such is often the case in the later stages of Alzheimer's disease or following a stroke, heightening the strain experienced by the child providing support. Unresolved conflict between parent and child or between siblings often surfaces, increasing the amount of emotion work as carers try to manage the conflict (MacRae, 1998).

At the same time, the emotion work that is fundamental to family caring is also the basis for assigning meaning to caregiving and for defining rewards as well as costs as part of this experience. In mother-and-daughter dyads, caregiving by the daughter is the basis for growing tolerance and acceptance of one another (Sheehan and Donorfio, 1999). The additional time together that the need for care requires is an opportunity to know one another better, put conflicts aside, and become more comfortable with one another. Similarly, among caregiving sons, the opportunity to "pay back" parents for past support, a sense of purpose and personal growth, and serving as a good role model for their children are positive outcomes of looking after parents (Harris, 1998).

Among children caring for parents or parents-in-law with long-term illnesses or disabilities, one third do not find caregiving stressful, two fifths find caregiving intermittently stressful, and one quarter experience constant stress

(Penning, 1998). What accounts for these variations? Counter to the usual assumption, multiple role involvements are a minor and inconsistent factor. Instead, gender (daughters experience greater stress than sons) and a parent's behavioral problems or need for extensive care are key determinants of stress. However, although daughters report more stress from caregiving, they do not report negative consequences for their physical or emotional health. Cognitive impairments and associated behavioral problems of parents have a particularly negative effect on caregiver well-being (Starrels, Ingersoll-Dayton, Dowler, and Neal, 1997) because they increase the amount of care provided (Yates, Tennstedt, and Chang, 1999). However, an emotionally close tie between parents and their children offsets the negative impact of caregiving as contributing to depression (Yates et al, 1999), highlighting the importance of a relationship's qualitative dimensions.

Gender Variations

The caregiving playing field is not even for men and women. At the onset, the pressure to provide care differs between them. The longstanding and persistent normative expectation that daughters rather than sons should make the adjustments necessary to care for a parent is an important component of strain among them. As well, the fact that caring is considered normative for women does not remove the feeling of ambivalence that results from meeting this obligation (Aronson, 1992). Unfortunately, the expectation that women should care may be resistant to change because older parents, a generation more committed to this view, are often the ones who determine which child will be their key helper (Merrill, 1997).

The emotional strain from caring for frail parents is experienced by sons and daughters, but the routes to this outcome differ (Mui, 1995), highlighting the fact that gender structures social life. Knowing the predictors of stress for men and women is at least as important to our understanding of family dynamics as knowing gender variations in the amount of stress. Both sons and daughters experience more strain as caregiving's impact on their personal and social lives increases (Mui, 1995). However, for daughters only, the spillover of caregiving into work and a poor relationship with their parent are critical determinants of emotional strain. For sons, more behavioral problems on the part of the parent and having fewer other informal helpers are key predictors of emotional strain. Once resources, parental impairment, caregiver tasks, and the interference of caregiving with personal and social life are taken into account, gender differences in degree of caregiver burden are reduced substantially (Kramer and Kipnis, 1995; Mui, 1995). In other words, all things being equal, men and women do not differ substantially in their experience of emotional strain. But all things are not equal. Daughters tend to have fewer resources, to provide more intensive support, and to experience more interference with work, all factors that contribute to stress (Merrill, 1997).

Employed men and women differ in their adaptations to work as a method of meeting obligations toward parents. Women more typically use sick days, miss work-based social events, and pass up opportunities for advancement; men more often interrupt their work days (Martin-Matthews and Campbell, 1995). Although both sons and daughters experience stress as a result of taking time off work (Starrels et al., 1997), lost opportunities for advancement have dire long-term consequences for women (Martin-Matthews, 1999). Another gender contrast is that parents who are cared for by sons tend to reciprocate by offering assistance more often than parents who are cared for by daughters, possibly because help from daughters is accepted as appropriate (Starrels et al., 1997). Such assistance lowers stress, so once again, sons may enjoy less stressful conditions when caring for a parent. These various gender differences must be placed within the broader social context of structured relations (Connidis and McMullin, 2000). On balance, the social construction of gender in the family and workplace creates different caregiving conditions for men and women, leading to greater stress on behalf of women that is not an inherent feature of being a man or woman.

The Relevance of Race

Race is also associated with caregiver stress. Some studies find lower levels of stress, burden, and depression among non-White caregivers (Connell and Gibson, 1997), whereas others report similar levels of stress (Aranda and Knight, 1997; Bowman et al., 1998; Young and Kahana, 1995). However, the causes of stress may differ by race, reflecting different life circumstances (Aranda and Knight, 1997). For example, among Whites but not African Americans, caregivers who are children suffer more strain than do other relatives (Bowman et al.,1998). Conversely, being married tends to reduce caregiver strain for Black but not White caregivers. The different impact of these factors may be an outcome of variations in family structures and arrangements, which reflect structured relations based on race.

Impact on Parents

Last, as this discussion has reflected, research on the consequences of caring focuses heavily on the caregiver's experience, in this case that of the child. What about older parents? How do they feel about being cared for by their children? Clearly, the loss of independence can be traumatic for older persons, who prefer to live on their own and take care of themselves for as long as possible. Nonetheless, as we have seen, many parents as well as children are committed to the notion of filial responsibility. Therefore, when care is necessary, receiving it from children can be considered a desirable option on behalf of parents. Indeed, those parents who anticipate a time when they can no longer live with their children believe that their lives will be worse as a result, particularly if they are unmarried (Coward, Albrecht, and Shapiro, 1996). Nonetheless, there is evidence that having children take on caregiving responsibilities takes a psychological toll on their parents.

Depression is higher among both mothers and fathers who receive support from a child than among parents who do not (Dunham, 1995), but marital status and level of care tend to mediate this relationship (Silverstein, Chen, and Heller, 1996). Unmarried parents initially benefit psychologically from receiving support, to a point. When support moves from moderate to high levels, children's caring lowers their well-being. An exception to this trend occurs among coresident parents when the older mother or father contributes to the family, thereby increasing a sense of personal control (Pruchno, Burant, and Peters, 1997b). Greater personal control, in turn, enhances the parent's psychological well-being.

Although having children, particularly a daughter, reduces the likelihood of institutionalization (Burr, 1990; Freedman, 1996), there are times when children simply cannot offer the support needed to sustain a parent's independence in the community. Institutionalization of an elderly parent can be a very difficult decision and transition period for the parent and child and is usually only entertained after families have tried other alternatives, including coresidence. Once in institutional settings, continued interaction with family improves the quality of life for older nursing-home residents (Kirkconnell and Tindale, 1986). Most of us will not see a day when our parents move to an institutional setting. Instead, for most of our lifetimes, the more familiar experience in our relationships with parents will be receiving help from them, not giving it to them. Let us now turn to consider the support that older parents offer their adult children.

Parental Support to Adult Children

> You know, when I first got my little boy, I wanted to live to bring him up, and
> here I am at 85 still worrying about him.
>
> —*85-year-old widow*

As noted earlier when discussing the nature of the parent-child tie, the happiness and success of one's children is very important to older parents, as it is for their younger counterparts (Demo and Acock, 1996). Later in life, parents tend to withdraw somewhat from active parenting, as their adult children are committed to their jobs, a partner, or children. That said, parenting never stops, and when children experience problems or are unable to be truly independent, the potentially active role of parenting in older age is evident. One transition in which this is particularly manifest is that of becoming a grandparent. The many contributions that older persons often make to their children's lives through their involvement with grandchildren are discussed in Chapter 10.

The recent intergenerational equity debate (see Chapter 14) has spawned greater attention to the various ways in which older parents continue to assist their children, a topic generally neglected in the growing concern about caregiving. Most older parents remain not only independent but also significant contributors to their children's lives, ranging from emotional support to providing a home (Bengtson and Harootyan, 1994; Logan & Spitze, 1996; Marshall, 1997; Rosenthal and Gladstone, 1993; Stone et al., 1998). Half of Canadian parents aged 55 to 64, and over a third of parents aged 65 to 74, provide their children with at least two types of instrumental help (personal care, transportation, finances, child care, meal preparation, laundry and cleaning, and house and yard maintenance; Stone et al., 1998). One third of the younger parents and one quarter of those aged 65 to 74 provide such help at least monthly. Exchanges of instrumental aid between parents and children either favor children or remain balanced until parents are aged 70 years or more; aid to children drops off markedly after the age of 75. Older parents continue to be a source of advice, as is evident when they serve as confidants for their adult children. They also often serve as the first personal example of later-life transitions, such as retirement or widowhood. In part based on experience, parents can be critical to their children's ability to weather such transitions.

Financial aid between the generations in the form of private wealth transfers strongly favor adult children over older parents (Stone et al., 1998). Add to this transfers through inheritance, and the imbalance is increased manifold (Marshall, 1997). This pattern of giving is established in middle age, when parents are more inclined to provide financial support to their children than to their parents (Wong et al., 1999). A child's need for support is an important determinant of how much money a parent provides (McGarry and Schoeni, 1997). Within families, children who are less well-off are more likely to receive financial help from their parents and to receive more of it than their more solvent siblings. Furthermore, such financial transfers are freely given and do not serve as payment for other forms of help received from children. Among White, African, and Hispanic Americans, Hispanics are most committed to the view that older parents should provide financial assistance to their children (Burr and Mutchler, 1999).

The tendency to provide help to children based on need means that older parents serve as effective troubleshooters and committed sources of support for their children. This is particularly evident in two situations that highlight the extent to which parents help their children when required: caring for children who have AIDS and caring for children with long-term disabilities. Although these are not typical situations for older parents, they stand as testament to the operation of "revocable detachment" (see Chapter 1) by which family members honor one another's independence but are ready to provide extensive support if and when it is needed. A third form of support, co-residence, is discussed separately.

Supporting Children With AIDS

The spread of AIDS among young and middle-aged adults has created a challenging and often tragic situation for many older parents who must confront their child's illness and, often, death, during the prime of life (Mullan, 1998). For many persons with AIDS, an older mother serves as a critical source of support, offering both emotional support and, when needed, hands-on caring. This is particularly true among homosexual and bisexual African American men who are less likely to be members of gay support networks than their White counterparts (Brown and Sankar, 1998). Similarly, African American women turn for help to their family of origin first and then to their partners. Generally, Hispanic men rely more on their family, whereas White men rely more on extrafamilial ties for support.

Among older mothers of children with AIDS, initial awareness of their child's illness tends to be met with the strong emotions of grief, sadness, shock, and fear, coupled with the practical response of seeking information (Thompson, 2000). Despite some older mothers' discomfort with the link between AIDS and being gay (see also Brennan and Moore, 1994), mothers tend to focus on their child's illness rather than their child's sexual orientation. One mother comments,

> I try . . . to think of . . . first of all, "What can I do to help?" and that's a mother's instinct, you know, "How can I help?" And "How can I be more understanding of it?," and that's been hard for me to understand—I want to understand more about the disease, and I don't want to know too much more about the lifestyle. (Thompson, 2000:161)

Many mothers whose children are either gay or intravenous drug users fully accept their children and do not assign any blame to them for contracting HIV. But they may have to manage the conflict with a spouse or child that this acceptance creates. A mother says this about her husband: "A little bit of rage comes out. . . . 'If he hadn't been indulging in this behavior it wouldn't have happened in the first place.' . . . I feel helpless . . . disgusted that he can't move past that" (Thompson, 2000:160). Mothers often blame themselves for their child's situation. For them, a key challenge is to establish parental boundaries that set limits to their responsibility for their adult children, permitting them to focus on the present and the support of their child.

Supporting Children With Special Needs

A particularly demanding case of ongoing support to a child occurs when children have a long-term disability or illness. Caring for children with a developmental disability represents a good example of this phenomenon. The demands of caring for these children as youngsters may be typical of all children, and parents often receive support from their parents, as illustrated in Photo 8.1. In stark contrast to the situation of adult children caring for their parents, caring for a child with a long-term disability is often a lifelong role for parents. Increases in survival at birth and longevity have heightened a parent's chances of looking after a child with a developmental disability into old age (Fullmer, Tobin, and Smith, 1997). Furthermore, policy shifts that encourage community living, in part to reduce the costs of providing services, have

Photo 8.1. Having a child with special needs typically means a life-long commitment to caring by parents, including living together.

increased the pressure on families to provide long-term care for those who are mentally ill and developmentally challenged (Greenberg, Seltzer, and Greenley, 1993).

The vast majority of caregivers to such adults are parents, and the vast majority of adults with developmental disabilities or mental illness live with their parent(s) (Greenberg et al., 1993). The longer life expectancy of women makes it more likely that older mothers will be carrying out this responsibility alone at a time in life when their own needs for support may be increasing.

Nonetheless, parents remain committed caregivers to their dependent children, sometimes to the point of remaining silent about abuse at the hands of their child for fear that their child will have nowhere else to live if the abuse is discovered (Pillemer, 1985).

Older parents caring for adult children with disabilities tend to receive little outside assistance (Roeher Institute, 1996). Even when such support is available, a number of factors inhibit its use by older mothers. The child's condition is one factor. Although most adult children with developmental disabilities living with their mothers are in day programs or employed, this is true for less than half of coresident children with a mental illness (Greenberg et al., 1993). Ironically, given their greater need, among mothers of adult children with developmental disabilities, increasing age and disability make it less likely that their children are in day programs (Fullmer et al., 1997). Furthermore, mothers who do not use this service are less inclined to use respite care or to make future plans for their children in the event that they can no longer look after them (Fullmer et al., 1997). Not surprisingly, they are more likely to feel burdened by caregiving (Greenberg et al., 1993).

Differences among children shape the nature of caregiving. A child's gender is influential. Mothers of daughters with developmental disabilities are more vigilant caregivers and experience more subjective burden as a consequence of looking after their children than do mothers of sons (Fullmer et al., 1997). One reason for this is that mothers of daughters are less likely to use day programs because they worry about their daughter being sexually exploited. Yet mothers of children who are mentally ill or developmentally challenged report better relationships with their daughters than sons (Greenberg et al., 1993). The child's condition also creates different care demands. Children with developmental disabilities receive a broader range of direct care from their mothers than do children who are mentally ill (Greenberg et al., 1993; Pruchno, Patrick, and Burant, 1996). However, mothers report better relationships with their children if their child has developmental disabilities than if their child is mentally ill, in part because children who are mentally ill exhibit more behavioral problems.

One family member's situation has repercussions for all family members. The majority of mothers report receiving substantial help from other children in meeting the needs of their child (Fullmer et al., 1997). Variations in such support make a crucial difference to how mothers experience caring for their child. Mothers with a smaller support group experience more caregiver burden from looking after children with developmental disabilities or mental illness (Greenberg et al., 1993). Lack of family cohesion also increases caregiving burden among mothers of children who are mentally ill. These mothers experience greater burden (Greenberg et al., 1993) and poorer well-being (Pruchno et al., 1996) than mothers of children with a developmental disability.

The Subjective Impact of Caring

Generally, providing support to children does not have negative consequences for parents' well-being. Indeed, among widowed and divorced parents, helping children may actually reduce depression (Silverstein et al., 1996). However, there are times when the needs of adult children can be intense and reach the point of being a burden. As well, a child's problems (mental or physical health, alcohol or drug related, or stress) have a direct effect on the well-being of their parents (Pillemer and Suitor, 1991). Parents with children who have problems are more depressed than parents of children who do not. Similarly, when parents with distant ties to their children are compared with parents who enjoy close ties, both mothers and fathers are significantly less happy, and fathers are also less satisfied with life (Connidis and McMullin, 1993; Koropeckyj-Cox, 1999).

Thus, there are qualitative benefits and costs to being parents in later life and no guarantees that having children will bring happiness at this stage of life. At the same time, parents derive rewards from successfully meeting commitments to their children. Even in the case of caring for a child with a long-term disability or illness, parents experience the gratification that stems

> from the intimacy of the relationship between the caregiver and care recipient, and from the knowledge that one has fulfilled an obligation to a family member, adapted successfully to a personal challenge or crisis, or made life better for a loved one in need of support. (Greenberg et al., 1993:543)

Coresidence of
Adult Children and Their Parents

The coresidence of parents and children is much more a function of children living with parents than parents living with children (Aquilino, 1990). About 16% of persons aged 60 and over live with an adult child in either the child or parent's home (Schmertmann, Boyd, Serow, and White, 2000). From the ages of 60 to 75 years, the likelihood of coresidence decreases, but beyond the age of 75 for women and 80 for men, the chances of living with a child increase (Schmertmann et al., 2000). This is especially true of mother-daughter co-residency; among women aged 90 and over, living with a daughter is two times more likely than it is for 75 year olds.

Parents Living With Children

An older parent's declining health, loss of a former caregiver or partner, desire for companionship, and lower income are the key reasons for moving into the home of a child (Brackbill and Kitch, 1991; Brody, Litvin, Hoffman, and Kleban, 1995; Hoyert, 1991; Wilmoth, 2000). In terms of current marital status, widowed mothers are more likely to live with a child than are women of other marital statuses (Roan and Riley, 1996). Following the general age trends noted earlier, women widowed between the ages of 65 and 74 are less likely to live with a child than are younger widows, possibly reflecting the greater interdependence of younger widows and their younger children (Bess, 1999). Counter to popular belief, having a widowed mother move in is more likely to improve than depress the economic well-being of the household, especially among non-Whites (Waehrer and Crystal, 1995). The marital status of daughters also alters the coresident caregiving situation (Brody et al., 1995). Married and widowed women more commonly have their mothers move in with them, whereas divorced and separated daughters more often move in with their mothers. Single women are most likely to have never left home and, hence, are also more likely to reside with and care for their mothers in the mothers' home. For a daughter, a mother's declining ability to cope independently is the primary motivation for coresidence. Because of its association with poorer health, coresidency typically means more intensive caregiving by the adult child (Boaz, Hu, and Ye, 1999; Call, Finch, Huck and Kane, 1999).

Sons and daughters are as likely to have an older parent live with them, but this is more common for sons if the household contains two generations (older parent and adult child) and more common for daughters in three-generation households (Coward and Cutler, 1991). As well, with increasing age, living with a daughter is more common than living with a son. Coresident older parents receive parallel levels of help from daughters and daughters-in-law, despite the fact that daughters feel closer to their parent(s) than daughters-in-law do to their parent(s)-in-law (Peters-Davis, Moss, and Pruchno, 1999). Sons and sons-in-law provide considerably less help than their spouses and feel equally close to their parent(s) and parents-in-law, but only sons feel guilty about not giving more help (Peters-Davis et al., 1999).

Coresidence is more likely among Black and Hispanic than among White older persons (Brown and Sankar, 1998; Burr and Mutchler, 1999). This reflects a stronger normative commitment among older Hispanic and African Americans to living together as an appropriate filial obligation (Burr and Mutchler, 1999; Lee, Peek, and Coward, 1998). The more common experience of multigenerational households among Black than White older parents (Belgrave and Bradsher, 1994) is also a function of variations in marital status, with older and younger Whites more likely to be married (Aquilino, 1990). Some argue that a stronger sense of responsibility to family among non-Whites is a coping mechanism for dealing with poverty, poor health, and discrimination (Burr and Mutchler, 1999). However, strong filial norms and multigenerational households cannot counteract the relative disadvantages faced by older Black parents, including poorer functional ability (see Waite and Hughes, 1999). Instead, these features of family life must be linked to the structurally created inequality that makes them necessary. Although research can "control for" the factors that help account for observed differences by race—income, health, living conditions, education, marital status—in real life, these factors operate simultaneously.

One's childhood experiences may also influence whether an older parent shares a child's home (Szinovacz, 1997). When compared with those who lived with both parents when they were growing up, those who grew up with remarried fathers are less likely to coreside. By contrast, growing up with mothers who were single or remarried makes coresidence more likely. For sons only, growing up with a single father makes it more likely that they will live together once the son is an adult. What about the experience of living with grandparents as a child? Multigenerational living arrangements while a child or young adult create more favorable attitudes toward sharing a home with either an older parent or adult child (Goldscheider and Lawton, 1998).

When parents live with their children, satisfaction with coresidency is higher for both parent and child when there is greater balance in their relationship (Brackbill and Kitch, 1991). In turn, greater dependence of the parent increases the risk of ending coresidency. Coresident daughters are especially subject to strain and are more overloaded, more resentful about providing care, and less satisfied than daughters whose parent lives elsewhere (Murphy et al., 1997).

Children Living With Parents

The growing trend for adult children to return to their parents' home has been dubbed "the refilling of the empty nest," and the children who return are sometimes labeled "boomerang kids." There is a corresponding trend for children to delay leaving the nest in the first place (Cherlin, Scabini, and Rossi, 1997). In the United States, where the trend is less pronounced than in Europe, 20% of men aged 25 to 29 years and 12% of women in this age group have yet to leave their parents' homes (Goldscheider, 1997). High unemployment rates and higher education are the key reasons for the delay in leaving home (Cherlin et al., 1997). Children who take longer to leave home are primarily the offspring of middle-aged parents. Children who return are more likely to be sharing the home of somewhat older parents. Among parents aged 65 years or more, close to 1 in 7 have a child living with them (White and Rogers, 1997).

Based on a very inclusive definition of returning home as living again with parents for 4 months or more, just over one quarter of adult Canadian children (aged 19 to 35) return to live with their parents (aged 35 to 60; Mitchell, 2000). Key reasons for their return are to save money, financial setbacks, finishing school, returning to school, a job ending, or a relationship ending (Mitchell, 2000; Mitchell and Gee, 1996). Returning home is accepted as appropriate following a daughter's divorce and doing so increases substantially the amount of support that she will receive from her parents (Hoyert, 1991). Generally, having an unmarried child, especially one who never married, increases the probability of a child living with an older parent; about half of parents who are 65 years or more have such a child, and one quarter of them have a coresident child (Aquilino, 1990; see also White and Rogers, 1997). These marital-status differences account for any variation between Black and White parents in the probability of having coresident children (with White children more likely to be married). Somewhat surprisingly, qualitative aspects of the parent-child relationship and of the parents' marriage do not alter the probability of adult children living with their parents, although the continuous marriage of parents does (White and Rogers, 1997). On balance, the factors that account for either delayed leaving of the parental home or a subsequent return demonstrate that the adult child's need for support is a key motivator for living with parents.

Although intergenerational exchanges occur when children return to their parents' homes, parents and children agree that parents give more support to their children than their children give to them (Mitchell, 2000). The modest contributions by children to housework and finances when living with parents are similar for sons and daughters, who both view living with their parents positively (Ward and Spitze, 1996). Although children who live with their parents tend to receive more support than they give, when compared with nonresident children, they exchange more support with their parents (White and Rogers, 1997). Among children aged 19 to 40 years, this difference does not affect the level of emotional closeness to parents. However, when compared with nonresident children, coresident children have lower evaluations of their mother's respect for them, their fairness, and of their trustworthiness. This suggests that sharing a home does create some strain between older parents and their adult children (White and Rogers, 1997). A significant problem in samples of coresident children is their substantial age range and the consequent range of experience among children. When age and circumstance are considered, older and employed children find living with their parents a more positive experience than their younger and unemployed counterparts (White and Rogers, 1997). Thus, it is unemployed, younger coresident children who tend to have less positive views of living with their parents.

Parents who have children living with them are generally satisfied with this arrangement (Aquilino and Supple, 1991; Mitchell, 2000). Mothers' and fathers' variations in satisfaction are accounted for by different aspects of their relationships with coresident children (Aquilino and Supple, 1991). Mothers are most satisfied when expressed hostility (shouting, heated arguments, etc.) is low and the time spent with children is frequent and enjoyable. Fathers' satisfaction also benefits from frequent pleasurable time together with children but is threatened by disagreements with children, although not by the hostility that may result from such disagreements. Thus, although mothers are unaffected by having disagreements with their children, fathers tolerate hostility more effectively. Nearly 75% of mothers and 50% of fathers list the companionship and friendship of their children as a key benefit of having a child living at home (Mitchell, 2000). Associated costs for mothers are lack of privacy and independence, the child's failure to help out with household tasks, and the child's lifestyle and dependence. For fathers, key detriments of coresidence are lack of privacy and independence, the child's personality or attitude, and the child's lifestyle. Thus, although most parents who have children living at home believe that the arrangement is working out very well, there can be tensions in the arrangement.

Summary

In summary, older parents and their adult children maintain active ties with one another. The meaning of parenthood shifts in old age as parents feel less responsibility for their children. However, a child's well-being continues to be a central source of concern to older parents and, should their children be in need, older parents provide extensive support. In turn, as their parents age, adult children typically provide more help, as needed. Most older persons maintain relatively independent life styles for most if not all of their lives. Consequently, the picture of the sandwiched generation, caught between the demands of two dependent generations, applies to a relatively small proportion of adult children.

Gender pervades intergenerational ties between older persons and their children, both qualitatively and in terms of support exchanges. This does not necessarily mean that one gender has better ties to parents than the other, rather that they are different. More recent work points out some of the advantages of sons' support to parents, correcting the bias implicit in the assumption that the type of support provided by daughters is best for parents.

As children age and have growing responsibilities to other family members or to work, parents are less central to their lives than they once were. At the same time, although children are a significant component of older parents' lives, they are not typically the hub of their lives, and having children does not guarantee their happiness. Nonetheless, older parents and their children are critical sources of support to one another, and should old age bring dependency, children serve as reliable sources of emotional and instrumental aid to their parents. If children are as important to the lives of older parents as they appear to be, what then of older persons who have never had children?

9

Childless Older Persons

When I was three, I decided not to have children. . . . As it turns out, my choice
not to have children has defined my adult life. It's been like hacking through
undergrowth while walking down a hardly used, perfectly paved way. . . . In fact,
on that path my choice not to be a mother became more of a *discovery* of a decision. . . . I had to make the choice from so far down in my own core that I was
never wholly aware of it. . . . For this is a decision you do not make once, but
many times. I would leave the idea of not having children behind, only to face it
again and again as I went on.

—Molly Peacock (1998:1, 9)

Molly Peacock's (1998) memoirs provide a vivid example of childlessness
as a transition rather than a discrete event. Indeed, even those who choose parenthood but cannot have children become childless over time (Matthews and
Martin Matthews, 1986). Among today's older persons, there are three primary routes to becoming childless: never marrying, involuntary childlessness
in a marriage, and voluntary childlessness in a marriage. For the vast majority
of older persons, remaining single meant not having children. Thus, these
individuals went through two transitions, one to singlehood (see Chapter 5)
and one to childlessness. For many involuntarily childless couples, considerable time and emotion are invested in becoming parents before becoming
childless. Once again, childlessness is likely to be experienced gradually, as

options for parenthood diminish, and one begins to view oneself as permanently rather than temporarily childless. In recent decades, involuntary childlessness has declined as health and treatments for sexually transmitted diseases have improved (Heaton, Jacobson, and Holland, 1999).

Perceptions of childlessness among men and women of childbearing ages involve dimensions of later life in two ways. First, considerations about having children among the childfree include the assumed pleasure of grandparenthood for their parents (Seccombe, 1991). Second, younger adults may anticipate the merits of having children to care for them in their own old age (Seccombe, 1991). These benefits of having children are offset by the perceived costs of parenting, including immediate financial costs as well as longer-term opportunity costs related to leisure time and the careers of one or both partners. The assumed long-term advantages of having children reflect strongly held cultural beliefs about filial responsibility and the pleasures of grandparenthood that have been highly resistant to changing social conditions.

However, although childless persons may still believe that they are negatively stereotyped by their family and friends (Somers, 1993), the longstanding stigma associated with being childless (Miall, 1986) has softened somewhat. This is evident in the fact that choosing to be childless has increased, with a persistently greater preference for this status among Whites than Blacks (Heaton et al.,1999). As well, current terms to describe childlessness, most notably *childfree* and *childless by choice,* were introduced to capture the more positive side of being without children. Cohabitation rather than marriage may increase the number of couples who do not have children, as marriage is a much stronger predisposing factor to having children than is cohabitation. A lower-key view of becoming a parent is also suggested by the decreasing stability of decisions about whether to have children, with some of childbearing age shifting from a preference for childlessness to either wanting or having children and others drifting into childlessness through perpetual delay (Heaton et al., 1999). Nonetheless, being childless remains an atypical experience for most couples and can no longer be assumed among the single (see Chapter 2). Given the focus of our discussion on older persons, remember that the pressure on married persons of that generation to have children was very strong and the stigma of not doing so very high when they were young adults.

Despite the pronatalist cultural pressures experienced by older persons, other factors operating at the time when they were younger meant significant cohort differences among them in levels of childlessness. There was a high rate of remaining childless (25%) among women born in 1910, who were of childbearing age during the Depression (Heaton et al., 1999). Some years later, rates of childlessness were unusually low (10% for women born in 1935) among women bearing babies during the Baby Boom. Thus, despite wide variations in the availability of effective birth control, social and economic conditions have had a profound effect on the fertility behavior of prospective parents. Among the current elderly, there is also considerable age variation in the reasons for being childless. For example, the relatively small percentage of persons who remained childless while the baby boom was born suggests that childlessness was mainly involuntary for this cohort.

Reasons for Being Childless

Typically, childlessness is assumed to be involuntary, primarily due to infertility, or voluntary, in which case an individual or couple has chosen not to have children. In fact, however, when asked, older childless persons give a much broader range of reasons for being childless, and their assessments of whether their reasons constitute a choice or circumstance does not always fit the conventional dichotomy of voluntary versus involuntary childlessness (Connidis and McMullin, 1996). Among childless persons aged 55 years or more, 28% define themselves as childless by choice and 72% as childless by circumstance. Only those who give physiological reasons for childlessness, the most common response among the ever married, uniformly define themselves as childless by circumstance.

About 70% of single persons give being single as their reason for not having children; one quarter of these individuals consider childlessness to be a choice (Connidis and McMullin, 1996). The other single childless persons who see their situation as a choice say that they have no children due to fate, altruism (e.g., not wanting to have children in an overcrowded world), and self-actualization (e.g., wanting to be free to travel). For the ever married who define being childless as a choice, key reasons for not having children are age, their spouse's preferences, and altruism or practical concerns.

Among those who consider being childless a matter of circumstance, single persons give being single and altruism as the key reasons for being childless; ever-married persons focus on physiological problems, age, and fate as their reasons (Connidis and McMullin, 1996). Widowed women are more likely than all other combinations of gender and marital status to consider childlessness an outcome of circumstances. Conversely, single and divorced women and single and widowed men are most likely to see being childless as a choice.

The Impact of Being Childless on
Social Activity and Support in Later Life

Married childless persons of younger and older ages tend to have particularly strong marital ties and rely extensively on one another rather than on an extended network of family and friends (Ishii-Kuntz and Seccombe, 1989; Somers, 1993; on childless men, Connidis and Davies, 1990). By contrast, single childless persons tend to be resourceful in negotiating an effective social support network over the years (Johnson and Catalano, 1981). Among older, unmarried, childless Canadians, there are no marital status differences in the likelihood of having support available if needed or in giving and receiving support (Wu and Pollard, 1998). The relative isolation and mutual dependence of some older, childless, married couples may be due to the greater closeness that develops among couples who share the stigma of being childless (Miall, 1986). Older single persons, on the other hand, would not face such stigma because children were equated with marriage.

Those with children have more friends and family, a higher number of family visits, and receive more help and support than the childless (Chapman, 1989; Rempel, 1985). Yet older parents and childless persons are equally likely to report having someone to confide in and to provide assistance, financial aid, emotional support, and companionship (Connidis and McMullin, 1994). The one difference by parental status is that childless women aged 55 and over are less likely than mothers to have someone who makes them feel needed and appreciated. Of older, unmarried, childless Canadians, 90% have support available to them from family, friends, or, most commonly, family and friends (Wu and Pollard, 1998). An important exception to these trends are the oldest old, those childless persons aged 85 and over (Johnson and Barer, 1995). They are less likely to have someone to take care of them when needed, although they remain creative in negotiating alternative ties in the absence of children. However, research generally suggests that differences in volume of support and number of supporters should not be treated as indicators of unmet need or discontent among childless persons.

Older, childless persons and parents share equal levels of involvement in going to public places and traveling, but the childless go on outings more often than do parents (Connidis and McMullin 1992). Childless persons are also more likely to find companionship with their friends and other relatives than are parents, indicating that childless persons negotiate social participation networks that enhance taking part in activities outside the home. However, there appear to be some gender differences, with friends composing a larger complement of childless women's confidant and companion networks and siblings more dominant in their confidant network than is true for either childless men or mothers (Connidis and Davies, 1990). The companion networks of childless men rely more heavily on friends, whereas their confidant network favors other relatives to a greater extent than the networks of fathers. As well, sibling pairs in which at least one sibling is childless talk on the phone and discuss important matters more often than do parents (Connidis, 1989a).

The greater likelihood of the childless living alone (re: widows, see Bess, 1999) has been used as evidence of their greater isolation (Bachrach, 1980). However, the greater economic resources of the childless (Rempel, 1985) may be as important in explaining their higher rates of independent living. As well, a key predictor of living alone later in life among widows is having done so earlier in life (Bess, 1999). Living alone as a younger adult due either to later age at marriage or to a spouse's temporary absence may have been a more common experience among childless widows than among widowed mothers.

The Impact of Being Childless on Quality of Life in Older Age

When asked about whether there are advantages or disadvantages to being childless, nearly three quarters of 267 older childless men and women said that there are advantages, whereas two thirds say that there are disadvantages (Connidis and McMullin, 1999). Forty-five percent report both advantages and disadvantages, 25% say that there are only advantages, and 20% see only disadvantages to being childless. These responses suggest a fairly balanced view of being childless that might be mirrored if similar questions were asked of parents about the merits of having children.

Although there are no variations in the probability of seeing disadvantages to childlessness, widowed, childless persons are less likely than married individuals to report advantages to being childless (Connidis and McMullin,

1999). Perhaps, the fact that the single and divorced typically spent more of their younger lives alone than did the widowed created a better opportunity for them to negotiate other ties, whereas the widowed were investing in their marriages. The other significant difference is the higher odds of the childless by choice (86%) reporting advantages to being without children when compared with those who are childless by circumstance (67%).

What are the perceived advantages and disadvantages of childlessness in later life? The top three advantages are fewer worries and problems, financial wealth, and greater freedom. The top-rated disadvantages are lack of companionship, being alone, and loneliness; a feeling of a missed experience or incompleteness; and lack of support and care (Connidis and McMullin, 1999; for similar results re: women, see Alexander, Rubinstein, Goodman, and Luborsky, 1992). The perception of financial advantage is supported by actual experience among those who hold this view; they are indeed better off than those who do not. However, the actual situations of those who report greater loneliness, incompleteness, and inadequate support as costs of being childfree do not differ from those who do not. They are no more lonely or less satisfied with what they have done in life, and they are as likely to have support available to them. The contrast between perceptions and actual experience, combined with the lack of variation in who reports disadvantages, "suggests that the costs of childlessness are less related to personal experience and more a function of learning widely-held cultural views supporting parenthood and the negative side of being childless" (Connidis and McMullin, 1999:462). For today's older women in particular, regrets about being childless occur in the context of failing to conform to strongly held expectations that women should have children (Alexander et al., 1992).

Despite objective differences in the number of family and friends and amount of help received, those with and without children in old age share similar levels of satisfaction and loneliness (McMullin and Marshall, 1996; Rempel, 1985). However, whereas childlessness itself is not directly linked to loneliness and depression, when marital and parental status are combined, divorced parents are more lonely than divorced, childless persons, and divorced mothers are more depressed than women who are divorced and childless (Koropeckyj-Cox, 1998). Those who are married with children are less lonely and depressed than parents and childless persons who are widowed or divorced. But married parents are no better off than either married or never-married, childless persons. Once again, greater opportunity to cultivate other relationships such as that enjoyed by single persons or by divorced childless persons, when compared with divorced parents, may explain why childlessness does not carry the same costs in loneliness and depression for these groups.

Last, although research shows no overall differences in well-being between parents and children, there may be variations among parents and among the childless. We have already seen that having children only improves subjective well-being when ties between parents and children are close. In parallel fashion, when compared with parents who have close ties with their children, those who are childless by choice are just as happy and satisfied with life (Connidis and McMullin, 1993). However, those who are childless by circumstance are less satisfied with life than are close parents, childless men are less happy than close fathers, and childless women are more depressed than close mothers. Clearly, it is not necessary to have children to have a satisfying old age. But for those who wanted to have children and could not, a sense of regret about being childless continues into later life and lowers subjective well-being. In short, neither having children nor remaining childless guarantees happiness in later life.

This chapter has focused on the experience of being childless among older persons, considering both the subjective and objective consequences of childlessness in later life. Unfortunately, we know very little about the intergenerational ties of childless persons. Yet those who do not have children engage in active relationships with their older parents and potentially with their aunts, uncles, and younger generations of nieces and nephews. Research on siblings (see Chapters 12 and 13) suggests that childless older persons are quite involved with the children of their siblings. However, childless persons are likely to be subject to the mediating role of their siblings in the cultivation of ties with nieces and nephews, much as grandparents must depend on their children to foster good ties with their grandchildren. Consider this possibility as we explore grandparent-grandchild ties in the next chapter.

10

Grandparents and Grandchildren

Research on the grandparent-grandchild tie has followed a route similar to that of parent-child relationships, with its increased emphasis on caregiving. This is especially true regarding grandparenthood in African American families (Hunter, 1997) because the long-overdue attention to Black families, in general, dovetailed with a shift in focus to caregiving. The ironic twist is that, whereas studies regarding parent-child exchanges pay disproportionate attention to the help provided *to* older parents, work on grandparent-grandchild exchanges concerns primarily the help provided *by* grandparents. Information about the availability of grandparents and contact between them and their grandchildren is now presented. We then explore the nature of grandparent-grandchild ties, the qualitative aspects of this relationship, and support exchanges. The impact of divorce and remarriage on grandparent-grandchild ties is addressed in Chapter 11.

Availability of and Contact With Grandparents

As we saw in Chapter 2, about 80% of older persons are grandparents. The likelihood of having grandparents increased dramatically over the 20th century. Estimates are that fewer than 1 in 4 children in 1900 had four grandparents at birth; by age 30, only 1 in 5 had any surviving grandparents (Uhlenberg, 1996). By the century's end, 2 in 3 children began life with four grandparents (and often more, when one includes stepgrandparents), and by age 30, 3 in 4 still had at least one grandparent. Over time, having grandmothers rather than

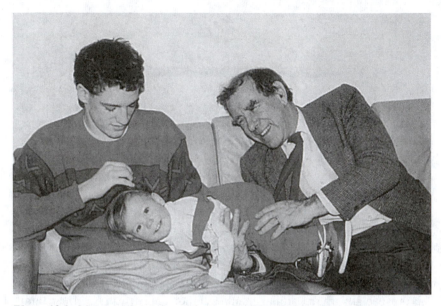

Photo 10.1. Most grandparents acquire grandchildren before they reach old age.

grandfathers has become even more likely, as women's life expectancy has increased more dramatically than men's (Uhlenberg, 1996). In 2000, two thirds of those aged 30 still had a grandmother, but just over one quarter had a grandfather. In the same year, of 40-year-old adults, 1 of 5 had a living grandparent. Although significant differences in life expectancy by race continue, the negative impact of mortality on the availability of grandparents is offset somewhat by younger ages of childbearing among non-Whites (Szinovacz, 1998).

One thing that has remained quite constant over the past 100 years is the age at which adults become grandparents; the transition to grandparenthood remains a phenomenon of middle, not old, age (Szinovacz, 1998). About half of all grandparents are under the age of 60 (Aldous, 1995). Thus, for the majority, grandparenthood is not new in old age (see Photo 10.1). In turn, the grandchildren of later-life grandparents are typically teenagers or young adults, a factor that has important implications for the type of relationship that is possible between grandparents and their grandchildren. Similarly, the age at which one becomes a grandparent influences the nature of grandparenting. Those who become grandparents at younger ages are more likely to be engaged in other activities, such as child-rearing and paid work; those who are relatively old for this transition tend not to engage in more demanding forms of support, such as looking after their grandchildren (Aldous, 1995).

Grandparents have been subject to the same social changes as all age groups. Most notable among them in terms of grandparent-grandchild relations are increased labor force participation among women and increased rates of divorce at all ages. Of married persons with adult children over the age of 18, 40% have a stepgrandparent in the family, and this is more likely to be a consequence of divorce and remarriage in the grandparent than the parent generation (Szinovacz, 1998). At the same time, two countertrends potentially increase the time that grandparents have to invest in their grandchildren. Retirement is now typical for all workers and is occurring at younger ages, and grandparenting and parenting tend not to be overlapping responsibilities (Szinovacz, 1998).

Regular contact with at least one grandchild is the norm, with over 80% of grandparents aged 50 or more seeing an adult grandchild in the past month (AARP, 2000). Among grandparents who are not caregivers to their grandchildren, nearly half (44%) see a grandchild once a week. Telephone contact is also common. Geographic distance is the key determinant of contact with grandchildren; increased distance diminishes both personal and phone contact (Aldous, 1995; Hodgson, 1995; Uhlenberg and Hammill, 1998). Baby boom granddaughters are in greater contact with their grandmothers than with their grandfathers (Mills, 1999), and grandmothers report greater contact and proximity with their grandchildren than do grandfathers (Silverstein and Long, 1998).

Among grandparents whose grandchildren still live with their parents, a number of factors influence the amount of contact with sets of grandchildren, a set being all grandchildren in one nuclear family (Uhlenberg and Hammill, 1998). Grandparents who have better relationships with their children, grandmothers, and maternal grandparents all enjoy more contact with their grandchildren than do their counterparts. Grandparents with more grandchild sets (i.e., those who have more children who have children) see any one family of grandchildren less often but have more overall contact with grandchildren than those with fewer grandchild sets. Last, married grandparents see their grandchildren most often, followed, in order, by widowed, remarried, and divorced grandparents. These marital-status differences are greater for grandfathers than for grandmothers, who are more likely to sustain contact whatever their marital status.

The grandchild's age is also related to contact frequency. Adult grandchildren see less of their grandparents than do younger grandchildren and less than they did when they were younger, often due to greater geographic distance between them (Cherlin and Furstenberg Jr., 1986; Mills, 1999; Silverstein and Long, 1998). However, a majority of grandchildren aged 18 or more have contact with their grandparents several times a month or more by phone, letter, or in person, with greater contact among those who feel emotionally closer to their grandparents (Hodgson, 1995). The growing popularity of E-mail is likely to enhance communication with all family members but perhaps especially between grandparents and grandchildren, given the greater appeal of the computer than letter writing to younger persons. Several age-related transitions affect grandparent-grandchild contact once grandchildren have grown up. Landing a job decreases contact with grandparents, whereas getting married and divorced both mean more contact with grandparents (Mills, 1999). In general, contact decreases over time, not because of emotional detachment but because grandchildren have other commitments, some of which lead them to live farther away (Silverstein and Long, 1998). Thus, despite sentimental attachments between them, once grandparents are very old (85 and over), grandchildren are not key sources of instrumental support (Johnson and Barer, 1997).

The Nature of
Grandparent-Grandchild Relations

As is true of all relationships, those between grandparents and grandchildren require negotiating an acceptable balance between noninterference and meeting the obligations of kinship (Aldous, 1995). When compared with ties between parents and children, however, the expressed obligation to provide support to either grandparents or grandchildren is lower (Rossi and Rossi, 1990). This suggests greater freedom in the parameters of the grandparent-grandchild relationship, with both parties more able to make choices about how involved they will be with one another. One consequence is considerable flexibility in the expectations of being a grandparent. At the same time, greater flexibility often means greater ambiguity about what is expected. Being a grandmother is regulated largely by uniform conceptions of the proscriptive norms (what one is not supposed to do) associated with grandparenting because the prescriptions of the role are less explicit (Johnson, 1983). More ambiguity is experienced by grandmothers who live farther away and by paternal rather than maternal grandmothers (Fischer, 1983).

Age of Grandchildren and Parents as Mediators

Three stages of the grandparent career correspond to the ages of grandchildren, but because most grandparents have several grandchildren, these stages often coincide (Cherlin and Furstenberg Jr., 1986). The first stage spans the time from birth to the teenage years, when grandparents are most involved, often babysitting and helping children in activities such as homework. In the second stage, teenagers withdraw somewhat from their grandparents. In turn, grandparents are less able to assist their grandchildren in their current activities, although adolescent grandchildren may perform errands for their grandparents. Last, grandchildren reach adulthood and may have children of their own. The difference that age of grandchildren makes to grandparenting is addressed in the comments of a 67-year-old grandmother in one of my studies:

> My two older granddaughters who live near here are 16 and 18. They have their own little worlds now. You don't expect to see as much of them. I miss them and I would love it if they would just drop in, you know. They do occasionally, but I know what it is to be young. I know that . . . they have their own schedules and they are working and going to school . . . and their social lives. But I do enjoy particularly the ones that are too young to be out on their own like that. And I think that they enjoy us. They love to come to Grandma's, and I like to keep it that way.

Age of grandchildren is also related to the extent of involvement of the middle generation, that is, their parents, in the negotiation of grandparent-grandchild ties. Becoming a grandparent is a contingent transition because having grandchildren is typically in the hands of one's children (Troll, 1985). This sets the stage for the central role of children as mediators in the relationship between grandparents and grandchildren, making the grandparent-grandchild link an indirect one. The extent to which parents are the linchpin in grandparent-grandchild interactions varies by the age of grandchildren (Sprey and Matthews, 1982). Virtually all interaction between young grandchildren and their grandparents is dependent on the parents. However, when grandchildren are pre- and early adolescents, they are less passive and may express to their parents a desire to see or not see their grandparents. In late adolescence and adulthood, grandchildren and grandparents often interact independently, and grandparents may play the role of mediators between their children and grandchildren.

Daughters are likely to be more influential mediators than sons when children are young, setting the stage early for more involvement with maternal than paternal grandparents. Mothers of young children tend to feel far greater affinity with their mothers than their mothers-in-law (Fischer, 1986). Consequently, the advice and involvement of their own mothers are welcomed, whereas that of their mothers-in-law are often resented. This foundation may limit the extent of subsequent independent interaction of older grandchildren with their paternal grandparents when compared with maternal grandparents. We have already seen the impact of the middle generation on contact between grandparents and grandchildren, and we shall consider it further in relation to support exchanges and qualitative dimensions of this relationship.

Dimensions of Grandparenting

Grandparents want to influence their grandchildren and are particularly committed to encouraging high morals and integrity, ambition, a commitment to success, and religious beliefs (AARP, 2000). The extent to which grandparents are indeed there in times of need has been the basis for labeling grandparents the family watchdogs (Troll, 1983) and the safety valve of the modern family (Hagestad, 1985). There are three components to being a grandparent: the meaning older people attach to being grandparents, the behaviors associated with grandparenting, and the degree of satisfaction derived from performing the role of grandparent (Kivnick, 1985). For some grandparents, particularly grandfathers (Thomas, 1995), the sense of immortality provided by grandchildren invests the relationship with special meaning. For others, the opportunity for reliving earlier parts of one's life is a valued component of grandparenting (Kivnick, 1985).

The link to an older person's younger years that is evoked by grandparenting is evident in the comments of a 65-year-old woman in my community study:

> The babe (grandson) was crying the second night he was home, and I got out of bed and tottled in, and my son is up looking after the babe. I said, "Here, give him to me." So I took him to a rocking chair, and I said, "This makes me think of my Grandma." Whenever we were upset or there was something that

we didn't like, or we were unhappy, Grandma used to take us and she would
sit one on here, one on one arm and one on the other arm or knee and just rock.
And she would sing.

As this grandmother's account suggests, experiences as a grandchild sometimes influence the ways in which grandparents are involved with their grandchildren. Grandparents who knew their own grandparents by spending time
with them and learning about them through family stories, reunions, and pho-
tographs are more active in the lives of their grandchildren as mentors, companions, providers of instrumental help, and people to talk to about problems
and future plans (King and Elder, 1997). It is not surprising that these grandparents feel they know their grandchildren better, even though their overall
contact and closeness is no greater.

Grandparenting styles have been described in different ways, based primarily on studies of White families. The *companionate style,* in which a
grandparent feels close to his or her grandchild(ren) without taking on a parental role, is most common (Cherlin and Furstenberg Jr., 1986). Half of a
national sample of grandparents were often a companion or friend to their
grandchild(ren), and about one third gave advice, talked about family history
and the parent's life as a child, and served as a confidant (AARP, 2000). This
parallels what others have termed an *apportioned style.* According to college-
aged grandchildren, such grandparents participate in their lives and development, while reserving the right to indulge them (Roberto and Stroes, 1995).
According to the middle generation of parents, the apportioned style is most
common among both maternal and paternal grandmothers (Henry, Ceglian,
and Matthews, 1992). The greater independence and financial security of
older people today fosters a companionate style of grandparenting, because
occupying a similar social status encourages ties that are informal, affection-
ate, and warm (Cherlin and Furstenberg Jr., 1986).

The next most prevalent pattern is the remote grandparent, who is less
involved (Roberto and Stroes, 1995), often because of geographic distance
from grandchildren (Cherlin and Furstenberg Jr., 1986). Other grandparents
have what is termed an *involved style;* they are in close geographic proximity
and often assume parentlike responsibilities, usually in response to a family
crisis, such as the separation or divorce of a child. From the point of view of
grandchildren, another style is the *individualized* grandparent who, although
emotionally closer than the remote grandparent, does not contribute much to
the lives of grandchildren (Roberto and Stroes, 1995).

In contrast, the predominant style of grandparenting in Black families is described as *authoritative* or influential and involves extensive support, sometimes to the point of assuming parental responsibilities (Hunter, 1997), particularly by grandmothers (Burton, 1992; Kivett, 1993). Some suggest that the greater involvement of grandmothers in Black families is best viewed as a family strategy in which both individuals and families are taking action within the context of the possibilities and constraints of their lives (Hunter, 1997). This view fosters recognition of both complementary and competing needs among individual family members and between individuals and the family as a unit. When combined with a life course view, the connections across generations are highlighted.

Gender also shapes grandparenting. Grandmothers and grandfathers are as likely to report aiding and being interested in grandchildren, but grandmothers emphasize closeness, warmth, and fun in their relationships with grandchildren (Russell, 1986). Grandfathers place more emphasis on their role as adviser, especially grandfathers on the paternal side. As well, grandfathers tend to focus on grandsons and the world of work, money, and social issues, whereas grandmothers do not differentiate between granddaughters and grandsons and focus on interpersonal and family issues (Hagestad, cited in Troll, 1983). These differences reflect the more instrumental approach of grandfathers compared to the more expressive approach of grandmothers (Hagestad, 1985).

Grandsons and granddaughters of college age engage more frequently in more activities with grandmothers than with grandfathers, whether paternal or maternal (Roberto and Stroes, 1995). These activities include short visits for conversation, family gatherings, talking about things that matter to them, and helping with chores. Grandmothers are also seen as having had a greater impact on their values as they grew up, as reflected in adulthood by greater mutual understanding, communication, and shared views of life.

Among the activities of grandmothers, babysitting, home recreation, and drop-in visits predominate (Gladstone, 1988). Although grandmothers would like to engage more often in other activities, they are reluctant to do so for fear of appearing meddlesome or intrusive. To avoid this perception, they concentrate on encounters that their children or grandchildren initiate rather than activities that they initiate (Robertson, 1977). There is some evidence of a preference among grandmothers for a fun-loving style, with the more domestic and nurturant traditional grandmother role seen as out of step with today's grandchildren (Johnson, 1983). Yet grandmothers in African American families are important sources of parental support for both mothers and fathers (Hunter, 1997). About a third of Black mothers and fathers turn to their mothers for parenting advice, almost half of mothers and over a third of fathers turn to them for child care and advice, and the remainder rely on their mothers for child care only. Being employed increases such support for fathers but not for mothers, whereas family characteristics, such as closeness and the number of surviving generations, are influential among mothers but not fathers. Thus, in the usual course of parenting, grandmothers are an important resource to their children in Black families.

Relying on a grandparent as the primary source of child care while at work is most common among Black mothers, followed by Hispanic and then White mothers (Ries and Stone, 1992). These differences reflect variations in cultural preferences, the immediate needs of working mothers, and the availability of relatives to provide care. For example, among Mexican and Black American mothers, one reason for turning to kin for child care is having unemployed family members, including grandmothers, who are both available and in need of the reciprocal arrangement of pay for child care (Uttal, 1999).

Qualitative Aspects of the Grandparent-Grandchild Relationship

If you can keep in touch with young people, it will rub off on you. I get a big kick. My grandchildren will come down tonight—three of them. Now, I will change and I will be laughing. And they are so natural and they are cheerful. And natural rubs off on you, and I think it keeps you young. But some people don't have grandchildren, and I say there is a certain amount of luck in life.

—66-year-old grandfather

I have three grandchildren, and my goodness me, there is no generation gap there at all.... I say they either make me feel old or they make me feel young. But I will say this, they certainly do keep the wheels lubricated—mentally and physically.

—76-year-old grandmother

Most grandparents are very satisfied with grandparenting and describe their relationships with their grandchildren as warm and close (Russell, 1986). The contentment of grandparents is mirrored by adult grandchildren's reports of very good relationships with their grandparents, characterized by closeness and feeling loved and appreciated (King and Elder, 1997). The general dissociation of today's grandparents from family authority enhances closeness between grandparents and grandchildren (Cherlin and Furstenberg, Jr., 1986).

The most pleasurable aspects of grandparenting include the company and affection of grandchildren, watching grandchildren acquire new skills and grow up, the feeling of pride about grandchildren, the meaning grandchildren give to life, and doing things with and for grandchildren (Russell, 1986). More involved grandparents are more satisfied with the amount of contact, emotional closeness, and conversations about important matters that they have with their grandchildren than are less involved grandparents (Cherlin and Furstenberg Jr., 1986). Among both Black and White grandparents, more time spent interacting with grandchildren increases the sense of being effective grandparents (Strom, Collinsworth, Strom, and Griswold, 1995). At the same time, grandchildren who share more time with their grandparents consider their grandparents better teachers and perceive them to be more satisfied with grandparenting.

Grandmothers tend to find their relationships with grandchildren more satisfying than do grandfathers (Silverstein and Long, 1998; Thomas, 1995) and are more involved with both grandsons and granddaughters (Cherlin and Furstenberg Jr., 1986; Hagestad, 1985). This helps account for the fact that adult grandchildren more often consider a grandmother their emotionally closest grandparent, even when they both grandmothers and grandfathers (Hodgson, 1995; Kennedy and Kennedy, 1993). The gendered nature of family ties is also reflected in greater closeness to maternal than paternal grandparents and to maternal than paternal grandmothers in particular (Hodgson, 1995). The ongoing advantage of maternal over paternal grandparents in having close relations with their grandchildren stems directly from the closer ties of mothers than fathers to their parents (Chan and Elder, 2000). Grandparents, in turn, are generally closer to their granddaughters than grandsons (Silverstein and Long, 1998).

The quality of grandparent-grandchild ties as reported by grandparents is strongly linked to the quality of the relationship between grandparents and their children (King and Elder, 1997). Similarly, older grandchildren who view the relationship between their parents and grandparents as positive and supportive also have more positive bonds with their grandparents (Hodgson, 1995; King and Elder, 1995). Furthermore, the involvement of mothers in activities with their adult children and warm relations between fathers and their adult children improve the quality of grandparent-grandchild ties (King and Elder, 1995). These findings attest to the significance of the middle generation's (particularly mother's) influence on relations between the oldest and youngest generations (Matthews and Sprey, 1985). Do grandparent-grandchild relations have a comparable impact on the middle generation?

Paternal grandfathers and maternal and paternal grandmothers all report greater closeness and more time together with their children following the arrival of grandchildren (Russell, 1986). Observations made by a 67-year-old woman in my community study suggest that the grandparent-grandchild bond can affect the behavior and views of the middle generation:

> When I was a nurse, I had a patient, and her grandson wanted to take her for a drive. She was recuperating, and they used to keep them in the hospital much longer then, but she was allowed to go out for a drive. The boy's mother, who was the patient's daughter, said, "We don't have time today, son," and he said, "Mum, I will have [more] time for you when you are older than you have for Grandma." Now, she [grandmother] went for the ride.

The arrival of grandchildren has different effects on parent-child relations, depending on gender. The closeness of ties between fathers and sons and between mothers and daughters seems to be unaffected by the arrival of grandchildren, and the transition to parenthood itself does not alter the closeness of parent-child relationships (Kaufman and Uhlenberg, 1998). However, additional children (that is, beyond the first child) improve mother-son relationships but weaken the father-daughter bond. Similarly, the transition to parenthood among grandchildren tends to draw grandchildren closer to grandmothers but decreases closeness to grandfathers (Mills, 1999). Thus, across the parent and grandparent generations, the arrival of children tends to have more positive consequences for women than for men.

What about patterns of closeness between grandparents and grandchildren over time? Grandparents tend to report closer ties to their grandchildren than grandchildren report to their grandparents. Although levels of closeness are generally high, grandparents' affections for their grandchildren follow a curvilinear pattern over a period of 23 years (Silverstein and Long, 1998). Closeness, mutual understanding, communication, and compatibility gradually decline from the ages of roughly 55 to 70 years and then increase modestly when grandparents are in their 70s and 80s. Yet among grandchildren aged 18 to 51 years, many report becoming closer to their grandparents over the years (Hodgson, 1995). Grandsons and granddaughters share the view that growing up heightened their ability to appreciate their grandparents. For example, one 24-year-old grandson explains his closer feelings toward his grandfather this way: "Now that I'm not a kid, I'm taking the time to really get to know him" (Hodgson, 1995:166). An exception to this trend occurs among grandchildren who have become a part of American culture but whose grandparents have not (Silverstein and Chen, 1999). Unlike their grandparents, acculturated Mexican American grandchildren report declines in affection for their grandparents over time but their grandparents do not.

Longitudinal work suggests that the impact of age on grandchildren's feelings about their grandparents also varies by gender of the grandparent (Mills,1999). Thus, as grandchildren age, they grow less close to their grandfathers but closer to their grandmothers. A personal crisis, more often on behalf of the grandparent, is sometimes the catalyst for greater closeness. One granddaughter reflects on her grandmother's support: "When my husband died, she really helped me through it, and now we're very close" (Hodgson, 1995:166). The combination of these results suggests that the feelings of grandparents, especially grandmothers, and grandchildren for one another become more similar over time.

Grandparents Caring for Grandchildren

More than 20 years ago, higher rates of divorce, single parenthood, and labor force participation among women were the basis for predicting a less symbolic and more functional role for middle-class grandparents as they met the changed needs of their children and grandchildren (Clavan, 1978). Indeed, this prediction has come true, as increasing numbers of older persons have taken on intensive support for their grandchildren, with the odds of caring for grandchildren for a minimum of 6 months now over 1 in 10 (Fuller-Thomson, Minkler, and Driver, 1997). This shift mimics long-established patterns in disadvantaged families, whose need for family support has always been greater. Caring for grandchildren can be a long-term commitment; over half of caregiving grandparents have looked after their grandchild(ren) for 3 or more years, and 1 in 5 have looked after a grandchild for 10 years or more (Fuller-Thomson et al., 1997).

Grandmothers who provide part-time care for their grandchildren are usually providing child care for working mothers (Bowers and Myers, 1999). They are more likely to be in the labor force themselves and to be satisfied with grandparenting than are grandmothers who are providing help to their grandchildren full time or not at all. These grandmothers tend to have excellent relationships with their grandchildren, would be willing to care for their grandchildren again if asked, and if married, report no ill effects on their relationships with their spouses (Bowers and Myers, 1999). Grandmothers who serve as child care providers for working daughters generally have offered to do so to help their child and to fulfill their own needs (Jendrek, 1994). However, growing numbers of grandparents are intensively involved in caring for their grandchildren. The increase in coresidence is one indicator of such commitment.

In the United States, 75% of families that include grandparents and grandchildren are maintained by a grandparent (Bryson and Casper, 1999). Similarly, in Canada, 55% of three-generation families maintained by one person are maintained by a grandparent (Che-Alford and Hamm, 1999). As well, in 54% of families with multiple maintainers, a grandparent contributes to household expenses. In 1997, almost 6% of American children up to the age of 18 lived in their grandparent(s)' home (Bowers and Myers, 1999; Bryson and Casper, 1999). In other words, almost four million grandchildren were living in homes maintained by their grandparent(s). Neither parent is present in over a third of these families, leaving the care of grandchildren primarily in the hands of their grandparent(s) (Bryson and Casper, 1999). Indeed, although still relatively rare, grandchildren living with grandparents without a parent in the household, often called "skipped generation" families, is the most rapidly growing coresidence arrangement.

Although there are more White children living in this arrangement, given population distribution by race and ethnicity, the odds of this situation are highest among African American children, followed by Hispanic and then White children (Minkler, 1999). Half of grandparent-maintained families include both grandparents, 43% have a grandmother only, and 6% have a grandfather only (Bryson and Casper, 1999). Grandchildren in families headed by their grandparent(s) are more likely to be poor, without health insurance, and to be in families receiving public assistance. The probability of poverty is highest in grandmother-maintained households, and such families most often have at least two generations of women (the grandmother and mother). Overall, the odds of becoming a caregiving grandparent are highest among women, African Americans, and grandparents whose children have died (Fuller-Thomson et al., 1997; Landry-Meyer, 1999). Grandmothers who are either the sole parental figure or share parenting with their spouse are most involved in caring for their grandchildren (Pearson, Hunter, Cook, Ialongo, and Kellam, 1997). Thus, the construction of social and family life by gender and race is reflected in grandparent-grandchild coresidence patterns.

The traumatic situations that typically precipitate caring for grandchildren represent a very challenging situation from the start. Grandparents who become parentlike figures to their grandchildren usually do so in response to their children's circumstances, including alcohol or drug abuse; divorce; emotional, mental, and physical health problems; the neglect or abuse of children; teen pregnancy; and imprisonment (Bowers and Myers, 1999; Fuller-Thomson et al., 1997; Hayslip, Shore, Henderson, and Lambert, 1998; Jendrek, 1994; Minkler, 1999; Pruchno, 1999; Sands and Goldberg-Glen, 2000). Less often, grandparents take over the care of their grandchildren following the death of their child, a factor of growing significance in the wake of the AIDS epidemic, especially among grandmothers of color (Minkler, 1999). As these reasons indicate, taking on full-time parental responsibilities for grandchildren is rarely a choice. Rather, it is a response to the needs of their grandchildren and children.

The factors associated with becoming a caregiving grandparent are reflected in the strategies and concerns of grandparents. Among Latino grandparents, multigenerational families typically include an adult child, but that child is most often the grandchild's aunt, not mother, and she provides considerable assistance with child care (Burnette, 1999). Unlike African American families, language may create a barrier to good grandparent-grandchild relations as Latino grandchildren become more assimilated, especially regarding language. The association of caregiving with poverty creates additional concerns among grandparents about the safety of their neighborhoods for their grandchildren, with particular worry about drugs in the streets (Burnette, 1999; Burton, 1992). A 67-year-old grandfather looking after his 4-year-old grandson describes the routine that he has developed to manage this concern:

> I make sure that I get all my business done before the dope dealers get busy around 4 in the afternoon. I let my grandson play outside till about noon. I get him in quick just in case there is some people on dope outside who got an early start. (Burton, 1992:748)

Grandparents worry also about whether they will stay healthy (Landry-Meyer, 1999) and live long enough to see their grandchildren into adulthood: "Every night I pray to God for ten more years of life. By then they [grandchildren] will be socialized to know what is good and bad. . . . I only hope I can see them through these difficult years" (Burnette, 1999:55). At the same time, looking ahead to the end of one's life often includes the resigned assumption that caring for younger generations will be a lifelong endeavor, as this 82-year-old great-grandmother observes:

> I had my great-grandbaby since she was 2 years old. Now she is 15. Her momma and daddy are still messing with that stuff [drugs]. That's a long time to have somebody's child. I guess she will be with me till I die. (Burton, 1992: 749)

Consequences of Caring

Grandmothers who look after their grandchildren full time tend to have good to excellent relationships with them, and some grow closer over time (Bowers and Myers, 1999). Despite this, when compared with grandmothers who provide no care or do so on a part-time basis, these grandmothers are much more likely to report behavior problems by their grandchildren. Grandparents report quite high rates of argumentative or aggressive behavior, discipline problems, psychological and medical problems, learning disabilities, and poor school performance among the grandchildren in their care (Pruchno, 1999; Sands and Goldberg-Glen, 2000). Such problems, in turn, increase burden and stress (Bowers and Myers, 1999; Sands and Goldberg-Glen, 2000), paralleling the experience of parents who care for adult children with a disability or mental illness (see Chapter 8). Thus, care in general, and care of grandchildren with various problems in particular, diminishes the positive sentiments and increases the stress of being a grandparent (Hayslip et al., 1998; Sands and Goldberg-Glen, 2000).

There are substantial health costs to caring for a grandchild. Grandparents of various backgrounds who look after grandchildren report poorer health, have a higher probability of depression, and more chronic health problems than those who do not (Minkler, 1999; Strawbridge et al., 1997). Low-income grandmothers who care for grandchildren full-time experience greater burden than their more affluent peers (Bowers and Myers, 1999). On the other hand, the greater likelihood that African American grandparents, especially grandmothers, will serve as parent surrogates makes them more likely to have a personal history of multigenerational living arrangements and to have peers who are also raising grandchildren (Pruchno, 1999). This helps account for the fact that Black grandparents experience less burden than White grandparents from caring for their grandchildren. Nonetheless, caregiving exacts an especially high toll among grandparents because they are much more likely than either caregiving spouses or adult children to have a history of stressful life events precede their experience of caring for grandchildren (Strawbridge et al., 1997).

Grandmothers who are expected to sustain ongoing parental responsibilities for children or grandchildren may grow to resent such demands on their time (Johnson and Barer, 1988). The considerable confusion about the place of caregiving grandparents in their relations with other family members may result in conflict among children concerning the respective parenting role of parents and grandparents and about the relative attention received by various grandchildren (Burnette, 1999). Indeed, grandmothers who assume parental responsibility for their grandchildren experience considerable ambivalence about doing so for two reasons (Jendrek, 1994). First, taking care of grandchildren contradicts the expectation of rest later in life. Second, acting on the desire to help their grandchildren means acknowledging that their child is an incompetent parent. Grandparents who care for their grandchildren also socialize less with friends and families (Burton, 1992; Minkler, 1999; Pruchno, 1999) and, if married, experience declines in marital satisfaction (Jendrek, 1993).

A frequently overlooked consequence of caring for grandchildren is the impact on the ties between grandparents and other grandchildren who are not care recipients (Hayslip et al., 1998). As well, assuming primary responsibility for a grandchild creates considerable ambivalence for grandmothers who find the demands of parenting clash with the expectations of grandmothering (Johnson and Barer, 1988). Differential treatment of grandchildren creates an additional complication to family dynamics for these grandmothers.

> I am the only one who sees that he gets his vitamins, that he has a normal life, that he gets to bed on time, that he doesn't run wild. Because of all that, I can never be a grandmother. I can't indulge him like I do my other grandchildren. I have to discipline him, so I can't be fun to be around. (Grandmother with full-time responsibility for her 5-year-old grandson; Johnson, 1988:112)

Like parents, the main concerns of grandparents are that their grandchildren are safe, healthy, and on their way to receiving a good education (Landry-Meyer, 1999). Despite the associated costs, most grandparents would make the decision to care for their grandchildren again and view caring for grandchildren as "the Lord's blessing" and an activity that gives life additional meaning (Burton, 1992; Hayslip et al., 1998). Caregiving grandmothers feel satisfied, happy, and rewarded by helping their grandchildren and enjoy their company and progress (Pruchno, 1999). Black grandmothers also feel closer to their grandchildren as a result of caring for them.

In turn, despite the challenging circumstances that typically lead grandparents to care for their grandchildren, grandchildren raised solely by grandparents fare very well when compared with those children raised by a single biological parent (Solomon and Marx, 1995). Even more striking, they do not differ markedly from children raised by both parents in terms of their relationships with teachers, general well-being, and health. Indeed, the only substantial difference is in school achievement, with children raised by grandparents performing less well than those raised by parents (Solomon and Marx, 1995). This seems to hold regardless of race or ethnicity. The benefits enjoyed by grandchildren may well come home to roost, as in the case of a granddaughter who helps her grandparents daily:

> I am thankful that I can do it. My mother was only 16 years old when I was born and my grandparents took care of me. I will never forget how she [my grandmother] always had time to do things with me (Dellmann-Jenkins, Blankemeyer, and Pinkard, 2000:183).

Summary

In sum, older grandparents derive considerable pleasure from their relationships with their grandchildren. In turn, adult children tend to enjoy good relations with their grandparents. For most older persons, grandparenting involves regular and emotionally rewarding contact. For some, being a grandparent involves intensive caring for grandchildren. One of the reasons that more grandparents are looking after grandchildren is the rising number of divorces among their children. In the final chapter of this section, the impact of divorce and remarriage on intergenerational ties is explored.

11

The Impact of Divorce and Remarriage on Intergenerational Relations

The Impact of Divorce on Ties Between Older Parents and Their Children

Unlike death, which is final, the problems of divorce go on and on.

—*Twice-married grandmother (Johnson and Barer, 1988:163)*

During the second half of the 20th century, there was a marked increase in divorce rates at all ages, including old age (see Chapter 2). However, divorcing later in life is still relatively uncommon. The more frequent experience for older parents is to have divorced earlier in life and to have either continued life as an unmarried person or to have remarried. For years, the focus of research about the impact of divorce has focused on the welfare of young children. More recently, this has been extended to a concern about the long-term consequences of long-ago events, in this case, the effects of parental divorce on the ties between parents and their adult children. Divorce often occurs while children are still living at home, but some parents divorce after their children have left. This variation may have consequences for parent-child ties. As part of the flurry of research about the support that children give their older parents, some researchers have also explored the impact of an adult child's divorce on intergenerational relationships.

Remarriage introduces additional complexity to family relationships, as stepkin and sometimes halfkin become a part of the family constellation. The impact of a parent's remarriage is likely to have variable repercussions, depending on the age of children at the time. In turn, the effect of a child's remarriage on ties with parents is likely to vary based on the child's age and whether the child or new partner has children. There is a firmly held view that parents have a stronger obligation to support their children than children have to support their parents, following the divorce or remarriage of parents (Coleman, Ganong, and Cable, 1997). As well, avowed obligations are stronger to biological kin than to in-laws and stepkin. Relationships between in-laws are unclear at best, but following divorce, they become even less clear. Like stepkin ties, the attitude that one is obliged to provide support following divorce is heavily swayed by the degree of emotional closeness between former in-laws (Ganong and Coleman, 1999). Thus, it would seem, divorce introduces some precariousness to familial ties. Let us now consider the reciprocal effects of parental and child divorce on the relationships between older parents and their adult children. The additional consequences for relationships between grandparents and grandchildren are explored later in this chapter.

The Impact of Parental Divorce

Transmission of Divorce

An ongoing concern about divorce is the greater risk of divorce among children whose parents divorced (Amato, 1996; Corak and Heisz, 1999; Feng, Giarrusso, Bengtson, and Frye, 1999). Longitudinal research indicates that a key reason for this greater risk is that children of divorced parents marry at a younger age (Ross and Mirowsky, 1999; re: daughters, see Feng et al., 1999). As well, a parent's divorce leads adult children to engage in forms of interpersonal behavior with their spouses, such as anger, jealousy, hurt feelings, and infidelity, which increase the probability of divorce (Amato, 1996). However, although parental divorce heightens the probability of children divorcing, neither marital quality among married children (Feng et al., 1999) nor the quality of children's adult intimate ties (Tayler, Parker, and Roy, 1995) appear to be adversely affected. Thus, it appears, children of divorced parents who remain married are no more or less likely to have good marriages than are children of parents who stay together.

When the child of divorced parents divorces, parents often feel both guilty and sad, taking the view that they bear some responsibility for their child's divorce through the example they set and knowing firsthand the challenges that face their child. In the words of a separated 66-year-old father of a divorced daughter,

> You are saddened by the thought of what your divorced child will have to go through. Well, you kinda know what's ahead for them in a marriage breakup after seeing your own deteriorate. You know there is disappointment; there's heartache, no peace, and your life is really upset . . . they don't know yet the agony of the months that go into years. . . . You see all that heavy stuff because you've been there, and they are just starting on that road. (Hamon and Cobb, 1993:83)

Parental Divorce and Support Exchanges

How are support exchanges between parents and children affected by parental divorce? Both divorced mothers and fathers, but especially fathers, have less contact than married parents with their adult children (Aquilino, 1994; Booth and Amato, 1994; Bulcroft, K. A., and Bulcroft, R. A., 1991; Cooney, 1994; Uhlenberg, 1990; Webster and Herzog, 1995). Although level of contact is generally unrelated to closeness between older parents and their children, among adult children of divorced parents, those who feel closer to their parents maintain greater contact with them (Cooney, 1994). This suggests that the tie between adult children and their divorced parents has a more voluntary and less obligatory character, potentially undermining the support exchanges typical of the parent-child relationship.

Among divorced parents aged 36 to 72, divorced mothers report receiving much more advice, financial help, emotional support, and service provision from their children than do divorced fathers (Wright and Maxwell, 1991). Reflecting on the divorce process itself, almost half of mothers but less than one fifth of the fathers found children to be their most helpful source of support. Among divorced fathers, parents outranked children as significant support providers. Older divorced fathers (aged 50 to 79) are far less likely than never-divorced fathers to consider their children likely sources of support should they be in need (Uhlenberg, 1990). Indeed, whereas a parent's widowhood prompts children to give more support, a parent's divorce does not

(Eggebeen, 1992; see also Aquilino, 1994). Thus, the lower expectations of divorced fathers are borne out in lower levels of support from adult children.

In turn, divorced parents generally provide less financial aid, instrumental support, advice, and companionship to their adult children than do their married peers, with a greater difference between fathers than mothers of the two marital statuses (White, 1992; see also Eggebeen, 1992). Compared with children whose parents remain married, children whose parents divorce are less likely to coreside with parents as young adults (Booth and Amato, 1994; re: fathers, see Uhlenberg, 1990) because the latter leave home at younger ages (Boyd and Norris, 1995) and are less likely to return after they have left (Aquilino, 1990). Later on, children who were adults at the time their parents divorced experience a decline in family gatherings and celebrations that would normally bring various factions of the family together (Campbell, 1995). Thus, the potential of midlife divorced parents to contribute to the cohesion of their extended family is undermined.

Among divorced parents, level of contact and relationship quality are crucial to the amount of support that they give to their adult children (White, 1992). Only financial aid is subject to the differential availability of resources, but even here, divorced parents provide more help to children with whom they are in greater contact and have stronger ties. These findings support the contention that the parent-child tie is characteristically more voluntary and less obligatory when parents are divorced. What remains unclear, however, is the extent to which parental divorce leads to less support to adult children because of limited resources, competing obligations (e.g., to a new spouse), or a decline in the commitment that divorced parents feel toward their children. What is clear is that the implications of divorce for intergenerational relations are quite different if divorced parents provide less support simply because they feel less compelled to help their children following divorce rather than because they have fewer resources. What about the quality of relationships between divorced parents and their adult children?

Parental Divorce and Relationship Quality

Among younger adults, both sons and daughters report more positive ties to their mothers than to their fathers before and after their parents' separation and divorce (Hoffman and Ledford, 1995; Kaufman and Uhlenberg, 1998). However, relationships with both parents are viewed more negatively by adult children whose parents have divorced (Kaufman and Uhlenberg, 1998).

Generally, adults consider their ties with parents as most positive prior to their separation and at their lowest ebb following separation, after which they tend to improve (Hoffman and Ledford, 1995). Divorce affects the quality of ties with fathers more adversely than ties with mothers, with father-child ties characterized by far greater detachment and less closeness, particularly with adult daughters (Aquilino, 1994; Hoffman and Ledford, 1995; Kaufman and Uhlenberg, 1998; Silverstein and Bengtson, 1997; Webster and Herzog, 1995; for daughters only, Booth and Amato, 1994; Cooney, 1994; for sons only, Kaufman and Uhlenberg, 1998).

The initial decline in the quality of parent-child relations following divorce is greater among opposite-sex (son-mother, daughter-father) than same-sex ties (Booth and Amato, 1994). Although over time, closeness rebounds to a greater extent for same-sex (son-father, daughter-mother) than opposite-sex ties, both adult sons and daughters are closer to their mothers than to their fathers after divorce (Hoffman and Ledford, 1995). Clearly, changing patterns in custodial arrangements may alter some of these long-term gender effects.

Generally, adult children of divorced parents have lower levels of well-being than children whose parents stay married (Amato and Keith, 1991). This relationship may be due to the association of parental divorce with lower socioeconomic status and poorer interpersonal relationships, factors that, in turn, heighten depression (Ross and Mirowsky, 1999). Although the long-term negative implications of parental divorce may foretell a bleak future, there is evidence that as divorce becomes more normative in society, its negative effects on individuals and family ties diminish (Amato and Keith, 1991). This suggests that at least some of the impact of divorce is the associated stigma. As the stigma of divorce declines, so too may the less positive consequences for parent-child relations.

The focus in studies of the impact of divorce is usually on the parent-child relationship itself. This tells us nothing about how children of divorced parents might negotiate other relationships differently as a consequence of their less involved ties with parents. When compared with those from intact families, adult children of divorce are almost 2 times more likely to have someone who is more like a mother to them than is their biological mother, and 13 times more likely to have someone who is more like a father than their biological father (Webster and Herzog, 1995). Blacks are less likely than Whites to have a motherlike figure and more likely to report a fatherlike figure. These intriguing results suggest that a parental divorce encourages investment in other relationships that may satisfy those needs that are not met by biological parents.

The Impact of a Child's Divorce

For most parents, a child's divorce is a distressing experience, evoking feelings of sadness, loss, powerlessness, disappointment, confusion, guilt, and, for some, bitterness (Hamon and Cobb, 1993; Pearson, 1993). Many parents are quite shocked to learn about their child's divorce, having been unaware of the inner workings of their child's marriage (Hamon and Cobb, 1993; Johnson and Barer, 1988; Matthews and Sprey, 1984). Having no foreknowledge of a child's marital problems and, later, not knowing why a child divorced, make parents' adjustment to the divorce more difficult (Hamon and Cobb, 1993). Lack of awareness reflects a cultural preference to maintain intimacy at a distance once children are adults, with both parents and children seeking to respect mutual independence. Indeed, a key challenge presented by a child's divorce is the need to renegotiate the parent-child relationship based on changed circumstances.

The reorganization that follows a child's divorce results in three general family forms (Johnson and Barer, 1988). The first focuses on the strong intergenerational bond between biological grandparents, the parent, and grandchildren. The second type revolves around the nuclear unit of parent and children. A third option is the formation of a loose-knit network that, unlike the other types, includes friendly relations with in-laws and the ex-spouse, less dependency on parents, and shifting boundaries. These family forms represent alternative and, in some cases, transitional strategies for renegotiating relationships following divorce. Heavy reliance on parents is for some an effective method of moving from a nuclear family with two parents to one with one parent. Although parents can be particularly helpful in making this transition, their involvement also means more scrutiny of the previously private domain of the child's family, creating ambivalence in the parent-child tie (Johnson and Barer, 1988).

A Child's Divorce and Support Exchanges

In-depth reports of older parents concerning the help that they give to their children suggest extensive emotional and instrumental support in the aftermath of divorce (Hamon, 1995). Divorce clearly introduces ambiguity in family boundaries, leaving parents confused about how to interact appropriately with both their child and former child-in-law (Hamon, 1995; Hamon and Cobb, 1993). Although parents share a strong desire to support divorced children, some feel overinvolved in the lives of their child following his or her divorce, whereas others are concerned about the impact it is having on their own marriage. One 70-year-old father of a divorced daughter with children observes,

> I don't have the companionship of my wife. I don't have her there to take trips and to do some of the things that I worked for and should be able to enjoy doing now. And instead, we're almost literally tied down with another family. . . . So, we're stuck. (Hamon and Cobb, 1993:81)

There are mixed results regarding the impact of a child's divorce on parent-child relations. Children in a happy marriage have better relationships with their parents than do single, divorced, and separated daughters and divorced and separated sons (Kaufman and Uhlenberg, 1998). Divorced adult children report receiving less support from their parents and having more strained ties with their mothers, but the strain of mother-child ties creates less distress for divorced than married children (Umberson, 1992b). Others find no difference among children who are married or divorced in the support that they receive from parents. The possible exception is daughters with custody of children, who may receive more contact and support from their parents (Logan and Spitze, 1996; see also Cooney and Uhlenberg, 1992). Results concerning the impact of a child's divorce on the help offered to parents are equally mixed, with some finding that divorced children provide less support than their married peers (Cicirelli, 1984) and others finding no change in parental support when children divorce (Dwyer, Henretta, Coward, and Burton, 1992). More recent work supports the view that divorced children provide as much parental support as married children (Logan and Spitze, 1996).

Observed differences in support exchanges may reflect the possibility that children's perceptions of the need for support from and to older parents are altered by divorce. Facing the challenges of divorce may make children less sensitive to the needs of their parents and elevate their own need for support. Lower perceptions of parental need among divorced children lead them to give less help to their parents (Cicirelli, 1983). Heightened perceptions of their own need may lead them to perceive less parental support than is actually given because some needs remain unmet. From the parents' perspective, responding to the perceived needs of divorced children creates an ambivalent situation when the desire to help is curbed by the fear of interfering (Hamon, 1995; Hamon and Cobb, 1993). This is suggested in the comments of one 55-year-old mother of two divorced children, who reported being cautious about providing support: "They have to live with the decisions they are making and I just didn't ever want to give them the opportunity to say that I'd interfered" (Hamon, 1995:177). For some, the particularly ambivalent situation created by divorce is resolved by redefining the mother-daughter tie as friendship (Johnson and Barer, 1988). For others, the conflict that ambivalence provokes is open and accepted as a given. Yet others define the daughter's dependency following divorce as expected and, therefore, a mother's help is defined as appropriate for the situation.

The Impact of Divorce on Grandparent-Grandchild Ties

Changes that occur in the grandparent-parent-grandchild network following divorce in the middle generation are indicative of the major contribution grandparents often make to the lives of their children and grandchildren and of the dependence of the grandparent-grandchild relationship on the parent as mediator. We shall explore the initial response of grandparents to the divorce of their children and the impact of divorce on grandparent-grandchild ties in terms of lineage (maternal versus paternal grandparents), the gendered nature of child custody, and variations based on when divorce occurred and the age of grandchildren.

Parents are generally saddened by the divorce of their children, but the presence of grandchildren creates additional concern. Whatever the view of their children's situation, grandparents tend to worry about their grandchildren's future. A 73-year-old grandmother observes,

> I think the kids want a stable background. They want a mother and a father in their homes together. . . . The kids need that security. You can't replace it with anything . . . I'm a happy woman for my [divorced] kids' sake. And I'm really unhappy for my grandchildren's sakes. (Hamon and Cobb, 1993:81)

The ambiguity created by divorce extends to grandparents as they wonder how to maintain close ties with their grandchildren (Hamon and Cobb, 1993).

Photo 11.1. A child's divorce may threaten special times between grandparents and their grandchildren. Grandmothers stay in touch with their grandchildren more than grandfathers do after the divorce.

When compared with those who do not have grandchildren, grandparents are more likely to express feeling responsible, guilty, or burdened following their child's divorce, and their mixed feelings about the divorce are more inclined to increase over time (Pearson, 1993). Although grandparents are eager to support their grandchildren, they do not hope to serve as parents to their grandchildren (Hamon and Cobb, 1993; Johnson and Barer, 1988). Yet as we have seen (Chapter 10), some do become intensively involved in caring for their grandchildren. Whatever their level of involvement, grandparents must negotiate a revised relationship with their grandchildren, in substantial measure through renegotiating relationships with their children and children-in-law.

Generally, grandmothers maintain more contact with their grandchildren than do grandfathers after their child's divorce (Hilton and Macari, 1997), as Photo 11.1 reflects. Many grandmothers have greater contact with their grandchildren after the divorce or separation of their child (Gladstone, 1987). Grandmothers often look after their younger grandchildren and serve as a confidant or mediator between teenage grandchildren and their parents (Hamon,

1995; Johnson, 1983; Johnson and Barer, 1988). Grandmothers over 65 have less contact than those under 65 with their grandchildren (Johnson and Barer, 1988), partly because the older age of their grandchildren reduces their need for parentlike support.

As before divorce, geographic distance decreases contact (Cooney and Smith, 1996; Hilton and Macari, 1997). In some cases, children move closer to, and sometimes into, the homes of their parents to receive support, or grandparents move closer to their children to provide support, thereby enhancing geographic proximity and contact between grandparents and grandchildren following divorce (Gladstone, 1987). Living nearer by (Matthews and Sprey, 1984) and having more frequent contact (Henry et al., 1992) are, in turn, associated with greater emotional closeness. Increased contact and greater closeness are most likely when grandchildren are in the custody of the child rather than child-in-law (Gladstone, 1988; Hilton and Macari, 1997; Matthews and Sprey, 1984). Thus, there is usually greater contact with and assistance from maternal than paternal grandparents following divorce. A less usual decrease in contact is due primarily to unresolved conflict between either the grandparent and his or her child (Hilton and Macari, 1997) or between the separated spouses (Gladstone, 1987).

A particularly challenging situation is presented to those grandparents whose children do not have custody of their grandchildren. Traditionally, when custody has gone to one parent, it has been to the mother (re: policy, see Chapter 14). A child-in-law's custody of grandchildren threatens contact between grandparents and grandchildren; rancor between parents and grandparents magnifies this threat (Kruk, 1995). Thus, grandparents, especially on the paternal side, are highly motivated to get along with their children-in-law. The extent to which grandparents struggle to maintain contact with their grandchildren is evident in the fact that, following the divorce of parents, contact between fathers and their children falls off more precipitously than between paternal grandfathers and their grandchildren (Kruk and Hall, 1995).

The key factor differentiating postdivorce grandparental involvement in a range of activities is child custody, not lineage. However, the fact that child custody is more often granted to women reinforces matrilineal ties. Maternal grandmothers are less likely than paternal grandmothers to maintain ties with their child-in-law, less likely to expand their kinship network, and more likely to increase both instrumental and expressive aid to grandchildren following divorce (Johnson and Barer, 1987). Meanwhile, the maintenance of ties with their daughters-in-law to secure access to grandchildren has the long-term effect of expanding paternal grandparents' kinship networks. The impact of child custody is reflected further in findings that paternal grandparents are more involved than maternal grandparents in single-father families, and maternal grandparents are more involved than paternal grandparents in single-mother families (Hilton and Macari, 1997).

Regardless of whether the father or mother has custody, there are also gender differences in grandparental support, with grandmothers more likely than grandfathers to provide child care, help grandchildren with problems, teach new skills, go on outings, and provide treats (Hilton and Macari, 1997). Nonetheless, grandfathers can be described as maintaining active ties with their grandchildren in these postdivorce families. Custodial mothers in the labor force are particularly prone to rely on their mothers to look after their children (Gladstone, 1987). However, the higher labor force participation rates of women of all ages make providing such support more difficult for many of today's grandmothers. Many grandmothers find striking the right balance a dilemma: "If I do too much, I will have to do it all. If I do too little, I might lose them" (Johnson, 1983:561; Johnson and Barer, 1988).

Despite the considerable concern that divorce will interfere with good relationships with grandchildren, research using young adult samples of grandchildren finds equally close and involved ties between grandchildren and grandparents, whether or not parents have divorced (Cogswell and Henry, 1995; Cooney and Smith, 1996). Among those with grandparents nearby, maternal grandmothers are seen as more engaged in nurturance and guidance activities by grandchildren whose parents are divorced (Cogswell and Henry, 1995). Current custodial arrangements mean that paternal grandparents tend to live farther away. One consequence is that paternal grandmothers are less likely to meet the expectations of their grandchildren. However, grandchildren who were aged 16 or more when their parents divorced act more autonomously, independently initiating contact with their grandparents and seeing their paternal grandparents on their own rather than with their fathers (Cooney and Smith, 1996). Thus, later age of parental divorce appears to minimize the impact of custodial arrangements and reliance on parents as mediators in grandparent-grandchild relations. Last, children of divorce are far more likely than those from intact families to have a significant, nonbiological grandparent figure in their lives, including stepgrandparents (Cogswell and Henry, 1995). This supports the contention that, for grandchildren at least, divorce may have the positive side effect of extending family networks (Riley and Riley, 1996).

The Impact of
Remarriage on Intergenerational Ties

> I've come to the sage knowledge that people who remarry have to make laws
> beforehand about their own families. No matter how hard I try, I can't make my
> husband's children like mine. It causes emotional dismemberment.
>
> —*Remarried grandmother (Johnson and Barer, 1988:165)*

Remarriage adds a constellation of new ties while creating permutations in old ones. For the person who remarries, a new spouse means, potentially, new in-laws (parents- and siblings-in-law) and new steprelations (acquiring stepchildren and becoming stepparents). In turn, other family members experience parallel changes in their family composition. Children may acquire stepsiblings and stepgrandparents, as well as a stepparent and, eventually, halfsiblings. Parents of the remarried child may now have stepgrandchildren, along with a new son- or daughter-in-law. Existing relationships are likely to be altered. For example, an adult child's remarriage may spur changes in the relationship between biological or adoptive grandparents and their grandchildren. Thus, there are many facets to the consequences of remarriage when one considers the range of relationships that are affected. Our focus here is on intergenerational ties.

Remarried parents provide less support to their adult children than do continuously married parents (White, 1992). Similarly, the remarriage of adult children following divorce may decrease contact with parents (Logan and Spitze, 1996). Fathers who remarry when their children are still young are less satisfied with parenting and less involved in their children's activities (Christensen and Rettig, 1995). This suggests that remarriage is likely to exacerbate the long-term negative impact of divorce on relations between fathers and their children.

The significance of family history (Finch, 1989) takes on new heights in the study of step relationships. The current dearth of information cannot be redressed by a simple call for more research. Important and unique conceptual issues regarding stepkin that do not apply to blood or, usually, adoptive ties must be addressed. Consider as a starting point the case of parent-child ties. In the case of biological and adoptive parents, the bond between parent and child typically begins at birth or when the child is very young and involves two parents who share the same relationship to the child, either biological or chosen.

Of course, there are exceptions, most notably, single mothers and lesbian or straight couples in which one partner is the biological parent. But the picture is more complex with step relations (see Ganong and Coleman, 1994). First, the age at which a child becomes a stepchild and siblings become stepsiblings will have a major impact on what we might term assimilation into a family. One would expect a range of experiences in step relations, depending on whether a step tie began in infancy, early childhood, adolescence, or adulthood.

Second, the gendered nature of family relations raises the question of who is biologically and who is step related. Is the combination a biological mother and stepfather or a biological father and stepmother? Third is the issue of custody and coresidence, which tends also to be gendered, especially for today's older persons. There are likely to be substantial differences in the degree of familial commitment established over the years based on whether children actually grew up with a stepparent. Fourth, this already complicated combination of factors is compounded further by variations in a parent's marital history; one parent may remarry and another not, either parent may remarry more than once, and either parent may have additional children with a new spouse, adding "half" siblings to the family constellation. Recognizing these conceptual challenges raises a red flag about the results from studies comparing biological and step ties because they typically fail to address these dimensions of step relations.

All these facets of parent-child step ties will have both short- and long-term consequences for family ties, including issues such as inheritance decisions by older parents with a mix of biological and step children (Bornat, Dimmock, Jones, and Peace, 1999) and care decisions by adult children who have both biological and step parents. Attitudes that stress biological kinship as a basis for inheritance except when stepkin have very close emotional relationships (Ganong and Coleman, 1999) suggest an additional burden of proof to step ties that parallels that of same-sex versus straight unions (see Chapter 4). The concept of ambivalence is particularly relevant to understanding the complex negotiations that must occur as families work out relatively uncharted territory.

In a U.S. sample of 1,200 persons aged 40 and over, 6% of sons and 9% of daughters are stepchildren (Logan and Spitze, 1996). Similarly, in Canada only 2% of all adult women and 4% of adult men have ever raised stepchildren (Burch, 1985), indicating that blended families still remain a somewhat special case. Stepchildren do not differ from other children in the amount of support that they give to and receive from parents (Logan and Spitze, 1996).

Another study found that parents give less support to stepchildren, but this includes those who became stepchildren in adulthood (Eggebeen, 1992). The presence of a stepparent leads children to leave home earlier and makes it less likely that they will return home (Goldscheider and Goldscheider, 1998). Thus, the net effect of remarriage while children are still young is to reduce coresidence between parents and adult children.

Attitudes concerning the obligation to help parents favor biological parents, but helping stepparents is also considered appropriate (Rossi and Rossi, 1990), particularly if contact has been maintained over the years (Ganong and Coleman, 1998) and if children feel close to their stepparents (Ganong, Coleman, McDaniel, and Killian, 1998). Similarly, expressed support for the obligation of stepparents to help their adult stepchildren is more substantial than the reverse obligation, but it still falls far short of obligations to biological children (Rossi and Rossi, 1990).

Remarriage has further implications for the grandparent-parent-grandchild network. Research on this topic is an added reminder of the need to pay attention to the source of information and the time frame that is examined. At first glance, information from grandparents presents a picture of declining contact between grandparents and grandchildren when a parent remarries (Gladstone, 1991). About half of grandparents whose child remarried report less contact with their grandchildren following their child's remarriage, whereas one quarter report more contact (Gladstone, 1991). However, key reasons for fewer visits are greater geographic distance, the grandchild getting older, and the ongoing consequences of their child not having custody of the grandchildren, rather than remarriage per se. The perception of grandchildren's shifting needs is also a factor. In some families, remarriage addresses needs of both the grandchildren and children that grandparents had previously sought to meet. Greater contact with children is also attributed to the increasing age of grandchildren, in this case, because grandchildren have reached an age when contact does not require the involvement of their parents.

The reports of adult grandchildren provide a good opportunity for assessing the impact of remarriage itself on ties between grandparents and their grandchildren. Among college students, the tie to the closest grandparent is strongest among grandchildren with a parent and stepparent (stepfamily), followed by those from single-parent families and then those from intact families (Kennedy and Kennedy, 1993). In 4 out of 5 stepfamilies, the closest grandparent is the parent of the coresident, biological parent. Grandchildren in stepfamilies have ties to their grandparents that are closer and more loving, expressive, supportive, enjoyable, and active. These findings are interpreted to mean an ever-deepening link with at least one grandparent as the grandchild moves from an intact family, to a single-parent family, to a stepfamily (Kennedy and Kennedy, 1993). However, the fact that grandchildren in stepfamilies are also more likely to have been cared for by grandparents or to have lived with them while growing up suggests that the support offered by grandparents may facilitate the remarriage of their children in the first place. More research is needed to determine whether and how grandparents' ties with grandchildren influence the middle generation's likelihood of marrying again.

There are three paths to stepgrandparenting: marrying someone who is a grandparent, acquiring stepgrandchildren through a child's marriage to someone who has children, and gaining stepgrandchildren through a stepchild's children (Ganong and Coleman, 1999). These multiple routes help explain the fact that 2 out of 5 American families include a stepgrandparent (Szinovacz, 1998), even though a comparatively small proportion of children are raised in stepfamilies. The transition to stepgrandparenthood has its own challenges. Before confronting the arrival of stepgrandchildren through their child's remarriage, older persons have had to deal with their child's divorce, subsequent status as a single parent, and the emerging relationship with a new partner (Henry, Ceglian, and Ostrander, 1993). Remarriage requires redefining family boundaries and negotiating expectations and opportunities for developing relationships with another child-in-law and stepchildren.

Another perspective on grandparent-grandchild relations following remarriage is that of the middle generation. An abiding concern of parents who form blended families is the relative attention received by children versus stepchildren, a concern that extends to ties with grandparents. Indeed, recently remarried mothers perceive both maternal and paternal grandmothers to be more engaged with original grandchildren than with stepgrandchildren, although they believe that their own mothers provide similar levels of instrumental support to their biological and step grandchildren (Henry et al., 1992). The apportioned grandmothering style (see Chapter 10) is most common between grandmothers and their grandchildren. However, among maternal grandmothers, stepgrandparenting is more likely to be remote (their stepchildren are the middle generation son-in-law's children). Paternal grandmothers are as likely to have an apportioned or remote style in relation to their stepchildren (middle-generation daughter-in-law's children). The greater involvement of paternal than maternal grandmothers with their stepchildren may reflect the fact that the mother's children are more likely than are the father's children to be coresident. Thus, sons are more likely to be living with their stepchildren than are daughters, potentially enhancing ties between paternal grandmothers and their stepgrandchildren through greater contact.

From the vantage point of adult stepchildren, ties to stepgrandparents are stronger and stepgrandparents are more likely to be considered important figures in their lives if the step relationship began earlier in life (Trygstad and Sanders, 1995). Nonetheless, the relative precariousness of step ties is evident in research regarding inheritance and obligation to care. Even in the case of very close ties with stepchildren and stepgrandchildren, biological children and grandchildren are often favored as beneficiaries (Bornat et al., 1999). Similarly, attitudes regarding obligations to care for older stepparents emphasize the significance of emotional closeness as a determining factor (Ganong and Coleman, 1999).

Summary

In sum, divorce and remarriage have effects that extend beyond the immediate parties involved. On balance, an adult child's divorce appears to have less impact on support exchanges between older parents and adult children than does the divorce of the parents. However, more research is needed to clarify our understanding of the consequences of divorce. In particular, much of the research focuses on quite young adults. Perhaps by the time divorced adult children are in middle age, they and their parents have renegotiated their relationship to involve more support in both directions.

The divorce of either generation, but especially of parents, tends to magnify the gendered nature of family life, reflecting in part gendered practices of custody and of responsibility toward raising children. As these shift, so too may the impact of gender on family ties. A far better understanding of how divorce affects the negotiation of other ties is needed before we can draw firm conclusions about the overall impact of divorce on the lives of older parents or their children.

In addition to their concerns about the welfare of their children following divorce, grandparents worry about their grandchildren's future. The response to this worry by many grandparents is to step in and offer support and stability to their grandchildren. This intervention appears to have lasting effects on the grandparent-grandchild tie, with good relations continuing after the remarriage of the middle-generation parent. In more extreme cases, divorce may result in the grandparent meeting parental responsibilities. More research is needed for us to better understand the consequences of remarriage for parents' relationships with their original children as well as biological and step children from a subsequent marriage. In turn, the implications of these ties for grandparent-grandchild relations require further study.

Summary and Conclusion to Part III

The majority of older persons have children and are engaged in exchange relationships with them. However, with age, parents and children become less focused on one another as they attend to other commitments and interests. However, should needs for support escalate in either generation, the other generation is generally available and willing to provide help, often at extensive levels.

The lives of adult children remain an ongoing concern for older parents, whose contentment can rise and fall depending on the successes and problems of their children. Having children, by itself, is no guarantee of happiness in old age, but having close relations with children enhances quality of life. Adult children with either temporary or long-term needs for housing, financial support, and care generally find ready allies and advocates in their parents. Increasing age and declining health may lead to an imbalance in the exchange, with parents more dependent on children toward the end of their lives. Although providing parental care may create considerable strain, a sense of filial duty motivates children, especially daughters, to provide care whether or not they have competing obligations, such as children and jobs.

There are many reasons for childlessness among older persons. Those who chose to be childless are happier in later life than those who did not, but on balance, most older childless persons lead contented lives. Comparisons of older persons with and without children indicate no differences in overall quality of life, although the childless have fewer sources of care and support in old age. However, although the size of their support network is smaller, childless older persons tend to meet their needs through the smaller number of support persons that they do have, and their social activity levels are at least as high as those of parents. Most older persons believe that there are both advantages and disadvantages to not having children. Perceived advantages are more likely to be founded on actual experience, whereas perceived disadvantages tend to reflect long-held cultural assumptions about the merits of having children. Just as having children is no guarantee of happiness, not having children does not spell unhappiness in later life.

Most older persons are grandparents and derive considerable pleasure from the flexibility and emotional focus of their relationship with grandchildren. Typically, grandparents engage in low-key, companionate ties with their grandchildren. Geographic proximity is important to this relationship, enhancing contact, emotional closeness, and involvement. Adult grandchildren tend to report close ties to their grandparents, especially on the maternal side and to grandmothers. Although grandparenting brings rewards, older parents are no closer to those of their children who produce grandchildren than those who do not. The potential extensiveness of support from the older to younger generations is most evident among the growing numbers of grandparents who effectively raise their grandchildren when their children cannot. Despite the costs of caring, grandparents find this experience satisfying and tend to be very close to the grandchildren who receive their care. However, there are important ways in which the burdens of caring can be redressed through social policy (see Chapter 14). As more grandparents see their grandchildren reach their 20s, 30s, and 40s, more attention should be paid to the support that adult grandchildren give to their grandparents.

Throughout this discussion of intergenerational relationships, several key themes have repeated themselves. First, gender fundamentally shapes familial ties because gender is the basis for structuring both family and work. The consequence is that women dominate in caregiving situations, particularly as adult children and grandmothers. Although they also dominate as spousal caregivers, this is in substantial measure a function of their availability because they are more likely to outlive their spouses. Even this case parallels the caregiving experience in other relationships, however. Men and women differ in terms of the nature of the care they provide, the support received from others when providing it, and the consequences of caring. Thus, change in the caregiving experience for men and women requires fundamental social change (see Chapter 14).

Second, race also structures the nature of intergenerational relations. Fundamental differences in family structure that are themselves a function of how race structures social life have profound implications for the nature of intergenerational ties. The association of race with disadvantage and with different cultural traditions creates additional complexity to understanding how families work. The greater involvement of non-White parents and grandparents in assisting and supporting younger generations presents a particular challenge, given their relative lack of resources. Yet cultural traditions appear to help offset the costs of caring in these families. Again, alleviating the burden of support can only occur through fundamental social change.

Third, meeting the substantial challenges that family members face in providing support to one another is either impeded or facilitated by access to resources. Class and economic situation are intricately bound to the demands on women and on family members of color as support providers. Limited access to resources and a position of disadvantage over generations combine to make support provision more necessary and more difficult to elude. In turn, providing extensive, unpaid support further undermines the capacity to improve one's resource base.

Last, social change in the form of divorce and remarriage is reshaping family structure across gender, class, and race divisions. Of course, variations based on gender, class, and race mean the these changes vary in their impact on both individuals and families. Focusing on change, rather than the judgmental assessments of change embedded in such terms as the decline of the family, deepens our understanding of different family forms and their relative strengths and weaknesses, from the vantage point of different players in the family. A family structure that better serves the interests of some groups is bound to be assessed as a better family form by those groups. Our examination of family ties following divorce suggests both costs and benefits for various family members, costs in terms of disrupting family ties; the increase in support demanded of others in the family, such as parents or grandparents; and the heartache that is associated with longer-term separation or isolation from loved ones. But there are also benefits: the satisfaction of seeing family members through difficult times, the greater closeness that comes from increased involvement, and the addition of new family members who enrich lives in unanticipated ways.

PART IV

Sibling Relationships

12

Sibling Ties
in Middle and Later Life

In my experience, it is often helpful to reflect on your own situation when considering research issues. Although you may not yet have a long-term partner, be married, or have children or grandchildren, you are very likely to have at least one brother or sister. If not, you are close to someone who does. Although personal observations have limited utility as a basis for drawing general conclusions about the nature of sibling ties, they do serve as important touchstones, providing a basis for comparison and for raising unanswered questions as one considers what is known to date. For most of us, the sibling relationship is the first experience of an intimate relationship with a peer. During childhood, siblings can serve as teachers, role models, confidants, and companions, and in cases where parents are not readily available, as parental figures. The nature of the relationships that children enjoy with one another in a family is likely to shape their perspective on family living as adults. Yet we know little of the sibling relationship once we become adults. In this chapter, we explore various facets of the sibling relationship in mid- and later life.

The place of siblings in our lives as adults has received very limited research attention. Those studies that have been done typically focus on either biological siblings or on all those who are considered siblings, without distinguishing among them. Consequently, we know even less about adult siblings who are related to each other through one biological parent (half siblings) or marriage (step siblings). As discussed in Chapter 11, several important facets of family history are likely to influence step and half relationships, including the age at which one becomes a step or half sibling, and whether one lived with step or half siblings while growing up. Another area of scant research attention is the impact of sexual orientation, if any, on sibling ties in adulthood. Do the unique features of the sibling tie make brothers and sisters important family ties for gay and lesbian adults? Or do differences in sexual orientation threaten sibling ties? Last, reflecting general inattention to in-law ties, there is little information about siblings-in-law. These topics are introduced to signal their importance and to highlight the fact that most studies of adult sibling ties do not address them.

A unique feature of the sibling relationship is its duration when compared to other family ties. As the longest-lasting tie most of us will have, there is the potential for shared experiences over a lifetime, providing a ready basis for reminiscence as we age. This enduring quality of the sibling relationship can also provide a sense of continuity over the life course, confirming a sense of ourselves in older age as persons still engaged in the world and as objects of affection and caring (Goetting, 1986; Moss and Moss, 1989; Ross and Milgram, 1982). In the wake of higher rates of divorce and of remaining single, these features may become especially valued. Studying the sibling tie makes a contribution to our general understanding of family ties in emphasizing the connection between our family lives as children and as adults.

Unlike other relationships, those among most siblings include the sharing of a common cultural background, early experiences of family belonging, and, for biological siblings, the same genetic pool (Cicirelli, 1982). Thus, siblings can play a substantial role in continuing the family sentiments of youth into adulthood and old age. In addition to shared sentiments, siblings generally share important structural positions in the larger social world, such as class and race. At the same time, there are often important differences between them, including gender (Sandmaier, 1994) and sexual orientation. As well, social mobility in adulthood may lead to significant variations in socioeconomic status that could have repercussions for sibling relations. Some have also argued that birth order has profound and long-lasting effects on individuals (Sulloway, 1996), but it is not clear that the significance of sibling ties varies accordingly. Clearly, we must be cautious not to overdraw the similarity of experience between siblings, especially once adults.

Another unique characteristic of the sibling relationship is its egalitarian nature. This reflects the horizontal nature of the tie between siblings, in contrast to the vertical tie between parents and children. Such horizontal ties are characterized by the relatively equal power of both parties and an emphasis on sociability (Cumming and Schneider, 1961). This suggests that, of all family ties, the sibling relationship most closely parallels the characteristics of friendship. Most sibling relationships weather a variety of changes and bear witness to many phases of family life (Connidis, 1992). Because of their unique features, exploring sibling ties contributes to a more sophisticated view of family relationships as continuously evolving over time, rather than as a fixed relationship in a particular family structure.

Availability of and Contact With Siblings

As we saw in Chapter 2, most of today's older persons have at least one living sibling (80% of those aged 65 and more). This will be even more true of the baby boom generation, whose older members are now in middle age. Most of us can expect to have at least one surviving brother or sister well into old age. The likelihood of having a sister in old age has increased most dramatically over the past 100 years (Uhlenberg, 1996). The greater complexity of family structure makes counting siblings more of a challenge, as individuals and researchers grapple with whether to include biological, half, and step siblings in one category; to count them separately; or to distinguish among siblings on qualitative grounds (White, 1998). The growing number of divorces and subsequent remarriages mean more adults will have both half and step sibling in the future (see Chapter 11).

As well as having siblings, many older persons have a sibling who lives nearby. In my community study, 70% of respondents aged 65 years or more who had living siblings, had at least one sibling less than a day's drive away. Geographic proximity tends to have a greater impact on sibling interaction (Lee and Ihinger-Tallman, 1980) and on participation in joint activities (Scott, 1983) than is true for parent-adult child involvement, with much higher contact among siblings who live near each other (Connidis, 1989a; Connidis and Campbell, 1995; Lee, Mancini, and Maxwell, 1990). As a 67-year-old sister puts it when comparing her closer tie to one sister than the other,

> Living in the same city, of course, you see each other every day or phone every day. I think that is the big bonus. With Susan, she was away for so many years. . . . You are not in touch or as close as you are when you are in the same city.

The greater significance of proximity is probably an outcome of the more voluntary nature of sibling relationships when compared with the more obligatory ties to parents or children.

In my study of persons aged 65 and over, 30% of those with siblings saw at least one of them several times a month or more, and 44% saw at least one sibling once a month or more. Although most siblings maintain contact with one another over the life span, the amount of sibling interaction is subject to competition from the family of procreation, so that when demands in the procreative family are higher, sibling interaction is lower. Thus, sibling contact goes down with the arrival of children and increases when children grow up (Gold, 1987; Leigh, 1982).

For many older individuals, retirement also affords an opportunity for greater sibling contact, and when an aging sibling suffers a health crisis, contact with that sibling often increases (Gold, 1987). When I asked a 70-year-old brother about his relationship with his younger sister since retiring, he replied,

> Oh, it hasn't changed any. Still have the geographic distance. . . . But it really doesn't matter because the telephone's a wonderful instrument, and she knows and I know that if either of us needs the other, why, we're on the next plane.

However, the confining impact of health problems and decreased mobility, especially where distance is a factor, generally leads to a decline in contact in the oldest stages of life (Cicirelli, 1982; Scott, 1983). Nonetheless, over a 12-year period, old rural women did not see less of their siblings, despite changes in proximity and the number of surviving siblings (Scott, 1996).

Gender influences contact with siblings. Whether examining contact with the sibling who is seen most often or contact with the entire sibling network, middle-aged and older women report seeing their siblings more frequently than do men (Connidis and Campbell, 1995). Furthermore, sisters interact more often than other gender combinations (Connidis, 1989a; Connidis and Campbell, 1995; Lee et al., 1990; Scott, 1983). Because brothers do not see each other more than brother-sister dyads do, the difference suggests a unique tie between sisters that transcends simply being the same gender. The fact that sisters discuss matters that are important to them more often than do brothers or brother-sister pairs supports this view (Connidis, 1989a).

Although married older persons maintain contact with their own brothers and sisters, for most couples, visits with the spouses' siblings either occur when spouses are together or not at all (Rosenberg and Anspach, 1973). Independent visiting (i.e., without one's spouse) occurs with siblings but not siblings-in-law, and contact is generally greater with the wife's than the husband's family (Irish, 1964). This matrilineal focus among married couples means that men are in greater contact with in-laws than are women. This is also one reason why contact between two sisters is more common than between two brothers.

Marital status also affects contact frequency. Older persons who are widowed, single, or without children have more contact with their siblings than do married parents (Chappell and Badger, 1987; Lee and Ihinger-Tallman, 1980). When compared with divorced older persons, single older persons see their siblings more often (Strain and Payne, 1992). The combination of marital statuses in a sibling dyad also makes a difference (Connidis and Campbell, 1995). Regarding the sibling seen most often, the greatest contact is between a single respondent and a single sibling, followed by divorced persons with a single sibling, and then widowed respondents with a single sibling. Interaction is lowest between married respondents and their married siblings (Connidis and Campbell, 1995; Lee et al., 1990) and between widowed individuals with either a widowed or a divorced sibling (Connidis and Campbell, 1995). Thus, being unmarried per se does not lead to greater interaction; rather, being single (never married) is key. Results for contact with all siblings are similar; interaction with their sibling network is greater for single respondents than for all other marital-status groups. Because these differences occur independent of emotional closeness (Connidis and Campbell, 1995), it appears that single individuals may feel a stronger sense of obligation to their siblings and, in turn, siblings may feel a stronger sense of obligation to their single siblings.

Parent status makes a difference to contact with siblings too. Those who have only childless siblings see their siblings more often than those whose sibling networks include parents (Connidis and Campbell, 1995). A pair of childless siblings sees each other most often, followed by pairs in which one sibling is a parent and one is childless, and then by two parents (Connidis, 1989a). Single persons, who are generally childless, are more likely to live near at least one sibling than are persons of other marital statuses (Connidis, 1989b), suggesting that the salience of siblings to single, childless persons shapes decisions about where to live.

The marital and childbearing history of parents may also have a bearing on sibling ties. Among siblings aged 18 and over, although siblings maintain some contact whether full siblings, half siblings, or step siblings, full siblings enjoy significantly greater levels of contact than half or step siblings (White and Riedmann, 1992a). Even the full siblings in families with step ties see each other less often than full siblings in original families do. More research is needed to determine the impact of the age at which siblings become step or half siblings, whether they coresided, and the age gaps between them to appreciate just what it is about not being full siblings or in intact families that accounts for these differences.

Last, the total family network often provides a basis for indirect interaction among siblings through intermediaries, usually parents, who keep family members informed about one another (Allan, 1977). There is also a considerable degree of information exchange among siblings who are not in direct contact with each other (Ross and Milgram, 1982). Thus, siblings are in touch with one another not only directly but also indirectly as part of a larger family network of parents and siblings.

Neither the amount of contact nor the frequency of interaction over time captures the nature of sibling ties. Different types of interaction may be possible or impossible depending on circumstances such as health or financial situation and do not bear upon the quality of the relationship. For example, an 81-year-old man in the London study observed,

> There are nine of us [brothers and sisters] in the family, and we kind of cling together. Especially when you move around, you know, you have got to stay together. I haven't made as many friends, but we have each other. . . . [T]hey are all so far away now . . . we don't see much of each other.

As well, there may be cases where high levels of interaction do not reflect closeness but rather are a function of a shared sense of family commitment among siblings (McGhee, 1985). Let us turn now to consider the nature and quality of sibling relationships as we age.

The Nature of Sibling Ties in Later Life

Social expectations pose major contradictions for sibling ties. Four major issues about childhood sibling relationship have been identified as equity, maturity, loyalty, and individuality (Handel, 1994). These issues reflect, in part, strongly held but conflicting cultural views about the nature of sibling ties and can be viewed as two pairs of dialectical opposites. In the first, the expectation that siblings should be treated equitably by their parents is made difficult by the fact that, being different ages, siblings are at different levels of maturity and cannot, therefore, be treated in the same way. In the second, the expectation of loyalty between siblings conflicts with the need to develop as individuals. These fundamental contradictions make sibling ties inherently ambivalent (Bedford, 1989).

To some extent, aging itself reduces ambivalence by minimizing the significance of maturity and individuality as issues to be dealt with in the sibling relationship. As siblings grow older, age ceases to be a major factor in their relationship, a shift observed frequently by respondents in my sibling dyad study. The following quote from a woman of 60 about her relationship with her 70-year-old brother is a good example:

> He left home when I was 9 years old so we had very little relationship growing up. He was 10 years older than I and so he was 19. He went away from home and then he was in the army and went overseas for 6 years. And then came back and went to university . . . so our relationship has become closer as we got older rather than a continuum. . . . It would have been 35 years ago [that our father died]. At that point, we hadn't seen much of each other and at that age a ten-year age difference . . . is quite an age difference. The age difference doesn't matter as much as you get older.

As well, despite stereotypical depictions that present a uniform image of older people, the older we become, the more diverse we are, partly because we accumulate a different array of life experiences. Thus, the need to actively strive for individuality declines with time. Nonetheless, expectations regarding the sibling tie in childhood are extended into adult life when the sibling relationship is viewed as egalitarian and more voluntary than ties to a spouse, parents, or children (Cicirelli, 1982).

The traditional focus on the nuclear family and on marriage as the essential units of family life lends itself to the treatment of relationships as working toward shared familial goals through the rational adaptations of individuals (McCall, 1988). Such a view is fundamental to earlier developmental approaches to studying relationships, with their view of a progression from one stage to the next and the idea of failure if progression does not occur. However, if development is viewed as transformation and relationships go through phases rather than stages, then attention can be paid to changes in relationships in response to changing circumstances (McCall, 1988). We are more readily able to see this quality of family relationships in the sibling tie because we have not imbued it with notions of success and progress toward goals to the degree we have marriage or parenthood. Consider this argument in relation to attempts to delineate a developmental sequence of sibling relationships.

Goetting (1986:708) argues that in early and middle adulthood, the sibling "tasks of nurturance, caretaking, and teaching," which dominated childhood, "must be transformed into tasks addressing adult needs as persons become spouses, parents, and children of aging parents." Old age involves four additional developmental tasks for siblings: companionship and emotional support, shared reminiscence and perceptual validation, resolution of sibling rivalry, and aid and direct services (Goetting, 1986). The outline of these staged tasks makes an important contribution by specifying several *forms* of the adult sibling relationship. But is the caretaking of childhood truly a different developmental task from the caretaking of old age? Must one wait until old age to resolve sibling rivalry or to provide emotional support to siblings or to reminisce with one another? These features of the sibling tie—nurturance, caretaking, and teaching—are better viewed as forms of the sibling relationship that resurface during various phases of the life course, in response to environmental influences.

Types of Sibling Relationships

There is considerable variation in the type of relationships that siblings negotiate with one another. These variations occur across and also within families, reflecting the varying points of view that can be held by members of one family. Qualitative data from 60 older individuals were used to create a typology of sibling relationships based on degrees of closeness, envy, resentment, instrumental support, emotional support, acceptance, psychological involvement, and contact (Gold, 1986, 1989; Gold, Woodbury, and George, 1990). Based on inductive analysis, five types of sibling ties were identified: intimate (17% of sample), congenial (28%), loyal (35%), apathetic (10%), and hostile (10%; Gold, 1986, 1989). Subsequent quantitative analysis suggests that the hostile and apathetic types can be combined into one because they have similar negative consequences for emotional and instrumental support (Gold et al., 1990). The small sample size in this study precludes generalizing about the actual distribution of these types of sibling relationships, but the variation that the types represent underlines the folly of attempting to develop one characterization of the sibling bond.

Intimate siblings share ardent devotion, psychological closeness, confidences, love, empathy, frequent and consistent contact, emotional and instrumental support, and often consider one another best friends (Gold, 1986). Congenial siblings share traits similar to intimate siblings but are somewhat less empathic, less likely to consider one another best friends, and less likely to be in daily contact. The loyal siblings are not especially loyal and devoted to one another as individuals but rather share a strong sense of loyalty to the importance of being siblings. In many respects, these loyal siblings are an example of intimacy at a distance (see Chapter 1). A strong sense of family obligation brings them together and evokes intense feelings of family solidarity during crises, but these feelings subside when normalcy returns (Gold, 1986).

The majority of older persons have intimate, congenial, or loyal ties with siblings. However, Blacks are more likely to emphasize positive and supportive dimensions of sibling ties, whereas Whites more often refer to envy and resentment when talking about their siblings (Gold, 1990). This contrast may reflect long-standing differences rooted in childhood and early adulthood, periods during which Black siblings offer extensive support to one another. Among Whites, sibling ties characterized as apathetic or hostile are most likely to occur between brother dyads but, counter to most work on gender and sibling ties, among Blacks, hostile ties are more likely between sisters.

Sibling Solidarity and Loyalty

In one of the earliest studies on older siblings, Cumming and Schneider (1961) argued that age grading in American society is based in part on an egalitarian ideology that makes us more comfortable with horizontal than vertical relationships. Consequently, horizontal ties tend to enjoy a greater degree of solidarity. In the kinship structure, the horizontal nature of the sibling relationship is the basis for solidarity among sisters and brothers. The degree of sibling solidarity is evident in the observation that, even when brothers and sisters either perceive themselves to be incompatible or actually dislike each other, the sibling relationship is not dramatically affected (Allan, 1977). The family network, particularly parents, is effective in keeping siblings together despite differences, and relatively little interaction is required to maintain most sibling relationships. Siblings also share very similar views on life, indicating high consensual solidarity (Suggs and Kivett, 1986-87).

Sibling loyalty, as distinguished from solidarity, is a deeper attachment that goes beyond friendly and companionate relations and "involves feeling and identification with the other person; it also requires tangible action and sacrifice" (Bank and Kahn, 1982:252). Loyal sibling relationships have several features parallel to those of friendship: actively trying to be with each other; cooperation, sympathy and mutual helpfulness; a unique language generally not shared with others; and defense of each other against outsiders (Bank and Kahn, 1982). Given that 77% of older individuals consider at least one sibling a close friend (Connidis, 1989b), many older persons appear to enjoy loyal sibling relationships.

Loyalty is often a feature of dyad relationships within a large family. Such loyalty tends to exceed sibling rivalry and conflict and is based in part on the perception that siblings can count on one another and treat one another more fairly than is true of parents (Bossard and Boll,1956). Large families tend not to promote sibling rivalry to the same extent as smaller ones, primarily because parents of many children do not have time to serve as arbitrators in disputes among siblings. Instead, siblings are left to sort things out on their own, thus promoting cooperation and minimizing rivalry. The more intimate ties evident among older persons with more living siblings show that the difference extends across the life course (Gold et al., 1990).

Closeness Among Siblings in Later Life

For many, the sibling tie has the potential for being a warm and close relationship in later life, as reflected in Photo 12.1. Among adults aged 55 and over, 70% say they are somewhat, very, or extremely close to at least one of their siblings (Connidis, 1994a). A strong sense of family membership and closeness to particular siblings is permanently shaped by shared childhood experiences for many adults, including eating and playing games together, going to church, family crises, and special events (Gold, 1987). Closeness rarely develops in old age; instead, siblings who are close as adults tend to have been close in childhood (Scott, 1983). However, growing older minimizes any barriers to closeness created by age differences between siblings when they were young (Gold, 1987).

Typically, sibling rivalry declines with age (Allan, 1977), and sibling ties are closer in old age (Cicirelli, 1995; Scott, 1983). During young and middle

Photo 12.1. For many brothers and sisters, sibling ties are closer in older age when there is time to invest in them once more.

adulthood, there is often greater focus on a spouse, children and, sometimes, on one or only a few siblings rather than all of them (Ross and Milgram, 1982). But by middle age, increasing age means greater closeness to siblings (Connidis and Campbell, 1995). These patterns over time are described by a married father, aged 64:

> When we were younger, we were all quite close. And I mean right up through our early married years. And then, for some reason that none of us know about—and we've actually discussed it—we drifted apart. We really did drift apart. And we had very little in common. I think Mary (wife) and I being out of town contributed to it. But starting again, oh, I don't know, 10, 12 years ago or something, we've really got back and got pretty much the relationship we had when we were kids. But we did come full circle and we've actually talked about it, you know, "How come?" There was a period of 6 or 8 years that we hardly ever even talked to each other on the telephone, never mind directly. We'd meet occasionally at family things and what not. I think it was partly . . . job related; I think it was partly because of what our children were involved in. Just for no real reason. Just drifted apart.

Despite the drifting apart noted by this brother, he also talks about working together with his siblings to handle the closing of their father's business after his death and to settle the estate of their mother after her death. In both instances, siblings were brought closer together. The various health problems of this man and his siblings have had a similar effect.

A widowed mother in her 60s describes a similar pattern of closeness over time but emphasizes changing responsibilities as the reason for growing closer again later in life:

> I think that you grow up, [and] naturally each one of us finds his own way or her own way during those stages. If you develop relationships in the community where you live and you're very involved with your family, you don't have much time for siblings. But then, after your children grow up, you probably think of your siblings more just because you are fond of each other, and you just want to maintain that relationship.... You don't want to lose it. After your responsibilities are fewer, you want to renew and strengthen the relationship with your siblings. That's the way I feel about it.

Closeness is enhanced by growing up in large families where children are forced into groups, often out of necessity (Ross and Milgram, 1982). However, the closeness that is fostered in large families may be confined to the group of greatest association. The comments of a 66-year-old man are illustrative:

> My father died when I was 2 and that makes a difference. And the different age groups in a large family, from the youngest—I'm the second youngest— to the oldest.... I never skated with any of them on the river or went swimming with them, so we have no memories of the things that we had done together when we were children. I am closer to the young one, my brother that died. I was quite close to him because we grew up together. And my sister. We used to go dancing together. Now, I was fairly close to those two, the ones that I grew up with. The other ones weren't there, so I couldn't be close to them.

This selectivity among siblings in a large family is evident in the fact that those who have more siblings are generally more likely to consider at least one of them a close friend but less likely to think of all of their siblings as close friends (Connidis, 1989b). Furthermore, those with more siblings are significantly closer to their emotionally closest sibling than are those from smaller families (Connidis and Campbell, 1995).

Although geographic distance tends to hamper sibling closeness (Lee et al., 1990), this appears to be true only when distance is maintained for a lengthy period (Ross and Milgram, 1982). Geographic proximity enhances closeness to the sibling network overall but not to the emotionally closest sibling (Connidis and Campbell, 1995). This suggests that having a proximate sibling increases the likelihood of indirect communication about the entire sibling network, enhancing general closeness to siblings. When siblings move nearer to one another, the consequence is generally more frequent communication and a heightened feeling of closeness. Speaking first of his sister and then of his brother, a 71-year-old man in one of my studies recounts,

> Then they [sister and her husband] came to live here permanently . . . and of course, we were physically close, and we saw more of them. My brother moved . . . and I saw much less of him . . . so that . . . changed the relationship. If you are going to continue a relationship, you have to see each other.

Indeed, the link of geographic proximity to greater contact is the key reason for greater emotional closeness (White and Riedmann, 1992a).

Marital and parent status also influence sibling intimacy. Widowed siblings stand out as the emotionally closest sibling of middle-aged and older persons (Connidis and Campbell, 1995). More generally, those who are widowed, single, or childless are closer than married parents to their siblings (Chappell and Badger, 1987; Lee and Ihinger-Tallman, 1980). The high rate of widowhood among older people makes siblings pivotal or focal kin for many in old age, particularly women. Furthermore, the special place of siblings in the lives of unattached and childless older persons may extend to other members of a sibling's family. For example, a childless aunt of 68 moved in order to be near to her sister and family. She says,

> I am very close to my nieces and nephews. They're like my own, and I'm very fond of them. They used to come to Toronto to stay with my mother and me. I'd take them around Toronto, and they really enjoyed that.

Compared to men, middle-aged and older women are closer to their siblings, regardless of gender (Connidis and Campbell, 1995). However, there are contradictory results about whether sisters, same-sex, or mixed-gender (sister-brother) siblings are closer to one another. The tie between sisters is generally seen to be closer (Cicirelli, 1995; Goetting, 1986), followed by brother-sister ties and then by brothers. However, some conclude that both men and women feel closer to a sibling of the same sex, with women feeling closer to their sisters than men do to their brothers (Gibson and Mugford, 1986). Two problems haunt studies of gender variations in emotional closeness. One is that there are likely to be gender differences in what closeness means and in willingness to speak openly about it, with men more reticent to discuss the emotional side of relationships (Matthews, 1994). When, for example, one focuses on the emotionally closest sibling, women report being closer to their sibling, whether brother or sister, than do men (Connidis and Campbell, 1995). In other words, the gender of the respondent rather than the gender combination may be more critical to determining closeness. The other problem is that the entire configuration of the sibling network is rarely taken into account when determining how close siblings are to one another. Families vary in gender composition so that some have siblings of the same sex only, some have opposite-sex siblings only, and some have both brothers and sisters. As we shall see when we discuss the sharing of parental care, such gender configurations are important in shaping sibling relationships.

This said, the tie between sisters tends to have a unique capacity for intimacy, starting early in life:

> Later in life, the close proximity of sisters in childhood may be recreated. Women tend to outlive their male partners by several years, and many widowed and retired sisters end up living together again in the same kind of intimacy as they shared in childhood. At the end of her life, as at the beginning, a sister may be privy to the small, personal details about the other—her eating, sleeping and washing habits—to which possibly no other person, except a long-term sexual partner, ever has access. Over a whole lifetime such intimacy contributes to a rare and special kind of closeness. (McConville, 1985:56)

Several respondents in my study of sibling dyads, both men and women, talk about the difference that gender makes, including the observation that gender simply makes a difference but does not make sibling ties better or worse. A 60-year-old woman with one sister and two brothers, speaking of her sister and one of her brothers, says,

> The person I talk to the most is Rose. But I'm definitely not fonder of her. Rose and John are both [close]—perhaps Rose a little bit more because I talk

to her a little bit more. And perhaps two women, you know, talk perhaps a little bit more. . . . I can say anything at all to John. Anything. . . . For a man, he is extremely understanding. I mean, there are very few men that would sit around and discuss relationships.

A 71-year-old man compares his relationships with his sister and brother and concludes,

They are different, but I wouldn't say one was closer. The distance, of course, and the fact that my brother is a male. There are some personal feelings that I don't confide in anyone, but I discuss some things with my brother that I wouldn't with my sister. It's just different.

Changing attitudes toward gender relations are sometimes raised as older persons reflect on their sibling ties. For example, a 72-year-old woman observes,

I imagine maybe [my brothers] were at one time closer than I was to either of them. . . . It used to be different, how you talk to a woman and a man, but nowadays, things are so much more open than it used to be. I guess you can say whatever, male or female.

Just as some childless older persons make culturally based assumptions about the benefits of having children (see Chapter 9), some older persons without a same-sex sibling make assumptions about how positive the experience would be. A woman of 72 with brothers only says,

Maybe if I had a sister, it would be different. I think having a sister would have been great. A sister you would feel closer to than you would brothers. Your interests would be more the same. They [my brothers] were always playing ball, and I wasn't much of a sports fan.

A 64-year-old man begins a similar reverie but catches himself:

I have to keep a balanced attitude. It's hard to do when you're a brother [with] sisters, because I don't have brothers. I've often speculated what it would have been like to have had a brother. But it's funny, I'm looking back now on the two sons I have. . . . They don't speak to each other. They don't get along.

Last, emotional closeness is usually regarded as a dependent variable, with researchers trying to understand what factors lead to closer ties. However, feeling close to siblings is also likely to encourage certain behaviors, such as contact and confiding. The focus on equal power and sociability in the sibling tie minimizes some of the obligatory component that typifies other family relationships, especially vertical ties (Cumming and Schneider, 1961). Thus, our sentiments or emotional attachment to siblings are likely to play an important role in our adult relationships with brothers and sisters. Indeed, among those aged 55 and over who have siblings, those who are emotionally closer to their siblings confide in and see each other more than those who are less close (Connidis and Campbell, 1995; see also Lee et al., 1990). Similarly, those who consider a sibling a friend see that sibling more often (White and Riedmann, 1992b). The significance of emotional closeness for increasing contact may make the sibling tie a more precarious source of support than those relationships imbued with a stronger sense of obligation.

Confiding Between Siblings

Confiding with someone is usually considered an indicator of a close relationship. Siblings are important confidants in later life, with a general preference for sisters over brothers (Wenger and Jerome, 1999). However, because siblings are peers, living into old age may require turning to younger kin to replace lost siblings. Among participants in my study of persons aged 65 and over who have someone that they trust and confide in, 22% list a sibling as one of their key confidants (Connidis and Davies, 1992). The chances of naming a sibling a confidant are higher among the childless, especially if single or previously married; among those who have more siblings; and among those who have a sibling living near by (Connidis and Davies, 1992). However, if we look at the composition of the confidant network, a somewhat different picture emerges (Connidis and Davies, 1990). Siblings comprise a larger portion of the confidant network of childless persons, as we would expect, but this is also true for single women and for parents whose children live farther away.

Similar analyses with persons aged 55 and over also reveal differences in the picture formed of confiding, depending on whether one examines the probability of considering a sibling a confidant or the overall composition of the confidant network (Campbell, Connidis, and Davies, 1999). The chances of confiding in a sibling are higher among women, the childless, those whose children live far away, and those whose siblings live near by. In terms of network composition, of those whose nearest sibling lives within an hour's drive, siblings are a larger portion of the confidant network of single men (55%) than single women (40%) and compose about one fifth of the network of divorced men and women (Campbell et al., 1999). Siblings are also more dominant in the confidant networks of women than of men among the married (25% versus 9%) and widowed (37% versus 23%). Once again, siblings emerge as especially salient in the lives of women, as well as among single and childless persons.

Siblings as Companions

Siblings are more likely to serve as confidants than companions in later life (Connidis and Davies, 1992), in part because companionship requires proximity, a feature more common among friends than siblings (Wellman and Wortley, 1989). Nonetheless, 5% of persons aged 65 or more list a sister or brother as someone who is a usual companion for activities outside the home (Connidis and Davies, 1992). Siblings compose a larger portion of the companion network of single women than of any other group (Connidis and Davies, 1990). Among those aged 55 and over, women and those with a proximate sibling are more likely than their counterparts to list a sibling as a companion (Campbell et al., 1999). If siblings are nearby, they follow friends as the second most dominant tie in the companion network of single persons and are a sizeable portion (23%) of this network for widowed women. Last, siblings are more dominant in the companion network of childless persons than of parents (see also, Scott, 1983). Again, siblings are particularly significant ties for women, single persons, and those who are child free.

The Sibling Ties of Gay and Lesbian Adults

As noted earlier, there has been very little exploration of the impact of sexual orientation on sibling ties. This is partly a function of the focus on gay and lesbian partnerships and parenting in discussions of gay family ties (Allen and Demo, 1995). This emphasis is understandable given the fact that both of these relationships have involved political struggle for formal legislation, for example, through legalization of same-sex marriage and the right of gay and lesbian individuals or couples to adopt children. This focus is also ironic because it follows the pattern of highlighting nuclear families that has typified traditional studies.

We have already discussed same-sex partnerships (see Chapter 4) and the extra challenge they may face in the absence of support from the partners' families of origin. Although accounts of rejection due to sexual orientation generally or living with a gay or lesbian partner in particular abound, we must be careful not to overstate the case. Joan Laird (1996:90), a mother, grandmother, and partner of a lesbian, argues,

> Ours is not an unusual story. Lesbian and gays come from families and are connected to these original families. . . . Most of us are not cut off from our families—not forever rejected, isolated, disinherited. We are daughters and sons, siblings, aunts and uncles, parents and grandparents. Like everyone else, most of us have continuing, complicated relationships with our families. We participate in negotiating the changing meanings, rituals, values, and connections that define kinship.

A key reason for framing the sentiment of families to their gay or lesbian members as one of rejection is the common focus on "coming out" as the defining moment of this relationship (Laird, 1996). Yet over time, many gay and lesbian persons with families work out good relations with both their parents and siblings. Indeed, as we saw earlier (Chapter 4), dominant family forms among older lesbian and gays include the family of origin (Fullmer, 1995).

Clearly, there is much to explore about sibling ties among gay and lesbian adults. Does the peership of siblings make acceptance of and support to a gay or lesbian sibling more likely than is true of a parent's response to a child? Does the coming out of a brother or sister mark a key transition in the sibling tie that persists over time? Are siblings important players in the family networks of older gays and lesbians? Such questions demand answers if we are to have a complete picture of family ties across the life course.

13

Life Transitions and Sibling Ties

Social expectations are never perfectly reproduced in our social relationships but are instead only one factor taken into account in the negotiation of family ties (Finch, 1989). Their variable interpretation is one reason for differences between and within families. Sibling relationships might be negotiated quite differently by those in large families than those in small ones or among those with spouses compared to those without. This possibility has been downplayed considerably by the two models of support that dominated gerontological work on social support for some time: the hierarchical compensatory model and the task-specific model (see Chapter 8). A third model, the functional-specificity-of-relationships model (Simons, 1983-1984), allows for variations in how particular relationships are negotiated by different groups of people (Campbell et al., 1999; Connidis, 1994b; Connidis and Campbell, 1995; Connidis and Davies, 1990; Connidis and McMullin, 1994). Thus, for some older persons, and at some points in time, siblings may be a particularly important source of support.

However, this does not mean that there is not a socially constructed view of an appropriate relationship hierarchy. A fairly widespread view of a hierarchy of obligation toward given family members is evident in Western culture, with children, a spouse, and parents at the top of the obligation hierarchy (see Rossi and Rossi, 1990). Other ties, including those to siblings, follow. Obligations to family members lower in the hierarchy can be avoided when claims of obligation to family members higher in the hierarchy can be made. Thus, the cost of a more voluntary relationship is that it carries less of an obligation for others to provide support. Also, as was true of the grandparent-grandchild relationship (Chapter 10), greater latitude in more voluntary relations makes for less certain expectations that must be clarified through negotiations.

Given the place of siblings in family networks, life transitions are likely to have an impact on sibling relationships. We have seen that involvement with siblings ebbs during the early and middle adult years. How do the transitions typical of the family life course affect the sibling tie? Entry to and exit from relationships usually involves renegotiating other ties, including those with siblings. What are the consequences of marrying, having children, losing one's spouse through divorce or widowhood, and the changing needs of parents and siblings as they age, for ties between sisters and brothers?

The Impact of
Changes in Marital and Parental Status

The transition from unmarried to married person signals a significant shift in focus, as a newly married couple creates their relationship from a combination of the habits and lifestyles accumulated from their respective families (Schvanaveldt and Ihinger, 1979). The net effect of this effort may be to create some distance between themselves and other family members, including siblings. Retrospective reports from older persons support the dominant view that marriage had a negative impact on sibling relationships (Ross and Milgram, 1982), although 33% believe that their marriage enhanced their sibling ties.

More recent retrospective data from my sibling dyad study show somewhat different patterns, in part perhaps because the participants range in age from 25 to 89 years and are, therefore, commenting on different stages in their lives (Connidis, 1994a). Among those who believed that the sibling tie was affected by their own or their sibling's marriage (roughly 40%), about half of the comments concerned enhancement of the sibling relationship and the other half its diminution. Positive comments refer to improved or enhanced relationships and becoming closer emotionally due to maturing, doing more together, sharing the experience of being married, and good relations with siblings-in-law. When asked about the impact of his marriage on his sibling relationships, a 63-year-old man replies,

> Oh God, much improved! Very simple . . . Rita, Mary, and Bob have said to me, "You know, you'd really have a problem if you decided to split from June. We like you very much, but we love June."

These observations also attest to the strong bonds that may build up between siblings-in-law over the years.

In some cases, getting married creates distance in sibling ties. A 53-year-old childless woman observes,

> I was more close with my sister when I was . . . living with her. After I got married, I moved out. . . . It's not the same as if you live in the same house. It takes you a little bit out of the family. . . . You've got another person to spend more time with.

However, comments regarding less closeness apply more often to the marriage of a sibling than a respondent's marriage (35% versus 20%). Conversely, contact with siblings comes up more often in comments about one's own marriage (24%) than about siblings' marriages (13%). Such observations are usually cast in neutral tones as an outcome of being busier, having other obligations, or being farther away. But for some, even though sibling ties remain close, there is regret about less contact, as a 67-year-old woman illustrates:

> When I got married, my husband didn't see it was all that necessary to see anybody that much, and I missed [my brother]. . . . It's funny, but I didn't ever think about it or even diagnose it really. But in later years, I sort of did.

These comments indicate how variable retrospective accounts can be, depending on the life stage at which they are reported.

The birth of a child tends to "open" a family initially composed of the marital dyad only (Schvanaveldt and Ihinger, 1979). This shift may in turn extend family boundaries to include siblings who have their own claims as aunts and uncles to their new niece or nephew (Connidis, 1994b). Once again, two fifths of the respondents in the sibling dyad study believed that the arrival of children, either theirs or their siblings', affected their sibling ties. In this case, however, the vast majority of comments focused on positive consequences: Almost 75% reported greater emotional closeness, improved relations, and greater contact. Children bring families together, provide new companions for younger siblings or cousins, and are the basis for common concerns. Greater sharing with siblings is noted by a 64-year-old father:

> After I had children, I guess there's more understanding, and there's more sharing in the same problems, "Oh, my child did this and my son did that." . . . When individuals . . . have children, they have common problems and common worries and common concerns. They're a little bit more able to share and to understand what the other people are going through and perhaps support one another.

For a minority, the arrival of children spelled less closeness and contact, primarily because they were the first to have children, so parenthood was a unique rather than a shared experience. Also, the new parent had less free time. As children grow older, contact with siblings often increases, as children become more independent. At the same time, some parents experience a decline in emotional closeness to their siblings as their more independent children prefer to spend major holidays at home and become companions to their parents in their own right (Connidis, 1994b). However, over a third of the observations concerning the impact of children growing up reflect greater emotional closeness, with a history of shared experiences with siblings and their children cementing the sibling bond.

Divorce and widowhood are more likely than either marriage or having children to affect sibling ties (Connidis, 1994b; see Chapter 6). The net effect is generally the strengthening of the sibling tie through greater emotional closeness, better relations, sibling support after the divorce, seeing siblings more often, and moving to live nearer by. The intimacy of sibling ties allows open sharing of painful transitions. A 61-year-old widow says, "you don't mind having them [siblings] know what you've gone through. This is something that you need to talk about inside the family." Indeed, among older divorced parents (Wright and Maxwell, 1991) and widowed women (Martin Matthews, 1991; Ross and Milgram, 1982), siblings are often a helpful source of support, bringing brothers and sisters closer together.

Sharing Caring for Parents

The growing need for support by aging parents can signal a transition in the sibling relationship, as sisters and brothers seek ways of providing support to their mother or father or both (Connidis, 1994a). Typically, this is a gradual transition, but a health crisis or death of one parent may mark a dramatic shift in sibling involvement to meet the immediate demands of the situation. Ideally, siblings, who are now primarily middle-aged adults, figure out ways of sharing responsibility for their parents. For some, however, negotiating commitments to parents is the basis for conflict about what constitutes equitable contributions (Strawbridge and Wallhagen, 1991), as letters to Ann Landers and her sister Abby regularly illustrate.

Helping older parents often involves mutual assistance among siblings (Cicirelli, 1992) and reestablishes greater interaction among siblings in middle and older age, as compared to the earlier adult years. Although they do not always do as they say, most children profess the view that the responsibility of supporting parents means "doing one's share of the caregiving as well as attending to the needs of other family members, not just those of the older person" (Piercy, 1998:116). Siblings who have always been on good terms are better able to weather any strain created by caring for a parent than are siblings who have tended not to get along in the past (Ross and Milgram, 1982). In fact, close sibling relations tend to facilitate the parent-caring process throughout, as those who are close are most likely to share the care of their parent(s) (Matthews, 1987b). Siblings unable to share equally in caring for parents can offer relief to the sibling shouldering the responsibility by visiting their parent(s). Typically, siblings do provide a wide range of support to a sibling who serves as the primary helper (Penrod, Kane, Kane, and Finch, 1995).

How do brothers and sisters work out caring arrangements for their parents? Before considering this general question, let us review key issues that influence the results of research on this topic. First, as you know, older persons vary greatly in their need for help. Similarly, the samples of older parents used in studies about social support differ in the amount of help that parents require. Thus, some samples contain a cross-section of older persons (Stoller, Forster, and Duniho, 1992), not all of whom need help. Others focus on parents who require daily help with basic activities, such as meal preparation, bathing, and moving around the house (Wolf, Freedman, and Soldo, 1997). Second, some research seeks to explain who is likely to help older persons (Stoller et al., 1992), whereas others examine what leads to differences in the amount of support provided to older parents (Connidis, Rosenthal, and McMullin, 1996; Wolf et al., 1997). Third, some studies obtain information from older parents (Stoller et al., 1992; Wolf et al., 1997), whereas others rely on the reports of the person providing support (Connidis et al., 1996). These variations influence the results and help explain some of the contradictory findings that are discussed. Thus, it is important to be aware of these methodological differences in sampling and in the research questions posed.

The earlier discussion about the help that adult children give to their older parents reviewed an array of individual characteristics that affect support to parents (see Chapter 8). We know, for example, that daughters are more likely than sons to provide support and in larger quantities. Thus, we can infer that sisters are more likely than brothers to be involved in extensive helping. Being the oldest sister further increases the likelihood of caregiving among women (Robison et al., 1995). When exploring the sibling relationship, the entire family is of greater interest than the traits of individual siblings, because we can address questions about how support to parents is determined within the context of family negotiations. What are the factors that shape which siblings provide what support to older parents? Examining the impact of family composition, such as number of brothers and sisters, is one way to approach this question.

Among parents aged 65 and over ($n = 584$) with varying levels of independence, having at least one proximate child is the most important determinant of reporting a child as one of their "biggest helpers" (Stoller et al., 1992). Although this seems straightforward enough, there may be differences among sisters and brothers in their likelihood of moving to be closer to their parents when help is needed. As well, parents, given a choice, may be more inclined to move near a daughter than a son when they require support. Thus, although the significance of geographic proximity appears to be gender neutral, proximity itself may be gendered, just as White adult children and their parents are less likely than their Black or Hispanic counterparts to live near one another.

For married parents, greater need for support and having a child living nearer by make naming a child a key or primary helper more likely (Stoller et al., 1992). Previously married mothers are more likely than married parents to name a child as a helper, even if children live far away. Parents who have both sons and daughters are most likely to consider a son the primary helper if there are proximate sons in combination with distant daughters. Married parents tend not to have a gender preference, but widowed mothers do, preferring daughters over sons when they are equally available. Thus, while both parents are living, sisters may feel no more pressure than their brothers to help their parents. But a father's death may precipitate gender-specific pressures to aid a widowed mother, altering the nature of sibling ties in the process. However, gender differences in providing care to parents are only partly because mothers prefer to be cared for by a daughter (Lee et al., 1993).

A Canadian study of 1,015 employed workers who help parents for at least 1 hour per week examined the effects of number of brothers and number of sisters on helping patterns (Connidis et al., 1996). Reports of children who help mothers only, fathers only, or both parents concern the amount of help they give, whether someone shares the caring, and whether they serve as the primary helper. Among women, particularly, those with more sisters provide *more* hours of help to both parents, but for both men and women, having more sisters makes sharing care for mothers more likely and being the primary helper less likely. The number of brothers also increases the amount of help given but only to fathers. Those with more brothers are more likely to have someone share in the help given to mothers and, for men and married women, less likely to be the primary helper. These findings underscore the fact that the help shared among siblings is not a zero-sum game; instead, the amount of help increases with family size. Differences based on sibling gender indicate that families with more sisters may have a stronger ethos of support (Connidis et al., 1996).

A study of unmarried parents who need help and have at least two children focused on the parent's report of the one person who helps "most of the time" with activities of daily living (e.g., bathing, getting out of bed, eating) and the two people who help most with instrumental activities of daily living (e.g., preparing meals, shopping, managing money; Wolf et al., 1997). In this case, the parents' need for care is most central to predicting the number of hours of care siblings provide to their parents. In addition, the more time that siblings invest in caring for a mother or father, the less time a given individual spends helping that parent, especially when there are more sisters in the family. However, again, the net effect of having more children is to receive more support because, for every additional hour one sibling helps his or her parent, other siblings reduce the care they give by only about 5 minutes. Because daughters provide more hours of help than do sons, networks with more sisters provide more support to an unmarried parent. What is unclear from this and other studies that focus on one point in time is the extent to which siblings rotate responsibility for the care of their parent(s) over time.

Qualitative analysis indicates differences in gender preference among parents, depending on the nature of the support that is required (Stoller et al., 1992). Parents whose needs are minimal do not favor sons or daughters, but parents who need help with household labor tend to favor daughters over sons. In cases where sons are the primary helpers, much of the help is actually provided by a woman, typically a daughter-in-law or granddaughter (see Chapter 8). When competing commitments are similar, sisters provide a range of help to their parents that equals or exceeds that given by their brothers. The exceptional cases where brothers provide more varied parental help than their sisters are explained by greater proximity. When sisters and brothers have different levels of commitment, sisters provide a broader range of support, whether their commitments are greater or fewer than those of their brothers.

The impact of gender structure and the number of siblings on the division of parent care is documented in both qualitative and quantitative studies (Coward and Dwyer, 1990; Dwyer and Coward, 1991; Matthews 1987a, 1987b; Matthews and Rosner,1988). Families with only two sisters share the care of parents most equitably (Matthews and Rosner, 1988). In larger families, two sisters provide most of the care, whereas the others provide periodic help when needed or none at all. In families of brothers and sisters, it is the sisters who provide most of the care, with brothers providing occasional or no care. Consequently, primary caregivers who have brothers only are most likely to receive little or no sibling support. This difference is magnified among sisters because they are reluctant to seek help from their siblings, taking the view that "I shouldn't have to ask; they should just pitch in" (Merrill, 1997:57). In contrast, brothers who serve as the primary helper tend to simply demand support from their siblings. As one brother puts it, "Family is family, but I won't let it take over my life. I make sure the others help, and they listen. I just tell them, 'This is the way it has to be'" (Merrill, 1997:57).

The discrepancy between the help offered by brothers versus sisters may also be exaggerated by a tendency to focus on the types of help more typically provided by sisters (Matthews, 1995). Although lone sisters with brothers are more likely to be "in charge" of parental care and to provide more of the personal and housekeeping support, brothers are active in providing the more traditionally male forms of help, such as financial management, visiting, and, sometimes, more personal forms of care for fathers but not mothers. Because such efforts do not fit the traditional image of caregiving, they tend to be minimized by the sister and her brothers.

Gender differences in approaches to caring for parents are also reflected in the way that men in families with brothers only negotiate care arrangements for their parents. Unlike sisters, brothers tend to deal directly with their parents rather than with each other about their parents' situation unless there is a crisis, in which case they coordinate their efforts (Matthews and Heidorn, 1998). Brothers are more reactive than proactive, leaving it to parents to let them know what help is needed rather than seeking out ways in which to assist. Usual forms of support are masculine or gender neutral, and sons typically minimize the significance of the help they provide. The approach taken by sons in brothers-only families fosters more independence among their parents, leading them to negotiate other sources of help to reduce their reliance on sons and to be active participants in decisions about what and how much help they receive (Matthews and Heidorn, 1998). Clearly, the gender configuration of siblings has a substantial impact on both the process and the form of providing care to older parents. Whether one configuration is better or worse from the parent's point of view is an open question.

The substantially greater involvement of sisters than brothers in the care of parents reflects the gendered nature of family care. In a cultural context where looking after family members is seen as women's work (Matthews, 1995), women are less able than men to claim legitimate excuses to avoid parental caring. In the family context, marital status is an additional source of inequality (Connidis and Campbell, 1995). Although inequities of marital status may be a central facet of the inequities based on gender, marital status provides a dimension to family dynamics that is not entirely reducible to gender. For example, when negotiating responsibilities toward parents, being married and having assumed obligations toward a spouse has currency as a legitimate excuse from providing support (see Finch, 1989), especially when compared to a single sibling. In this sense, marital status is a source of differential power in negotiating family relationships. The fact that unmarried children outstrip their married counterparts in the amount of support that they provide to their parents (Silverstein and Litwak, 1993), especially among women (Connidis et al., 1996), supports this argument. Indeed, an unmarried child is more likely to be the only one assisting a mother and to be the primary helper to a father. Gay and lesbian siblings may be especially likely to care for their parents, in part because of their assumed single status (Kimmel, 1992).

There is also an affective component to the provision of parent care. Siblings who are emotionally close to one another are more likely to share in the care they provide to parents and to accept inequities among siblings in the division of parental care (Matthews, 1987a). A 60-year-old married mother in my sibling dyad study said that her family was close during her childhood, but, she observes,

We probably drew closest together during the time that we looked after our elderly mother. We shared responsibility for looking after her. He [respondent's brother] looked after her, and I would take her for a month or so. Then, I looked after her for a couple of years or so, and he would take her. We did it together. It was a joint decision. And the finances. We decided jointly and then we agreed that if she outlived her money, then we would jointly do whatever needed to be done. And she did outlive her money, but, you know, it all worked out.

In this case, a history of closeness was the basis for sharing parental care amicably.

In other families, the need to support parents leads to conflict and stress. This usually concerns the relative amount of help offered by siblings but stems as well from having one's caregiving efforts criticized or from having different views about the option of institutionalization (Avioli, 1989; Bedford, 1995; Lerner, Somers, Reid, Chiriboga, and Tierney, 1991; Merrill, 1997; Strawbridge and Wallhagen, 1991). When asked general questions about caring, sibling pairs in which both members were involved in parental support reported the situation as reasonably manageable and fair to both siblings (Lerner et al., 1991). Yet when addressing specific questions about whether caregiving is equitable and whether the sharing of care could be more fair, substantial discrepancies between siblings arise. Most siblings believe that their own contribution is greater than their sibling's and that they cannot increase the amount of help that they give their parent(s). They also believe that their sibling could contribute more but will not. Such sentiments are more common among women than men, among those who are less close to their sibling, and when caregiving is more demanding. However, even in families described as close, the needs of parents can be the basis for disagreement. A 56-year-old married father with six siblings observes:

> . . . what my mother should do with her house. . . . We're all telling her different things, and I had a bit of an argument with my brother . . . about trying to get things done and sorted out for her. So I've just sort of withdrawn and let him run things.

Here, disagreement is the basis for different levels of involvement in parental support but not necessarily for animosity between siblings. Indeed, general reports of fairness in the sharing of care to parents, despite believing that contributions are unequal, suggest a shared desire among siblings to maintain good relations with one another during trying times (Lerner et al., 1991).

Of course, the impact of parental support may vary among siblings within a family. Two sisters in their 60s from my dyad study both noted that their mother demanded a lot of support after she was widowed and this support was provided primarily by two other sisters who lived close by. One consequence of sharing the care of their mother was greater closeness between these two helpers. Social class also alters the effect of caring for parents on sibling relations. Working-class siblings more often note conflict, in part perhaps because failure to care violates a more strongly held commitment to filial obligation (Merrill, 1997).

Following the death of a parent, previously weak ties may lead to the dissolution of the sibling relationship. However, more often, ties are strengthened on the loss of parents, in part because siblings offer the only remaining ties to the original family (Connidis, 1994b). Following the death of a mother, a sibling, usually an older sister, may take on some of the responsibilities for maintaining family ties formerly carried out by the mother (Cicirelli, 1982). However, a parental death may lead to new or renewed conflict among siblings as they debate appropriate inheritance from their parents or feel bitterness about their parents' legacy. Again, such conflict and its extent will depend on the nature of sibling ties prior to the parent's death. Now, let us consider the extent to which siblings are sources of support to one another in later life.

Support Exchanges Between Siblings

Bessie and I have been together since time began, or so it seems. Bessie is my little sister, only she's not so little. She is 101 years old, and I am 103. . . . Neither one of us ever married, and we've lived together most all of our lives and probably know each other better than any two human beings on this Earth. After so long, we are in some ways like one person. She is my right arm. If she were to die first, I'm not sure if I would want to go on living because the reason I am living is to keep *her* living.

—*Sadie Delany*

To tell you the truth, I wouldn't be here without sister Sadie. We are companions. But I'll tell you something else: Sadie has taken on this business of getting
old like it's a big *project*. She has it all figured out, about diet and exercise.
Sometimes, I just don't want to do it, but she is my big sister, and I really don't
want to disappoint her.

—Bessie Delany
(Delany, Delany, and Hill Hearth, 1993:207-208;
Bessie died in 1995, Sadie died in 1999.)

The family serves as a fairly reliable source of support, in part, because we
learn to have a strong sense of obligation to other family members. This sentiment is encouraged and reinforced in general terms by societal norms and,
more specifically, by the state, especially during times of fiscal crisis (see
Chapter 14). However, as we have seen, the extent of this sense of obligation
varies and tends to be strongest toward children and parents (Rossi and Rossi,
1990). The ability to avoid responsibility toward siblings is supported by the
fact that the sibling tie is more voluntary and, hence, lower in the hierarchy of
perceived responsibility toward family members (see Connidis and Campbell,
1995). As Finch (1989:45) notes, whether siblings provide support "depends
very much upon personal circumstances and personal liking. . . . Except perhaps in rather trivial matters, there is no real sense that one can expect assistance from someone just because they are your brother or sister." Yet as the
Delany sisters exemplified, for some, the tie to siblings is very powerful and
supportive.

Among adults aged 65 to 90, siblings are more likely to share social activities than to assist one another (Scott, 1983). Indeed, the primary motivation for
maintaining contact with siblings is enjoyment rather than obligation, a motivation particularly characteristic of sibling relationships when compared to
other kin (Cicirelli, 1982; Leigh, 1982). This reinforces the view that sibling
relationships are based more on voluntary choice and interest than is true
of other kin ties and are characteristically egalitarian rather than reflecting
dependency relations. Consequently, there is considerable variability in the
likelihood of helping siblings (Wellman, 1992), siblings tend to keep their
exchanges equitable (Scott, 1983), and help from siblings in older age is usually in response to specific situational demands (Goetting, 1986). Even when
siblings live together, they are typically quite independent (Chappell and
Badger, 1987).

Nonetheless, a very important facet of the sibling relationship in older age is the common view that siblings are potential caregivers (Chappell and Badger, 1987), particularly in the absence of a spouse or child who can provide help (Cicirelli, 1992). Among persons aged 55 or more, one fifth of those with one sibling and one quarter of those with two or more siblings report that they could live with one of their siblings if needed (Connidis, 1994b). In turn, 60% of respondents say that a sibling could live with them if needed. Over half of those with one sibling and three quarters of those with two or more say that their siblings would provide help during a crisis. In addition, longer-term help due to illness is perceived to be available from a brother or sister by one fifth of those who have one sibling and one third of those who have two or more. Single and widowed persons are more likely than married individuals to consider siblings a potential source of long-term support due to illness. On the other hand, single, widowed, and divorced persons are also more likely than their married counterparts to say that a sibling could live with them, thereby serving as a resource in later life. As well, having sisters rather than brothers and living near a sibling heighten the view that siblings are potential sources of help. Thus, for many, having a sibling provides a sense of having an "insurance policy" for support in older age (Hochschild, 1973) and helps to stave off loneliness in old age (Gold, 1987).

What about actual exchanges of support between siblings in later life? Generally, siblings are more active as providers of emotional than instrumental support (Miner and Uhlenberg, 1997). Only a minority of persons aged 55 and over report having received support from their siblings (Connidis, 1994b). At most, 24% have received aid, and this is among individuals with two or more siblings who have received "other" help (15% of those with one sibling have done so). About one fifth have received help when ill, and fewer than 1 in 10 have received financial aid from siblings.

As our previous discussion would suggest, the most emotionally supportive ties are between sisters (Lee et al., 1990; White and Riedmann, 1992b). Generally, siblings are more likely to be providers of emotional and instrumental support and to serve as confidants and companions for middle-aged and older women than men (Campbell et al., 1999; Miner and Uhlenberg, 1997). Among those with only one sibling, help during an illness is more likely between a pair of sisters than any other gender combination (Connidis, 1994b).

Marital status has a substantial bearing on sibling support. Those with only one sibling have a higher incidence of receiving support when sick if that sibling is divorced (Connidis, 1994b). Among those with two or more siblings, single and widowed respondents are more likely than those who are married to have received sibling support during an illness. More generally, single older persons exceed married individuals in the probability of receiving instrumental help from siblings (Campbell et al., 1999). Siblings are also the largest portion of the instrumental support networks of single persons, especially for single women, and place second (after children) in the networks of widowed persons and divorced women when siblings live nearby.

Parent status also plays a role in sibling support. Older adults who have siblings but who do not have children have a much higher likelihood of both receiving help from and giving help to siblings (Scott, 1983). For respondents with two or more siblings, childless persons are more likely than parents to have received help from siblings during an illness (Connidis, 1994b). In terms of overall network composition, siblings compose a larger portion of the instrumental support networks of childless persons than of those who are parents (Campbell et al., 1999), demonstrating that childless individuals negotiate particularly supportive sibling ties that continue into old age. On the other hand, those who have at least one childless sibling are more likely to have received other forms of help from a sibling (Connidis, 1994b). In younger adult years, single mothers, particularly those who are divorced, stand out as an exceptional group of parents who receive significantly higher levels of emotional and instrumental support from their siblings (Marks and McLanahan, 1993). This may bode well for support in old age for the growing number of single mothers.

Older individuals who are unmarried and childless, especially those who have always been single, are most likely to live with siblings (Chappell and Badger, 1987; Lee and Ihinger-Tallman, 1980). A 72-year-old widow from one of my studies highlights the full family membership of a coresident brother:

> My brother and I get along very well. . . . He has lived with me a number of years. He never got married, and my mother died when he was just a baby, you see. When I got married, he came to live with me about 2 years after. . . . Yes, he's family, with the grandchildren and everything. He's one of our family. He is not excluded from anything. That's the way we live.

There are important differences in the features of coresidence, depending on whether older persons are living with a brother or sister. Siblings may live together and not have a particularly good relationship, as is the case of a 79-year-old widow and her widowed brother: "We get along all right, but he is very short tempered, and sometimes it doesn't work too well. I am just beginning to get to the stage where I am thinking seriously about selling my home." Among persons aged 60 and over, those who live with a brother both perceive their sibling as available for support and receive support from him (Chappell, 1991). Those who live with a sister are generally well off, are more likely to be women, and are more likely to profess independence but actually receive support from their sister.

On balance, the results concerning sibling support lend support to the view that the same relationship can be negotiated quite differently, depending on an individual's circumstances. The fact that siblings are particularly good at offering emotional support suggests that the sibling tie is best suited to socioemotional support, in keeping with the task-specificity model (see Chapter 8). However, the variability among older persons in the relative significance of siblings as support providers illustrates considerable flexibility in how particular ties are negotiated. For those who are not married, especially single (Cicirelli, Coward, and Dwyer, 1992) and widowed persons, and for childless older persons, siblings can be especially important sources of support in later life. At the same time, older persons without a spouse or children are also distinguished by their greater availability as potential helpers to their siblings.

Summary and Conclusion to Part IV

Most older people have a living sibling. Sibling contact is typically pleasurable, motivated by seeking enjoyable company, and there is evidence of sibling solidarity and loyalty, most notably between older sisters. Of the five types of sibling ties—intimate, congenial, loyal, apathetic, and hostile—apathetic and hostile ties are least common. Sibling ties are especially significant ties for women, those who are not married (particularly, single persons), and the childless. These groups both rely more on their siblings and are more available to them. Generally, support exchanges between siblings are restricted to extreme circumstances.

The more voluntary nature of sibling ties makes them more variable. Consequently, differences in geographic proximity, marital status, and parent status all affect the amount and nature of sibling interaction. Nonetheless, most older persons enjoy warm ties with their siblings, often reestablishing contact and closeness with them once the demands of the early and middle adult years are met. Working out the care of parents involves negotiating new understandings with siblings, often bringing siblings together. However, this situation can trigger conflict as well.

The concepts of intimacy at a distance and revocable detachment, developed to characterize the North American family, apply particularly well to the adult sibling relationship (see Chapter 1). Intimacy at a distance is the ability to maintain family ties despite limited interaction, whereas revocable detachment means that dormant emotional ties can be mobilized if needed or wanted (George, 1980:79; Rosenmayr and Kockeis, 1963). Although a relatively small proportion of older persons actually receive extensive support from siblings, many more consider a sibling someone they could turn to should the need arise. The supportive behavior of many siblings following a divorce or widowhood suggests that siblings can, and do, become more involved when demanded by the situation.

Examining the sibling relationship illustrates that the hierarchical depiction of family relationships provides an overly monolithic, static, and deterministic representation of relationships in action. At the very least, one must take into account that different groups are likely to have different hierarchies of relationships. Moreover, the hierarchies themselves vary, depending on the nature or form of the interaction (for example, companionship versus confiding versus help during an illness). Several other factors combine to make the negotiation of family obligations a very dynamic process. Circumstances change. Various family members have different needs at different times. Obligations to someone higher in the obligation hierarchy might be met by someone else, freeing siblings to support each other. A married mother in her fifties addresses this possibility:

> Because of my sister's circumstances—and I certainly would never want her to know this—but because she is on her own, I think that if my sister were sick and one of the [children] were ill, I know where I'd be. I'd be with my sister because there are other people that would be with my [children]. My husband would go to my kids, but I would be with my sister. And that may sound strange to you but . . . I just feel she hasn't married, and . . . my husband is always here if something happens to me or the children. And so, it would be my sister I would go to.

The sibling tie links our present to our past, providing a sense of continuity over time that very few relationships can rival.

Several trends may have important implications for sibling ties in the future. Because larger families tend to promote sibling loyalty and reduce sibling rivalry, the tendency toward smaller families in the past two decades could result in reduced loyalty and increased competition between siblings. This possibility may be heightened by the combination of full sibling ties with half and step siblings in a growing number of families. Conversely, having one sibling may heighten the interdependence and intensity of the sibling relationship. The increased labor force participation of women may offset or reinforce these possibilities. On the one hand, work outside the home can be expected to limit the amount of time mothers spend with their children, including time spent mediating sibling disputes. This mimics the situation found in larger families where parents cannot play such a role, with the consequence that cooperation among siblings is necessary. On the other hand, if age-graded day care outside the home is required, the opportunity for sibling interaction is also limited. This may minimize the development of strong sibling loyalties based on accessibility and shared experiences. Among children for whom care is provided in the home, the effect of mothers working outside the home could be the enhancement of sibling closeness. Divorce may also be expected to have a surprisingly positive effect on sibling relationships. The absence of one parent and the decreased availability of the remaining parent may lead to a greater reliance on siblings, thereby engendering greater sibling closeness and loyalty. Again, this may be offset by the arrival of step and half siblings. Such differences in childhood experiences would probably extend into the later years.

Among divorced adults, the absence of a spouse may lead to reestablishing sibling bonds earlier than usual. The importance of sisters to women following divorce suggests that this support and bonding may be more common among women than men. In general, heightened awareness of the possibility of divorce among children and adults alike may enhance the importance of the durability of the sibling relationship over time. Last, the greater longevity of women means more years of living without a spouse and more years spent in the company of other women, including sisters.

PART V

Research and
Policy Issues and Directions

14

Research and
Policy Issues and Directions

A national conversation on aging needs to be based on an understanding of the broader context in which aging is occurring. . . . It also needs to proceed with a broad recognition of values that may drive the debate and the range of choices before the body politic. . . . Without an established moral context, our national dialogue will be void of values which respond to such basic issues as the meaning and purposes of life, individual and societal responsibilities, and even the kind of society the people of the country desire for people of all ages.

—*Cornman and Kingson (1996:15)*

Although the focus of this book has been aging in the context of family ties, I echo these sentiments about the type of conversation needed to address research and policy on this subject. In the preceding chapters, the nature and quality of various family ties were examined by exploring the availability of each tie, degree of contact, support exchanges, and the subjective meaning and impact of the relationship. Maintaining a focus on these themes required temporarily suspending comment on research issues and social policy. With the earlier chapters as a foundation, research and social policy issues related to older persons and their families are now considered. Most research is not motivated by a desire to address questions of social policy. However, good research provides essential, valid, and reliable information about issues and, ideally,

counters incorrect assumptions and cultural biases that can shape social policy. Unsubstantiated biases are especially likely to run deep on the topic of
family relationships because these ties are so central to our daily lives and so
close to morally loaded issues, such as sexuality. Improving research and theory on aging and family ties enhances both our understanding of the older person in a family context and the knowledge base necessary for formulating
more effective and innovative social policy. Thus, while research and policy
issues are discussed separately, one outcome of attending to the research concerns outlined in the discussion to follow is to provide a more informed basis
for establishing programs and policies suited to the varying needs of older persons and their families. In the end, of course, research results cannot be left to
speak for themselves. They are read, interpreted, and politicized by those who
take an active interest in promoting various visions of family life.

Research Issues

Research concerns can be divided into three categories. The first is the questions we ask: the topics we choose for exploration. The second is methodology: the type and method of data collection and analysis. The third is theory:
the frameworks we use to direct our questions and interpret our results. We
will discuss each of these in turn.

Research Questions

The questions we choose to address have a way of creating a sense of
urgency about some topics while minimizing the importance of others. When
many researchers decide that a particular topic warrants their attention, the
proliferation of results that are produced shapes priorities about the pressing
and common experiences related to aging and family ties about which something must be done. Some examples over the past few decades are the negative
consequences of retirement for men, including spillover effects for their families; the emptiness of the nest when children grow up and leave home; the
crisis of the sandwiched generation, caught in the middle of competing demands for care by their old parents and their dependent children; and the
burden of caregiving, especially for the sandwiched generation. Are these
important issues? Yes. Do they reflect the real experiences of most older persons and their families? No. Instead, these questions typically arose from

deeply embedded social beliefs about what matters (or should matter) to various groups in our society and inadequate information about how prevalent particular situations were and are.

Research about family ties and aging has made remarkable progress over the past 20 years. Greater sophistication and flexibility in thinking, researching, and theorizing about families, about aging, and about their interconnection have advanced our understanding and orientation to this topic markedly. Based on sound research, we can now conclusively dispel many myths and downplay many exaggerations about family life:

The vast majority of old people are active family members, including those who are single, divorced, and childless.

The typical experience of being an older family member is to be engaged in relationships characterized by reciprocity, not dependency.

Across the life course, relationships are negotiated and renegotiated in response to life transitions, changing circumstances, and the availability of various ties.

Older persons have not been deserted by their families.

Diversity in family life does not necessarily denote superior and inferior alternatives but, rather, proactive strategies for dealing with varying circumstances.

Family forms that are yet to be officially legitimated carry many of the hallmarks of idealized family life, such as the caring, support, and love evident in gay and lesbian partnerships or between stepparents and their stepchildren.

The field has also matured to the point where researchers can admit to overzealous attempts to convince others of the significance of aging and family life. Several authors have documented the various ways in which we have unwittingly "oversold" the "problems" related to changes in family life (Rosenthal, 2000), intergenerational caregiving (Martin-Matthews, 2000b), the refilled nest (Mitchell, 2000), and intergenerational equity (McDaniel, 2000). For example, only a minority of families are in the structural position of having both older parents and children of young ages, and even fewer experience the simultaneous dependence of parents and children to the point of requiring care (see Chapter 8). Clearly, for those who do, the demands are pressing and sometimes overwhelming. But even here, our focus on caregiver burden has only recently been countered by recognizing the rewards of caring and the genuine interest that family members have in helping ensure the comfort and well-being of their loved ones, including older parents.

Our questions tend to be tradition bound, particularly when it comes to older persons. Thus, we have a long history of asking questions about relationships between married partners, between parents and children, and between grandparents and grandchildren. Typically, only married older persons are asked questions about their intimate partners. The separated, divorced, and widowed may be asked about their former spouse, but neither they nor single persons are likely to be asked about current lovers. The outcome is that we know virtually nothing about the intimate relationships of the unmarried in later life.

We have only recently begun to explore questions about other ties, such as those between siblings, or to consider the place of single and childless individuals as family members rather than as individuals left behind when others marry and have children. The greater instability of the spousal bond provides additional incentive for paying increased attention to the sibling tie. We have seen that siblings are central to the lives of older persons who do not have partners or children. We have also seen that siblings without such attachments are particularly valuable resources for other family members. To best appreciate what it is to be single in later life, we should explore variations in the experience of being single over the life course, for different groups and for different cohorts.

We have only recently begun to conceive of alternative family forms as simply alternatives rather than as dysfunctional versions of an ideal family. This includes asking new and different research questions about families headed by single parents, about the impact of divorce on family life, and about the rights of gay and lesbian persons to have their partnerships and families formally recognized. One reason that we know very little of the family lives of older gay and lesbian individuals is that we have failed to ask about them.

Studies are needed that examine the impact of divorce on the lives of older persons. Such research must take into account the duration of the marriage prior to divorce, the age at divorce, and differences across cohorts in the repercussions of divorce. The long-term consequences of remarriage earlier in life and of remarriage in older age require further investigation. To date, we have focused on remarriage following divorce rather than widowhood and on the consequences for younger children of both divorce and remarriage. What are the long-term effects on ties between parents and children and between siblings who are biologically linked to two parents versus one parent or who are step-relations (see Chapter 11)? Related questions concern cohabitation involving older couples. How prevalent is cohabitation in later life? What is the nature of these relationships? What are their consequences for other family ties?

Another trend with significant implications for family life is women's participation in the labor force. Although the impact of women's paid work on caregiving to young children and to old parents has received considerable attention, we know little about the impact of lifelong work on partnerships, on ties with adult children, and on relationships with grandchildren. The combination of older women working and higher divorce rates among their children could have major repercussions for the transitions that occur after divorce in both generations.

Methodological Issues

At the same time that we limit our understanding of the full range of family life through the questions that we ask and do not ask, we also obscure our perception through the kinds of research that we do. Confining ourselves to favored research methodologies hampers our ability to observe the complexity and dynamism of family life. Our ability to witness family processes is dampened by our focus on individuals rather than family relationships. As you have read, we have moved forward in our attempts to take into account the bigger family picture through examinations of family composition and through having multiple sources of information about one family or relationship. Nonetheless, much research continues to focus on a key informant (such as the "primary" caregiver; the child or sibling of greatest contact; the grandchild who lives nearest by) rather than an entire family. Because we have yet to develop one research methodology that addresses all of our concerns about family life, we must combine multiple research strategies to create a better composite picture. This involves valuing the important contributions that *both* quantitative and qualitative research can make to our understanding of family ties and aging.

A major problem in aging research, including that related to family ties, is the dependence on results from cross-sectional studies. A cross-sectional design involves obtaining information from a sample at one point in time. Therefore, one can only reach definitive conclusions about the state of affairs at the time the study was conducted. Cross-sectional designs provide an uncertain basis for drawing conclusions about change over time. Longitudinal studies, on the other hand, involve obtaining data at different times, either from the same sample or from different samples that represent the same population.

The development of several longitudinal studies using both local and national samples has made a substantial contribution to our understanding of family ties over the life course. Knowing which changes over the life course are a function of aging and which are responses to other situational factors will improve our understanding and the accuracy of our projections for the future. The strong push for a life course perspective on aging and family ties encourages more longitudinal work and emphasizes the need to consider the link between individual lives and social structure.

Theoretical Issues

Last, whereas these suggested strategies should improve our understanding of family ties and of families as a network of relationships rather than of individuals, they do not guarantee that we will place families within a larger social context. This connection can be achieved partly through the research that we do but is most likely to occur through the application of theoretical frameworks that focus on the ways in which broader social processes shape family life. Inequitable structural arrangements based on gender (including sexual orientation), race, ethnicity, and class are reproduced in families and often overpower individual objectives and initiatives, making it very difficult for some to create and maintain desired familial arrangements. For example, differential expectations of familial commitment based on gender, extreme differences in economic resources based on race and class, and varying legal rights based on age, marital status, and sexual orientation cross-cut one another to create ambivalent and sometimes conflicting situations for family members. Yet, remarkably in some cases, the family has remained resilient, in part, because of the strong efforts of family members to make their families work, despite structural pressures that mitigate against their success. Our theoretical work must incorporate this essential tension between individual agency and social structure, in part, with the objective of recommending ways in which social arrangements can be altered to reduce inequity and better support a range of family forms.

Just as appreciating diversity is central to our understanding of family life at the societal level, so too is diversity in relationships essential to all family members, including older persons. As our discussion has clearly shown, family ties remain central to the social life of Americans and Canadians. At the same time, all of us benefit from having social networks that extend beyond family. The often dire circumstances that women face in old age after a lifetime of committing themselves to family members attest to the shortcomings of extreme dependence on the family. Changes such as the increases in paid work among women and in divorce have been treated primarily as threats to the welfare of families, in general, and of children, in particular. Yet one might argue that these changes represent important transitions toward an expanded ability to negotiate a lifetime of varied relationships more independently. Social policy has an important role to play in enhancing such independence, as we see in the following discussion.

Social Policy

Reforms always are the product of political struggle and negotiation. Hence, they invariably generate positive as well as negative effects that, in turn, are mediated by gender, race, class, sexual orientation, age, and (dis)ability. On the one hand, then, law and public policy help maintain the status quo of structured inequalities by buttressing particular forms of social and family organization. At the same time, law and public policy are not merely unitary instruments of oppression wielded by white, bourgeois, heterosexual men.

—*Chunn (2000:226)*

Public Issue or Private Trouble?

Problems encountered by members of society can be perceived and treated as private troubles or public issues (Mills, 1959). Private troubles are the problems of individuals for which they are typically held responsible. Much of the explicit treatment of situations as private troubles surrounds responsibility for solving problems. However, holding individuals account-able for solving their problems can have the effect of implicitly blaming them for their problems, thereby abdicating society of the responsibility for provid-ing remedies (Ryan, 1971). When problems are treated as public issues, there is acceptance at the social level for some responsibility in providing solutions. Only rarely is a particular event or circumstance entirely a private trouble or a public issue. Instead, most situations have elements of both.

Perhaps, no area better exemplifies the delicate balance between private troubles and public issues than problems that arise within the family. When families are considered the logical source for solutions to the problems of their members, this is essentially treating problems as private troubles. When social polices are developed to support individuals and families in the resolution of problems, there is evidence of treating problems as public issues. The privacy and autonomy accorded the family and its members complicate the treatment of the family as a target for social policy. At the same time, the family's importance as a social institution has been the basis for considering it the ideal focus for policy initiatives.

Widowhood, a predominantly female experience, provides a good example of these issues. Although a widow is rarely blamed for the death of her husband, the initial adjustment to widowhood is an intensely personal process of bereavement (a private trouble) to be surmounted by the widow, with support from her family and close friends. However, some of the repercussions of widowhood, such as the poverty experienced by many widows, are more accurately considered public issues because they are, in substantial measure, socially created.

The distinction between private and public responsibility has taken on new urgency in debates about support to older persons and their families. We have observed the great extent to which older individuals and their families treat changes accompanying aging as private troubles for which they assume responsibility. Family members actively support one another under usual circumstances and increase their support in response to changes in needs brought about by poor health, divorce, the birth of a child, retirement, widowhood, remarriage, and so on. However, several factors combine to potentially limit the future ability of families to provide care for older members. First, the net effect of fewer children (except for parents of the baby boom) and living longer is an increase in the proportion of old individuals who do not have working-age children, typically the best source of support. Second, although labor force participation has not led women to abandon their parents, it has altered the ways in which care is provided and has increased the need for support from other sources. Third, divorce clearly negates the support of a spouse but also lowers the amount of support exchanged between generations, further undermining adult children as a resource in old age.

At the same time that the reservoir of familial support is shrinking (except for the parents of the baby boom), the potential needs of the older population are expanding. Ongoing differences in life expectancy between men and women and greater longevity mean there will continue to be a large number of widows and an ever-aging older population. Thus, although the older population as a whole (i.e., those over 65) may be healthier, wealthier, and more educated in the future, the more rapid growth of the oldest age group (those 75 plus) will counterbalance some of this improvement, because health and income are lower in this age cohort, especially among widows. Yet at a time when the very trends that increase the need for support also impede the ability of family members to provide more of it, governments are cutting back publicly funded programs, effectively transferring care to families (Gerstel and Gallagher, 1994).

The Intergenerational Equity Debate

The intergenerational equity debate centers on the view that each generation must receive its fair share of government spending (public transfers). On one side are those who argue that the old are receiving too much, at the expense of the young. On the other are those who disagree and believe that discussions of equity must include more than current government expenditures. The view of intergenerational inequity as a problem has strong roots in the United States where, in 1984, Americans for Generational Equity (AGE) was formed with the objective of applying Thomas Jefferson's view that each generation should ensure that the succeeding one enjoys similar or greater levels of prosperity (Bengtson, 1993). In Britain, Johnson, Conrad, and Thomson (1989) argued that elderly people are "parasitic upon the state and ultimately on taxpayers" and paralleled AGE's effect in the United States of enabling "governments already committed to cuts in state benefits and services to justify these to lay part of the blame for the economic crisis on elderly people" (Arber and Ginn, 1991:54).

Comparisons of Canadian and U.S. policy have cast Canada as more publicly minded, collectivist, and egalitarian (Clark, 1993; Myles, 1989). Sadly, however, claims that the intergenerational equity debate does not apply to Canada (Marshall et al., 1993; Schulz, 1997) now ring hollow as both countries have shared trends in deficit reduction, downsizing, and cost cutting in the public and private spheres. An outcome of these trends is a renewed focus on methods for reducing public support, such as espousing a philosophy of community-based rather than institutional care. However, in an economic climate where funds do not match rhetoric (Chappell, 1993), this typically means an increased reliance on family members who are often already overextended. Another result is further entrenchment of the intergenerational equity debate, as one age group is cast against another as more or less deserving of government funds in the face of a general reluctance to increase support to all age groups. Debates about public sector support center on the claim that imbalanced governmental transfers favor the old (Marshall et al., 1993).

Claims of intergenerational inequity might be supportable if one focused narrowly on one point in time and on only public transfers to old people, particularly the very old (Cornman and Kingson, 1996). But these claims stand up very poorly if one expands the horizon to include a lifetime of contributions to society, including to the public purse (Cornman and Kingson, 1996), as well as the private transfers that older people make, particularly to their families, over their lifetimes (Marshall, 1997; Marshall et al., 1993; McDaniel, 1997; Stone et al., 1998).

These lifelong and continuing efforts of older people make it impossible to claim lack of individual initiative. Yet the push for "fiscal responsibility," and the resulting cuts in programs of all kinds that have ensued, have stymied the groundswell of growing demands to humanize, personalize, integrate, and expand social programs that arose in the eighties (Dobell and Mansbridge, 1986). In Canada, for example, public protests, mainly led by older persons, successfully halted the federal government's plan to fix pension benefits in 1985. By the end of the century, much broader pension changes were introduced without incident. Similarly, in the United States, where one third of federal spending goes to programs for older persons, a general willingness to expand benefits to the aged can no longer be assumed (Steckenrider, 1999).

Age-Based Versus Needs-Based Social Policy

There is some debate concerning whether or not social policy should be age based. Some time ago, Marshall (1981) discussed two scenarios of what the future holds for older persons, a best case and a worst case, mirroring current discussions of whether we are moving toward an age-integrated society (Riley and Riley, 2000; Uhlenberg, 2000). In the best case, described more recently as the scenario of postmodern optimism (Giddens, 1991), age will become irrelevant because of the improved health, education, and status of older people. Thus, age-based policies will become increasingly unnecessary and, indeed, are to be avoided both now and in the future because they reinforce age segregation. In the worst case, also dubbed the nightmare scenario (Giddens, 1991), the one that Marshall predicts will occur, significant differences among age groups will continue and, because these differences place older persons at a disadvantage, age-based policies to counter them will also continue to be required.

As long as there are age-based limits to labor market accessibility in the form of the common practice of retirement by the age of 65 and a reluctance to hire older workers, claims of age irrelevance are hard to justify. Indeed, the expectation of retirement and the inability of some to continue working for health reasons suggest some responsibility on behalf of the state to ensure economic viability in later life. The age set for either mandatory (in Canada) or customary retirement (indirectly through age requirements for benefits such as Social Security in the United States) can serve as an economic safety valve. In times of high unemployment, an earlier age is either encouraged or required. An economic upswing results in both increased employment and a move to an older retirement age. If current moves to delay both retirement and eligibility for pension benefits continue (Henretta, 2000), government responsibility may once again be replaced by private earnings. However, if subtle or overt discrimination against older workers continues (Guillemard, 2000), it is unlikely that such changes in policy will be met by corresponding changes in employment eligibility of more than a year or two beyond current retirement ages.

Provision of services in response to need reflects a view recommended by Cain (1987:291) that the "proper quest for policy makers is to provide equal concern and respect—not necessarily equal resources or access to services—to members of various age categories." Hence, groups of any age who have particular circumstances that necessitate public support should receive it. The rising poverty rates among children in both Canada and the United States and a failure to contend adequately with this trend in two of the world's richest nations are cause for concern.

> It is hard to imagine that a society that does not respond to the plight of its children will look kindly on its frail and older members. At the same time, it is hard to imagine an effective response to children's needs that will not involve public values that will in turn affect older persons. (Cornman and Kingson, 1996:19)

In other words, supporting the young and old need not be treated as a zero-sum game; meeting the needs of one group will assist the other, and meeting the needs of both groups is essential.

Social policies that provide for one age group tend to benefit other generations because assets are shared within families. Consequently, financial transfers to older persons do not only decrease their dependence on family members. They also increase older persons' financial contributions to children and grandchildren (Foner, 2000). We have seen that grandparents are especially important resources to grandchildren in families experiencing a spate of challenges, including poverty, racial discrimination, drug use, and divorce. These same grandparents often face considerable hardship in providing this support. Social policies that support either children or older persons help the other generation; helping both children and older persons multiplies the reciprocal benefits to both generations. As well, the personal concern of younger persons for their older relatives fosters a willingness to contribute to public programs for older people (Attias-Donfut, 2000; Foner, 2000).

For older persons, the principles of basing support on age and on need are reflected in social policy. Eligibility for social insurance programs rests on age and is exemplified in the United States by Social Security and Medicare (Meyer and Bellas, 1995). Social assistance programs are based on need, as in the case of Supplemental Security Income and Medicaid. Determining whether older persons are in need tends to be a humiliating process, and such social assistance programs are likely to pit taxpayer against welfare recipient. Social insurance programs, although expensive, are generally more popular because all contributors are beneficiaries. Despite their apparent universality, both Social Security and Medicare leave some groups, most notably women, Blacks, Hispanics, and the poor, vulnerable because social security is tied to previous labor force involvement; long-term care can quickly deplete their limited benefits (Meyer and Bellas, 1995). The safety net provided by assistance programs does not catch all of those who need additional support.

Tax-based programs, such as deductions for retirement savings plans, are another form of public support (Cornman and Kingson, 1996). Tax deductions for those who care for relatives, which may be used as an incentive for informal caring, yield limited results (Linsk, Keigher, England, and Simon-Rusinowitz, 1995). As well, there are private transfers, including private and public pension plans, employment-based health benefits, and the extensive range of support offered by family and friends (Cornman and Kingson, 1996).

The need for support is the most compelling reason that public programs should be augmented. It is also inconsistent to encourage older persons' dependence on family members, particularly children, in a culture that places such high value on independence. We know that parents derive greater satisfaction from their relationships with children when there is reciprocity rather than dependency. As well, studies from several Western nations show that today's older population favors formal over informal support for personal and long-term care (Daatland, 1990; Wielink et al., 1997). Providing assistance, including funds, directly to older individuals helps them to maintain their position in exchange relations with others instead of becoming more dependent and subservient (Brubaker and Brubaker, 1995; Kane and Penrod, 1995; Pyke, 1999). Furthermore, intergenerational investment has been proposed as a counter to the concept of intergenerational equity and views age-based public supports to older persons as a large insurance benefit that protects younger generations from the personal debt they would accrue if their older relatives were sick or poor (Greene and Marty, 1999).

Support for Caregivers

A key reason that the family cannot be considered a true substitute for other social programs for the elderly is that caregivers also require support, especially if care is given for a long time. On balance, family caregivers want to help older persons, and formal support does not serve as a substitute for their efforts (Brody, 1995; Miller, 1998). Like the cared for, caregivers also receive extensive help from other family members, but they require help from formal services as well. The more extensive support to and from older persons evident among ethnic and racial minorities, particularly through coresidence (Brotman, 1998; Clarke and Neidert, 1992; Minkler, 1999), means that special efforts must be made to provide support to these caregivers. Because qualifying for limited formal support services often requires children to emphasize the burden of caring for their parents, relations between older parents and their adult children can be undermined. As well, the complicated access routes to fragmented services lead many caregivers to give up trying to obtain formal support (Miller, 1998).

Formal services are essential, not only because there are limits to the support that family can provide but also because some types of care are best provided personally or informally and others formally. Rather than viewing any form of care as the ideal, we must instead work toward coordinating complementary support from various sources. A value shift in this direction is evident in policy paradigms that focus on caring partnerships, in which all caregivers, whether formal or informal, coordinate their efforts; and on client-centered care, in which older persons are clients rather than patients and are considered partners in the caring process (Keating, Fast, Connidis, Penning, and Keefe, 1997). Although this orientation is laudable, there is the risk of a subtext that will have the net effect of shifting more responsibility to older persons and their families.

Meeting Diverse Needs

One of the central critiques of the intergenerational-equity premise is the focus on differences *between* age groups rather than the substantial differences *within* age groups based on gender, race, class, and health status (Bengtson and Murray, 1993; Marshall, 1997; Stone et al., 1998). Increasing inequity is the foundation for ongoing cleavages that cut across age groups and affect the daily lives of families (Jackson and Kalavar, 1993). One appeal of focusing on intergenerational equity is the greater simplicity of altering age-based government transfers than of tackling more fundamental but thorny challenges, such as poverty and racism. Nonetheless, the most wrenching demands on familial relationships tend to be made on those who have the fewest resources. As well, it is in these families that the older generation is most likely to be giving more support than it is receiving (Jackson and Kalavar, 1993).

The substantial drop in financial status experienced by older persons generally, and the high poverty rates among visible minority seniors and older women in particular (Brotman, 1998), can only be redressed if treated as public issues rather than private troubles. The growing ethnic and racial diversity among older persons (Angel, 1999; Cornman and Kingson, 1996) is one reason that the improved standard of living among today's seniors must not be the basis for a complacent stance toward cutbacks in publicly funded support to older persons. Yet dealing with inequality based on race and ethnicity poses a unique quandary. How does one strike the right balance between recognizing the negative consequences of socially created structural conditions that leave some in a position of relative disadvantage and respecting the effective adaptations of familial arrangements as a proactive strategy? If too much emphasis is placed on the disadvantages faced by particular groups, such as Black and Hispanic Americans, there is a risk of promoting the view that their familial arrangements are dysfunctional. But if the focus is placed too heavily on successful culturally based reliance on extended family relationships, there is the risk of relying too much on strong family ties and failing to acknowledge social responsibility for structurally created conditions (Burnette, 1999). An overly monolithic view of particular minority groups also risks minimizing the substantial historical and cultural diversity within them (Dilworth-Anderson and Burton, 1999). However, on balance, the impact of minority status, poverty, and accessibility appear to loom larger than cultural preferences in explaining the long-term care arrangements of older persons (Mui, Choi, and Monk, 1998).

This quandary is reflected in debates such as whether to encourage marriage among African Americans by minimizing support to single parents and maximizing support to those who marry (Cherlin, 1992). In the end, forcing a choice between how much support to give single versus married parents does not address the issue satisfactorily, in part, because of the moral judgments implicit in either strategy. Instead, addressing issues of unemployment among young Black men, a fundamental structural issue, is likely to be a more fruitful approach (Cherlin, 1992). One net effect of this support is to lighten the load of grandparents caring for their grandchildren. In Hispanic families, such change would also spell relief for the far higher proportion of aunts and great aunts who provide intensive help to their (great) nieces and nephews (Minkler, 1999).

In the longer term, more racial and gender equality in the labor force today will benefit younger generations, reducing their dependency on older generations. However, such initiatives at the early stages of employment must extend as well to the end of work careers. Although Black and White men and women have all retired at earlier ages over the past few decades (Gendell and Siegel, 1996), Black and Hispanic older persons and women are more likely to experience early involuntary exit from the labor force. This early exit often becomes retirement and reduces years of earnings and subsequent pensions in old age (Flippen and Tienda, 2000). Poverty lies at the heart of many of the dilemmas confronted by older persons and their families and is particularly high among those who engage most in support exchanges with kin (Minkler, 1999).

Just as is true of race, gender cross-cuts concerns about social policy from the perspective of both the older person and the caregiver. In old age, women face more economic hardship, in substantial measure because they are more likely to be alone for longer periods as a result of being widowed or divorced (Holden and Kuo, 1996). Of course, the reason that being on their own has such dramatic consequences is that most of today's older women did not accumulate their own wealth during their younger years. Instead, they spent most of their lives engaged in caring for others, work that is both undervalued and unpaid (Hooyman and Gonyea, 1995).

Like all groups, women's circumstances in old age are the outcome of a lifetime of experience. Limited paid work minimizes access not only to benefits through work but also to state-based support that rests on financial contributions in earlier years, such as social security in the United States or old age security in Canada. Even among middle-aged, full-time paid workers with pension coverage, men's accumulated pension wealth is significantly greater than women's, reflecting the dual labor market and the more checkered employment histories of women (Johnson, Sambamoorthi, and Crystal, 1999). The treatment of caring as a personal trouble for families (women) to manage continues to have a firm hold, despite other social changes. Yet only when caring is respected as an issue to be dealt with at the societal level can women escape the costs of caring that follow them into old age (Hooyman and Gonyea, 1995; Neysmith, 1991).

Women are particularly in need of financial support through public policy and through changes in the private sector, such as improvements in eligibility for and value of work-based pensions. However, the gendered structure of our society also oppresses men but in quite different ways. For example, divorced men tend to be especially isolated in old age, a situation shaped considerably by the fact that, during their younger years, their former spouses typically received custody of their children. Restructuring society based on equitable gender relations is likely to enhance the social networks of men, giving them the opportunity to develop more involved familial ties. As the case of old divorced men illustrates, such changes must occur across the life course, including caring for children. Inequities cannot be corrected at the end of life through targeted social programs—for women or men.

The gendered nature of caregiving is reflected in the fact that women provide more care to older persons and are expected to do so, weakening their negotiating position when families work out who will help. The collision between caring responsibilities and labor force participation reveals the essential tension between work and family when they are treated as two independent, rather than overlapping, spheres of social life. When the labor market was primarily the domain of men and the family the domain of women, the stark realities of meeting demands in both arenas was hidden because far fewer workers were affected. Now, it is clear that, if family caregiving is to remain viable, there must be more latitude in the work place. Such change moves slowly, particularly during times of high unemployment and when there are still widely held views among employers that work and family should remain separate (Rosenthal, 1997).

As economic prospects brighten and as combining paid work and family become normative for women and men, employers are becoming more aware of and responsive to the needs of those employees caring for older family members (Neal, Chapman, Ingersoll-Dayton, and Emlen, 1993). Nonetheless, in both the United States and Canada, there is much room for expanding work-based policies that facilitate meeting the simultaneous demands of employment and family caring. Favored benefits to help balance work and family commitments among employees include time off without pay, flexible time, compressed work weeks, personal days with pay, part-time work that permits maintenance of regular benefits (Martin-Matthews, 1999), and being able to work at home (Merrill, 1997).

A hallmark of social policy must be diversity. I have noted the substantial differences in family dynamics and old age that result from inequities based on gender, race, ethnicity, and class. When these intersect with each other and with old age, relative social disadvantage is compounded. A strategy of serving older persons and their families that rests on promoting one approach, however popular that approach might be, cannot succeed, because the needs and situations of older individuals are too variable.

Community-Based Support

What types of formal support do older persons and their families need? Direct financial support to caregiving family members, through tax incentives or actual payment, is primarily beneficial in relieving some of the strain and enhancing the autonomy of those committed to caring for an older member. However, financial assistance is unlikely to encourage more families to provide care or to avert institutionalization, and the ethical debate about paying individuals who already have a moral obligation to care is one reason that many states forbid financial compensation to family caregivers (Kapp, 1995). Yet paying family caregivers who have few resources has the merit of redistributing income (Kane and Penrod, 1995; Linsk et al., 1995).

A number of programs share the common goal of bolstering the ability of older individuals to remain in the community, either independently or with the support of family. These include homemaker services, meal preparation (meals-on-wheels, wheels-to-meals), personal in-home care, telephone information and assistance, assistance for minor household repairs, transportation, and day care and respite care programs. To the extent that some of these services (e.g., transportation) enhance the independence of elderly individuals, they reduce dependence on families. Support such as day care and respite care provide either daily or periodic relief from caregiving. Although respite care does not alter caregiver well-being appreciably, it is lauded by those who use it and serves a useful function in meeting short-term needs for additional support (Kane and Penrod, 1995; Linsk et al., 1995). Day care programs have the additional advantage of providing the older individual with a social outlet. As well, these programs are an independent source of activity that is not family based and are, therefore, more likely to enhance self-esteem.

Although a number of these services and programs are available in many communities, a key problem is their coordination. Elders and their families often face difficulties in finding services, not because they do not exist but because they cannot locate them. Furthermore, the support provided by family and by the formal sector is far more effective if properly coordinated (Brubaker and Brubaker, 1995). Involving the family caregiver as a case manager, along with the older person as client, is one strategy for enhancing the coordination of informal and formal help. Historically, the success of many community- and institution-based services has relied heavily on an active volunteer sector. Higher labor force participation rates among women threaten the viability of this resource in the future because volunteers are predominantly women. At the same time, however, paid work among women increases the ability of many families to purchase care for their members, young and old.

The Ongoing Need for Institutional Support

Thus far, we have focused attention on family caregiving and community-based care. But the philosophical and financial appeal of community-based programs must not divert attention from the ongoing and potentially heightened need for improvements in institutional care, as the oldest of the old are the fastest growing segment of the older population. Over 40% of those who were aged 65 in 1990 are expected to spend some time in a nursing home over the course of their lives (Brubaker and Brubaker, 1995). More and better institutional alternatives are needed for those with limited options for familial support and for those whose care requirements exceed what family members and community-based programs can handle.

Legal Intervention in Family Ties

Looking beyond social policy itself, the law serves as a vehicle for change and a reflection of our cultural beliefs about family life and the obligations of family members to one another. In Canada, all 10 provinces have legislation regarding support obligations of adult children to their older parents, either as a separate Parents' Maintenance Act, or as part of a Family Law Reform Act. Such acts reflect a belief in reciprocity between parent and child and, unlike earlier acts, do not require evidence of parental destitution due to specified circumstances, such as mental illness. However, very few cases under parents' maintenance acts are ever brought to court. When parents do succeed at obtaining support from children through the courts, the cases typically involve financial need by the parents, financial capacity of the children, and a history of adequate parental support to the child (Martin-Matthews, 2000a). Two cases exemplify the unusual circumstances that lead to successful litigation. In the first (*In re Blum and Blum,* January 21, 1982, Dominion Law Reports, 132 (3d):69-73), a mother petitioned for support from her son because her husband had avoided support payments by divesting himself of all assets. Meanwhile, the son was supporting his father and had been assisting his mother as well, up to the time when she took her husband to court. The mother was granted support from her son. Higher divorce rates might increase the number of such cases.

In a second case (*St. Joseph's Health Centre v. Sauro et al.,* 1984, 45 Ontario Reports (2d)221-224), the plaintiff was not the parent but an institution that had provided chronic care to the father. The institution's claim against the children was for the costs of their father's care prior to his death. The court ruled that the Family Law Reform Act of Ontario did not extend the obligation of children to their parents' creditors but only concerned direct support from child to parent. Therefore, the children were not required to pay their father's hospital bill. This decision contrasts somewhat with legislative efforts in the United States where the Health Care Financing Administration allows state Medicaid offices to curtail nursing home expenses by passing "family responsibility" laws that require family members to help cover costs (Linsk et al., 1995). However, to date, attempts to apply such statutes have been few and have resulted in very little capital accruing to nursing homes (Kapp, 1995).

Although legislation that directly concerns family caregiving to older persons is very limited, there are other ways in which the law has been used as a vehicle to change family ties across the life course. Two current issues stand as examples: attempts to secure visitation rights for grandparents and attempts to have gay and lesbian relationships legally recognized.

Efforts to gain visitation rights by grandparents have a long history. In 1984, grandparent contact with grandchildren was declared a moral rather than a legal obligation, so parents were not required to permit grandparent visitation (Wacker, 1995). However, by 1991, statutes concerning grandparents' visitation rights were in place in all 50 states, but they usually require a divorce, separation, or death of parent(s) for grandparents to make a claim. If parents and children are together, grandparents cannot seek visitation rights in any state. Parental rights continue to take precedence, and grandparents may well be denied access when parents argue their rights to privacy and to judge appropriate levels of grandparental access to their child(ren) (Aldous, 1995). The isolation of grandparents from their grandchildren, particularly following the awarding of custody to their child-in-law, has prompted the creation of advocacy groups aimed at securing additional grandparent rights (Bender and Brannon, 1994; Hilton and Macari, 1997). The policy implications of growing numbers of single-parent families is one incentive for governmental support of grandparents' desire to carry out their ongoing commitment to their grandchildren (Aldous, 1995).

A related issue for grandparents is their status as caregivers. The mixed experience of caring for grandchildren is one reason for differing views of how much it should be encouraged (Johnson, 1997; Robertson, 1997). On balance, assuming full parental responsibility for grandchildren is not an experience welcomed by most grandparents (Johnson, 1997). Although grandparents do not have the rights of access to grandchildren that parents do to children, when serving as caregivers, the fact that they are relatives often limits accessibility to financial assistance (Landry-Meyer, 1999). Given that grandparents caring for grandchildren are often poor, it is not surprising that one of their overwhelming concerns is whether they can afford to look after their grandchildren. Obtaining legal custody of grandchildren, a process that can prove difficult and costly, is a significant issue for grandparents who are raising their grandchildren (Landry-Meyer, 1999). Some states have instituted alternative legal relationships between grandparents and grandchildren that grant grandparents parental authority without going through a custody case.

The changing role of grandparents in the lives of their grandchildren is but one outcome of the changing face of families. Rising numbers of divorce, remarriage, and cohabitation have meant changes in family structure, including a growing number of families that involve various step relationships (Milan, 2000). Changes in public policy, including legal rights and obligations, must keep pace with the emergence of these new ties (Mason and Mauldon, 1999). Current inconsistencies include the contrast between the "stranger" model of some policies, in which coresident stepparents have no rights or responsibilities, and the "dependency" model, in which it is assumed that a coresident father is providing financial support (Mason, 1998).

The fight for gay and lesbian rights has included efforts to obtain legal standing for same-sex relationships to garner the social, legal, and economic benefits that go with marriage (Dean, 1994; Rubenstein, 1996; Schwartz and Rutter, 1998). Resistance to instituting gay and lesbian relationships as marriage in both the United States and Canada demonstrates the significance of gender and sexual orientation as a basis for establishing rights and obligations.

> Gender difference is central to the social control of intimacy. Indeed, homosexual marriage provides the perfect experimental design. Only one crucial variable—gender—has been altered, and all others remain constant (love, commitment, concern for property, union of two families). Varying gender in the context of marriage, it turns out, is a highly provocative innovation. (Schwartz and Rutter, 1998:184-185)

So strong was the backlash following the 1996 passage of same-sex unions in Hawaii (repealed in a 1999 final ruling) and the rise of the family values debate during the Dole-Clinton campaign, that the Defense of Marriage Act was passed (Schwartz and Rutter, 1998). This federal law explicitly does not recognize same-sex relationships as marriage, thus denying access to related benefits. Furthermore, states are not required to recognize same-sex marriages that take place in another state. This sets a precedent of federal involvement in state powers by breaking with the long-standing requirement of the states to recognize marriages and divorces that occur in another state.

As we have seen in earlier chapters, being in unsanctioned same-sex partnerships can undermine the familial commitments that these couples desire. For example, financial security in old age or after the death of one partner is threatened when couples are not treated as though married, and the right to be treated as a family member when one partner is ill is not guaranteed (Rubenstein, 1996). Legal marriage includes myriad state and federal entitlements, including a spouse's pension, social security survivor benefits, inheritance, bereavement leave, child custody, divorce protection, and sick leave to care for a spouse (Demian, 2000). Although there is not uniform support for same-sex marriage in the gay and lesbian community, these tangible disadvantages to not having legal status as married couples led some gay and lesbian individuals to use the courts to gain access to benefits, regardless of marital status. A growing number of employers now offer spousal benefits to same-sex partners of their employees, and some municipalities have legal domestic partnerships that give cohabiting couples access to benefits, whatever their gender or sexual orientation (Stacey, 1998). Some government jurisdictions, such as the state of Vermont in the United States and the province of Ontario in Canada, have extended the benefits of married couples to same-sex couples. But they do not recognize their unions as marriage.

Failure to sanction same-sex couple relationships undermines the parental rights of both biological and nonbiological lesbian or gay parents, whose intimate relationships often serve as justification for denying custody (Millbank, 1997; Rubenstein, 1996). Parenthood remains more common among lesbians than gays and, among older persons, is most often the consequence of a former heterosexual marriage (Stacey, 1998). In addition to maintaining custody, current legal efforts by lesbians and gays include obtaining second-parent (the nonbiological parent) adoption rights.

In terms of social programs targeted at older people, gay and lesbian individuals face difficult situations as they confront discriminatory attitudes among those who administer resources and services (Ehrenberg, 1997). Although all sexual activity in institutional settings tends to be shunned by staff, this is particularly true of gay and lesbian relations. Limited acceptance is one reason that older gay and lesbian persons generally favor living in a gay or lesbian retirement community over one for gay and straight residents (Quam and Whitford, 1992). Thus, the progress that has been made in increasing the number of social, educational, and outreach services directed toward older gay and lesbian persons (Jacobson and Grossman, 1996) must continue.

Conclusion

The family values debate of the past two decades and the rise of postmodernism in various disciplines has highlighted the family as an institution in decline. Yet although considerable change in family relations over the years has occurred, it is difficult to conclude that this change has been uniformly negative. Instead, the greater diversity of family life and the variations in family form that have occurred over the past 50 years also mean new options and strengths (Johnson, 1995) as we begin a new century. A long view of family life, aided by taking the vantage point of older family members, suggests a timelessness in the quest to develop and invest in familial relationships. As this chapter has illustrated, policy initiatives designed to benefit older persons and their families can cast a broad net. Although some programs are clearly targeted at meeting the immediate demands of particular situations, these can only be effective if built on a foundation of income adequacy and accessibility to health care—regardless of age, race, gender, sexual orientation, ethnicity, class, and marital status. Thus, to address the challenges faced by older persons and their family members, we must address these fundamental social issues.

Ultimately, a caring environment cannot be legislated. In a society valuing the independence and support of all adult members, policies that increase the ability of older persons to help themselves and that support families in the comprehensive help they offer their senior members best serve the interests of all family members. Direct financial assistance to older individuals and their care providers permits autonomous decision making regarding purchased services. More active promotion of existing services would help seniors and family members avoid undue delays in discovering appropriate community support. More broadly, however, there is a need for greater recognition of the obligations of family members caring for an older person. If the family is to continue to meet the needs of its members, young and old, family interests must be permitted to coexist with, and sometimes supersede, those of other domains.

References

Adelman, Marcy. 1991. Stigma, gay lifestyles, and adjustment to aging: A study of later-life gay men and lesbians. Pp. 7-32 in John Alan Lee (Ed.), *Gay midlife and maturity*. New York: Haworth.

Ade-Ridder, Linda. 1990. Sexuality and marital quality among older married couples. Pp. 48-67 in Timothy H. Brubaker (Ed.), *Family relationships in later life* 2nd ed. Newbury Park, CA: Sage.

Ade-Ridder, Linda, and Timothy H. Brubaker. 1983.The quality of long-term marriages. Pp. 77-90 in Timothy H. Brubaker (Ed.), *Family relationships in later life*. Beverly Hills, CA: Sage.

Aldous, Joan. 1994. Someone to watch over me: Family responsibilities and their realization across family lives. Pp. 42-68 in Eva Kahana, David Biegel, and May Wykle (Eds.), *Family caregiving across the lifespan*. Thousand Oaks, CA: Sage.

Aldous, Joan. 1995. New views of grandparents in intergenerational conflict. *Journal of Family Issues* 16:1:104-122.

Alexander, Baine B., Robert L. Rubinstein, Marcene Goodman, and Mark Luborsky. 1992. A path not taken: A cultural analysis of regrets and childlessness in the lives of older women. *The Gerontologist* 32:5:618-625.

Allan, Graham. 1977. Sibling solidarity. *Journal of Marriage and the Family* 39:Feb: 177-183.

Allen, Katherine R. 1989. *Single women/family ties: Life histories of older women*. Newbury Park, CA: Sage.

Allen, Katherine R., and David H. Demo. 1995. The families of lesbians and gay men: A new frontier in family research. *Journal of Marriage and the Family* Feb:11-127.

Allen, Katherine R., and Robert S. Pickett. 1987. Forgotten streams in the family life course: Utilization of qualitative retrospective interviews in the analysis of life-long single women's family careers. *Journal of Marriage and the Family* 49:Aug: 517-526.

Allen, Susan M. 1994. Gender differences in spousal caregiving and unmet need for care. *Journal of Gerontology: Social Sciences* 49:4:S187-S195.

Allen, Susan M., Frances Goldscheider, and Desiree A. Ciambrone. 1999. Gender roles, marital intimacy, and nomination of spouse as primary caregiver. *The Gerontologist* 39:2:150-158.

Amato, Paul R. 1996. Explaining the intergenerational transmission of divorce. *Journal of Marriage and the Family* 58:3:628-640.

Amato, Paul R., and Bruce Keith. 1991. Parental divorce and adult well-being: A meta-analysis. *Journal of Marriage and the Family* 53:1:43-58.

Ambert, Anne-Marie. 1998. Divorce: Facts, figures, and consequences. *Contemporary family trends.* Ottawa: Vanier Institute of the Family.

American Association of Retired Persons. 1999a. Modern maturity talks about sex! *Modern Maturity* Web edition. Sept-Oct. (Web site:www.aarp.org/mmaturity/sep_oct 99).

American Association of Retired Persons. 1999b. Ms.behavin' again. *Modern Maturity* Web edition. May-June. (Web Site: www.aarp.org/mmaturity/may_jun99).

American Association of Retired Persons. 1999c. Life lines: Everything you wanted to know about sex after 50. *Modern Maturity* Web edition. Sept-Oct. (Web site: www.aarp.org/mmaturity/sep_oct99).

American Association of Retired Persons. 2000. AARP survey: *Grandparents, grandchildren have strong bond, visit often.* News release, January 4. Web Site: www.aarp.org/press/2000/nr010400.html.

Angel, Ronald J. 1999. Cultural sensitivity—Who needs it? Book review. *The Gerontologist* 39:3:376-378.

Angel, Ronald J., Jacqueline L. Angel, and Christine L. Himes. 1992. Minority group status, health transitions, and community living arrangements among the elderly. *Research on Aging* 14:4:496-521.

Angel, Ronald J., Jacqueline L. Angel, Judi L. McClellan, and Kyriakos S. Markides. 1996. Nativity, declining health, and preferences in living arrangements among elderly Mexican Americans: Implications for long-term care. *The Gerontologist* 36:4:464-473.

Antonucci, Toni C. 1990. Social supports and social relationships. Pp. 205-226 in Robert H. Binstock and Linda K. George (Eds.), *Handbook of Aging and the Social Sciences.* 3rd ed. New York: Academic Press.

Antonucci, Toni C., and Hiroko Akiyama. 1995. Convoys of social relations: Family and friendship within a life span context. Pp. 355-372 in Rosemary Blieszner and Victoria Hilkevitch Bedford (Eds.), *Handbook of aging and the family.* Westport, CN: Greenwood.

Antonucci, Toni C., Rebecca Fuhrer, and James S. Jackson. 1990. Social support and reciprocity: A cross-ethnic and cross-national perspective. *Journal of Social and Personal Relationships* 7:519-530.

Aquilino, William S. 1990.The likelihood of parent-adult child coresidence: Effects of family structure and parental characteristics. *Journal of Marriage and the Family* 52:May:405-419.

Aquilino, William S. 1994. Later life parental divorce and widowhood: Impact on young adults' assessment of parent-child relations. *Journal of Marriage and the Family* 56:Nov:908-922.

Aquilino, William S., and Khalil R. Supple. 1991. Parent-child relations and parent's satisfaction with living arrangements when adult children live at home. *Journal of Marriage and the Family* 53:1:13-27.

Aranda, Maria P., and Bob G. Knight. 1997. The influence of ethnicity and culture on the caregiver stress and coping process: A sociocultural review and analysis. *The Gerontologist* 37:3:342-354.

Arber, Sara, and Jay Ginn. 1991. *Gender and later life*. London: Sage.

Arbuckle, Nancy Weber, and Brian de Vries. 1995. The long-term effects of later life spousal and parental bereavement on personal functioning. *The Gerontologist* 35: 5:637-647.

Aronson, Jane. 1992. Women's sense of responsibility for the care of old people: "But who else is going to do it?" *Gender and Society* 6:1:8-29.

Askham, Janet. 1995. The married lives of older people. Pp. 86-97 in Sara Arber and Jay Ginn (Eds.), *Connecting gender and ageing: A sociological approach*. Buckingham, UK: Open University Press.

Atchley, Robert C., and M. Powell Lawton. 1997. Is gerontology biased toward a negative view of the aging process and old age? YES: Robert C. Atchley, NO: M. Powell Lawton. Pp. 197-208 in Andrew E. Scharlach and Lenard W. Kaye (Eds.), *Controversial issues in aging*. Boston: Allyn and Bacon.

Atchley, Robert C., and Sheila J. Miller. 1983. Types of elderly couples. Pp. 77-90 in Timothy H. Brubaker (Ed.), *Family relationships in later life*. Beverly Hills: Sage.

Atkinson, Maxine P., Vira R. Kivett, and Richard T. Campbell. 1986. Intergenerational solidarity: An examination of a theoretical model. *Journal of Gerontology* 41:3: 408-416.

Attias-Donfut, Claudine. 2000. Cultural and economic transfers between generations: One aspect of age integration. *The Gerontologist* 40:3:270-272.

Auger, Jeanette A. 1995. Lesbians and aging: Triple trouble or tremendous thrill. Pp. 105-114 in Robynne Neugebaurer-Visano (Ed.), *Seniors and sexuality: Experiencing intimacy in later life*. Toronto: Canadian Scholar's Press.

Avioli, Paula S. 1989. The social support functions of siblings in later life: A theoretical model. *American Behavioral Scientist* 33:45-57.

Bachrach, Christine A. 1980. Childlessness and social isolation among the elderly. *Journal of Marriage and the Family* 42:627-637.

Bank, Stephen, and Michael D. Kahn. 1982. Intense sibling loyalties. Pp. 251-266 in Michael E. Lamb and Brian Sutton-Smith (Eds.), *Sibling relationships: Their nature and significance across the lifespan*. Hillside, NJ: Lawrence Erlbaum.

Barrett, Anne E. 1999. Social support and life satisfaction among the never married. *Research on Aging* 21:1:46-72.

Barrett, Anne E., and Scott M. Lynch. 1999. Caregiving networks of elderly persons: Variation by marital status. *The Gerontologist* 39:6:695-704.

Bedford, Victoria H. 1989. Sibling ambivalence in adulthood. *Journal of Family Issues* 10:211-224.

Bedford, Victoria H. 1992. Memories of parental favoritsm and the quality of parent-child ties in adulthood. *Journal of Gerontology: Social Sciences* 47:3:S149-S155.

Bedford, Victoria H. 1995. Sibling relationships in middle and old age. Pp. 201-222 in Rosemary Blieszner and Victoria Hilkevitch Bedford (Eds.), *Handbook of aging and the family*. Westport, CT: Greenwood.

Belgrave, Linda Liska, and Julia E. Bradsher. 1994. Health as a factor in institutionalization: Disparities between African Americans and Whites. *Research on Aging* 16:2:115-141.

Belgrave, Linda Liska, May L. Wykle, and Jung M. Choi. 1993. Health, double jeopardy, and culture: The use of institutionalization by African-Americans. *The Gerontologist* 33:3:379-385.

Bender, William N., and Lynn Brannon. 1994. Victimization and non-custodial parents, grandparents, and children as a function of sole custody: Views of the advocacy groups and research support. *Journal of Divorce and Remarriage* 21:3/4: 81-114.

Bengtson, Vern L. 1993. Is the "contract across generations" changing? Effects of population aging on obligations and expectations across age groups. Pp. 3-23 in V. L. Bengtson and W. A. Achenbaum (Eds.), *The changing contract across generations*. New York: Aldine De Gruyter.

Bengtson, Vern L., Roseann Giarrusso, Merril Silverstein, and Haitao Wang. 2000. Families and intergenerational relationships in aging societies. *Hallym International Journal of Aging* 2:1:3-10.

Bengtson, Vern L., and Robert A. Harootyan. 1994. *Intergenerational linkages: Hidden connections in American society*. New York: Springer.

Bengtson, Vern L., and Tonya M. Murray. 1993. "Justice" across generations (and cohorts): Sociological perspectives on the life course and reciprocities over time. Pp. 111-138 in Lee M. Cohen (Ed.), *The changing contract across generations*. New York: Aldine De Gruyter.

Bengtson, Vern L., Carolyn J. Rosenthal, and Linda M. Burton. 1996. Paradoxes of family and aging. Pp. 253-282 in R. H.Binstock and L. K. George (Eds.), *Handbook of aging and the social sciences*. 4th ed. New York: Academic Press.

Bengtson, Vern L., and S. Schrader. 1982. Parent-child relations: The measurement of intergenerational interaction and affect in old age. In D. J. Mangen and W. Peterson (Eds.), *Research instruments in social gerontology*. Minneapolis: University of Minnesota Press.

Berger, Raymond M. 1996. What are older homosexual men like? Pp. 155-199 in Raymond M. Berger (Ed.), *Gay and grey: The older homosexual man*. 2nd ed. New York: Harrington Park.

Berger, Raymond M., and James J. Kelly. 1996. Gay and grey revisited. Pp. 1-22 in Raymond M. Berger (Ed.), *Gay and grey: The older homosexual man*. 2nd ed. New York: Harrington Park.

Berman, Harry J. 1987. Adult children and their parents: Irredeemable obligation and irreplaceable loss. *Journal of Gerontological Social Work* 10:1/6:2:21-34.

Bernard, Jessie. 1972. *The future of marriage*. New York: Bantam.

Bess, Irwin. 1999. Widows living alone. *Canadian Social Trends* Summer: 2-5. Statistics Canada Cat. No. 11-008.

Black, M. 1985. Health and social support of older adults in the community. *Canadian Journal on Aging* 4:4:213-226.

Blieszner, Rosemary. 1993. A socialist-feminist perspective on widowhood. *Journal of Aging Studies* 7:2:171-182.

Blieszner, Rosemary, Paula M. Usita, and Jay A. Mancini. 1996. Diversity and dynamics in late-life, mother-daughter relationships. Pp. 5-24 in Karen A. Roberto (Ed.), *Relationships between women in later life*. New York: Harrington Park.

Boaz, Rachel F., Jason Hu, and Yongjia Ye. 1999. The transfer of resources from middle-aged children to functionally limited elderly parents: Providing time, giving money, sharing space. *The Gerontologist* 39:6:648-657.

Broman, Clifford L. 1993. Race differences in marital well-being. *Journal of Marriage and the Family* 55:Aug:724-732.

Booth, Alan, and Paul R. Amato. 1994. Parental marital quality, parental divorce, and relations with parents. *Journal of Marriage and the Family* 56:1:21-34.

Bornat, Joanna, Brian Dimmock, David Jones, and Sheila Peace. 1999. The impact of family change on older people: The case of stepfamilies. Pp. 248-262 in Susan McRae (Ed.), *Changing Britain: Families and households in the 1990s*. New York: Oxford University Press.

Bossard, James H.S., and Eleanor S. Boll. 1956. *The large family system*. Philadelphia: University of Pennsylvania Press.

Bould, Sally. 1993. Familial caretaking: A middle-range definition of family in the context of social policy. *Journal of Family Issues.* 14:1:133-151.

Bowers, Bonita F., and Barbara J. Myers. 1999. Grandmothers providing care for grandchildren: Consequences of various levels of caregiving. *Family Relations* 48:3:303-311.

Bowman, Karen F., C. Seth Landefeld, Linda M. Quinn, Robert M. Palmer, Jerome Kowal, and Richard H. Fortinsky. 1998. Strain in African American and White American caregivers of hospitalized elderly: Implications for discharge planning. *Research on Aging* 20:5:547-568.

Boyd, Monica, and Doug Norris. 1995. Leaving the nest? The impact of family structure. *Canadian Social Trends* 28:14-19. Ottawa.

Brackbill, Yvonne, and Donna Kitch. 1991. Intergenerational relationships: A social exchange perspective on joint living arrangements among the elderly and their relatives. *Journal of Aging Studies* 5:1:77-97.

Brennan, Patricia Flatley, and Shirley M. Moore. 1994. Caregivers of persons with AIDS. Pp. 159-177 in Eva Kahana, David E. Biegel, and May L. Wykle (Eds.), *Family caregiving across the lifespan*. Thousand Oaks, CA: Sage.

Brody, Elaine M. 1995. Prospects for family caregiving. Pp. 15-28 in Rosalie A. Kane and Joan D. Penrod (Eds.), *Family caregiving in an aging society: Policy perspectives*. Thousand Oaks, CA: Sage.

Brody, Elaine M., Morton H. Kleban, Pauline T. Johnsen, Christine Hoffman, and Claire B. Schoonover. 1987. Work status and parent care: A comparison of four groups of women. *The Gerontologist* 27:2:201-208.

Brody, Elaine M., Sandra J. Litvin, Christine Hoffman, and Morton Kleban. 1995. Marital status of caregiving daughters and co-residence with dependent parents. *The Gerontologist* 35:1:75-85.

Broman, Clifford L. 1993. Race differences in marital well-being. *Journal of Marriage and the Family* 55:Aug:724-732.

Brotman, Shari. 1998. The incidence of poverty among seniors in Canada: Exploring the impact of gender, ethnicity and race. *Canadian Journal on Aging* 17:2:166-185.

Brown, Diane R., and Andrea Sankar. 1998. HIV/AIDS and aging minority populations. *Research on Aging* 20:6:865-884.

Brown, Lester B., Steven G. Sarosy, Terry Clark Cook, and J. Gerramy Quarto. 1997.
Gay men and aging. New York: Garland.

Brubaker, Ellie, and Timothy H. Brubaker. 1995. Critical policy issues. Pp. 235-247 in
G. C. Smith, S. S. Tobin, E. A. Robertson-Tchabo and P. W. Power (Eds.)

Brubaker, Timothy H. 1985. Responsibility for household tasks: A look at golden anni-
versary couples aged 75 years and older. In Warren A. Peterson and Jill Quadagno
(Eds.), *Social bonds in later life.* Beverly Hills: Sage.

Brubaker, Timothy H. 1990. An overview of family relationships in later life. Pp. 13-26
in Timothy H. Brubaker (Ed.), *Family relationships in later life.* 2nd ed. Newbury
Park, CA: Sage.

Strengthening aging families: Diversity in practice and policy. Thousand Oaks, CA:
Sage.

Bryant, Chalandra M., and Rand D. Conger. 1999. Marital success and domains of
social support in long-term relationships: Does the influence of network members
ever end? *Journal of Marriage and the Family* 61:2:437-450.

Bryson, Ken, and Lynne M. Casper. 1999. Coresident grandparents and grandchildren.
Pp. 23-198. *Current population reports,* Special studies. Washington, DC: U.S.
Census Bureau.

Bulcroft, Kris A., and Richard A. Bulcroft. 1991. The timing of divorce: Effects on parent-child relationships in later life. *Research on Aging* 13:2:226-243.

Bulcroft, Kris, and M. O'Conner. 1986. The importance of dating relationships on
quality of life for older persons. *Family Relations* 35:397-401.

Bulcroft, Richard A., and Kris A. Bulcroft. 1991. The nature and functions of dating in
later life. *Research on Aging* 13:2:244-260.

Burch, Thomas K. 1985. *Family history survey: Preliminary findings.* Ottawa: Ministry of Supply and Services Canada.

Burch, Thomas K. 1990. Remarriage of older Canadians: Description and interpretation. *Research on Aging* 12:4:546-559.

Burch, Thomas K., and Beverley J. Matthews. 1988. *Decomposing crude headship
rate: A theoretical note.* Unpublished manuscript. London, Ontario, Canada: University of Western Ontario.

Burnette, Denise. 1999. Social relationships of Latino grandparent caregivers: A role
theory perspective. *The Gerontologist* 39:1:49-58.

Burr, Jeffrey A. 1990. Race/sex comparisons of elderly living arrangements: Factors
influencing the institutionalization of the unmarried. *Research on Aging* 12:4:
507-530.

Burr, Jeffrey A., and Jan E. Mutchler. 1999. Race and ethnic variations in norms of filial
responsibility among older persons. *Journal of Marriage and the Family* 61:3:
674-687.

Burton, Linda. 1992. Black grandparents rearing grandchildren of drug-addicted parents: Stressors, outcomes, and social service needs. *The Gerontologist* 32:6:744-
751.

Burton, Linda, Judith Kasper, Andrew Shore, Kathleen Cagney, Thomas LaVeist,
Catherine Cubbin, and Pearl German. 1995. The structure of informal care: Are
there differences by race? *The Gerontologist* 35:6:744-752.

Bury, Michael. 1995. Ageing, gender and sociological theory. Pp. 15-29 in Sara Arber and Jay Ginn (Eds.), *Connecting gender and ageing: A sociological approach.* Philadelphia: Open University Press.

Buunk, Bram P., and Barry van Driel. 1989. *Variant lifestyles and relationships.* Newbury Park, CA: Sage.

Cain, Leonard D. 1987. Alternative perspectives on the phenomena of human aging: Age stratification and age status. *Journal of Applied Behavioral Science* 23:2: 277-294.

Calasanti, Toni M. 1996. Incorporating diversity: Meaning, levels of research, and implications for theory. *The Gerontologist* 36:2:147-156.

Calasanti, Toni M., and Anna M. Zajicek. 1993. A socialist-feminist approach to aging: embracing diversity. *Journal of Aging Studies* 7:2:117-131.

Call, Kathleen T., Michael A. Finch, Shirley M. Huck, and Rosalie Kane. 1999. Caregiver burden from a social exchange perspective: Caring for older people after hospital discharge. *Journal of Marriage and the Family* 61:3:688-699.

Campbell, Lori D., Ingrid Arnet Connidis, and Lorraine Davies. 1999. Sibling ties in later life: A social network analysis. *Journal of Family Issues* 20:1:114-148.

Campbell, Marjory. 1995. Divorce at mid-life: Intergenerational issues. *Journal of Divorce and Remarriage* 23:1/2:185-202.

Cantor, Marjorie. 1979. Neighbors and friends: An overlooked resource in the informal support system. *Research on Aging* 1:434-463.

Carrière, Yves, and Louis Pelletier. 1995. Factors underlying the institutionalization of elderly persons in Canada. *Journal of Gerontological Sciences* 50B:3:S164-S172.

Cassidy, Margaret L. 1985. Role conflict in the postparental period. *Research on Aging* 7:3:433-454.

Causey, Kelly A., and Candan Duran-Aydintug. 1997. Tendency to stigmatize lesbian mothers in custody cases. *Journal of Divorce and Remarriage* 28:1/2:171-182.

Chan, Christopher G., and Glen H. Elder. 2000. Matrilineal advantage in grandchild-grandparent relations. *The Gerontologist* 40:2:179-190.

Chapman, Nancy J. 1989. Gender, marital status and childlessness of older persons and the availability of informal assistance. Pp. 277-328 in M. D. Petersen and D. L. White (Eds.), *Health care of the elderly: An information sourcebook.* Newbury Park, CA: Sage.

Chappell, Neena L. 1991. In-group differences among elders living with friends and family other than spouses. *Journal of Aging Studies* 5:1:61-76.

Chappell, Neena L. 1992. *Social support and aging.* Toronto: Butterworths.

Chappell, Neena L. 1993. Implications of shifting health care policy for caregiving in Canada. *Journal of Aging and Social Policy* 5:1&2:39-55.

Chappell, Neena L., and Mark Badger. 1987. *Non-traditional living arrangements among the elderly.* Unpublished Manuscript.

Chappell, Neena, and Valerie K. Kuehne. 1998. Congruence among husband and wife caregivers. *Journal of Aging Studies* 12:3:239-254.

Chapple, M. J., S. Kippax, and G. Smith. 1998. "Semi-straight sort of sex:" Class and gay community attachment explored within a framework of older homosexually active men. *Journal of Homosexuality* 35:2:65-83.

Cheal, David. 1991. *Family and the state of theory.* Toronto: University of Toronto Press.

Cheal, David. 1993. Unity and difference in postmodern families. *Journal of Family Issues* 14:1:5-19.

Che-Alford, Janet, and Brian Hamm. 1999. Under one roof: Three generations living together. *Canadian Social Trends* Summer:6-9. Ottawa: Statistics Canada.

Cherlin, Andrew J. 1992. *Marriage, divorce, remarriage.* 2nd ed. Cambridge, MA: Harvard University Press.

Cherlin, Andrew J., and Frank F. Furstenberg, Jr. 1986. *The new American grandparent: A place in the family, a life apart.* New York: Basic Books.

Cherlin, Andrew J., Eugenia Scabini, and Giovanna Rossi. 1997. Still in the nest: delayed home leaving in Europe and the United States. *Journal of Family Issues* 18:6:572-575.

Chevan, Albert. 1995. Holding on and letting go: Residential mobility during widowhood. *Research on Aging* 17:3:278-302.

Chevan, Albert. 1996. As cheaply as one: Cohabitation in the older population. *Journal of Marriage and the Family* 58:Aug:656-667.

Christensen, Donna Hendrickson, and Kathryn D. Rettig. 1995. The relationship of remarriage to post-divorce co-parenting. *Journal of Divorce and Remarriage* 24: 1/2:73-88.

Chunn, Dorothy E. 2000. Politicizing the personal: Feminism, law, and public policy. Pp. 225-259 in Nancy Mandell and Ann Duffy (Eds.), *Canadian families: Diversity, conflict, and change.* 2nd ed. Toronto: Harcourt Brace.

Cicirelli, Victor G. 1982. Sibling influence throughout the lifespan. Pp. 267-284 in Michael E. Lamb and Brian Sutton-Smith (Eds.), *Sibling relationships: Their nature and significance across the lifespan.* Hillsdale, NJ: Lawrence Erlbaum.

Cicirelli, Victor G. 1983. Adult children's attachment and helping behavior to elderly parents: A path model. *Journal of Marriage and the Family* 45:4:815-822.

Cicirelli, Victor G. 1984. Marital disruption and adult children's perception of their siblings' help to elderly parents. *Journal of Family Relations* 33:4:613-621.

Cicirelli, Victor G. 1992. *Family caregiving: Autonomous and paternalistic decision making.* Newbury Park, CA: Sage.

Cicirelli, Victor G. 1995. *Sibling relationships across the life span.* New York: Plenum.

Cicirelli, Victor G., Raymond T. Coward, and Jeffrey W. Dwyer. 1992. Siblings as caregivers for impaired elders. *Research on Aging* 14:3:331-350.

Clark, Phillip G. 1993. Moral discourse and public policy in aging: Framing problems, seeking solutions, and "public ethics." *Canadian Journal on Aging* 12:4:485-508.

Clarke, Clifford J., and Lisa J. Neidert. 1992. Living arrangements of the elderly: An examination of differences according to ancestry and generation. *The Gerontologist* 32:6:796-804.

Clarke, Edward J., Mar Preston, Jo Raksin, and Vern L. Bengtson. 1999. Types of conflict and tensions between older parents and adult children. *The Gerontologist* 39:3:261-270.

Clavan, Sylvia. 1978. The impact of social class and social trends on the role of grandparent. *The Family Coordinator* October:351-357.

Cochran, Donna L., Diane R. Brown, and Karl C. McGregor. 1999. Racial differences in the multiple social roles of older women: Implications for depressive symptoms. *The Gerontologist* 39:4:465-472.

Cogswell, Carolyn, and Carolyn S. Henry. 1995. Grandchildren's perceptions of grandparental support in divorced and intact families. *Journal of Divorce and Remarriage* 23:3/4:127-149.

Cohler, Bertram J., and Karen Altergott. 1995. The family of the second half of life: Connecting theories and findings. Pp. 59-94 in Rosemary Blieszner and Victoria Hilkevitch Bedford (Eds.), *Handbook of aging and the family.* Westport, CT: Greenwood.

Coleman, Marilyn, Lawrence Ganong, and Susan M. Cable. 1997. Beliefs about women's intergenerational family obligations to provide support before and after divorce and remarriage. *Journal of Marriage and the Family* 59:1:165-176.

Connell, Cathleen M., and Gloria D. Gibson. 1997. Racial, ethnic, and cultural differences in dementia caregiving: review and analysis. *The Gerontologist* 37:3: 355-364.

Connidis, Ingrid. 1989a. Contact between siblings in later life. *Canadian Journal of Sociology* 14:4:429-442.

Connidis, Ingrid Arnet. 1989b. Siblings as friends in later life. *American Behavioral Scientist* 33:1:81-93.

Connidis, Ingrid Arnet. 1992. Life transitions and the adult sibling tie: A qualitative study. *Journal of Marriage and the Family* 54:Nov:972-982.

Connidis, Ingrid Arnet. 1994a. Growing Up and Old Together: Some Observations on Families in Later Life. Pp. 195-205 in Victor Marshall and Barry McPherson (Eds.), *Aging: Canadian Perspectives.* Peterborough, Ontario: Broadview.

Connidis, Ingrid Arnet. 1994b. Sibling support in older age. *Journal of Gerontology: Social Sciences* 49:6:S309-S317.

Connidis, Ingrid Arnet. 1999a. Anticipating change in family ties and aging: The implications of demographic trends. In L.E. Stone (Ed.), *Cohort flow and the consequences of population aging, an international analysis and review.* CD Edition. Ottawa: Statistics Canada.

Connidis, Ingrid Arnet. 1999b. *The impact of demographic and social trends across age groups on informal support for older persons.* Paper presented at the National Seminar: Demographic Change and Population Ageing. Moncton, New Brunswick, Canada, April 22-24.

Connidis, Ingrid Arnet, and Lori D. Campbell. 1995. Closeness, confiding, and contact among siblings in middle and late adulthood. *Journal of Family Issues* 16:6:722-745.

Connidis, Ingrid Arnet, and Lorraine Davies. 1990. Confidants and companions in later life: The place of family and friends. *Journal of Gerontology: Social Sciences* 45:4:S141-149.

Connidis, Ingrid Arnet, and Lorraine Davies. 1992. Confidants and companions: Choices in later life. *Journal of Gerontology: Social Sciences* 47:3:S115-122.

Connidis, Ingrid Arnet, and Julie Ann McMullin. 1992. Getting out of the house: The effect of childlessness on social participation and companionship in later life. *Canadian Journal on Aging* 11:4:370-386.

Connidis, Ingrid Arnet, and Julie Ann McMullin. 1993. To have or have not: Parent status and the subjective well-being of older men and women. *The Gerontologist* 33: 5:630-636.

Connidis, Ingrid Arnet, and Julie Ann McMullin. 1994. Social support in older age: Assessing the impact of marital and parent status. *Canadian Journal on Aging* 13: 4:510-527.

Connidis, Ingrid Arnet, and Julie Ann McMullin. 1996. Reasons for and perceptions of childlessness among older persons: Exploring the impact of marital status and gender. *Journal of Aging Studies* 10:3:205-222.

Connidis, Ingrid Arnet, and Julie Ann McMullin. 1999. Permanent childlessness: Perceived advantages and disadvantages among older persons. *Canadian Journal on Aging* 18:4:447-465.

Connidis, Ingrid Arnet, and Julie Ann McMullin. 2000. *Sociological ambivalence and family ties: A critical perspective.* Unpublished manuscript.

Connidis, Ingrid, and Judith Rempel. 1983. The living arrangements of older residents: The role of gender, marital status, age, and family size. *Canadian Journal on Aging* 2:3:91-105.

Connidis, Ingrid Arnet, Carolyn J. Rosenthal, and Julie Ann McMullin. 1996. The impact of family composition on providing help to older parents: A study of employed adults. *Research on Aging* 18:4:402-429.

Cooney, Theresa M. 1994. Young adults' relations with parents: The influence of recent parental divorce. *Journal of Marriage and the Family* 56:1:45-56.

Cooney, Theresa M., and Lori Ann Smith. 1996. Young adults' relations with grandparents following recent parental separation. *Journal of Gerontology: Social Sciences* 51B:2:S91-S95.

Cooney, Theresa M., and Peter Uhlenberg. 1992. Support from parents over the life course: The adult child's perspective. *Social Forces* 71:1:63-84.

Corak, Miles, and Andrew Heisz. 1999. *Death and divorce: The long-term consequences of parental loss on adolescents.* June 9. Ottawa: Statistics Canada, Analytic Studies Branch. Cat. No. 11F0019MPE99135.

Cornman, John M., and Eric R. Kingson. 1996. Trends, issues, perspectives, and values for the aging of the baby boom. *The Gerontologist* 36:1:15-26.

Cotten, Shelia. 1999. Marital status and mental health revisited: Examining the importance of risk factors and resources. *Family Relations* 48:3:225-233.

Counts, Robert M. 1992. Second and third divorces: The flood to come. *Journal of Divorce and Remarriage* 17:1/2:193-200.

Coward, Raymond T., Stan L. Albrecht, and Adam Shapiro. 1996. The perceptions of elderly parents about the possibility of discontinuing their coresidence with children. *Research on Aging* 18:3:325-348.

Coward, Raymond T., and Stephen J. Cutler. 1991. The composition of multigenerational households that include elders. *Research on Aging* 13:1:55-73.

Coward, Raymond T., and Jeffrey W. Dwyer. 1990. The association of gender, sibling network composition, and patterns of parent care by adult children. *Research on Aging* 12:158-181.

Crompton, Susan, and Anna Kemeny. 1999. In sickness and in health: The well-being of married seniors. *Canadian Social Trends.* Winter. Statistics Canada Catalogue No. 11-008.

Cruikshank, Margaret. 1991. Lavender and grey: A brief survey of lesbian and gay aging studies. Pp. 77-87 in John Alan Lee (Ed.), *Gay midlife and maturity.* New York: Haworth.

Cumming, Elaine, and W. E. Henry. 1961. *Growing old: The process of disengagement* New York: Basic Books.

Cumming, Elaine, and Charles Lazer. 1981. Kinship structure and suicide: A theoretical link. *Canadian Review of Sociology and Anthropology* 18:3:271-282.

Cumming, Elaine, and M. Schneider. 1961. Sibling solidarity: A property of American kinship. *American Anthropologist* 63:498-507.

Daatland, Svein Olav. 1990. What are families for? On family solidarity and preferences for help. *Aging and Society* 10:1-15.

Darroch, A. Gordon, and Michael Ornstein. 1984. Family and household in nineteenth-century Canada: Regional patterns and regional economics. *Journal of Family History* Summer 158-179.

Davies, Lorraine. 1995. A closer look at gender and distress among the never married. *Women and Health* 23:2:13-30.

Davies, Lorraine. 2000. *Transitions and singlehood: The forgotten life course.* Unpublished manuscript.

Davis, James A., and Tom W. Smith. *General social surveys, 1972-1996* (Cumulative File). Chicago: National Opinion Research Center.

Davis, Maradee A., Deborah J. Moritz, John M. Neuhaus, and John D. Barclay. 1996. The influence of sociodemographic characteristics and morbidity on the likelihood of living alone among older U.S. adults who become unmarried: A comparison of women and men. *Journal of Women and Aging* 8:2:3-17.

Dean, Craig R. 1994. Gay marriage: A civil right. *Journal of Homosexuality* 27:3/4: 111-115.

Delany, Sarah, E. Elizabeth Delany, with Amy Hill Hearth. 1993. *Having our say: The Delany sisters' first 100 years.* New York: Kodansha America, Inc.

Dellmann-Jenkins, Mary, Maureen Blankemeyer, and Odessa Pinkard. 2000. Young adult children and grandchildren in primary caregiver roles to older relatives and their service needs. *Family Relations* 49:2:177-186.

Demian. 2000. Quick facts on legal marriage for same-sex couples: Partners task force for gay and lesbian couples. Web Site: *www.buddybuddy.com/quick.html.*

Demo, David H., and Alan C. Acock. 1996. Singlehood, marriage, and remarriage. *Journal of Family Issues* 17:3:388-407.

Depner, Charlene E., and Berit Ingersol-Dayton. 1985. Conjugal social support: Patterns in later life. *Journal of Gerontology* 40:6: 761-766.

DeWit, David J., Andrew V. Wister, and Thomas K. Burch. 1988. Physical distance and social contact between elders and their adult children. *Research on Aging* 10:1: 56-80.

Dietz, Tracy L. 1995. Patterns of intergenerational assistance within the Mexican American family: Is the family taking care of the older generation's needs? *Journal of Family Issues* 16:3:344-356.

Dilworth-Anderson, Peggye, and Linda Burton. 1999. Critical issues in understanding family support and older minorities. Pp. 93-105 in Toni P. Miles (Ed.), *Full-color aging: Facts, goals, and recommendations for America's diverse elders.* Washington, DC: Gerontological Society of America.

Dobell, A. R., and S. H. Mansbridge. 1986. *The social policy process in Canada.* Montreal: The Institute for Research on Public Policy.

Dorfman, Lorraine T. 1992. Couples in retirement: Division of household work. Pp. 159-173 in Maximiliane Szinovacz, David J. Ekerdt, and Barbara H. Vinick (Eds.), *Families and retirement.* Newbury Park, CA: Sage.

Doty, Pamela, Mary E. Jackson, and William Crown. 1998. The impact of female caregivers' employment on patterns of formal and informal eldercare. *The Gerontologist* 38:3:331-341.

Doudna, Christine, and Fern McBride. 1981. Where are the men for the women at the top? Pp. 21-34 in Peter J. Stein (Ed.), *Single life: Unmarried adults in social context.* New York: St. Martin's.

Dowd, James J. 1980. *Stratification among the aged.* Monterey, CA: Brooks/Cole.

Dugan, Elizabeth, and Vira R. Kivett. 1994. The importance of emotional and social isolation to loneliness among very old rural adults. *The Gerontologist* 34:3:340-346.

Duncan, Stephen F. 1986. Why some men do not marry. Pp. 55-72 in Robert A. Lewis and Robert E. Salt (Eds.), *Men in families.* Beverly Hills, CA: Sage.

Dunham, Charlotte Chorn. 1995. A link between generations: Intergenerational relations and depression in aging parents. *Journal of Family Issues* 16:4:450-465.

Duvall, Evelyn Mills. 1967. *Family development.* 3rd ed. Toronto: J. B. Lippincott.

Dwyer, Jeffrey W., and Raymond T. Coward. 1991. Multivariate comparisons of the involvement of adult sons versus daughters in the care of impaired parents. *Journal of Gerontology: Social Sciences* 46:5:S259-S269.

Dwyer, Jeffrey W., John C. Henretta, Raymond T. Coward, and Amy J. Barton. 1992. Changes in the helping behaviors of adult children as caregivers. *Research on Aging* 14:351-75.

Dwyer, Jeffrey W., Gary R. Lee, and Thomas B. Jankkowski. 1994. Reciprocity, elder satisfaction, and caregiver stress and burden: The exchange of aid in the family caregiving relationship. *Journal of Marriage and the Family* 56:1:35-43.

Dwyer, Jeffrey W., and Karen Seccombe. 1991. Elder care as family labor. *Journal of Family Issues* 12:2:229-247.

Dykstra, Pearl A. 1990. Disentangling direct and indirect gender effects on the supportive network. Pp. 55-65 in C. P. M. Knipscheer and T. C. Antonucci (Eds.), *Social network research: Substantive issues and methodological questions.* Amsterdam: Swets and Zeitlinger.

Dykstra, Pearl A. 1995. Loneliness among the never and formerly married: The importance of supportive friendships and a desire for independence. *Journal of Gerontology: Social Sciences* 50B:5:S321-S329.

Eggebeen, David J. 1992. Family structure and intergenerational exchanges. *Research on Aging* 14:4:427-447.

Ehrenberg, Miriam. 1997. Living with aging: Review and prospects. Pp. 627-638 in Martin Duberman (Ed.), *A queer world: The Center for Lesbian and Gay Studies reader.* New York: New York University Press.

Eisenhandler, Susan A. 1992. Lifelong roles and cameo appearances: Elderly parents and relationships with adult children. *Journal of Aging Studies* 6:3:243-257.

Faludi, Susan. 1991. *Backlash: The undeclared war against American women.* New York: Crown.

Farkas, Janice I., and Dennis P. Hogan. 1995. The demography of changing inter-generational relationships. Pp. 1-25 in Vern L. Bengtson, K. Warner Schaie, and Linda M. Burton (Eds.), *Adult intergenerational relations: Effects of societal change.* New York: Springer.

Feng, Du, Roseann Giarrusso, Vern L. Bengtson, and Nancy Frye. 1999. Inter-generational transmission of marital quality and marital instability. *Journal of Marriage and the Family* 61:2:451-463.

Finch, Janet. 1989. *Family obligations and social change.* Cambridge, MA: Basil Blackwell.

Finch, Janet, and Jennifer Mason. 1990. Divorce, remarriage, and family obligations. *Sociological Review* 38:2:219-246.

Finch, Janet, and Jennifer Mason. 1991. Obligations of kinship in contemporary Britain: Is there normative agreement? *British Journal of Sociology* 42:3:345-367.

Finch, Janet, and Jennifer Mason. 1993. *Negotiating family responsibilities.* New York: Tavistock/Routledge.

Fischer, Lucy Rose. 1983. Transition to grandparenthood. *International Journal of Aging and Human Development* 26:3:248-252.

Fischer, Lucy Rose. 1985. Elderly parents and the caregiving role: An asymmetrical transition. Pp. 105-114 in Warren A. Peterson and Jill Quadagno (Eds.), *Social bonds in later life.* Beverly Hills, CA: Sage.

Fischer, Lucy Rose. 1986. *Linked lives: Adult daughters and their mothers.* New York: Harper.

Fitting, Melinda, Peter Rabins, M. Jane Lucas, and James Eastham. 1986. Caregivers for dementia patients: A comparison of husbands and wives. *The Gerontologist* 26:3:248-252.

Flippen, Chenoa, and Marta Tienda. 2000. Pathways to retirement: Patterns of labor force participation and labor market exit among the pre-retirement population by race, Hispanic origin, and sex. *Journal of Gerontology: Social Sciences* 55B:1: S14-S27.

Foner, Anne. 2000. Age integration or age conflict as society ages? *The Gerontologist* 40:3:272-276.

Frankel, B. Gail, and David J. DeWit. 1988. Geographic distance and intergenerational contact: Methodological issues. *Journal of Aging Studies* 3:2:139-162.

Franklin, Susan T., Barbara D. Ames, and Sharon King. 1994. Acquiring the family eldercare role: Influence on female employment adaptation. *Research on Aging* 16:1:27-42.

Freedman, Vicki A. 1996. Family structure and the risk of nursing home admission. *Journal of Gerontology: Social Sciences* 51B:2:S61-S69.

Friedland, Robert B., and Laura Summer. 1999. *Demography is not destiny.* Washington, DC: National Academy on an Aging Society: A Policy Institute of the Gerontological Society of America.

Friend, Richard A. 1996. Older lesbian and gay people: A theory of successful aging. Pp. 277-298 in Raymond Berger (Ed.), *Gay and grey: The older homosexual man.* 2nd ed. New York: Harrington Park.

Fuller-Thomson, Esme, Meredith Minkler, and Diane Driver. 1997. A profile of grand-parents raising grandchildren in the United States. *The Gerontologist* 37:3:406-411.

Fullmer, Elise M. 1995. Challenging biases against families of older gays and lesbians. Pp. 99-119 in G. C. Smith, S. S. Tobin, E. A. Robertson-Tchabo, and P. W. Power (Eds.), *Strengthening aging families: Diversity in practice and policy.* Thousand Oaks, CA: Sage.

Fullmer, Elise M., Sheldon S. Tobin, and Gregory C. Smith. 1997. The effects of off-spring gender on older mothers caring for their sons and daughters with mental retardation. *The Gerontologist* 37:6:795-803.

Ganong, Lawrence H., and Marilyn Coleman. 1994. *Remarried family relationships.* Thousand Oaks, CA: Sage.

Ganong, Lawrence H., and Marilyn Coleman. 1998. Attitudes regarding filial respon-sibilities to help elderly divorced parents and stepparents. *Journal of Aging Studies* 12:3:271-290.

Ganong, Lawrence H., and Marilyn Coleman. 1999. *Changing families, changing responsibilities: Family obligations following divorce and remarriage.* Mahwah, NJ: Lawrence Erlbaum.

Ganong, Lawrence H., Marilyn Coleman, and Dennis Mapes. 1990. A meta-analytic review of family structure stereotypes. *Journal of Marriage and the Family* 52: May:287-297.

Ganong, Lawrence H., Marilyn Coleman, Annette Kusgen McDaniel, and Tim Killian. 1998. Attitudes regarding obligations to assist an older parent or stepparent fol-lowing later-life remarriage. *Journal of Marriage and the Family* 60:3:595-610.

Gee, Ellen. 1995. Families in later life. Chapter 3, pp. 77-113 in Roderic Beaujot, Ellen M. Gee, Fernando Rajulton, and Zenaida R. Ravanera (Eds.), *Family over the life course: Current demographic analysis.* Ottawa: Statistics Canada Demography Division.

Gendell, Murray, and Jacob S. Siegel. 1996. Trends in retirement age in the United States, 1955-1993, by sex and race. *Journal of Gerontology Social Sciences* 51B: 3:S132-S139.

George, Linda. 1980. *Role transitions in later life.* Monterey, CA: Brooks-Cole.

Gerstel, N., and S. Gallagher. 1994. Caring for kith and kin: Gender, employment and the privatization of care. *Social Problems* 41:519-539.

Gibson, Diane, and Stephen Mugford. 1986. Expressive relations and social support. Pp. 63-84 in Hal L. Kendig (Ed.), *Aging and families: A social networks perspec-tive.* Boston: Allen & Unwin.

Giddens, Anthony. 1992. *The transformation of intimacy: Sexuality, love and eroti-cism in modern societies.* Stanford, CA: Stanford University Press.

Giddens, Anthony. 1991. *Modernity and self-identity.* Cambridge, MA: Polity.

Gillis, John R. 1996. *A world of their own making: Myth, ritual, and the quest for family values.* Cambridge, MA: Harvard University Press.

Ginn, Jay, and Sara Arber. 1995. "Only connect": Gender relations and aging. Pp. 1-14 in Sara Arber and Jay Ginn (Eds.), *Connecting gender and aging: A sociological approach.* Philadelphia: Open University Press.

Gladstone, James W. 1987. Factors associated with changes in visiting between grandmothers and grandchildren following an adult child's marriage breakdown. *Canadian Journal on Aging* 6:2:117-127.

Gladstone, James W. 1988. Perceived changes in grandmother-grandchild relations following a child's separation or divorce. *The Gerontologist* 28:1:66-72.

Gladstone, James W. 1991. An analysis of changes in grandparent-grandchild visitation following an adult child's remarriage. *Canadian Journal on Aging* 10:2:113-126.

Glenn, Norval D. 1998. The course of marital success and failure in five American 10-year marriage cohorts. *Journal of Marriage and the Family* 60:August:569-576.

Goetting, Anne. 1986. The developmental tasks of siblingship over the life cycle. *Journal of Marriage and the Family* 48:703-714.

Gold, Deborah T. 1986, November. *Sibling relationships in old age: A typology.* Paper presented at the Gerontological Society of America annual meeting, Chicago.

Gold, Deborah T. 1987. Siblings in old age: Something special. *Canadian Journal on Aging* 6:3:199-215.

Gold, Deborah T. 1989. Sibling relations in old age: A typology. *International Journal of Aging and Human Development* 28:1:37-51.

Gold, Deborah T. 1990. Late-life sibling relationships: Does race affect typological distribution? *The Gerontologist* 30:6:741-748.

Gold, Deborah T., Max A. Woodbury, and Linda K. George. 1990. Relationship classification using grade of membership analysis: A typology of sibling relationships in later life. *Journal of Gerontology: Social Sciences* 45:2:S43-S51.

Goldman, Noreen, Sanders Korenman, and R. Weinstein. 1995. Marital status and health among the elderly. *Social Science and Medicine* 40:1717-1730.

Goldscheider, Frances. 1990. The aging of the gender revolution: What do we know and what do we need to know? *Research on Aging* 12:4:531-545.

Goldscheider, Frances. 1997. Recent changes in U.S: Young adult living arrangements in comparative perspective. *Journal of Family Issues* 18:6:708-724.

Goldscheider, Frances K., and Calvin Goldscheider. 1998. The effects of childhood family structure on leaving and returning home. *Journal of Marriage and the Family* 60:3:745-756.

Goldscheider, Frances K., and Leora Lawton. 1998. Family experiences and the erosion of support for intergenerational coresidence. *Journal of Marriage and the Family* 60:3:623-632.

Goodman, Marcene, and Robert L. Rubinstein. 1996. Parenting in later life: Adaptive illusion in elderly mothers of one child. *Journal of Aging Studies* 10:4:295-311.

Gordon, Tuula. 1994. *Single women: On the margins?* New York: New York University Press.

Gough, Kathleen. 1971. The origin of the family. *Journal of Marriage and the Family* 33:Nov:760-771.

Gouldner, Alvin J. 1967. Reciprocity and autonomy in functional theory. Pp. 141-169 in N. J. Demerath, III, and Richard A. Peterson (Eds.), *System, change and conflict.* New York: Free Press.

Gratton, Brian, and Carole Haber. 1993. In search of "intimacy at a distance": Family history from the perspective of elderly women. *Journal of Aging Studies* 7:2:183-194.

Greenberg, Jan S., Marsha Mailick Seltzer, and James R. Greenley. 1993. Aging parents of adults with disabilities: The gratifications and frustrations of later-life caregiving. *The Gerontologist* 33:4:542-550.

Greene, Vernon L., and Kristina Marty. 1999. Editorial essay. Generational investment and social insurance for the elderly: Balancing the accounts. *The Gerontologist* 39:6:645-647.

Greenwell, Lisa, and Vern L. Bengtson. 1997. Geographic distance and contact between middle-aged children and their parents: The effects of social class over 20 years. *Journal of Gerontology: Social Sciences* 52B:1:S13-S26.

Grossman, Arnold H. 1997. The virtual and actual identities of older lesbians and gay men. Pp. 615-626 in Martin Duberman (Ed.), *A queer world: The Center for Lesbian and Gay Studies reader.* New York: New York University Press.

Guberman, Nancy, and Pierre Maheu. 1999. Combining employment and caregiving: An intricate juggling act. *Canadian Journal on Aging* 18:1:84-106.

Gubrium, Jaber F. 1975. Marital dissolution and the evaluation of everyday life in old age. *Journal of Marriage and the Family* 36:1:107-113.

Gubrium, Jaber F. 1975. Being single in old age. *International Journal of Aging and Human Development* 6:1:29-41.

Guillemard, Anne-Marie. 2000. Age integration in Europe: Increasing or decreasing? *The Gerontologist* 40:3:301-302.

Hagestad, Gunhild O. 1985. Continuity and connectedness. Pp. 31-48 in Vern L. Bengtson and Joan F. Robertson (Eds.), *Grandparenthood.* Beverly Hills, CA: Sage.

Hahn, Beth A. 1993. Marital status and women's health—The effect of economic marital acquisitions. *Journal of Marriage and the Family* 55:495-504.

Hamon, Reanna R. 1995. Parents as resources when adult children divorce. *Journal of Divorce and Remarriage* 23:1/2:171-183.

Hamon, Reanna R., and Laurel L. Cobb. 1993. Parents' experience of and adjustment to their adult children's divorce: Applying family stress theory. *Journal of Divorce and Remarriage* 21:1/2:73-94.

Hammond, Ron J., and Greg O. Muller. 1992. The late-life divorced: Another look. *Journal of Divorce and Remarriage* 16:3/4:135-150.

Handel, Gerald. 1994. Central issues in the construction of sibling relationships. Pp. 493-523 in Gerald Handel and Gail G. Whitchurch (Eds.), *The psychosocial interior of the family.* 4th ed. New York: Aldine de Gruyter.

Hareven, Tamara K. 1991. The history of the family and the complexity of social change. *American Historical Review.* 96:95-124.

Hareven, Tamara K. 1996. Introduction: Aging and generational relations over the life course. Pp. 1-12 in Tamara K., Hareven (Ed.), *Aging and Generational Relations Over the Life Course.* New York: Walter de Gruyter.

Hareven, Tamara K., and Kathleen Adams. 1996. The generation in the middle: Cohort comparisons in assistance to aging parents in an american community. Pp. 272-293 in Tamara K., Hareven (Ed.), *Aging and Generational Relations Over the Life Course.* New York: Walter de Gruyter.

Harris, Phyllis Braudy. 1998. Listening to caregiving sons: Misunderstood realities. *The Gerontologist* 38:3:342-352.

Hayslip, Jr., Bert, R. Gerald Shore, Craig E. Henderson, and Paul L. Lambert. 1998. Custodial grandparenting and the impact of grandchildren with problems on role satisfaction and role meaning. *Journal of Gerontology: Social Sciences* 53B:3: S164-S173.

Heaton, Tim B., Cardell K. Jacobson, and Kimberlee Holland. 1999. Persistence and change in decisions to remain childless. *Journal of Marriage and the Family* 61:2: 531-539.

Heinemann, Gloria D., and Patricia L. Evans. 1990. Widowhood: Loss, change, and adaptation. Pp. 142- 168 in Timothy H. Brubaker (Ed.), *Family relationships in later life.* 2nd ed. Newbury Park, CA: Sage.

Henkens, Kene. 1999. Retirement intentions and spousal support: A multi-actor approach. *Journal of Gerontology: Social Sciences* 54B:2:S63-S73.

Henretta, John C. 2000. The future of age integration in employment. *The Gerontologist* 40:3:286-292.

Henry, Carolyn S., Cindi Penor Ceglian, and D. Wayne Matthews. 1992. The role behavior, role meanings, and grandmothering styles of grandmothers and step-grandmothers: Perceptions of the middle generation. *Journal of Divorce and Remarriage* 17:3/4:1-22.

Henry, Carolyn S., Cindi Penor Ceglian, and Diane L. Ostrander. 1993. The transition to stepgrandparenthood. *Journal of Divorce and Remarriage* 19:3/4:25-44.

Hiedemann, Bridget, Olga Suhomlinova, and Angela M. O'Rand. 1998. Economic independence, economic status, and empty nest in midlife marital disruption. *Journal of Marriage and the Family* 60:Feb:219-231.

Hilton, Jeanne M., and Daniel P. Macari. 1997. Grandparent involvement following divorce: A comparison in single-mother and single-father families. *Journal of Divorce and Remarriage* 28:1/2:203-224.

Himes, Christine L. 1994. Parental caregiving by adult women: A demographic perspective. *Research on Aging* 16:2:191-211.

Himes, Christine L., Dennis P. Hogan, and David J. Eggebeen. 1996. Living arrangements of minority elders. *Journal of Gerontology: Social Sciences* 15:1:S42-S48.

Himes, Christine L., Anne K. Jordan, and Janice I. Farkas. 1996. Factors influencing parental caregiving by adult women: Variations by care intensity and duration. *Research on Aging* 18:3:349-370.

Hochschild, Arlie R. 1973. *The unexpected community.* Berkeley: University of California Press.

Hochschild, Arlie R. 1983. *The managed heart.* Berkeley: University of California Press.

Hodgson, Lynne Gershenson. 1995. Adult grandchildren and their grandparents: The enduring bond. Pp. 155-170 in Jon Hendricks (Ed.), *The ties of later life.* Amityville, NY: Baywood.

Hoffman, Charles D., and Debra K. Ledford. 1995. Adult children of divorce: relationships with their mothers and fathers prior to, following parental separation, and currently. *Journal of Divorce and Remarriage* 24:3/5:41-57.

Holden, Karen C., and Hsiang-Hui Daphne Kuo. 1996. Complex marital histories and economic well-being: The continuing legacy of divorce and widowhood as the HRS cohort approaches retirement. *The Gerontologist* 36:3:383-390.

Hong, Lawrence K., and Robert W. Duff. 1994. Widows in retirement communities: The social context of subjective well-being. *The Gerontologist* 34:3:347-352.

Hooker, Karen, Deborah J. Monahan, Sally R. Bowman, Leslie D. Frazier, and Kim Shifren. 1998. Personality counts for a lot: Predictors of mental and physical health of spouse caregivers in two disease groups. *Journal of Gerontology: Psychological Sciences* 53B:2:P73-P85.

Hooyman, Nancy R., and Judith Gonyea. 1995. *Feminist perspectives on family care: Policies for gender justice.* Thousand Oaks, CA: Sage.

Hooyman, Nancy, and J. Asuman Kiyak. 1999. *Social gerontology: A multidisciplinary perspective* 5th ed. Boston: Allyn & Bacon.

Hoyert, Donna L. 1991. Financial and household exchanges between generations. *Research on Aging* 13:2:205-225.

Hunter, Andrea G. 1997. Counting on grandmothers: Black mothers' and fathers' reliance on grandmothers for parenting support. *Journal of Family Issues* 18:3:251-269.

Huyck, Margaret Hellie. 1995. Marriage and close relationships of the marital kind. Pp. 181-200 in Rosemary Blieszner and Victoria Hilkevitch Bedford (Eds.), *Handbook of aging and the family.* Westport, CT: Greenwood.

Ikkink, Karen Klein, Theo van Tilberg, and Kees C. P. M. Knipscheer. 1999. Perceived instrumental support exchanges in relationships between elderly parents and their adult children: Normative and structural explanations. *Journal of Marriage and the Family* 61:4:831-844.

Ingersoll-Dayton, Berit, Ruth Campbell, Yikiko Kurokawa, and Masahiko Saito. 1996. Separateness and togetherness: Interdependence over the life course in Japanese and American marriages. *Journal of Social and Personal Relationships* 13:3:385-398.

Ingersoll-Dayton, Berit, Marjorie E. Starrels, and David Dowler. 1996. Caregiving for parents and parents-in-law: Is gender important? *The Gerontologist* 36:4:483-491.

Irish, Donald P. 1964. Sibling interaction a neglected aspect in family life research. *Social Forces* 42:3:279-288.

Ishii-Kuntz, Masako, and Karen Seccombe. 1989. The impact of children upon social support networks throughout the life course. *Journal of Marriage and the Family* 51:Aug:777-790.

Jackson, James S., and Jyotsna Kalavar. 1993. Equity and distributive justice across age cohorts—A life-course family perspective: Comment on Bengtson and Murray. Pp. 175-183 in Lee M. Cohen (Ed.), *Justice across generations: What does it mean?* Washington, DC: American Association of Retired Persons.

Jacobson, Sharon, and Arnold H. Grossman. 1996. Older lesbians and gay men: old myths, new images, and future directions. Pp. 345-373 in Ritch C. Savin-Williams and Kenneth M. Cohen (Eds.), *The lives of lesbians, gays, and bisexuals.* New York: Harcourt Brace.

Jendrek, Margaret Platt. 1993. Grandparents who parent their grandchildren: Effects on lifestyles. *Journal of Marriage and the Family* 55:609-621.

Jendrek, Margaret Platt. 1994. Grandparents who parent their grandchildren: Circumstances and decisions. *The Gerontologist* 34:2:206-216.

Johnson, Colleen Leahy. 1983. A cultural analysis of the grandmother. *Research on Aging* 5:4:547-567.

Johnson, Colleen Leahy. 1985. The impact of illness on late-life marriages. *Journal of Marriage and the Family* 47:Feb:165-172.

Johnson, Colleen Leahy. 1988a. Active and latent functions of grandparenting duties during the divorce process. *The Gerontologist* 28:2:185-191.

Johnson, Colleen Leahy. 1988b. *Ex familia: Grandparents, parents, and children adjust to divorce.* New Brunswick, NJ: Rutgers University Press.

Johnson, Colleen L. 1997. Should grandparents assume full parental responsibility? Pp. 178-183 in Andrew E. Scharlach and Lenard W. Kaye (Eds.), *Controversial issues in aging.* Boston: Allyn & Bacon.

Johnson, Colleen L., and Barbara M. Barer. 1995. Childlessness and kinship organization: Comparisons of very old Whites and Blacks. *Journal of Cross-Cultural Gerontology* 10:289-306.

Johnson, Colleen L., and Barbara M. Barer. 1997. *Life beyond 85 years: The aura of survivorship.* New York: Springer.

Johnson, Colleen Leahy, and Donald J. Catalano. 1981. Childless elderly and their family supports. *The Gerontologist* 21:6:610-618.

Johnson, Malcolm L. 1995. Interdependency and the generational compact. *Ageing and Society.* 15:243-265.

Johnson, Paul, Christopher Conrad, and David Thomson. 1989. *Workers versus pensioners: Intergenerational justice in an ageing world.* Manchester, UK: Manchester University Press.

Johnson, Richard W., Usha Sambamoorthi, and Stephen Crystal. 1999. Gender differences in pension wealth: Estimates using provider data. *The Gerontologist* 39:3: 320-333.

Julien, Danielle, Elise Chartrand, and Jean Begin. 1999. Social networks, structural interdependence, and conjugal adjustment in heterosexual, gay, and lesbian couples. *Journal of Marriage and the Family* 61:May:516-530.

Kaganoff, Penny, and Susan Spano. 1995. Introduction. Pp. xiii-xx in Penny Kaganoff and Susan Spano (Eds), *Women on divorce: A bedside companion.* New York: Harcourt Brace.

Kane, Rosalie A., and Joan D. Penrod. 1995. Toward a caregiving policy for the aging family. Pp. 144-185 in Rosalie A. Kane and Joan D. Penrod (Eds.), *Family caregiving in an aging society: Policy perspectives.* Thousand Oaks, CA: Sage.

Kapp, Marshall B. 1995. Legal and ethical issues in family caregiving and the role of public policy. Pp. 123-143 in Rosalie A. Kane and Joan D. Penrod (Eds.) *Family caregiving in an aging society: Policy perspectives.* Thousand Oaks, CA: Sage.

Kaufman, Gayle, and Peter Uhlenberg. 1998. Effects of life course transitions on the quality of relationships between adult children and their parents. *Journal of Marriage and the Family* 60:Nov:924-938.

Keating, Norah C., and Priscilla Cole. 1980. What do I do with him 24 hours a day? Changes in the housewife role after retirement. *The Gerontologist* 20:1:84-89.

Keating, Norah C., Janet E. Fast, Ingrid A. Connidis, Margaret Penning, and Janice Keefe. 1997. Bridging policy and research in eldercare. *Canadian Journal on Aging/Canadian Public Policy* Supplement: 22-41.

Keith, Pat M. 1985. Financial well-being of older divorced/separated men and women: Findings from a panel study. *Journal of Divorce* 9:1:61-72.

Keith, Pat M. 1986. Isolation of the unmarried in later life. *Family Relations* 35:3:389-395.

Keith, Patricia M., and Robert B. Schafer. 1985. Equity, role strains, and depression among middle-aged and older men and women. Pp. 37-39 in Warren A. Peterson and Jill Quadagno (Eds.), *Social bonds in later life.* Beverly Hills, CA: Sage.

Keith, Pat M., Robert B. Schafer, and Robbyn Wacker. 1995. Outcomes of equity/inequity among older spouses. Pp. 9-19 in Jon Hendricks (Ed.), *The ties of later life.* Amityville, NY: Baywood.

Kelley, Harold H. 1981. Marriage relationships and aging. Pp. 275-300 in James G. March (Ed.-in-chief), Robert W. Fogel, Elaine Hatfield, Sara B. Kiesler, and Ethel Shanas (Eds.), *Aging, stability and change in the family.* Toronto: Academic Press.

Kendig, Hal L. 1986. Intergeneration exchange. Pp. 85-109 in Hal L. Kendig (Ed.), *Ageing and families: A social networks perspective.* Boston: Allen & Unwin.

Kennedy, Gregory E., and C. E. Kennedy. 1993. Grandparents: A special resource for children in stepfamilies. *Journal of Divorce and Remarriage* 19:3/4:45-68.

Kimmel, D. C. 1992. The families of older gay men and lesbians. *Generations* Summer:37-38.

King, Valarie, and Glen H. Elder, Jr. 1995. American children view their grandparents: Linked lives across three rural generations. *Journal of Marriage and the Family* 57:1:165-178.

King, Valarie, and Glen H. Elder, Jr. 1997. The legacy of grandparenting: Childhood experiences with grandparents and current involvement with grandchildren. *Journal of Marriage and the Family* 59:Nov.:848-859.

Kinsella, Kevin. 1995. Aging and the family: Present and future demographic issues. Pp. 32-56 in Rosemary Blieszner and Victoria Hilkevitch Bedford (Eds.), *Handbook of aging and the family.* Westport, CT: Greenwood.

Kirkconnell, Ross D., and Joseph A. Tindale. 1986, November 1-17. *The importance of continuing family relations after admission to a long term care setting.* Paper presented at the 15th Educational and Scientific Meeting of the Canadian Association on Gerontology, Quebec City..

Kitson, Gay C., Karen Benson Babri, Mary Joan Roach, and Kathleen S. Placidi. 1989. Adjustment to widowhood and divorce: A review. *Journal of Family Issues* 10:1:5-32.

Kivett, Vira. 1993. Racial comparisons of the grandmother role: Implications for strengthening the family support system of older Black women. *Family Relations* 42:165-178.

Kivnick, Helen Q. 1985. Grandparenthood and mental health: Meaning, behavior, and satisfaction. Pp. 151-158 in Vern L. Bengtson and Joan R. Robertson (Eds.), *Grandparenthood.* Beverly Hills, CA: Sage.

Koropeckyj-Cox, Tanya. 1998. Loneliness and depression in middle and old age: Are the childless more vulnerable? *Journal of Gerontology: Social Sciences* 53B:6:S303-S312.

Koropeckyj-Cox, Tanya. 1999, August. *Distressed parents and happy childless: The conditional link between parental status and subjective well-being.* Paper presented at the American Sociological Association Annual Meetings, Chicago.

Kramer, Betty J. 1997. Differential predictors of strain and gain among husbands caring for wives with dementia. *The Gerontologist* 37:2:239-249.

Kramer, Betty J., and Stuart Kipnis. 1995. Eldercare and work conflict: Toward an understanding of gender differences in caregiver burden. *The Gerontologist* 35:3: 340-348.

Kruk, Edward. 1995. Grandparent-grandchild contact loss: Findings from a study of "Grandparent Rights" members. *Canadian Journal on Aging* 14:4:737-754.

Kruk, Edward, and Barry L. Hall. 1995. The disengagement of paternal grandparents subject to divorce. *Journal of Divorce and Remarriage* 23:1/2:131-147.

Kurdek, Lawrence A. 1991. The relations between reported well-being and divorce history, availability of a proximate partner, and gender. *Journal of Marriage and the Family* 53:Feb:71-78.

Kurdek, Lawrence A. 1992. Relationship stability and relationship satisfaction in cohabiting gay and lesbian couples: A prospective longitudinal test of the contextual and interdependence models. *Journal of Social and Personal Relationships* 9:125-142.

Kurdek, Lawrence A. 1994. Conflict resolution styles in gay, lesbian, heterosexual nonparent, and heterosexual parent couples. *Journal of Marriage and the Family* 56:Aug:705-722.

Kurdek, Lawrence A. 1998. Relationship outcomes and their predictors: Longitudinal evidence from heterosexual married, gay cohabiting, and lesbian cohabiting couples. *Journal of Marriage and the Family* 60:Aug:553-568.

Laird, Joan. 1996. Invisible ties: Lesbians and their families of origin. Pp. 89-122 in Joan Laird and Robert-Jay Green (Eds.), *Lesbians and gays in couples and families: A handbook for therapists.* San Francisco: Jossey-Bass.

Landry-Meyer, Laura. 1999. Research into action: Recommended intervention strategies for grandparent caregivers. *Family Relations* 48:4:381-389.

Laslett, Barbara.1978. Family membership, past and present. *Social Problems* 25:5: 476-490.

Lauer, Robert H., Jeanette C. Lauer, and Sarah T. Kerr. 1995. The long-term marriage: Perceptions of stability and satisfaction. Pp. 35-41 in Jon Hendricks (Ed.), *The ties of later life.* Amityville, NY: Baywood.

Lawton, Leora, Merril Silverstein, and Vern Bengtson. 1994. Affection, social contact, and geographic distance between adult children and their parents. *Journal of Marriage and the Family* 56:1:57-68.

Lee, John Alan. 1989. Invisible men: Canada's aging homosexuals. Can they be assimilated into Canada's "liberated" gay communities? *Canadian Journal on Aging* 8: 1:79-97.

Lee, John Alan. 1990. Can we talk? Can we really talk? Communication as a key factor in the maturing homosexual couple. *Journal of Homosexuality* 20:3-4:143-168.

Lee, Gary R., Jeffrey W. Dwyer, and Raymond T. Coward. 1993. Gender differences in parent care: Demographic factors and same gender preferences. *Journal of Gerontology: Social Sciences* 48:1:S9-S16.

Lee, Gary R., and Marilyn Ihinger-Tallman. 1980. Sibling interaction and morale: The effects of family relations on older people. *Research on Aging* 2:3:367-391.

Lee, Gary R., Chuck W. Peek, and Raymond T. Coward. 1998. Race differences in filial responsibility expectations among older parents. *Journal of Marriage and the Family* 60:2:404-412.

Lee, Gary R., Marion C. Willetts, and Karen Seccombe. 1998. Widowhood and depression: Gender differences. *Research on Aging* 20:5:611-630.

Lee, Thomas R., Jay A. Mancini, and Joseph W. Maxwell. 1990. Sibling relationships in adulthood: Contact patterns and motivations. *Journal of Marriage and the Family* 52:May:431-440.

Leigh, Geoffrey K. 1982. Kinship interaction over the family life span. *Journal of Marriage and the Family* 44:Feb:197-208.

Lerner, Melvin J., Darryl G. Somers, David Reid, David Chiriboga, and Mary Tierney. 1991. Adult children as caregivers: Egocentric biases in judgments of sibling contributions. *The Gerontologist* 31:6:746-755.

Letter to the editor. 1999. *Maclean's Magazine.* Aug 23:4.

Lever, Janet. 1994. The 1994 survey of sexuality and relationships: The men. *The Advocate: The National Gay and Lesbian Newsmagazine* Aug 23:17-24.

Lever, Janet. 1995. The 1994 Survey of sexuality and relationships: The women. *The Advocate: The National Gay and Lesbian Newsmagazine* Aug 22: 22-30.

Lieberman, Morton A., and Lawrence Fisher. 1999. The effects of family conflict resolution and decision making on the provision of help for an elder with Alzheimer's disease. *The Gerontologist* 39:2:159-166.

Lin, Ge, and Peter A. Rogerson. 1995. Elderly parents and the geographic availability of their adult children. *Research on Aging* 17:3:303-331.

Linsk, Nathan L., Sharon M, Keigher, Suzanne E. England, and Lori Simon-Rusinowitz. 1995. Compensation of family care for the elderly. Pp. 64-91 in Rosalie A. Kane and Joan D. Penrod (Eds.), *Family caregiving in an aging society: Policy perspectives.* Thousand Oaks, CA: Sage.

Litwak, Eugene. 1985. *Helping the elderly: The complementary roles of informal networks and formal systems.* New York: Guilford.

Logan, John R., and Glenna D. Spitze. 1996. *Family ties: Enduring relations between parents and their grown children.* Philadelphia: Temple University Press.

Longino, Jr., Charles F., and Aaron Lipman. 1981. Married and spouseless men and women in planned retirement communities: Support network differentials. *Journal of Marriage and the Family* 43:169-177.

Loomis, Laura Spencer, and Alan Booth. 1995. Multigenerational caregiving and well-being: The myth of the beleaguered sandwich generation. *Journal of Family Issues* 16:2:131-148.

Lopata, Helena Znaniecka. 1996. *Current widowhood: Myths and realities.* Thousand Oaks, CA: Sage.

Luescher, Kurt, and Karl Pillemer. 1998. Intergenerational ambivalence: A new approach to the study of parent-child relations in later life. *Journal of Marriage and the Family* 60:2:413-425.

Lugaila, Terry. 1992. *Households, families, and children: A 30-year perspective.* Current Population Reports, P23-181. Washington: U.S. Department of Commerce.

Lupri, Eugen, and James Frideres. 1981. The quality of marriage and the passage of time: Marital satisfaction over the family life cycle. *Canadian Journal of Sociology* 6:3:282-305.

Lynott, Patricia Passuth, and Robert E. L. Roberts. 1997. The developmental stake hypothesis and changing perceptions of intergenerational relations. *The Gerontologist* 37:3:394-405.

Mack, Ruthanna, Alan Salmoni, Gloria Viverais-Dressler, Elaine Porter, and Rashmi Garg. 1997. Perceived risks to independent living: The views of older, community-dwelling adults. *The Gerontologist* 37:6:729-736.

MacRae, Hazel. 1992. Fictive kin as a component of the social networks of older people. *Research on Aging* 14:2:226-247.

MacRae, Hazel. 1998. Managing feelings: Caregiving as emotion work. *Research on Aging* 20:1:137-160.

Manalansan, Martin F., IV. 1996. Double minorities: Latino, Black, and Asian men who have sex with men. Pp. 393-415 in Ritch C. Savin-Williams and Kenneth M. Cohen (Eds.), *The lives of lesbians, gays, and bisexuals.* Fort Worth, TX: Harcourt Brace.

Mann, Susan A., Michael D. Grimes, Alice Abel Kemp, and Pamela J. Jenkins. 1997. Paradigm shifts in family sociology? Evidence from three decades of family textbooks. *Journal of Family Issues* 18:3:315-349.

Marks, Nadine F. 1996. Flying solo at midlife: Gender, marital status, and psychological well-being. *Journal of Marriage and the Family* 58:Nov:917-932.

Marks, Nadine F. 1998. Does it hurt to care? Caregiving, work-family conflict, and midlife well-being. *Journal of Marriage and the Family* 60:4:951-966.

Marks, Nadine F., and Sara S. McLanahan. 1993. Gender, family structure, and social support among parents. *Journal of Marriage and the Family* 55:2:481-493.

Marshall, Victor W. 1981. Societal tolerance of aging: Sociological theory and social response to population aging. Pp. 85-104 in *Adaptability and aging 1.* Paris: International Centre of Social Gerontology/Centre International de Gerontologie Sociale.

Marshall, Victor W. 1997. *The generations: Contributions, conflict, equity.* Report prepared for the Division of Aging and Seniors. Ottawa: Health Canada.

Marshall, Victor W., Fay Lomax Cook, and Joanne Gard Marshall. 1993. Conflict over intergenerational equity: Rhetoric and reality in a comparative context. Pp. 119-140 in Vern L. Bengtson and W. A. Achenbaum (Eds.), *The changing contract across generations.* New York: Aldine de Gruyter.

Marshall, Victor W., Sarah H. Matthews, and Carolyn J. Rosenthal. 1993. Elusiveness of family life: A challenge for the sociology of aging. Pp. 39-72 in G. L. Maddox and M. Powell Lawton (Eds.), *Annual review of gerontology and geriatrics, 13.* New York: Springer.

Marsiglio, William, and Denise Donnelly. 1991. Sexual relations in later life: A national study of married persons. *Journal of Gerontology: Social Sciences* 46:6: S338-344.

Martin Matthews, Anne. 1991. *Widowhood in later life.* Toronto: Butterworths/Harcourt.

Martin-Matthews, Anne. 1996. Why I dislike the term "eldercare." *Transition* Sept:16.

Martin-Matthews, Anne. 1999. Widowhood: Dominant renditions, changing demography, and variable meaning. Pp. 27-46 in Sheila M. Neysmith (Ed.), *Critical issues for future social work practice with aging persons.* New York: Columbia University Press.

Martin-Matthews, Anne. 2000a. Change and diversity in aging families and intergenerational relations. Pp. 323-359 in Nancy Mandell and Ann Duffy (Eds.), *Canadian families: Diversity, conflict, and change.* 2nd ed. Toronto: Harcourt Brace.

Martin-Matthews, Anne. 2000b. Intergenerational caregiving: How apocalyptic and dominant demographies form the questions and shape the answers. Pp. 80-79 in Ellen M. Gee and Gloria M. Guttman (Eds.), *The overselling of population aging: apocalyptic demography, intergenerational challenges, and social policy.* Don Mills, Ontario: Oxford University Press.

Martin Matthews, Anne, and Lori D. Campbell. 1995. Gender roles, employment, and informal care. Pp. 129-143 in Sara Arber and Jay Ginn (Eds.), *Connecting gender and aging: Sociological reflections.* Philadelphia: Open University Press.

Martin Matthews, Anne, and Janice M. Keefe. 1995. Work and care of elderly people: A Canadian perspective. Pp. 116-138 in J. Phillips (Ed.), *Working carers: International perspectives on working and caring for older people.* Aldershot, England: Avebury.

Martin Matthews, Anne, and Carolyn J. Rosenthal. 1993. Balancing work and family in an aging society: The Canadian experience. Pp. 96-122 in George Maddox and M. Powell Lawton (Eds.), *Annual review of gerontology and geriatrics, 13.* New York: Springer.

Masheter, Carol. 1991. Postdivorce relationships between ex-spouses: The roles of attachment and interpersonal conflict. *Journal of Marriage and the Family* 53: Feb:103-110.

Masheter, Carol. 1997. Healthy and unhealthy friendship and hostility between ex-spouses. *Journal of Marriage and the Family* 59:May:463-475.

Mason, Mary Ann. 1998. The modern American stepfamily: Problems and possibilities. Pp. 95-115 in Mary Ann Mason, Arlene Skolnick, and Stephen D. Sugarman (Eds.), *All our families: New policies for a new century.* New York: Oxford University Press.

Mason, Mary Ann, and Jane Mauldon. 1999. The new stepfamily requires a new public policy. Pp. 387-394 in Cheryl M. Albers (Ed.), *Sociology of families: Readings.* Thousand Oaks, CA: Pine Forge.

Matthews, Ralph D., and Anne Martin Matthews. 1986. Infertility and involuntary childlessness: The transition to nonparenthood. *Journal of Marriage and the Family* 48:641-649.

Matthews, Sarah H. 1987a. Perceptions of fairness in the division of responsibility for old parents. *Social Justice Review* 1:425-437.

Matthews, Sarah H. 1987b. Provision of care to old parents: Division of responsibility among adult children. *Research on Aging* 9:45-60.

Matthews, Sarah H. 1994. Men's ties to siblings in old age: Contributing factors in availability and quality. Pp. 178-196 in Edward H. Thompson (Ed.), *Older men's lives.* Thousand Oaks, CA: Sage.

Matthews, Sarah H. 1995. Gender and the division of filial responsibility between lone sisters and their brothers. *Journal of Gerontology: Social Sciences* 50B:5:S312-S320.

Matthews, Sarah H., and Jenifer Heidorn. 1998. Meeting filial responsibilities in brothers-only sibling groups. *Journal of Gerontology: Social Sciences* 53B:5:S278-S286.

Matthews, Sarah H., and Tena Tarler Rosner. 1988. Shared filial responsibility: The family as the primary caregiver. *Journal of Marriage and the Family* 50:185-195.

Matthews, Sarah H., and Jetse Sprey. 1984. The impact of divorce on grandparenthood: An exploratory study. *The Gerontologist* 24:1:41-47.

Matthews, Sarah H., and Jetse Sprey. 1985. Adolescents' relationships with grandparents: An empirical contribution to conceptual clarification. *Journal of Gerontology* 40:5:621-626.

Matthias, Ruth E., James E. Lubben, Kathryn A. Atchison, and Stuart O. Schweitzer. 1997. Sexual activity and satisfaction among very old adults: Results from a community-dwelling medicare population survey. *The Gerontologist* 37:1:6-14.

McCall, George J. 1988. The organizational life cycle of relationships. Pp. 467-484 in Steve Duck (Ed.), *Handbook of personal relationships: Theory, research, and interventions.* Toronto: John Wiley.

McConville, Brigid. 1985. *Sisters: Love and conflict within the lifelong bond.* London: Pan Books.

McDaniel, Susan A. 1997. Intergenerational transfers, social solidarity, and social policy: Unanswered questions and policy challenges. *Canadian Public Policy/ Canadian Journal on Aging* Supplement: 1-21.

McDaniel, Susan A. 2000. What did you ever do for me?: Intergenerational linkages in a restructuring Canada. Pp. 130-152 in Ellen M. Gee and Gloria M. Gutman (Eds.), *The overselling of population aging: Apocalyptic demography, intergenerational challenges, and social policy.* Don Mills, Ontario: Oxford University Press.

McDonald, Lynn. 1997. The invisible poor: Canada's retired widows. *Canadian Journal on Aging* 16:3:553-583.

McGarry, Kathleen, and Robert F. Schoeni. 1997. Transfer behavior within the family: Results from the asset and health dynamics study. *Journal of Gerontology* Series B:52B:Special Issue:82-92.

McGhee, Jerrie L. 1985. The effects of siblings on the life satisfaction of the rural elderly. *Journal of Marriage and the Family* 47:Feb:85-91..

McKain, Walter. 1972. A new look at older marriages. *The Family Coordinator* 21:1: 61-69.

McLaren, Leah. 2000, February 12. The man glut. *The Globe and Mail* R1, R6.

McMullin, Julie. 1995. Theorizing age and gender relations. Pp. 30-41 in Sara Arber and Jay Ginn (Eds.), *Connecting gender and aging: A sociological approach.* Philadelphia: Open University Press.

McMullin, Julie Ann, and Victor W. Marshall. 1996. Family friends, stress, and well-being: Does childlessness make a difference? *Canadian Journal on Aging* 15:3: 355-373.

McPherson, Barry D. 1998. *Aging as a social process.* 3rd ed. Toronto: Harcourt Brace.

Medley, Morris L. 1977. Marital adjustment in the post-retirement years. *The Family Coordinator* 26:1:5-11.

Merrill, Deborah M. 1993. Daughters-in-law as caregivers to the elderly. *Research on Aging* 15:1:70-91.

Merrill, Deborah M. 1997. *Caring for elderly parents: Juggling work, family, and caregiving in middle and working class families.* Westport, CT: Auburn House.

Meyer, Madonna Harrington, and Marcia L. Bellas. 1995. U.S. old-age policy and the family. Pp. 264-283 in Rosemary Blieszner and Victoria Hilkevitch Bedford (Eds.), *Handbook of aging and the family.* Westport, CT: Greenwood.

Miall, Charlene E. 1986. The stigma of involuntary childlessness. *Social Problems* 33:4:268-282.

Milan, Anne. 2000. One hundred years of families. *Canadian Social Trends* Spring: 4-17.

Millbank, Jenni. 1997. Lesbians, child custody, and the long lingering gaze of the law. Pp. 280-301 in Susan B. Boyd (Ed.), *Challenging the public/private divide: Feminism, law, and public policy.* Toronto: University of Toronto Press.

Miller, Baila. 1990. Gender differences in spouse caregiver strain: Socialization and role explanations. *Journal of Marriage and the Family* 52:May:311-321.

Miller, Baila. 1998. Family caregiving: Telling it like it is. *The Gerontologist* 38:4:510-513.

Miller, Baila, and Julie E. Kaufman. 1996. Beyond gender stereotypes: Spouse caregivers of persons with dementia. *Journal of Aging Studies* 10:3:189-204.

Mills, C. Wright. 1959. *The sociological imagination.* New York: Oxford University Press.

Mills, Terry L. 1999. When grandchildren grow up: Role transition and family solidarity among baby boomer grandchildren and their grandparents. *Journal of Aging Studies* 13:2:219-239.

Miner, Sonia, and Peter Uhlenberg. 1997. Intergenerational proximity and the social role of sibling neighbors after midlife. *Family Relations* 46:2:145-153.

Minkler, Meredith. 1999. Intergenerational households headed by grandparents: Contexts, realities, and implications for policy. *Journal of Aging Studies* 13:2:199-218.

Mitchell, Barbara A. 2000. The refilled "nest": Debunking the myth of families in crisis. Pp. 80-99 in Ellen M. Gee and Gloria M. Guttman (Eds.), *The overselling of population aging: Apocalyptic demography, intergenerational challenges, and social policy.* Don Mills, Ontario: Oxford University Press.

Mitchell, Barbara A., and Ellen M. Gee. 1996. "Boomerang kids" and midlife parental marital satisfaction. *Family Relations* 45:Oct.:442-448.

Moore, Eric G., and Mark W. Rosenberg. 1997. *Growing old in Canada: Demographic and geographic perspectives.* Ottawa: Statistics Canada and ITP Nelson.

Morgan, Leslie A. 1992. Marital status and retirement plans: Do widowhood and divorce make a difference? Pp. 114-126 in Maximiliane Szinovacz, David J. Ekerdt, and Barbara H. Vinick (Eds.), *Families and retirement.* Newbury Park, CA: Sage.

Morrison, Peter A. 1990. Demographic factors reshaping ties to family and place. *Research on Aging* 12:4:399-408.

Moss, Miriam S., and Sidney Z. Moss. 1992. Themes in parent-child relationships when elderly parents move nearby. *Journal of Aging Studies* 6:3:259-271.

Moss, Sydney Z., and Miriam Moss. 1989. The impact of the death of an elderly sibling: Some considerations of a normative loss. *American Behavioral Scientist* 33: 1:94-106.

Mugford, Stephen, and Hal L. Kendig.1986. Social relations: Networks and ties. Pp. 38-59 in Hal L. Kendig (Ed.), *Aging and families: Social networks perspectives*. Boston: Allen & Unwin.

Mui, Ada C. 1995. Caring for frail elderly parents: A comparison of adult sons and daughters. *The Gerontologist* 35:1:86-93.

Mui, Ada C., Namkee G. Choi, and Abraham Monk. 1998. *Long-term care and ethnicity* Westport, CT: Auborn House.

Mullan, Joseph T. 1998. Aging and informal caregiving to people with HIV/AIDS. *Research on Aging* 20:6:712-738.

Murphy, Barbara, Hilary Schofield, Julie Nankervis, Sidney Bloch, Helen Herrman, and Bruce Singh. 1997. Women with multiple roles: The emotional impact of caring for ageing parents. *Ageing and Society* 17:277-291.

Murphy, Mike, Karen Glaser, and Emily Grundy. 1997. Marital status and long-term illness in Great Britain. *Journal of Marriage and the Family* 59:Feb:156-164.

Mutchler, Jan E. 1990. Household composition among the nonmarried elderly: A comparison of black and white women. *Research on Aging* 12:4:487-506.

Mutschler, Phyllis H. 1994. From executive suite to production line: How employees in different occupations manage elder care responsibilities. *Research on Aging* 16: 1:7-26.

Myles, John. 1989. *Old age and the welfare state: The political economy of pensions*. Lawrence, KS: University Press of Kansas.

Nakosteen, Robert A., and Michael A. Zimmer. 1997. Men, money, and marriage: Are high earners more prone than low earners to marry? *Social Science Quarterly* 78: 1:66-82.

National Economic Council. 1998. *Women and retirement security*. Washington, DC: National Economic Council Interagency Working Group on Social Security.

Neal, Margaret B., N. J. Chapman, Berit Ingersoll-Dayton, and A. C. Emlen. 1993. *Balancing work and caregiving for children, adults, and elders*. Newbury Park, CA: Sage.

Neal, Margaret B., Berit Ingersoll-Dayton, and Marjorie E. Starrels. 1997. Gender and relationship differences in caregiving patterns and consequences among employed caregivers. *The Gerontologist* 37:6:804-816.

Nett, Emily M. 1993. *Canadian families: Past and present*. 2nd ed. Toronto: Butterworths.

Neugebauer-Visano, Robynne. 1995. Seniors and sexuality? Confronting cultural contradictions. Pp. 17-34 in Robynne Neugebauer-Visano (Ed.), *Seniors and sexuality: Experiencing intimacy in later life*. Toronto: Canadian Scholars' Press.

Neysmith, Sheila M. 1991. From community care to a social model of care. Pp. 272-299 in C. T. Baines, P. M. Evans, and S. M. Neysmith (Eds.), *Women's caring: Feminist perspectives on social welfare*. Toronto: McClelland & Stewart.

Norgard, Theresa M., and Willard L. Rodgers. 1997. Patterns of in-home care among elderly black and white Americans. *The Journal of Gerontology* Series B:52B:93-101.

Norris, Joan E. 1980. The social adjustment of single and widowed older women. *Essence* 4:3:135-144.

Nydegger, Corinne N. 1983. Family ties of the aged in cross-cultural perspective. *The Gerontologist* 23:1:26-32.

O'Brien, Carol-Anne, and Aviva Goldberg. 2000. Lesbians and gay men inside and outside families. Pp. 115-145 in Nancy Mandell and Ann Duffy (Eds.), *Canadian families: Diversity, conflict, and change*. Toronto: Harcourt Brace.

O'Brien, Mary. 1991. Never married older women. *Social Indicators Research* 24: 301-315.

O'Bryant, Shirley. 1991. Older widows and independent lifestyles. *International Journal on Aging and Human Development* 32:1:41-51.

O'Connor, Pat. 1990. The adult mother/daughter relationship: A uniquely and universally close relationship? *The Sociological Review* 38:2:293-323.

Ory, Marcia G., Richard R. Hoffman, III, Jennifer L. Yee, Sharon Tennstedt, and Richard Schulz. 1999. Prevalence and impact of caregiving: A detailed comparison between dementia and nondementia caregivers. *The Gerontologist* 39:2:177-185.

Ory, Marcia G., Diane L. Zablotsky, and Stephen Crystal. 1998. HIV/AIDS and aging: Identifying a prevention research and care agenda. *Research on Aging* 20:6:637-652.

Parrott, Tonya M., and Vern L. Bengtson. 1999. The effects of earlier intergenerational affection, normative expectations, and family conflict on contemporary exchanges of help and support. *Research on Aging* 21:1:73-105.

Patterson, Charlotte J. 1996. Lesbian and gay parents and their children. Pp. 274-302 in Ritch C. Savin-Williams and Kenneth M. Cohen (Eds.), *The lives of lesbians, gays, and bisexuals: Children to adults*. New York: Harcourt Brace.

Peacock, Molly. 1998. *Paradise, piece by piece*. Toronto: McClelland & Stewart.

Pearson, Jane L. 1993. Parents' reactions to their children's separation and divorce at two and four years: Parent gender and grandparent status. *Journal of Divorce and Remarriage* 20:3/4:25-43.

Pearson, Jane L., Andrea G. Hunter, Joan M. Cook, Nicholas S. Ialongo, and Sheppard G. Kellam. 1997. Grandmother involvement in child caregiving in an urban community. *The Gerontologist* 37:5:650-657.

Peek, Chuck W., John C. Henretta, Raymond T. Coward, R. Paul Duncan, and Molly C. Dougherty. 1997. Race and residence variations in living arrangements among unmarried older adults. *Research on Aging* 19:1:46-68.

Peek, Kristen M., Raymond T. Coward, and Chuck W. Peek. 2000. Race, aging, and care: Can differences in family and household structure account for race variations in informal care. *Research on Aging* 22:2:117-142.

Penning, Margaret J. 1998. In the middle: Parental caregiving in the context of other roles. *Journal of Gerontology: Social Sciences* 53B:4:S188-S197.

Penrod, Joan D., Rosalie A. Kane, Robert L. Kane, and Michael D. Finch. 1995. Who cares: The size, scope, and composition of the caregiver support system. *The Gerontologist* 35:4:489-497.

Peplau, Letitia Anne, Rosemary C. Veneigas, and Susan Miller Campbell. 1996. Gay and lesbian relationships. Pp. 250-269 in Ritch C. Savin-Williams and Kenneth

M. Cohen (Eds.), *The lives of lesbians, gays, and bisexuals.* Fort Worth, TX: Harcourt Brace.

Peters, Arnold, and Aart C. Liefbroer. 1997. Beyond marital status: Partner history and well-being in old age. *Journal of Marriage and the Family* 59:Aug:687-699.

Peters-Davis, Norah D., Miriam S. Moss, and Rachel A. Pruchno. 1999. Children-in-law in caregiving families. *The Gerontologist* 39:1:66-75.

Peterson, Candida C. 1995. Husbands' and wives' perceptions of marital fairness across the family life cycle. Pp. 43-53 in Jon Hendricks (Ed.), *The ties of later life.* Amityville, NY: Baywood.

Peterson, Nancy L. 1982. *The ever single woman: Life without marriage.* New York: Quill.

Piercy, Kathleen W. 1998. Theorizing about family caregiving: The role of responsibility. *Journal of Marriage and the Family* 60:Feb:109-118.

Pillemer, Karl. 1985. The dangers of dependency: New findings on domestic violence against the elderly. *Social Problems* 33:2:146-158.

Pillemer, Karl, and J, Jill Suitor. 1991. "Will I ever escape my child's problems?" Effects of adult children's problems on elderly parents. *Journal of Marriage and the Family* 53:Aug:585-594.

Pina, Darlene L., and Vern Bengtson. 1995. Division of household labor and the well-being of retirement-aged wives. *The Gerontologist* 35:3:308-317.

Pope, Mark, and Richard Schulz. 1990. Sexual attitudes and behavior in mid-life and aging homosexual males. *Journal of Homosexuality* 20:3/4:169-177.

Pruchno, Rachel A. 1999. Raising grandchildren: The experience of black and white grandmothers. *The Gerontologist* 39:2:209-221.

Pruchno, Rachel A., Christopher Burant, and Norah D. Peters. 1997a. Typologies of caregiving families: Family congruence and individual well-being. *The Gerontologist* 37:2:157-167.

Pruchno, Rachel A., Christopher Burant, and Norah D. Peters. 1997b. Understanding the well-being of care receivers. 1997. *The Gerontologist* 37:1:102-109.

Pruchno, Rachel A., Julie Hicks Patrick, and Christopher J. Burant. 1996. Mental health of aging women with children who are chronically disabled: Examination of a two-factor model. *Journal of Gerontology: Social Sciences* 51B:6:S284-S296.

Pyke, Karen. 1999. The micropolitics of care in relationships between aging parents and adult children: Individualism, collectivism, and power. *Journal of Marriage and the Family* 61:3:661-672.

Pyke, Karen, and Vern L. Bengtson. 1996. Caring more or less: Individualistic and collectivist systems of family elder care. *Journal of Marriage and the Family.* 58:2:379-392.

Quam, Jean K., and Gary S. Whitford. 1992. Adaptation and age-related expectations of older gay and lesbian adults. *The Gerontologist* 32:3:367-374.

Quirouette, Cecile, and Delores Pushkar Gold. 1995. Spousal characteristics as predictors of well-being in older couples. Pp. 21-33 in Jon Hendricks (Ed.), *The ties of later life.* Amityville, NY: Baywood.

Rempel, Judith. 1985. Childless elderly: What are they missing? *Journal of Marriage and the Family* 43:2:941-955.

Rhyne, Darla. 1981. Bases of marital satisfaction among men and women. *Journal of Marriage and the Family* 43: 941-955.

Ries, Paula, and Anne J. Stone. Editors. 1992. *The American woman 1992-93: A status report.* New York: Norton.

Riley, Matilda White, and John W. Riley, Jr. 1996. Generational relations: A future perspective. Pp. 283-291 in Tamara K. Hareven (Ed.), *Aging and generational relations: Life-course and cross-cultural perspectives.* New York: Aldine De Gruyter.

Riley, Matilda White, and John W. Riley, Jr. 2000. Age integration: Conceptual and historical background. *The Gerontologist* 40:3:266-270.

Roan, Carol L., and R. Kelly Riley. 1996. Intergenerational coresidence and contact: A longitudinal analysis of adult children's response to their mother's widowhood. *Journal of Marriage and the Family* 58:3:708-717.

Roberto, Karen A., and Johanna Stroes. 1995. Grandchildren and grandparents: Roles, influences, and relationships. Pp. 141-154 in Jon Hendricks (Ed.), *The ties of later life.* Amityville, NY: Baywood.

Robertson, Joan. 1977. Grandparenthood: A study of role conceptions. *Journal of Marriage and the Family* 39:1:165-74.

Robertson, Joan. 1997. Should grandparents assume full parental responsibility? Pp. 174-178, 183-184 in Andrew E. Scharlach and Lenard W. Kaye (Eds.), *Controversial issues in aging.* Boston: Allyn & Bacon.

Robison, Julie, Phyllis Moen, and Donna Dempster-McClain. 1995. Women's caregiving: Changing profiles and pathways. *Journal of Gerontology: Social Sciences* 50B:S362-S373.

Roeher Institute. 1996. *Disability, community and society: Exploring the links.* North York, Ontario: The Roehr Institute.

Rose, Hilary, and Errolyn Bruce. 1995. Mutual care but differential esteem: Caring between older couples. Pp. 114-128 in Sara Arber and Jay Ginn (Eds.), *Connecting gender and ageing: A sociological approach.* Buckingham, UK: Open University Press.

Rosenberg, George S., and Donald F. Anspach. 1973. Sibling solidarity in the working class. *Journal of Marriage and the Family* 35:Feb:108-113.

Rosenmayr, Leopold, and E. Kockeis. 1963. Propositions for sociological theory of aging and the family. *International Social Sciences Journal* 15:410-426.

Rosenthal, Carolyn J. 1985. Kinkeeping in the familial division of labor. *Journal of Marriage and the Family* 47:4:965-974.

Rosenthal, Carolyn J. 1987. Generational succession: The passing on of family headship. *Journal of Comparative Family Studies* 18:1:61-77.

Rosenthal, Carolyn J. 1997. The changing contexts of family care in Canada. *Ageing International* Summer:13-31.

Rosenthal, Carolyn J. 2000. Aging families: Have current changes and challenges been "oversold?" Pp. 45-63 in Ellen M. Gee and Gloria M. Guttman (Eds.), *The overselling of population aging: Apocalyptic demography, intergenerational challenges, and social policy.* Don Mills, Ontario: Oxford University Press.

Rosenthal, Carolyn J., and James Gladstone. 1993. Family relationships and support in later life. *Journal of Canadian Studies* 28:1:138-151.

Rosenthal, Carolyn J., Anne Martin-Matthews, and Sarah Matthews. 1996. Caught in the middle? Occupancy in multiple roles and help to parents in a national probability sample of Canadian adults. *Journal of Gerontology: Social Sciences* 51B: 6:S274-S283.

Rose-Rego, Sharon K., Milton E. Strauss, and Kathleen A. Smyth. 1998. Differences in the perceived well-being of wives and husbands caring for persons with Alzheimer's disease. *The Gerontologist* 389:2:224-230.

Ross, Catherine E. 1995. Reconceptualizing marital status as a continuum of social attachment. *Journal of Marriage and the Family* 57:Feb:129-140.

Ross, Catherine E., and John Mirowsky. 1999. Parental divorce, life-course disruption, and adult depression. *Journal of Marriage and the Family* 61:4:1034-1045.

Ross, Helgola G., and Joel I. Milgram. 1982. Important variables in adult sibling relationships: A qualitative study. Pp. 225-249 in Michael E. Lamb and Brian Sutton-Smith (Eds.), *Sibling relationships: Their nature and significance across the lifespan.* Hillsdale, NJ: Lawrence Erlbaum.

Ross, Margaret M., Carolyn J. Rosenthal, and Pamela G. Dawson. 1997. Spousal caregiving in the institutional setting: Task performance. *Canadian Journal on Aging* 16:1:51-69.

Rossi, Alice S., and Peter H. Rossi. 1990. *Of human bonding: Parent-child relations across the life course.* New York: Aldine de Gruyter.

Rubenstein, William B. 1996. Lesbians, gay men, and the law. Pp. 331-344 in Ritch C. Savin-Williams and Kenneth M. Cohen (Eds.), *The lives of lesbians, gays, and bisexuals.* New York: Harcourt Brace.

Rubinstein, Robert L. 1987. Never married elderly as a social type: Re-evaluating some images. *The Gerontologist* 27:1: 08-113

Rubinstein, Robert L., Baine B. Alexander, Marcene Goodman, and Mark Luborsky. 1991. Key relationships of never married, childless older women: A cultural analysis. *Journal of Gerontology: Social Sciences* 46:5:S270-S277.

Ruggles, Steven. 1996. Living arrangements of the elderly in America: 1880-1980. Pp. 254-271 in Tamara K. Hareven (Ed.), *Aging and Generational Relations Over the Life Course.* New York: Walter de Gruyter.

Russell, Graeme. 1986. Grandfathers: Making up for lost opportunities. Pp. 233-259 in Robert A. Lewis and Robert E. Salt (Eds.), *Men in families.* Beverly Hills, CA: Sage.

Ryan, William. 1971. *Blaming the victim.* New York: Vintage.

Ryff, Carol D., Young Hyun Lee, Marilyn J. Essex, and Pamela S. Schmutte. 1994. My children and me: Midlife evaluations of grown children and self. *Psychology and Aging* 9:2:195-205.

Saluter, Arlene. 1992. Marital status and living arrangements: March 1991. *Current Population Reports, Series P-20, Population Characteristics No. 461.* Washington: Government Printing Office, U.S. Bureau of the Census.

Saluter, Arlene. 1996. Marital status and living arrangements: March 1995. *Current Population Reports, Series P-20, Population Characteristics No. 461.* Washington: Government Printing Office, U.S. Bureau of the Census.

Sandmaier, Marian. 1994. *Original kin: The search for connection among adult sisters and brothers.* New York: Dutton.

Sands, Roberta, and Robin S. Goldberg-Glen. 2000. Factors associated with stress among grandparents raising their grandchildren. *Family Relations* 49:1:97-105.

Scanzoni, John, and William Marsiglio. 1993. New action theory and contemporary families. *Journal of Family Issues* 14:1:105-132.

Scharlach, Andrew E. 1994. Caregiving and employment: Competing or complementary roles? *The Gerontologist* 34:3:378-385.

Schmertmann, Carl P., Monica Boyd, William Serow, and Douglas White. 2000. Elder-child coresidence in the United States: Evidence from the 1990 census. *Research on Aging* 22:1:23-42.

Schone, Barbara Steinberg, and Robin M. Weinick. 1998. Health-related behaviors and the benefits of marriage for elderly persons. *The Gerontologist* 38:5:618-627.

Schulz, James H. 1997. The real crisis of the century: Growing inequality, not stealing from our children. Book Review. *The Gerontologist* 37:1:130-131.

Schvanaveldt, Jay D., and Marilyn Ihinger. 1979. Sibling relationships in the family. Pp. 453-467 in W. Burr, R. Hill, F. I. Nye, and I. L. Reiss (Eds.), *Contemporary theories about the family* Vol. 1. New York: Free Press.

Schwartz, Pepper, and Virginia Rutter. 1998. *The gender of sexuality*. Thousand Oaks, CA: Pine Forge.

Scott, Jean Pearson. 1983. Siblings and other kin. Pp. 47-62 in Timothy H. Brubaker (Ed.), *Family relationships in later life*. Beverly Hills: Sage.

Scott, Jean Pearson. 1996. Sisters in later life: Changes in contact and availability. *Journal of Women and Aging* 8:3/4:41-53.

Seccombe, Karen. 1991. Assessing the costs and benefits of children: Gender comparisons among childfree husbands and wives. *Journal of Marriage and the Family* 53:1:191-202.

Seccombe, Karen, and Masako Ishii-Kuntz. 1994. Gender and social relationships among the never-married. *Sex Roles* 30:7/8:585-603.

Sev'er, Aysan. 1992. *Women and divorce in Canada*. Toronto: Canadian Scholars' Press.

Sex and marriage: Can passion survive kids, careers and the vagaries of aging? 1999. *Maclean's* Aug 9:24-29.

Shanas, Ethel. 1979. Social myth as hypothesis: The case of the family relations of old people. *The Gerontologist* 19:1:3-9.

Shanks, Lela Knox. 1996. *Your name is Hughes Hannibal Shanks: A caregiver's guide to Alzheimer's*. Lincoln, NE: University of Nebraska Press.

Sheehan, Nancy W., and Laura M. Donorfio. 1999. Efforts to create meaning in the relationship between aging mothers and their caregiving daughters: A qualitative study of caregiving. *Journal of Aging Studies* 13:2:161-176.

Shernoff, Michael. 1998. Gay widowers: Grieving in relation to trauma and social supports. *Journal of the Gay and Lesbian Medical Association* 2:1:27-33.

Siegel, Judith M. 1995. Looking for Mr. Right? Older single women who become mothers. *Journal of Family Issues* 16:2:194-211.

Silverstein, Merril, and Joseph J. Angelleli. 1998. Older parents' expectations of moving closer to their children. *Journal of Gerontology: Social Sciences* 53B:3: S153-S163.

Silverstein, Merril, and Vern L. Bengtson. 1997. Intergenerational solidarity and the structure of adult child-parent relationships in American families. *American Journal of Sociology* 103:2:429-460.

Silverstein, Merril, and Xuan Chen, 1999. The impact of acculturation in Mexican American families on the quality of adult grandchild-grandparent relationships. *Journal of Marriage and the Family* 61:1:188-198.

Silverstein, Merril, Xuan Chen, and Kenneth Heller. 1996. Too much of a good thing? Integenerational social support and the psychological well-being of older parents. *Journal of Marriage and the Family* 58:4:970-982.

Silverstein, Merril, and Eugene Litwak. 1993. A task-specific typology of intergenerational family structure in later life. *The Gerontologist* 33:2:258-264.

Silverstein, Merril, and Jeffrey D. Long. 1998. Trajectories of grandparents' perceived solidarity with adult grandchildren: A growth curve analysis over 23 years. *Journal of Marriage and the Family* 60:Nov:912-923.

Silverstein, Merril, Tonya M. Parrott, and Vern L. Bengtson. 1995. Factors that predispose middle-aged sons and daughters to provide social support to older parents. *Journal of Marriage and the Family* 57:May:465-475.

Simons, Ronald. 1984. Specificity and substitution in the social networks of the elderly. *International Journal of Aging and Human Development* 18:2:121-139.

Smerglia, Virginia L., and Gary T. Deimling. 1997. Care-related decision-making satisfaction and caregiver well-being in families caring for older members. *The Gerontologist* 37:5:658-665.

Smith, Deborah, and Phyllis Moen. 1998. Spousal influence on retirement: His, her, and their perceptions. *Journal of Marriage and the Family* 60:Aug:734-744.

Snell, James G. 1996. *The citizen's wage: The state and the elderly in Canada, 1900-1951.* Toronto: University of Toronto Press.

Solomon, Jennifer Crew, and Jonathan Marx. 1995. "To grandmother's house we go": Health and school adjustment of children raised solely by grandparents. *The Gerontologist* 35:3:386-394.

Somers, Marsha D. 1993. A comparison of voluntarily childfree adults and parents. *Journal of Marriage and the Family* 55:3:643-650.

Spitze, Glenna, and John R. Logan. 1990. More evidence on women (and men) in the middle. *Research on Aging* 12:182-198.

Sporakowski, Michael J., and George A. Hughston. 1978. Prescriptions for happy marriage: Adjustments and satisfactions of couples married for 50 or more years. *The Family Coordinator* October:27:321-327.

Sprey, Jetse, and Sarah H. Matthews. 1982. Contemporary grandparenthood: A systemic transition. *Annals of the American Academy of Political and Social Science* 464:Nov:91-103.

Stacey, Judith. 1998. Gay and lesbian families: Queer like us. Pp. 117-143 in Mary Ann Mason, Arlene Skolnick, and Stephen D. Sugarman (Eds.), *All our families: New policies for a new century.* New York: Oxford University Press.

Stack, Steven, and J. Ross Eshleman. 1998. Marital status and happiness: A 17-nation study. *Journal of Marriage and the Family* 60:May:527-536.

Starrels, Marjorie, Berit Ingersoll-Dayton, David W. Dowler, and Margaret B. Neal. 1997. The stress of caring for a parent: Effects of the elder's impairment on an employed adult child. *Journal of Marriage and the Family* 59:4:860-872.

Statistics Canada. 1973. *Families: Families by size and type.* Catalogue 93-714. Ottawa: Statistics Canada (1971 Census of Canada).

Statistics Canada. 1982. *Census families in private households: Persons, children at home, structure and type, living arrangements.* Catalogue 92-905. Ottawa: Ministry of Supply and Services Canada (1981 Census of Canada).

Statistics Canada. 1991. *Census of Canada.* Ottawa: Statistics Canada.

Statistics Canada. 1992. *Families, number, type and structure: The nation.* Catalogue 93-312. Ottawa: Ministry of Industry, Science, and Technology (1991 Census of Canada).

Statistics Canada. 1996. *Canadian census data: Census '96 dimension series.* [Online Database]. Available: 94F0008XCB. Ottawa: Statistics Canada.

Statistics Canada. 1996. *General social survey of Canada* (Cycle 10, 1995). Ottawa: Statistics Canada.

Steckenrider, Janie S. 1999. Entitlement fever. Book Review. *The Gerontologist* 39:3: 373-375.

Stein, Peter J. 1981. Understanding single adulthood. Pp. 9-21 in Peter J. Stein (Ed.), *Single life: Unmarried adults in social context.* New York: St. Martin's.

Stern, Steven. 1996. Measuring child work and residence adjustments to parents' long-term care needs. *The Gerontologist* 36:1:76-87.

Stevens, Nan. 1995. Gender and adaptation to widowhood in later life. *Ageing and Society* 15:37-58.

Stoller, Eleanor Palo. 1990. Males as helpers: The role of sons, relatives, and friends. *The Gerontologist* 30:2:228-235.

Stoller, Eleanor Palo, and Stephen J. Cutler. 1992. The impact of gender on configurations of care among married elderly couples. *Research on Aging* 14:3:313-330.

Stoller, Eleanor Palo, Lorna Earl Forster, and Tamara Sutin Duniho. 1992. Systems of parent care within sibling networks. *Research on Aging* 14:1:28-49.

Stommel, Manfred, Charles W. Given, and Barbara A. Given. 1998. Racial differences in the division of labor between primary and secondary caregivers. *Research on Aging* 20:2:199-217.

Stone, Leroy O., Carolyn J. Rosenthal, and Ingrid Arnet Connidis. 1998. *Parent-child exchanges of supports and intergenerational equity.* Ottawa: Statistics Canada.

Strain, Laurel, and Neena L. Chappell. 1982. Confidants—Do they make a difference in quality of life? *Research on Aging* 4:479-502.

Strain, Laurel, and Barbara J. Payne. 1992. Social networks and patterns of interaction among ever-single and separated/divorced elderly Canadians. *Canadian Journal on Aging* 11:1:31-53.

Strawbridge, William J., and Margaret I. Wallhagen. 1991. Impact of conflict on adult child caregivers. *The Gerontologist* 31:6:770-777.

Strawbridge, William J., Margaret I. Wallhagen, Sarah J. Shema, and George A. Kaplan. 1997. New burdens or more of the same? Comparing grandparent, spouse, and adult-child caregivers. *The Gerontologist* 37:4:505-510.

Strom, Robert, Pat Collinsworth, Shirley Strom, and Diane Griswold. 1995. Strengths and needs of black grandparents. Pp. 195-207 in Jon Hendricks (Ed.), *The ties of later life.* Amityville, NY: Baywood.

Stull, Donald E., and Annemarie Scarisbrick-Hauser. 1989. Never-married elderly: A reassessment with implications for long-term care policy. *Research on Aging* 11: 1:124-139.

Suggs, Patricia K., and Vira R. Kivett. 1986-87. Rural-urban elderly and siblings: Their value consensus. *International Journal of Aging and Human Development* 24:2:49-159.

Suitor, J. Jill. 1991. Marital quality and satisfaction with the division of household labor across the family life cycle. *Journal of Marriage and the Family* 53:Feb: 221-230.

Suitor, J. Jill, and Karl Pillemer. 1994. Family caregiving and marital satisfaction: Findings from a one-year panel study. *Journal of Marriage and the Family* 56: 681-690.

Sulloway, Frank J. 1996. *Born to rebel: Birth order, family dynamics, and creative lives.* New York: Pantheon.

Sweeney, Megan M. 1997. Remarriage of women and men after divorce: The role of socioeconomic prospects. *Journal of Family Issues* 18:5:479-502.

Sweet, James, Larry Bumpass, and Vaughn Call. 1988. *The design and content of the National Survey of Families and Households.* NSFH Working Paper No. 1. Madison: University of Wisconsin, Center for Demography and Ecology.

Szinovacz, Maximiliane. 1996. Couples' employment/retirement patterns and perceptions of marital quality. *Research on Aging* 18:2:243-268.

Szinovacz, Maximiliane. 1997. Adult children taking parents into their homes: Effects of childhood living arrangements. *Journal of Marriage and the Family* 59:3:700-717.

Szinovacz, Maximiliane E. 1998. Grandparents today: A demographic profile. *The Gerontologist* 38:1:37-52.

Szinovacz, Maximiliane. 2000. Changes in housework after retirement: A panel analysis. *Journal of Marriage and the Family* 62:Feb:78-92.

Talbott, Maria M. 1998. Older widows' attitudes towards men and remarriage. *Journal of Aging Studies* 12:4:429-449.

Tayler, Lyn, Gordon Parker, and Kay Roy. 1995. Parental divorce and its effects on the quality of intimate relationships in adulthood. *Journal of Divorce and Remarriage* 24:2/4:181-202.

Tedebrand, Lars-Goran. 1996. Gender, rural-urban and socio-economic differences in coresidence of the elderly with adult children: The case of Sweden 1860-1940. Pp. 158-190 in Tamara K, Hareven (Ed.), *Aging and generational relations over the life course.* New York: Walter de Gruyter.

Thomas, Jeanne L. 1995. Gender and perceptions of grandparenthood. Pp. 181-193 in Jon Hendricks (Ed.), *The ties of later life.* Amityville, NY: Baywood.

Thompson, Elizabeth. 2000. Mothers' experiences of an adult child's HIV/AIDS diagnosis: Maternal responses to and resolution of accountability for AIDS. *Family Relations* 49:2:155-164.

Thompson, Linda. 1993. Conceptualizing gender in marriage: The case of marital care. *Journal of Marriage and the Family* 55:Aug:557-569.

Thompson, Linda, and Alexis J. Walker. 1989. Gender in families: Women and men in marriage, work, and parenthood. *Journal of Marriage and the Family* 51:845-871.

Thurnher, Majda. 1976. Middle marriage: Sex differences in evaluation and perspective. *International Journal of Aging and Human Development* 7:2:29-135.

Too late for Prince Charming? 1986. *Newsweek* June 2:54-61.

Traupmann, Jane, and Elaine Hatfield. 1981. Love and its effect on mental and physical health. Pp. 253-274 in James G. March (Ed.-in-chief), Robert W. Fogel, Elaine Hatfield, Sara B. Kiesler, and Ethel Shanas (Vol. Eds.), *Aging: Stability and change in the family*. Toronto: Academic Press.

Treas, Judith, and Anke Van Hilst. 1976. Marriage and remarriage rates among older Americans. *The Gerontologist* 16:2:132-135.

Troll, Lillian E. 1983. Grandparents: The family watchdogs. Pp. 135-149 in Timothy H. Brubaker (Ed.), *Family relationships in later life*. Beverly Hills: Sage.

Troll, Lillian E. 1985. The contingencies of grandparenting. Pp. 63-74 in Vern L. Bengtson and Joan F. Robertson (Eds.), *Grandparenthood*. Beverly Hills, CA: Sage.

Trygstad, Debra W., and Gregory F. Sanders. 1995. The significance of stepgrandparents. Pp. 209-224 in Jon Hendricks (Ed.), *The ties of later life*. Amityville, NY: Baywood.

Uhlenberg, Peter. 1990. The role of divorce in men's relations with their adult children after mid-life. *Journal of Marriage and the Family* 52:Aug:677-688.

Uhlenberg, Peter. 1993. Demographic change and kin relationships in later life. Pp. 219-238 in George Maddox and M. Powell Lawton (Eds.), *Annual review of gerontology and geriatrics, 13*. New York: Springer.

Uhlenberg, Peter. 1996. Mortality decline in the twentieth century and supply of kin over the life course. *The Gerontologist* 36:5:681-685.

Uhlenberg, Peter. 2000. Introduction: Why study age integration? *The Gerontologist* 40:3:261-266.

Uhlenberg, Peter, Teresa Cooney, and Robert Boyd. 1990. Divorce for women after midlife. *Journal of Gerontology: Social Sciences* 45:1:S3-S11.

Uhlenberg, Peter, and Bradley G. Hammill. 1998. Frequency of grandparent contact with grandchild sets: Six factors that make a difference. *The Gerontologist* 38:3: 276-285.

Uhlenberg, Peter, and Mary Anne P. Myers. 1981. Divorce and the elderly. *The Gerontologist* 21:3:276-282.

Umberson, Debra. 1992a. Gender, marital status and the social control of health behavior. *Social Sciences and Medicine* 34:907-917.

Umberson, Debra. 1992b. Relationships between adult children and their parents: Psychological consequences for both generations. *Journal of Marriage and the Family* 54:3:664-674.

U.S. Bureau of the Census. 1972. *Marital status and living arrangements: March 1971. Current Population Reports. Series P-20, Population Characteristics No. 242*. Washington: Government Printing Office.

U.S. Bureau of the Census. 1981. *Marital status and living arrangements: March 1981. Current Population Reports. Series P-20, Population Characteristics No. 372*. Washington: Government Printing Office.

U.S. Bureau of the Census. 1991. *Marital status and living arrangements: March 1991. Current Population Reports. Series P-20, Population Characteristics No. 461*. Washington: Government Printing Office.

U.S. Bureau of the Census. 1995. *Marital status and living arrangements: March 1995. Current Population Reports. Series P-20, Population Characteristics No. 491*. Washington: Government Printing Office.

U.S. Bureau of the Census. 1990. *United States Census* (Public use microdata sample). Washington, DC: Author.

U.S. Bureau of the Census. 1996. *Current population reports: Marital status and living arrangements*. Washington, DC: Author.

Uttal, Lynet. 1999. Using kin for child care: Embedment in the socioeconomic networks of extended families. *Journal of Marriage and the Family* 61:4:845-857.

Vaillant, Caroline, and George E. Vaillant. 1993. Is the u-curve of marital satisfaction an illusion? A 40-year study of marriage. *Journal of Marriage and the Family* 55: Feb: 230-239.

Verbrugge, Lois M. 1979. Marital status and health. *Journal of Marriage and the Family* 41:2:267-285.

Vinick, Barbara H. 1978. Remarriage in old age. *The Family Coordinator* October: 359-363.

Vinick, Barbara H., and David J. Ekerdt. 1992. Couples view retirement activities: Expectation versus experience. Pp. 129-144 in Maximiliane Szinovacz, David J. Ekerdt, and Barbara H. Vinick (Eds.), *Families and retirement*. Newbury Park, CA: Sage.

Wacker, Robbyn R. 1995. Legal Issues and family involvement in later-life families. Pp. 284-306 in Rosemary Blieszner and Victoria Hilkevitch Bedford (Eds.), *Handbook of aging and the family*. Westport, CT: Greenwood.

Waehler, Charles A. 1996. *Bachelors: The psychology of men who haven't married*. Westport: Praeger.

Waehrer, Keith, and Stephen Crystal. 1995. The impact of coresidence on economic well-being of elderly widows. *Journal of Gerontology: Social Sciences* 50B:4: S250-S258.

Waite, Linda J. 1995. Does marriage matter? *Demography* 32:483-507.

Waite, Linda J., and Scott C. Harrison. 1992. Keeping in touch: How women in mid-life allocate social contacts among kith and kin. *Social Forces* 70:3:637-655.

Waite, Linda J., and Mary Elizabeth Hughes. 1999. At risk on the cusp of old age: Living arrangements and functional status among Black, White, and Hispanic adults. *Journal of Gerontology: Social Sciences* 54B:3:S136-S144.

Walker, Alexis J., and Clara C. Pratt. 1991. Daughters' help to mothers: Intergenerational aid versus caregiving. *Journal of Marriage and the Family* 53:1:3-12.

Walker, Kenneth N., Arlene MacBride, and Mary L. S. Vachon. 1977. Social support networks and the crisis of bereavement. *Social Science and Medicine* 11:1:35-41.

Wallace, Steven P., Lene Levy-Storms, Raynard S. Kington, and Ronald M. Andersen. 1998. The persistence of race and ethnicity in the use of long-term care. *Journal of Gerontology: Social Sciences* 53B:2:S104-S112.

Wallsten, Sharon S. 2000. Effects of caregiving, gender, and race on the health, mutuality, and social supports of older couples. *Journal of Aging and Health* 12:1:90-111.

Ward, Russell A. 1993. Marital happiness and household equity in later life. *Journal of Marriage and the Family* 55:May:427-438.

Ward, Russell A., and Glenna Spitze. 1996. Gender differences in parent-child coresidence experiences. *Journal of Marriage and the Family* 58:3:718-725.

Webster, Pamela S., and A. Regula Herzog. 1995. Effects of parental divorce and memories of family problems on relationships between adult children and their parents. *Journal of Gerontology: Social Sciences* 50B:1:S24-S34.

Weiss, Robert S. 1973. *Loneliness: The experience of emotional and social isolation.* Cambridge, MA: MIT Press.

Wellman, Barry. 1990. The place of kinfolk in personal community networks. *Marriage and Family Review* 15:1/2:195-228.

Wellman, Barry. 1992. Which types of ties and networks provide what kinds of social support? *Advances in Group Processes* 9:207-235.

Wellman, Barry, and Scot Wortley. 1989. Brothers' keepers: Situating kinship relations in broader networks of social support. *Sociological Perspectives* 32:3:273-306.

Wells, Yvonne D., and Hal L. Kendig. 1997. Health and well-being of spouse caregivers and the widowed. *The Gerontologist* 37:5:666-674.

Wenger, G. Clare, and Dorothy Jerome. 1999. Change and stability in confidant relationships: Findings from the Bangor Longitudinal Study of Ageing. *Journal of Aging Studies* 13:3:269-294.

White, Lynn. 1992. The effect of parental divorce and remarriage on parental support for adult children. *Journal of Family Issues* 13:2:234-250.

White, Lynn. 1998. Who's counting? Quasi-facts and stepfamilies in reports of number of siblings. *Journal of Marriage and the Family* 60:3:725-733.

White, Lynn K., and Agnes Riedmann. 1992a. When the Brady Bunch grows up: Step-/half- and full sibling relations in adulthood. *Journal of Marriage and the Family* 54:1:197-208.

White, Lynn K., and Agnes Riedmann. 1992b. Ties among adult siblings. *Social Forces* 7:1:85-102.

White, Lynn K., and Stacy L. Rogers. 1997. Strong support but uneasy relationships: Coresidence and adult children's relationships with their parents. *Journal of Marriage and the Family* 59:1:62-76.

Wielink, Gina, Robbert Huijsman, and Joseph McDonnell. 1997. Preferences for care: A study of the elders living independently in the Netherlands. *Research on Aging* 19:2:174-198.

Wilkie, Jane Riblett, Myra Marx Ferree, and Kathryn Strothers Ratcliff. 1998. Gender and fairness: Marital satisfaction in two-earner couples. *Journal of Marriage and the Family* 60:Aug:577-594.

Wilmoth, Janet M. 2000. Unbalanced social exchanges and living arrangement transitions among older adults. *The Gerontologist* 40:1:64-74.

Wilson, Gail. 1995. "I'm the eyes and she's the arms": Changes in advanced old age. Pp. 98-113 in Sara Arber and Jay Ginn (Eds.), *Connecting gender and ageing: A sociological approach.* Buckingham, UK: Open University Press.

Wineberg, Howard, and James McCarthy. 1998. Living arrangements after divorce. *Journal of Divorce and Remarriage* 29:1/2:131-146.

Wister, Andrew, and Laurel Strain. 1986. Social support and well-being: A comparison of older women and widowers. *Canadian Journal on Aging* 5:3:205-220.

Wolf, Douglas A. 1990. Household patterns of older women. *Research on Aging* 12:4:463-486.

Wolf, Douglas A. 1995. Changes in the living arrangements of older women: An international study. *The Gerontologist* 35:6:724-731.

Wolf, Douglas A., Vicki Freedman, and Beth J. Soldo. 1997. The division of family labor: Care for elderly parents. *The Journal of Gerontology* Series B:52B:Special Issue:102-109.

Wolfson, Christina, Richard Handfield-Jones, Kathleen Cranley Glass, Jacqueline McClaran, and Edward Keyserlingk. 1993. Adult children's perceptions of their responsibility to provide care for dependent elderly parents. *The Gerontologist* 33:3:315-323.

Wolinsky, Frederic D., and Robert J. Johnson. 1992. Widowhood, health status, and the use of health services by older adults: A cross-sectional and prospective approach. *Journal of Gerontology: Social Sciences* 47:1:S8-16.

Wong, Rebeca, Chiara Capoferro, and Beth J. Soldo. 1999. Financial assistance from middle-aged couples to parents and children: Racial-ethnic differences. *Journal of Gerontology: Social Sciences* 54B:3:S145-S153.

Wright, Carol L., and Joseph W. Maxwell. 1991. Social support during adjustment to later-life divorce: How adult children help their parents. *Journal of Divorce and Remarriage* 15:3/4:21-48.

Wu, Zheng. 1995. Remarriage after widowhood: A marital history study of older Canadians. *Canadian Journal on Aging* 14:4:719-736.

Wu, Zheng, and Margaret Penning. 1997. Marital instability after midlife. *Journal of Family Issues* 18:5:459-478.

Wu, Zheng, and Michael S. Pollard. 1998. Social support among unmarried childless elderly persons. *Journal of Gerontology: Social Sciences* 53B:6:S324-S335.

Yates, Mary Ellen, Sharon Tennstedt, and Bei-Hung Chang. 1999. Contributors to and mediators of psychological well-being for informal caregivers. *Journal of Gerontology: Psychological Sciences* 54B:1:P12-P22.

Young, Rosalie F., and Eva Kahana. 1995. The context of caregiving and well-being outcomes among African and Caucasian Americans. *The Gerontologist* 35:2: 225-232.

Zick, Cathleen D., and Ken R. Smith. 1991. Marital transitions, poverty, and gender differences in mortality. *Journal of Marriage and the Family.* 53:327-336.

Zsembik, Barbara A. 1993. Determinants of living alone among older Hispanics. *Research on Aging* 15:4:449-464.

Zsembik, Barbara A. 1996. Preferences for coresidence among older Latinos. *Journal of Aging Studies* 10:1:69-81.

Zube, Margaret. 1982. Changing behavior and outlook of aging men and women: Implications for marriage in the middle and later years. *Family Relations* 31: January:147-156.

Index

About the Author

Ingrid Arnet Connidis is Professor of Sociology at the University of Western Ontario, London, Canada. In 2001, she spent a term at Oregon State University where she conducted research on aging and the family as the recipient of the Petersen Visiting Scholar Award. Her research articles on various facets of family ties and aging, including sibling ties and childlessness, have been published in a range of journals, including *Journal of Marriage and the Family, Journal of Gerontology: Social Sciences, The Gerontologist, Journal of Family Studies, Research on Aging, Canadian Journal on Aging,* and *Journal of Aging Studies.* Her current research interests include family ties across generations, trends in family relationships over time, the family ties of older gay and lesbian persons, and step relationships. She has served on the board of the Canadian Association on Gerontology and is a long-term member of the American Sociological Association and the Gerontological Society of America.